Approaches
To
Shakespeare

by Norman Rabkin

McGRAW-HILL Book Company, New York • Toronto • London

Library of Congress Catalog Card Number 64-19675

4 5 6 7 8 9 - MU - 9 8

ACKNOWLEDGMENTS

"The Substance of Shakespearean Tragedy" by permission from A. C. Bradley, *Shakespearean Tragedy*, second edition, Macmillan & Co., Ltd., and St. Martin's Press, Inc., 1956.

"On the Principles of Shakespeare Interpretation" reprinted with permission of the Macmillan Company and Methuen & Co., Ltd., from *The Wheel of Fire* by G. Wilson Knight. *The Wheel of Fire* was originally published by Oxford University Press in 1930; fourth revised and enlarged edition published by Methuen & Co., Ltd., in 1949.

L. C. Knights, "The Question of Character in Shakespeare" by permission from John Garrett, ed., *More Talking of Shakespeare*, London: Longmans, Green & Co., Ltd.; New York: Theatre Arts Books, 1959.

"The Naked Babe and the Cloak of Manliness" from *The Well-Wrought Urn*, copyright 1947, by Cleanth Brooks. Reprinted by permission of Harcourt, Brace & World, Inc., and Dobson Books Ltd.

"A Reply to Cleanth Brooks" by permission from Helen Gardner, *The Business of Criticism*, The Clarendon Press, Oxford, 1959.

"Monistic Criticism and the Structure of Shakespearean Drama" by permission from R. S. Crane, *The Languages of Criticism and the Structure of Poetry*, Toronto: University of Toronto Press, 1953.

Francis Fergusson, "Macbeth as the Imitation of an Action" reprinted by permission from *English Institute Essays 1951*, New York: Columbia University Press, 1952.

"Ripeness Is All" reprinted from J. V. Cunningham, *Tradition and Poetic Structure* by permission of the publisher, Alan Swallow. Copyright 1960 by J. V. Cunningham.

"The Cosmic Background" reprinted with permission of Mr. Stephen Tillyard and the publishers from *Shakespeare's History Plays* by E. M. W. Tillyard. First published by Chatto & Windus, London, in 1944. Copyright 1946 by the Macmillan Company.

"Shakespeare: A Marxist Interpretation" by permission from A. A. Smirnov, *Shakespeare: A Marxist Interpretation,* translated by Sonia Volochova et al., New York: Critics Group, 1936.

Robert Ornstein, "Historical Criticism and the Interpretation of

CONTENTS

To Alfred Harbage

Shakespeare," *Shakespeare Quarterly,* X (1959), 3–9. Reprinted by permission of the author and the Shakepeare Association of America, Inc.

Ernst Kris, "Prince Hal's Conflict" by permission from *The Psychoanalytic Quarterly,* Vol. XVII, 1948, pp. 487–506.

Roy W. Battenhouse, "Shakespearean Tragedy: A Christian Approach" by permission from Nathan A. Scott, Jr., ed., *The Tragic Vision and the Christian Faith,* New York: Association Press, 1957.

"Some Limitations of a Christian Approach to Shakespeare" by permission from *ELH,* Vol. XXII (1955), published by the Johns Hopkins Press.

"The Saturnalian Pattern" reprinted from *Shakespeare's Festive Comedy* by C. L. Barber, by permission of Princeton University Press. Copyright 1959 by Princeton University Press.

"Shakespeare's Prose Style" reprinted by permission of the publishers from Jonas Alexander Barish, *Ben Jonson and the Language of Prose Comedy,* Cambridge, Mass.: Harvard University Press, Copyright 1960, by the President and Fellows of Harvard College.

Fredson Bowers, "What Shakespeare Wrote" by permission of the edition Quelle & Meyer, Heidelberg, from *Shakespeare Jahrbuch,* XCVIII (1962).

F. W. Bateson, "Shakespeare's Laundry Bills: The Rationale of External Evidence" by permission of the edition Quelle & Meyer, Heidelberg, from *Shakespeare Jahrbuch,* XCVIII (1962).

John Russell Brown, "Theatrical Research and the Criticism of Shakespeare and His Contemporaries," *Shakespeare Quarterly,* XIII (1962), 451–461. Reprinted by permission of the author and the Shakespeare Association of America, Inc.

"The Role of the Shakespearean Producer" by permission from Alfred Harbage, *Theatre for Shakespeare,* Toronto: University of Toronto Press, 1953.

INTRODUCTION

Shakespeare Quarterly publishes annually a bibliography of the year's work on Shakespeare: editions, biographies, reviews, interpretations, and studies of all sorts. The list for a recent year included no fewer than 1159 items—an increase of 110 over the bibliography for the preceding year, which in turn reflected an increase of 75 over the year before that. Naturally, when so much activity is expended by so many people on a single subject, one may legitimately expect that a good deal of it will not be very good. On the other hand, a good deal is, and the scholar is no less likely than the layman to be distressed by the sheer quantity of intellection which he will never have the time or the energy to absorb. Even more depressing is one's sense that all of this work constitutes a chaotic mess, a battlefield filled with eccentric knights rushing off in all directions, bearing only the vaguest sort of relationships to each other and scarcely understanding one another's language. But, for all the apparent anarchy, the situation is not what the numbers suggest. As a matter of fact, one of the rewards of the academic study of Shakespeare is the discovery that the knights are very much aware of each other, that the principles each serves ally him with others, and that most of the controversy which flourishes so vigorously, though it is nowhere near being reconciled, centers about a surprisingly small number of discrete critical issues.

It is the purpose of this book to isolate and clarify those issues by presenting a series of statements definitive of each of the major approaches to Shakespeare now being taken by intelligent and articulate scholar-critics. Though his sympathies lie more with some approaches than with others, the editor makes no attempt to take sides; the quantity and the quality of the modern criticism of Shakespeare are almost proof in themselves that no single approach answers the problems that Shakespeare raises. For all the atmosphere of controversy, no essay in this volume is a straw man, set up so that another essay can knock it down. Each piece has its own merits and provides its own challenge.

In introductory headnotes the editor attempts briefly to place each of the essays here reprinted in the context both of the writer's own work and of the area of criticism which he frequents. Wherever possible, each essay defines, exemplifies, or attacks a critical position relevant to all or a good many of Shakespeare's plays; the most notable exception, though it is certainly exemplary, is Ernst Kris' Freudian essay on *Henry IV,* which was selected because it is the most interesting achievement of this approach to date and because, unlike other kinds of critics, the Freudians have not yet produced a sufficiently impressive theoretical defense of their approach to Shakespeare.

Like Freudian criticism, the so-called New Criticism has been more interesting and influential in practice than in theory. Cleanth Brooks' essay, therefore, though it deals generally with the availability of Shakespeare's work to the kind of criticism he advocates, represents its author's approach best in its particular study of *Macbeth;* and because that approach can be opposed in specific terms, Helen Gardner's rejoinder, an analysis of the same passage in *Macbeth* that Professor Brooks discusses, has been chosen to follow the Brooks essay. The editor has taken the opportunity thus offered to make *Macbeth* a recurring point of comparison among critical methodologies. R. S. Crane and A. A. Smirnov are both represented, therefore, not only by theoretical definitions of their own approaches but also by concise interpretations of *Macbeth* which exemplify their theories, and Francis Fergusson illustrates his critical methodology in a study of the play.

As said above, the apparent welter of theories and counter-theories is not as confusing as might seem to be the case. Both chronologically and intellectually, twentieth-century approaches to Shakespeare begin with Bradley. From Bradley to the present, the majority of critics have assumed that the plays constitute complex and intelligible wholes which they can talk about in terms of meaning without falling into the trap of forgetting that whatever a play means, it means as a work of art. Moreover, the historian looking back on the course of criticism in the twentieth century can see lines of continuity and indebtedness which may not have been apparent to the critics themselves. Certainly the most forceful influence on critics for a good part of the century has been, surprisingly enough, the work of Samuel Taylor Coleridge, and through him the intellectual heritage of German romanticism. Bradley's avowedly Hegelian interpretations of the tragedies rest on a notion of imagination, in both Shakespeare and his audience, that, in Coleridge's terms, "reveals itself in the balance or reconciliation of opposite or discordant qualities."

The recognition of Bradley's debt to Coleridge leads to an interesting realization. Shakespearean critics of the early thirties, L. C. Knights and G. Wilson Knight for example, sounded a note of revolt against Bradley, and that note continued to be heard throughout the next two decades as an articulate generation of critics first rose up against the attitudes they felt to be entrenched in the academies and then moved into positions of authority themselves. Despite the fact that members of the new generation prided themselves on their originality and independence and often disagreed with each other, their audience perceived in their work a large area of shared ground, and John Crowe Ransom's appellation of the group as practitioners of the New Criticism provided a fixed point from which that area was immediately and clearly visible. It is becoming more and more clear that the intellectual roots of the movement lie in the assumptions of Coleridge. For better or worse, the New Critics' achievement consists in the objectification of an essentially subjective approach to literary works on the grounds that they possess a *unity* which can be identified and analyzed. Moreover, such key terms of the New Critics as *ambiguity, tension, paradox,* and *irony* all share not only Coleridge's interest in the workings of the mind but also his sense of imagination—which is the source and domain of literature—as the ability to reconcile "opposite or discordant qualities."

The first section of *Approaches to Shakespeare* is devoted to essays which reveal or reject the Coleridgean assumptions. The extent of the controversy possible on any single subject is well suggested by the fate of Cleanth Brooks' "The Naked Babe and the Cloak of Manliness": that famous essay was answered directly not only by Helen Gardner, whose rebuttal appears here, but also by Oscar James Campbell, and Professor Campbell's rejoinder has most recently been itself rebutted by L. C. Knights in *Some Shakespearean Themes.* In one way or another, however, as R. S. Crane points out, a good many such discussions really do not represent as much theoretical disagreement as their authors believe. A more radical disagreement is the assertion that valid criticism of Shakespeare is to be found only in historical scholarship which to some degree rejects the assumptions shared by such critics as Bradley, Knight, Knights, and Brooks.

The sense of historical responsibility, advocated here in different ways by Helen Gardner, R. S. Crane, and above all, J. V. Cunningham, can affect our understanding of Shakespeare in various ways. As "Ripeness Is All" shows, it can sweep away from the text the obscuring dust of misleading "meanings" which time inevitably silts onto it. It can, as the large part of Professor Cunningham's *Tradition and Poetic Structure* demonstrates, make us sufficiently at home in the esthetic world of the artist and his audience that we can share their assumptions about and expectations of a work in a given genre. And it can provide us with an indispensable knowledge of the philosophical positions and attitudes available to Shakespeare, of the popular assumptions he could accept or challenge, the kinds of questions he could ask, and the kinds of answers he could find in the world around him.

During the very years in which the New Critics were extending and deepening our understanding of one aspect of Shakespeare's technique, a number of scholar-critics with a more historic orientation were bringing to life for Shakespeare's modern readers the intellectual world of sixteenth- and seventeenth-century England and attempting to define the playwright's place in that world. Many useful books have been (and continue to be) published on this enormous subject. Three of the most important are Hardin Craig's *The Enchanted Glass* (1936), E. M. W. Tillyard's *The Elizabethan World Picture* (1943), and Theodore Spencer's *Shakespeare and the Nature of Man* (1942); an essay from Tillyard's *Shakespeare's History Plays* here represents the historical school which has been exploring the world of Renaissance humanism. Another kind of historical criticism is reflected in the Marxist interpretation of Shakespeare, practiced for the most part in the Soviet Union and represented here by Professor Smirnov. But historical criticism has its own pitfalls, as Robert Ornstein acutely demonstrates. It cannot be reiterated too often that there is no single key to Shakespeare interpretation.

The essays that follow Professor Ornstein's illustrate the pros and cons of another half-dozen significant approaches to Shakespeare. They reflect the strengths and weaknesses of our criticism. If their authors reveal more interest in tragedy than in comedy, that is because our age does so. If in their variety they suggest that the academy is no longer the comfortable home of any orthodoxy, that is because the university in our day reflects the intellectual uneasiness of the society which supports it. If they do not have the belletristic charm—and often vapidity—of critics of an earlier day, that is because they live in an age in which literature must prove that it is not a luxury before it can make a serious claim on our intellectual and moral attention.

Professor Barber's use of anthropology, Professor Barish's concern with prose style, others' interest in intellectual history or character or imagery or structure or theater or religion may seem, in the turmoil of a moment populated by hundreds of cantankerous writers, to be the work of antagonists fruitlessly engaged in a chaotic and wearisome set of struggles to the death. But all of these techniques, qualified by the warnings of those not blinded by adherence to a single position, add up to the pluralistic and rich approach to Shakespeare that can and should be cultivated by twentieth-century readers. We are lucky to have so many avenues. It is not insignificant that each time a new approach is developed, Shakespeare turns out to be the chief exemplar of the virtues which that approach recognizes for the first time. Like his continual popularity, this fact is testimony to his enduring greatness. The criticism of the twenty-first century will invent methods of which we have not yet dreamed, and again it will be discovered that Shakespeare preeminently has achieved what his critics are learning to perceive. This is in the nature of literary art, which flies while analysis, conceptual, rational, and selective, marches on the ground. But the more marches we take the more we understand of Shakespeare's flight. The controversy is exciting and we are the richer for it.

The Substance
of Shakespearean Tragedy

A. C. BRADLEY

Andrew Cecil Bradley (1851–1935), professor of poetry at Oxford from 1901 to 1906 and brother of the idealist philosopher F. H. Bradley, has perhaps been the single most important twentieth-century critic of Shakespeare. His interests, assumptions, and methods have aroused generations of writers to emulation or to an equally seminal rebellion. The introductory lecture in a series published as Shakespearean Tragedy *in 1904, this essay typifies Bradley's approach and exemplifies his strengths and his weaknesses. He starts with character, asserting that the calamities of tragedy proceed from the actions of men. The logic and the laws of the plays' universes are based in Bradley's scheme on the assumption of the primacy of character. But from character he moves to the argument, on which he insists with equal force and insight, that the universe of the tragedies is consistent and meaningful, and in no simple way. If Bradley stresses character both here and in his discussions of particular plays, thereby bringing down the wrath of critics who would in later years react against him, he also anticipates many of the issues that will be central in later controversy. Thus in "The Substance of Shakespearean Tragedy" he raises the question of whether Shakespeare's tragedies are religious, and more specifically Christian; and* Shakespearean Tragedy *begins the modern treatment of such matters as imagery and structure. Bradley's influence will be apparent in the essays that follow.*

The question we are to consider in this lecture may be stated in a variety of ways. We may put it thus: What is the substance of a Shakespearean tragedy, taken in abstraction both from its form and from the differences in point of substance between one tragedy and another? Or thus: What is the nature of the tragic aspect of life as represented by Shakespeare? What is the general fact shown now in this tragedy and now in that? And we are putting the same question when we ask: What is Shakespeare's tragic conception, or conception of tragedy?

These expressions, it should be observed, do not imply that Shakespeare himself ever asked or answered such a question; that he set himself to reflect on the tragic aspects of life, that he framed a tragic conception, and still less that, like Aristotle or Corneille, he had a theory of the kind of poetry called tragedy. These things are all possible; how far any one of them is probable we need not discuss; but none of them is presupposed by the question we are going to consider. This question implies only that, as a matter of fact, Shakespeare in writing tragedy did represent a certain aspect of life in a certain way, and that through examination of his writings we ought to be able, to some extent, to describe this aspect and way in terms addressed to the understanding. Such a description, so far as it is true and adequate, may, after these explanations, be called indifferently an account of the substance of Shakespearean tragedy, or an account of Shakespeare's conception of tragedy or view of the tragic fact.

Two further warnings may be required. In the first place, we must remember that the tragic aspect of life is only one aspect. We cannot arrive at Shakespeare's whole dramatic way of looking at the world from his tragedies alone, as we can arrive at Milton's way of regarding things, or at Wordsworth's or at Shelley's, by examining almost any one of their important works. Speaking very broadly, one may say that these poets at their best always look at things in one light; but *Hamlet* and *Henry IV.* and *Cymbeline* reflect things from quite distinct positions, and Shakespear's whole dramatic view is not to be identified with any one of these reflections. And, in the second place, I may repeat that in these lectures, at any rate for the most part, we are to be content with his *dramatic* view, and are not to ask whether it corresponded exactly with his opinions or creed outside his poetry —the opinions or creed of the being whom we sometimes oddly call "Shakespeare the man." It does not seem likely that outside his poetry he was a very simple-minded Catholic or Protestant or Atheist, as some have maintained; but we cannot be sure, as with those other poets we can, that in his works he expressed his deepest and most cherished convictions on ultimate questions, or even that he had any. And in his dramatic conceptions there is enough to occupy us.

1

In approaching our subject it will be best, without attempting to shorten the path by referring to famous theories of the drama, to start directly from the facts, and to collect from them gradually an idea of Shakespearean Tragedy. And first, to begin from the outside, such a tragedy brings before us a considerable number of persons (many more than the persons in a Greek play, unless the members of the Chorus are reckoned among them); but it is preeminently the story of one person, the "hero," [1] or at most of two, the "hero" and "heroine." Moreover, it is only in the love-tragedies, *Romeo and Juliet* and *Antony and Cleopatra*, that the heroine is as much the centre of the action as the hero. The rest, including *Macbeth*, are single stars. So that having noticed the peculiarity of these two dramas, we may henceforth, for the sake of brevity, ingore it, and may speak of the tragic story as being concerned primarily with one person.

The story, next, leads up to, and includes, the *death* of the hero. On the one hand (whatever may be true of tragedy elsewhere), no play at the end of which the hero remains alive is, in the full Shakespearean sense, a tragedy; and we no longer class *Troilus and Cressida* or *Cymbeline* as such, as did the editors of the Folio. On the other hand, the story depicts also the troubled part of the hero's life which precedes and leads up to his death; and an instantaneous death occuring by "accident" in the midst of prosperity would not suffice for it. It is, in fact, essentially a tale of suffering and calamity conducting to death.

The suffering and calamity are, moreover, exceptional. They befall a conspicuous person. They are themselves of some striking kind. They are also, as a rule, unexpected, and contrasted with previous happiness or glory. A tale, for example, of a man slowly worn to death by disease, poverty, little cares, sordid vices, petty persecutions, however piteous or dreadful it might be, would not be tragic in the Shakespearean sense.

Such exceptional suffering and calamity, then, affecting the hero, and—we must now add—generally extending far and wide beyond him, so as to make the whole scene a scene of woe, are an essential ingredient in tragedy, and a chief source of the tragic emotions, and especially of pity. But the proportions of this ingredient, and the direction taken by tragic pity, will naturally vary greatly. Pity, for example, has a much larger part in *King Lear* than in *Macbeth,* and is directed in the one case chiefly to the hero, in the other chiefly to minor characters.

Let us now pause for a moment on the ideas we have so far reached. They would more than suffice to describe the whole tragic fact as it presented itself to the mediaeval mind. To the mediaeval mind a tragedy meant a narrative rather than a play, and its notion of the matter of this narrative may readily be gathered from Dante or, still better, from Chaucer. Chaucer's *Monk's Tale* is a series of what he calls "tragedies"; and this means in fact a series of tales *de Casibus Illustrium Virorum*—stories of the Falls of Illustrious Men, such as Lucifer, Adam, Hercules, and Nebuchadnezzar. And the Monk ends the tale of Croesus thus:

> *Anhanged was Cresus, the proudè kyng;*
> *His roial tronè myghte hym nat availle.*
> *Tragédie is noon oother maner thyng,*
> *Ne kan in syngyng criè ne biwaille*
> *But for that Fortune alwey wole assaile*
> *With unwar strook the regnès that been proude;*
> *For whan men trusteth hire, thanne wol she faille,*
> *And covere hire brighte facè with a clowde.*

A total reverse of fortune, coming unawares upon a man who "stood in high degree," happy and apparently secure—such was

the tragic fact to the mediaeval mind. It appealed strongly to
common human sympathy and pity; it startled also another feeling, that of fear. It frightened men and awed them. It made them
feel that man is blind and helpless, the plaything of an inscrutable
power, called by the name of Fortune or some other name—a
power which appears to smile on him for a little, and then on a
sudden strikes him down in his pride.

Shakespeare's idea of the tragic fact is larger than this idea
and goes beyond it; but it includes it, and it is worth while to
observe the identity of the two in a certain point which is often
ignored. Tragedy with Shakespeare is concerned always with
persons of "high degree"; often with kings or princes; if not, with
leaders in the state like Coriolanus, Brutus, Antony; at the least,
as in *Romeo and Juliet*, with members of great houses, whose
quarrels are of public moment. There is a decided difference here
between *Othello* and our three other tragedies [*Hamlet, Lear,
Macbeth*, the subjects of Bradley's *Shakespearean Tragedy*], but
it is not a difference of kind. Othello himself is no mere private
person; he is the General of the Republic. At the beginning we
see him in the Council-Chamber of the Senate. The consciousness
of his high position never leaves him. At the end, when he is
determined to live no longer, he is as anxious as Hamlet not to
be misjudged by the great world, and his last speech begins

> Soft you; a word or two before you go.
> I have done the state some service, and they know it.[2]

And this characteristic of Shakespeare's tragedies, though not
the most vital, is neither external nor unimportant. The saying
that every death-bed is the scene of the fifth act of a tragedy has
its meaning, but it would not be true if the word "tragedy" bore
its dramatic sense. The pangs of despised love and the anguish
of remorse, we say, are the same in a peasant and a prince; but,
not to insist that they cannot be so when the prince is really a
prince, the story of the prince, the triumvir, or the general, has
a greatness and dignity of its own. His fate affects the welfare of
a whole nation or empire; and when he falls suddenly from the
height of earthly greatness to the dust, his fall produces a sense

of contrast, of the powerlessness of man, and of the omnipotence
—perhaps the caprice—of Fortune or Fate, which no tale of
private life can possibly rival.

Such feelings are constantly evoked by Shakespeare's tragedies
—again in varying degrees. Perhaps they are the very strongest
of the emotions awakened by the early tragedy of *Richard II.*,
where they receive a concentrated expression in Richard's famous
speech about the antic Death, who sits in the hollow crown

> *That rounds the mortal temples of a king,*

grinning at his pomp, watching till his vanity and his fancied
security have wholly encased him round, and then coming and
boring with a little pin through his castle wall. And these feelings,
though their predominance is subdued in the mightiest tragedies,
remain powerful there. In the figure of the maddened Lear we see

> *A sight most pitiful in the meanest wretch,*
> *Past speaking of in a king;*

and if we would realize the truth in this matter we cannot do
better than compare with the effect of *King Lear* the effect of
Tourgénief's parallel and remarkable tale of peasant life, *A King
Lear of the Steppes.*

2

A Shakespearean tragedy as so far considered may be called a
story of exceptional calamity leading to the death of a man in
high estate. But it is clearly much more than this, and we have
now to regard it from another side. No amount of calamity which
merely befell a man, descending from the clouds like lightning,
or stealing from the darkness like pestilence, could alone provide
the substance of its story. Job was the greatest of all the children
of the East, and his afflictions were well-nigh more than he could
bear; but even if we imagined them wearing him to death, that
would not make his story tragic. Nor yet would it become so, in
the Shakespearean sense, if the fire, and great wind from the

wilderness, and the torments of his flesh were conceived as sent by a supernatural power, whether just or malignant. The calamities of tragedy do not simply happen, nor are they sent; they proceed mainly from actions, and those the actions of men.

We see a number of human beings placed in certain circumstances; and we see, arising from the cooperation of their characters in these circumstances, certain actions. These actions beget others, and these others beget others again, until this series of inter-connected deeds leads by an apparently inevitable sequence to a catastrophe. The effect of such a series on imagination is to make us regard the sufferings which accompany it, and the catastrophe in which it ends, not only or chiefly as something which happens to the persons concerned, but equally as something which is caused by them. This at least may be said of the principal persons, and, among them, of the hero, who always contributes in some measure to the disaster in which he perishes.

This second aspect of tragedy evidently differs greatly from the first. Men, from this point of view, appear to us primarily as agents, "themselves the authors of their proper woe"; and our fear and pity, though they will not cease or diminish, will be modified accordingly. We are now to consider this second aspect, remembering that it too is only one aspect, and additional to the first, not a substitute for it.

The "story" or "action" of a Shakespearean tragedy does not consist, of course, solely of human actions or deeds; but the deeds are the predominant factor. And these deeds are, for the most part, actions in the full sense of the word; not things done " 'tween asleep and wake," but acts or omissions thoroughly expressive of the doer—characteristic deeds. The centre of the tragedy, therefore, may be said with equal truth to lie in action issuing from character, or in character issuing in action.

Shakespeare's main interest lay here. To say that it lay in *mere* character, or was a psychological interest, would be a great mistake, for he was dramatic to the tips of his fingers. It is possible to find places where he has given a certain indulgence to his love of poetry, and even to his turn for general reflections; but it would be very difficult, and in his later tragedies perhaps impossible, to detect passages where he has allowed such freedom to the interest in character apart from action. But for the opposite extreme, for the abstraction of mere "plot" (which is a very different thing from the tragic "action"), for the kind of interest which predominates in a novel like *The Woman in White*, it is clear that he cared even less. I do not mean that this interest is absent from his dramas; but it is subordinate to others, and is so interwoven with them that we are rarely conscious of it apart, and rarely feel in any great strength the half-intellectual, half-nervous excitement of following an ingenious complication. What we do feel strongly, as a tragedy advances to its close, is that the calamities and catastrophe follow inevitably from the deeds of men, and that the main source of these deeds is character. The dictum that, with Shakespeare, "character is destiny" is no doubt an exaggeration, and one that may mislead (for many of his tragic personages, if they had not met with peculiar circumstances, would have escaped a tragic end, and might even have lived fairly untroubled lives); but it is the exaggeration of a vital truth.

This truth, with some of its qualifications, will appear more clearly if we now go on to ask what elements are to be found in the "story" or "action," occasionally or frequently, beside the characteristic deeds, and the sufferings and circumstances, of the persons. I will refer to three of these additional factors.

(*a*) Shakespeare, occasionally and for reasons which need not be discussed here, represents abnormal conditions of mind; insanity, for example, somnambulism, hallucinations. And deeds issuing from these are certainly not what we call deeds in the fullest sense, deeds expressive of character. No; but these abnormal conditions are never introduced as the origin of deeds of any dramatic moment. Lady Macbeth's sleepwalking has no influence whatever on the events that follow it. Macbeth did not murder Duncan because he saw a dagger in the air: he saw the dagger because he was about to murder Duncan. Lear's insanity is not the cause of a tragic conflict any more than Ophelia's; it is, like Ophelia's, the result of a conflict; and in both cases the effect is mainly pathetic. If Lear were really mad when he divided his kingdom, if Hamlet were really mad at any time in the story, they would cease to be tragic characters.

(*b*) Shakespeare also introduces the supernatural into some of

his tragedies; he introduces ghosts, and witches who have supernatural knowledge. This supernatural element certainly cannot
in most cases, if in any, be explained away as an illusion in the
mind of one of the characters. And further, it does contribute to
the action, and is in more than one instance an indispensable part
of it: so that to describe human character, with circumstances,
as always the *sole* motive force in this action would be a serious
error. But the supernatural is always placed in the closest relation
with character. It gives a confirmation and a distinct form to inward movements already present and exerting an influence; to
the sense of failure in Brutus, to the stifled workings of conscience
in Richard, to the half-formed thought or the horrified memory
of guilt in Macbeth, to suspicion in Hamlet. Moreover, its influence is never of a compulsive kind. It forms no more than an
element, however important, in the problem which the hero has
to face; and we are never allowed to feel that it has removed
his capacity or responsibility for dealing with this problem. So far
indeed are we from feeling this, that many readers run to the
opposite extreme, and openly or privately regard the supernatural
as having nothing to do with the real interest of the play.

(c) Shakespeare, lastly, in most of his tragedies allows to
"chance" or "accident" an appreciable influence at some point in
the action. Chance or accident here will be found, I think, to
mean any occurrence (not supernatural, of course) which enters
the dramatic sequence neither from the agency of a character,
nor from the obvious surrounding circumstances.[3] It may be called
an accident, in this sense, that Romeo never got the Friar's message about the potion, and that Juliet did not awake from her
long sleep a minute sooner; an accident that Edgar arrived at the
prison just too late to save Cordelia's life; an accident that Desdemona dropped her handkerchief at the most fatal of moments;
an accident that the pirate ship attacked Hamlet's ship, so that he
was able to return forthwith to Denmark. Now this operation of
accident is a fact, and a prominent fact, of human life. To exclude
it *wholly* from tragedy, therefore, would be, we may say, to fail
in truth. And besides, it is not merely a fact. That men may start
a course of events but can neither calculate nor control it, is a
tragic fact. The dramatist may use accident so as to make us feel

this; and there are also other dramatic uses to which it may be put. Shakespeare accordingly admits it. On the other hand, any *large* admission of chance into the tragic sequence [4] would certainly weaken, and might destroy, the sense of the causal connection of character, deed, and catastrophe. And Shakespeare really uses it very sparingly. We seldom find ourselves exclaiming, "What an unlucky accident!" I believe most readers would have to search painfully for instances. It is, further, frequently easy to see the dramatic intention of an accident; and some things which look like accidents have really a connection with character, and are therefore not in the full sense accidents. Finally, I believe it will be found that almost all the prominent accidents occur when the action is well advanced and the impression of the causal sequence is too firmly fixed to be impaired.

Thus it appears that these three elements in the "action" are subordinate, while the dominant factor consists in deeds which issue from character. So that, by way of summary, we may now alter our first statement, "A tragedy is a story of exceptional calamity leading to the death of a man in high estate," and we may say instead (what in its turn is one-sided, though less so), that the story is one of human actions producing exceptional calamity and ending in the death of such a man.[5]

Before we leave the "action," however, there is another question that may usefully be asked. Can we define this "action" further by describing it as a conflict?

The frequent use of this idea in discussions on tragedy is ultimately due, I suppose, to the influence of Hegel's theory on the subject, certainly the most important theory since Aristotle's. But Hegel's view of the tragic conflict is not only unfamiliar to English readers and difficult to expound shortly, but it had its origin in reflections on Greek tragedy and, as Hegel was well aware, applies only imperfectly to the works of Shakespeare.[6] I shall, therefore, confine myself to the idea of conflict in its more general form. In this form it is obviously suitable to Shakespearean tragedy; but it is vague and I will try to make it more precise by putting the question. Who are the combatants in this conflict?

Not seldom the conflict may quite naturally be conceived as

lying between two persons, of whom the hero is one; or, more fully, as lying between two parties or groups, in one of which the hero is the leading figure. Or if we prefer to speak (as we may quite well do if we know what we are about) of the passions, tendencies, ideas, principles, forces, which animate these persons or groups, we may say that two of such passions or ideas, regarded as animating two persons or groups, are the combatants. The love of Romeo and Juliet is in conflict with the hatred of their houses, represented by various other characters. The cause of Brutus and Cassius struggles with that of Julius, Octavius and Antony. In *Richard II.* the King stands on one side, Bolingbroke and his party on the other. In *Macbeth* the hero and heroine are opposed to the representatives of Duncan. In all these cases the great majority of the *dramatis personae* fall without difficulty into antagonistic groups, and the conflict between these groups ends with the defeat of the hero.

Yet one cannot help feeling that in at least one of these cases, *Macbeth*, there is something a little external in this way of looking at the action. And when we come to some other plays this feeling increases. No doubt most of the characters in *Hamlet, King Lear, Othello,* or *Antony and Cleopatra* can be arranged in opposed groups;[7] and no doubt there is a conflict; and yet it seems misleading to describe this conflict as one *between these groups.* It cannot be simply this. For though Hamlet and the King are mortal foes, yet that which engrosses our interest and dwells in our memory at least as much as the conflict between them, is the conflict *within* one of them. And so it is, though not in the same degree, with *Antony and Cleopatra* and even with *Othello;* and, in fact, in a certain measure, it is so with nearly all the tragedies. There is an outward conflict of persons and groups, there is also a conflict of forces in the hero's soul; and even in *Julius Caesar* and *Macbeth* the interest of the former can hardly be said to exceed that of the latter.

The truth is, that the type of tragedy in which the hero opposes to a hostile force an undivided soul, is not the Shakespearean type. The souls of those who contend with the hero may be thus undivided; they generally are; but, as a rule, the hero, though he pursues his fated way, is, at least at some point in the action, and

sometimes at many, torn by an inward struggle; and it is frequently at such points that Shakespeare shows his most extraordinary power. If further we compare the earlier tragedies with
the later, we find that it is in the latter, the maturest works, that
this inward struggle is most emphasised. In the last of them,
Coriolanus, its interest completely eclipses towards the close of
the play that of the outward conflict. *Romeo and Juliet, Richard
III., Richard II.*, where the hero contends with an outward force,
but comparatively little with himself, are all early plays.

If we are to include the outer and the inner struggle in a conception more definite than that of conflict in general, we must
employ some such phrase as "spiritual force." This will mean
whatever forces act in the human spirit, whether good or evil,
whether personal passion or impersonal principle; doubts, desires,
scruples, ideas—whatever can animate, shake, possess, and drive
a man's soul. In a Shakespearean tragedy some such forces are
shown in conflict. They are shown acting in men and generating
strife between them. They are also shown, less universally, but
quite as characteristically, generating disturbance and even conflict in the soul of the hero. Treasonous ambition in Macbeth
collides with loyalty and patriotism in Macduff and Malcolm:
here is the outward conflict. But these powers or principles equally
collide in the soul of Macbeth himself: here is the inner. And
neither by itself could make the tragedy.[8]

We shall see later the importance of this idea. Here we need
only observe that the notion of tragedy as a conflict emphasises
the fact that action is the centre of the story, while the concentration of interest, in the greater plays, on the inward struggle
emphasises the fact that this action is essentially the expression
of character.

3

Let us now turn from the "action" to the central figure in it;
and, ignoring the characteristics which distinguish the heroes
from one another, let us ask whether they have any common
qualities which appear to be essential to the tragic effect.

One they certainly have. They are exceptional beings. We have seen already that the hero, with Shakespeare, is a person of high degree or of public importance, and that his actions or sufferings are of an unusual kind. But this is not all. His nature also is exceptional, and generally raises him in some respect much above the average level of humanity. This does not mean that he is an eccentric or a paragon. Shakespeare never drew monstrosities of virtue; some of his heroes are far from being "good"; and if he drew eccentrics he gave them a subordinate position in the plot. His tragic characters are made of the stuff we find within ourselves and within the persons who surround them. But, by an intensification of the life which they share with others, they are raised above them; and the greatest are raised so far that, if we fully realise all that is implied in their words and actions, we become conscious that in real life we have known scarcely anyone resembling them. Some, like Hamlet and Cleopatra, have genius. Others, like Othello, Lear, Macbeth, Coriolanus, are built on the grand scale; and desire, passion, or will attains in them a terrible force. In almost all we observe a marked one-sidedness, a predisposition in some particular direction; a total incapacity, in certain circumstances, of resisting the force which draws in this direction; a fatal tendency to identify the whole being with one interest, object, passion, or habit of mind. This, it would seem, is, for Shakespeare, the fundamental tragic trait. It is present in his early heroes, Romeo and Richard II., infatuated men, who otherwise rise comparatively little above the ordinary level. It is a fatal gift, but it carries with it a touch of greatness; and when there is joined to it nobility of mind, or genius, or immense force, we realise the full power and reach of the soul, and the conflict in which it engages acquires that magnitude which stirs not only sympathy and pity, but admiration, terror, and awe.

The easiest way to bring home to oneself the nature of the tragic character is to compare it with a character of another kind. Dramas like *Cymbeline* and *The Winter's Tale*, which might seem destined to end tragically, but actually end otherwise, owe their happy ending largely to the fact that the principal characters fail to reach tragic dimensions. And conversely, if these persons were put in the place of the tragic heroes, the dramas in which they appear would cease to be tragedies. Posthumus would never have acted as Othello did; Othello, on his side, would have met Iachimo's challenge with something more than words. If, like Posthumus, he had remained convinced of his wife's infidelity, he would not have repented her execution; if, like Leontes, he had come to believe that by an unjust accusation he had caused her death, he would never have lived on, like Leontes. In the same way the villain Iachimo has no touch of tragic greatness. But Iago comes nearer to it, and if Iago had slandered Imogen and had supposed his slanders to have led to her death, he certainly would not have turned melancholy and wished to die. One reason why the end of the *Merchant of Venice* fails to satisfy us is that Shylock is a tragic character, and that we cannot believe in his accepting his defeat and the conditions imposed on him. This was a case where Shakespeare's imagination ran away with him, so that he drew a figure with which the destined pleasant ending would not harmonise.

In the circumstances where we see the hero placed, his tragic trait, which is also his greatness, is fatal to him. To meet these circumstances something is required which a smaller man might have given, but which the hero cannot give. He errs, by action or omission; and his error, joining with other causes, brings on him ruin. This is always so with Shakespeare. As we have seen, the idea of the tragic hero as a being destroyed simply and solely by external forces is quite alien to him; and not less so is the idea of the hero as contributing to his destruction only by acts in which we see no flaw. But the fatal imperfection or error, which is never absent, is of different kinds and degrees. At one extreme stands the excess and precipitancy of Romeo, which scarcely, if at all, diminish our regard for him; at the other the murderous ambition of Richard III. In most cases the tragic error involves no conscious breach of right; in some (*e.g.* that of Brutus or Othello) it is accompanied by a full conviction of right. In Hamlet there is a painful consciousness that duty is being neglected; in Antony a clear knowledge that the worse of two courses is being pursued; but Richard and Macbeth are the only heroes who do what they themselves recognise to be villainous. It is important to observe that Shakespeare does admit such heroes,[9] and also that he appears to feel, and exerts himself to meet, the difficulty that arises from their admission. The difficulty is that the spectator must desire their defeat and even their destruction; and yet this desire, and the satisfaction of it, are not tragic feelings. Shakespeare gives to Richard therefore a power which excites astonishment, and a courage which extorts admiration. He gives to Macbeth a similar, though less extraordinary, greatness, and adds to it a conscience so terrifying in its warnings and so maddening in its reproaches that the spectacle of inward torment compels a horrified sympathy and awe which balance, at the least, the desire for the hero's ruin.

The tragic hero with Shakespeare, then, need not be "good," though generally he is "good" and therefore at once wins sympathy in his error. But it is necessary that he should have so much of greatness that in his error and fall we may be vividly conscious of the possibilities of human nature.[10] Hence, in the first place, a Shakespearean tragedy is never, like some miscalled tragedies, depressing. No one ever closes the book with the feeling that man is a poor mean creature. He may be wretched and he may be awful, but he is not small. His lot many be heart-rending and mysterious, but it is not contemptible. The most confirmed of cynics ceases to be a cynic while he reads these plays. And with this greatness of the tragic hero (which is not always confined to him) is connected, secondly, what I venture to describe as the centre of the tragic impression. This central feeling is the impression of waste. With Shakespeare, at any rate, the pity and fear which are stirred by the tragic story seem to unite with, and even to merge in, a profound sense of sadness and mystery, which is due to this impression of waste. "What a piece of work is man," we cry; "so much more beautiful and so much more terrible than we knew! Why should he be so if this beauty and greatness only tortures itself and throws itself away?" We seem to have before us a type of the mystery of the whole world, the tragic fact which extends far beyond the limits of tragedy. Everywhere, from the crushed rocks beneath our feet to the soul of man, we see power, intelligence, life, and glory, which astound us and seem to call for our worship. And everywhere we see them perishing, devouring one another and destroying themselves, often with dreadful pain, as though they came into being for no other end. Tragedy is the typical form of this mystery, because that greatness of soul which it exhibits oppressed, conflicting, and destroyed, is the highest existence in our view. It forces the mystery upon us, and it makes us realise so vividly the worth of that which is wasted that we cannot possibly seek comfort in the reflection that all is vanity.

4

In this tragic world, then, where individuals, however great they may be and however decisive their actions may appear, are so evidently not the ultimate power, what is this power? What account can we give of it which will correspond with the imaginative impressions we receive? This will be our final question.

The variety of the answers given to this question shows how difficult it is. And the difficulty has many sources. Most people, even among those who know Shakespeare well and come into real contact with his mind, are inclined to isolate and exaggerate some one aspect of the tragic fact. Some are so much influenced by their own habitual beliefs that they import them more or less into their interpretation of every author who is "sympathetic" to them. And even where neither of these causes of error appears to operate, another is present from which it is probably impossible wholly to escape. What I mean is this. Any answer we give to the question proposed ought to correspond with, or to represent in terms of the understanding, our imaginative and emotional experience in reading the tragedies. We have, of course, to do our best by study and effort to make this experience true to Shakespeare; but, that done to the best of our ability, the experience is the matter to be interpreted, and the test by which the interpretation must be tried. But it is extremely hard to make out exactly what this experience is, because, in the very effort to make it out, our reflecting mind, full of everyday ideas, is always tending to transform it by the application of these ideas, and so to elicit a result which, instead of representing the fact, conventionalises it. And the consequence is not only mistaken theories;

it is that many a man will declare that he feels in reading a tragedy what he never really felt, while he fails to recognise what he actually did feel. It is not likely that we shall escape all these dangers in our effort to find an answer to the question regarding the tragic world and the ultimate power in it.

It will be agreed, however, first, that this question must not be answered in "religious" language. For although this or that *dramatis persona* may speak of gods or of God, of evil spirits or of Satan, of heaven and of hell, and although the poet may show us ghosts from another world, these ideas do not materially influence his representation of life, nor are they used to throw light on the mystery of its tragedy. The Elizabethan drama was almost wholly secular; and while Shakespeare was writing he practically confined his view to the world of non-theological observation and thought, so that he represents it substantially in one and the same way whether the period of the story is pre-Christian or Christian.[11] He looked at this "secular" world most intently and seriously; and he painted it, we cannot but conclude, with entire fidelity, without the wish to enforce an opinion of his own, and, in essentials, without regard to anyone's hopes, fears, or beliefs. His greatness is largely due to this fidelity in a mind of extraordinary power; and if, as a private person, he had a religious faith, his tragic view can hardly have been in contradiction with this faith, but must have been included in it, and supplemented, not abolished, by additional ideas.

Two statements, next, may at once be made regarding the tragic fact as he represents it: one, that it is and remains to us something piteous, fearful and mysterious; the other, that the representation of it does not leave us crushed, rebellious, or desperate. These statements will be accepted, I believe, by any reader who is in touch with Shakespeare's mind and can observe his own. Indeed such a reader is rather likely to complain that they are painfully obvious. But if they are true as well as obvious, something follows from them in regard to our present question.

From the first it follows that the ultimate power in the tragic world is not adequately described as a law or order which we can see to be just and benevolent—as, in that sense, a "moral order": for in that case the spectacle of suffering and waste could

not seem to us so fearful and mysterious as it does. And from
the second it follows that this ultimate power is not adequately
described as a fate, whether malicious and cruel, or blind and indifferent to human happiness and goodness: for in that case the
spectacle would leave us desperate or rebellious. Yet one or other
of these two ideas will be found to govern most accounts of
Shakespeare's tragic view or world. These accounts isolate and
exaggerate single aspects, either the aspect of action or that of
suffering; either the close and unbroken connection of character,
will, deed and catastrophe, which, taken alone, shows the individual simply as sinning against, or failing to conform to, the
moral order and drawing his just doom on his own head; or else
that pressure of outward forces, that sway of accident, and those
blind and agonised struggles, which, taken alone, show him as
the mere victim of some power which cares neither for his sins
nor for his pain. Such views contradict one another, and no third
view can unite them; but the several aspects from whose isolation
and exaggeration they spring are both present in the fact, and a
view which would be true to the fact and to the whole of our
imaginative experience must in some way combine these aspects.

Let us begin, then, with the idea of fatality and glance at some
of the impressions which give rise to it, without asking at present
whether this idea is their natural or fitting expression. There can
be no doubt that they do arise and that they ought to arise. If
we do not feel at times that the hero is, in some sense, a doomed
man; that he and others drift struggling to destruction like helpless creatures borne on an irresistible flood towards a cataract;
that, faulty as they may be, their fault is far from being the sole
or sufficient cause of all they suffer; and that the power from
which they cannot escape is relentless and immovable, we have
failed to receive an essential part of the full tragic effect.

The sources of these impressions are various, and I will refer
only to a few. One of them is put into words by Shakespeare
himself when he makes the player-king in *Hamlet* say:

Our thoughts are ours, their ends none of our own;

"their ends" are the issues or outcomes of our thoughts, and these,
says the speaker, are not our own. The tragic world is a world

of action, and action is the translation of thought into reality. We see men and women confidently attempting it. They strike into the existing order of things in pursuance of their ideas. But what they achieve is not what they intended; it is terribly unlike it. They understand nothing, we say to ourselves, of the world on which they operate. They fight blindly in the dark, and the power that works through them makes them the instrument of a design which is not theirs. They act freely, and yet their action binds them hand and foot. And it makes no difference whether they meant well or ill. No one could mean better than Brutus, but he contrives misery for his country and death for himself. No one could mean worse than Iago, and he too is caught in the web he spins for others. Hamlet, recoiling from the rough duty of revenge, is pushed into blood-guiltiness he never dreamed of, and forced at last on the revenge he could not will. His adversary's murders, and no less his adversary's remorse, bring about the opposite of what they sought. Lear follows an old man's whim, half generous, half selfish; and in a moment it looses all the powers of darkness upon him. Othello agonises over an empty fiction, and, meaning to execute solemn justice, butchers innocence and strangles love. They understand themselves no better than the world about them. Coriolanus thinks that his heart is iron, and it melts like snow before a fire. Lady Macbeth, who thought she could dash out her own child's brains, finds herself hounded to death by the smell of a stranger's blood. Her husband thinks that to gain a crown he would jump the life to come, and finds that the crown has brought him all the horrors of that life. Everywhere, in this tragic world, man's thought, translated into act, is transformed into the opposite of itself. His act, the movement of a few ounces of matter in a moment of time, becomes a monstrous flood which spreads over a kingdom. And whatsoever he dreams of doing, he achieves that which he least dreamed of, his own destruction.

All this makes us feel the blindness and helplessness of man. Yet by itself it would hardly suggest the idea of fate, because it shows man as in some degree, however slight, the cause of his own undoing. But other impressions come to aid it. It is aided by everything which makes us feel that a man is, as we say, terribly unlucky; and of this there is, even in Shakespeare, not a

little. Here come in some of the accidents already considered,
Juliet's waking from her trance a minute too late. Desdemona's
loss of her handkerchief at the only moment when the loss would
have mattered, that insignificant delay which cost Cordelia's life.
Again, men act, no doubt, in accordance with their characters;
but what is it that brings them just the one problem which is
fatal to them and would be easy to another, and sometimes brings
it to them just when they are least fitted to face it? How is it
that Othello comes to be the companion of the one man in the
world who is at once able enough, brave enough, and vile enough
to ensnare him? By what strange fatality does it happen that
Lear has such daughters and Cordelia such sisters? Even character itself contributes to these feelings of fatality. How could
men escape, we cry, such vehement propensities as drive Romeo,
Antony, Coriolanus, to their doom? And why is it that a man's
virtues help to destroy him, and that his weakness or defect is so
intertwined with everything that is admirable in him that we can
hardly separate them even in imagination?

If we find in Shakespeare's tragedies the source of impressions
like these, it is important, on the other hand, to notice what we
do *not* find there. We find practically no trace of fatalism in its
more primitive, crude, and obvious forms. Nothing, again, makes
us think of the actions and sufferings of the persons as somehow
arbitrarily fixed beforehand without regard to their feelings,
thoughts, and resolutions. Nor, I believe, are the facts ever so
presented that it seems to us as if the supreme power, whatever
it may be, had a special spite against a family or an individual.
Neither, lastly, do we receive the impression (which, it must be
observed, is not purely fatalistic) that a family, owing to some
hideous crime or impiety in early days, is doomed in later days
to continue a career of portentous calamities and sins. Shakespeare, indeed, does not appear to have taken much interest in
heredity, or to have attached much importance to it. . . .

What, then, is this "fate" which the impressions already considered lead us to describe as the ultimate power in the tragic
world? It appears to be a mythological expression for the whole
system or order, of which the individual characters form an in-
considerable and feeble part; which seems to determine, far more

than they, their native dispositions and their circumstances, and, through these, their action; which is so vast and complex that they can scarcely at all understand it or control its workings; and which has a nature so definite and fixed that whatever changes take place in it produce other changes inevitably and without regard to men's desires and regrets. And whether this system or order is best called by the name of fate or no,[12] it can hardly be denied that it does appear as the ultimate power in the tragic world, and that it has such characteristics as these. But the name "fate" may be intended to imply something more—to imply that this order is a blank necessity, totally regardless alike of human weal and of the difference between good and evil or right and wrong. And such an implication many readers would at once reject. They would maintain, on the contrary, that this order shows characteristics of quite another kind from those which made us give it the name of fate, characteristics which certainly should not induce us to forget those others, but which would lead us to describe it as a moral order and its necessity as a moral necessity.

5

Let us turn, then, to this idea. It brings into the light those aspects of the tragic fact which the idea of fate throws into the shade. And the argument which leads to it in its simplest form may be stated briefly thus: "Whatever may be said of accidents, circumstances and the like, human action is, after all, presented to us as the central fact in tragedy, and also as the main cause of the catastrophe. That necessity which so much impresses us is, after all, chiefly the necessary connection of actions and consequences. For these actions we, without even raising a question on the subject, hold the agents responsible; and the tragedy would disappear for us if we did not. The critical action is, in greater or less degree, wrong or bad. The catastrophe is, in the main, the return of this action on the head of the agent. It is an example of justice; and that order which, present alike within the agents and outside them, infallibly brings it about, is therefore just. The rigour of its justice is terrible, no doubt, for a tragedy is a terrible story; but, in spite of fear and pity, we acquiesce, because our sense of justice is satisfied."

Now, if this view is to hold good, the "justice" of which it speaks must be at once distinguished from what is called "poetic justice." "Poetic justice" means that prosperity and adversity are distributed in proportion to the merits of the agents. Such "poetic justice" is in flagrant contradiction with the facts of life, and it is absent from Shakespeares tragic picture of life; indeed, this very absence is a ground of constant complaint on the part of Dr. Johnson. Δρασαντι παθειν, "the doer must suffer"—this we find in Shakespeare. We also find that villainy never remains victorious and prosperous at the last. But an assignment of amounts of happiness and misery, an assignment even of life and death, in proportion to merit, we do not find. No one who thinks of Desdemona and Cordelia; or who remembers that one end awaits Richard III. and Brutus, Macbeth and Hamlet; or who asks himself which suffered most, Othello or Iago; will ever accuse Shakespeare of representing the ultimate power as "poetically" just.

And we must go further. I venture to say that it is a mistake to use at all these terms of justice and merit or desert. And this for two reasons. In the first place, essential as it is to recognise the connection between act and consequence, and natural as it may seem in some cases (e.g. Macbeth's) to say that the doer only gets what he deserves, yet in very many cases to say this would be quite unnatural. We might not object to the statement that Lear deserved to suffer for his folly, selfishness and tyranny; but to assert that he deserved to suffer what he did suffer is to do violence not merely to language but to any healthy moral sense. It is, moreover, to obscure the tragic fact that the consequences of action cannot be limited to that which would appear to us to follow "justly" from them. And, this being so, when we call the order of the tragic world just, we are either using the word in some vague and unexplained sense, or we are going beyond what is shown us of this order, and are appealing to faith.

But, in the second place, the ideas of justice and desert are, it seems to me, in *all* cases—even those of Richard III. and of Macbeth and Lady Macbeth—untrue to our imaginative experience.

When we are immersed in a tragedy, we feel towards dispositions, actions, and persons such emotions as attraction and repulsion, pity, wonder, fear, horror, perhaps hatred; but we do not *judge*. This is a point of view which emerges only when, in reading a play, we slip, by our own fault or the dramatist's, from the tragic position, or when, in thinking about the play afterwards, we fall back on our everyday legal and moral notions. But tragedy does not belong, any more than religion belongs, to the sphere of these notions; neither does the imaginative attitude in presence of it. While we are in its world we watch what is, seeing that so it happened and must have happened, feeling that it is piteous, dreadful, awful, mysterious, but neither passing sentence on the agents, nor asking whether the behaviour of the ultimate power towards them is just. And, therefore, the use of such language in attempts to render our imaginative experience in terms of the understanding is, to say the least, full of danger.[13]

Let us attempt then to re-state the idea that the ultimate power in the tragic world is a moral order. Let us put aside the ideas of justice and merit, and speak simply of good and evil. Let us understand by these words, primarily, moral good and evil, but also everything else in human beings which we take to be excellent or the reverse. Let us understand the statement that the ultimate power or order is "moral" to mean that it does not show itself indifferent to good and evil, or equally favourable or unfavourable to both, but shows itself akin to good and alien from evil. And, understanding the statement thus, let us ask what grounds it has in the tragic fact as presented by Shakespeare.

Here, as in dealing with the grounds on which the idea of fate rests, I choose only two or three out of many. And the most important is this. In Shakespearean tragedy the main source of the convulsion which produces suffering and death is never good: good contributes to this convulsion only from its tragic implication with its opposite in one and the same character. The main source, on the contrary, is in every case evil; and, what is more (though this seems to have been little noticed), it is in almost every case evil in the fullest sense, not mere imperfection but plain moral evil. The love of Romeo and Juliet conducts them to death only because of the senseless hatred of their houses. Guilty ambition, seconded by diabolic malice and issuing in murder, opens the action in *Macbeth*. Iago is the main source of the convulsion in *Othello*; Goneril, Regan, and Edmund in *King Lear*. Even when this plain moral evil is not the obviously prime source within the play, it lies behind it: the situation with which Hamlet has to deal has been formed by adultery and murder. *Julius Caesar* is the only tragedy in which one is even tempted to find an exception to this rule. And the inference is obvious. If it is chiefly evil that violently disturbs the order of the world, this order cannot be friendly to evil or indifferent between evil and good, any more than a body which is convulsed by poison is friendly to it or indifferent to the distinction between poison and food.

Again, if we confine our attention to the hero, and to those cases where the gross and palpable evil is not in him but elsewhere, we find that the comparatively innocent hero still shows some marked imperfection or defect—irresolution, precipitancy, pride, credulousness, excessive simplicity, excessive susceptibility to sexual emotions, and the like. These defects or imperfections are certainly, in the wide sense of the word, evil, and they contribute decisively to the conflict and catastrophe. And the inference is again obvious. The ultimate power which shows itself disturbed by this evil and reacts against it, must have a nature alien to it. Indeed its reaction is so vehement and "relentless" that it would seem to be bent on nothing short of good in perfection, and to be ruthless in its demand for it.

To this must be added another fact, or another aspect of the same fact. Evil exhibits itself everywhere as something negative, barren, weakening, destructive, a principle of death. It isolates, disunites, and tends to annihilate not only its opposite but itself. That which keeps the evil man [14] prosperous, makes him succeed, even permits him to exist, is the good in him (I do not mean only the obviously "moral" good). When the evil in him masters the good and has its way, it destroys other people through him, but it also destroys *him*. At the close of the struggle he has vanished, and has left behind him nothing that can stand. What remains is a family, a city, a country, exhausted, pale and feeble, but alive through the principle of good which animates it; and, within it, individuals who, if they have not the brilliance or greatness of the tragic character, still have won our respect and confidence. And the inference would seem clear. If existence in an order depends on good, and if the presence of evil is hostile to such existence, the inner being or soul of this order must be akin to good.

These are aspects of the tragic world at least as clearly marked as those which, taken alone, suggest the idea of fate. And the idea which they in their turn, when taken alone, may suggest, is that of an order which does not indeed award "poetic justice," but which reacts through the necessity of its own "moral" nature both against attacks made upon it and against failure to conform to it. Tragedy, on this view, is the exhibition of that convulsive reaction; and the fact that the spectacle does not leave us rebellious or desperate is due to a more or less distinct perception that the tragic suffering and death arise from collision, not with a fate or blank power, but with a moral power, a power akin to all that we admire and revere in the characters themselves. This perception produces something like a feeling of acquiescence in the catastrophe, though it neither leads us to pass judgment on the characters nor diminishes the pity, the fear, and the sense of waste, which their struggle, suffering, and fall evoke. And, finally, this view seems quite able to do justice to those aspects of the tragic fact which give rise to the idea of fate. They would appear as various expressions of the fact that the moral order acts not capriciously or like a human being, but from the necessity of its nature, or, if we prefer the phrase, by general laws—a necessity or law which of course knows no exception and is as "ruthless" as fate.

It is impossible to deny to this view a large measure of truth. And yet without some amendment it can hardly satisfy. For it does not include the whole of the facts, and therefore does not wholly correspond with the impressions they produce. Let it be granted that the system or order which shows itself omnipotent against individuals is, in the sense explained, moral. Still—at any rate for the eye of sight—the evil against which it asserts itself, and the persons whom this evil inhabits, are not really something outside the order, so that they can attack it or fail to conform to it; they are within it and a part of it. It itself produces them—produces Iago as well as Desdemona, Iago's cruelty as well as Iago's courage. It is not poisoned, it poisons itself. Doubtless it shows by its violent reaction that the poison *is* poison, and that its health lies in good. But one significant fact cannot remove another, and the spectacle we witness scarcely warrants the assertion that the order is responsible for the good in Desdemona, but Iago for the evil in Iago. If we make this assertion we make it on grounds other than the facts as presented in Shakespeare's tragedies.

Nor does the idea of a moral order asserting itself against attack or want of conformity answer in full to our feelings regarding the tragic character. We do not think of Hamlet merely as failing to meet its demand, of Antony as merely sinning against it, or even of Macbeth as simply attacking it. What we feel corresponds quite as much to the idea that they are *its* parts, expressions, products; that in their defect or evil *it* is untrue to its soul of goodness, and falls into conflict and collision with itself; that, in making them suffer and waste themselves, *it* suffers and wastes itself; and that when, to save its life and regain peace from this intestinal struggle, it casts them out, it has lost a part of its own substance—a part more dangerous and unquiet, but far more valuable and nearer to its heart, than that which remains—a Fortinbras, a Malcolm, an Octavius. There is no tragedy in its expulsion of evil: the tragedy is that this involves the waste of good.

Thus we are left at last with an idea showing two sides or aspects which we can neither separate nor reconcile. The whole or order against which the individual part shows itself powerless seems to be animated by a passion for perfection: we cannot otherwise explain its behaviour towards evil. Yet it appears to engender this evil within itself, and in its effort to overcome and expel it it is agonised with pain, and driven to multilate its own substance and to lose not only evil but priceless good. That this idea, though very different from the idea of a blank fate, is no solution of the riddle of life is obvious; but why should we expect it to be such a solution? Shakespeare was not attempting to justify the ways of God to men, or to show the universe as a Divine

Comedy. He was writing tragedy, and tragedy would not be tragedy if it were not a painful mystery. Nor can he be said even to point distinctly, like some writers of tragedy, in any direction where a solution might lie. We find a few references to gods or God, to the influence of the stars, to another life: some of them certainly, all of them perhaps, merely dramatic—appropriate to the person from whose lips they fall. A ghost comes from Purgatory to impart a secret out of the reach of its hearer—who presently meditates on the question whether the sleep of death is dreamless. Accidents once or twice remind us strangely of the words, "There's a divinity that shapes our ends." More important are other impressions. Sometimes from the very furnace of affliction a conviction seems borne to us that somehow, if we could see it, this agony counts as nothing against the heroism and love which appear in it and thrill our hearts. Sometimes we are driven to cry out that these mighty or heavenly spirits who perish are too great for the little space in which they move, and that they vanish not into nothingness but into freedom. Sometimes from these sources and from others comes a presentiment, formless but haunting and even profound, that all the fury of conflict, with its waste and woe, is less than half the truth, even an illusion, "such stuff as dreams are made on." But these faint and scattered intimations that the tragic world, being but a fragment of a whole beyond our vision, must needs to be a contradiction and no ultimate truth, avail nothing to interpret the mystery. We remain confronted with the inexplicable fact, or the no less inexplicable appearance, of a world travailing for perfection, but bring to birth, together with glorious good, an evil which it is able to overcome only by self-torture and self-waste. And this fact or appearance is tragedy.[15]

1 *Julius Caesar* is not an exception to this rule. Caesar, whose murder comes in the third act, is in a sense the dominating figure in the story, but Brutus is the "hero."

2 *Timon of Athens,* we have seen, was probably not designed by Shakespeare, but even *Timon* is no exception to the rule. The subplot is concerned with Alcibiades and his army, and Timon himself is treated by the Senate as a man of great importance. *Arden of Feversham* and *A Yorkshire Tragedy* would certainly be exceptions to the rule; but I assume that neither of them is Shakespeare's; and if either is, it belongs to a different species from his admitted tragedies. See, on this species, Symonds, *Shakspere's Predecessors,* ch. xi.

3 Even a deed would, I think, be counted an "accident," if it were the deed of a very minor person whose character had not been indicated; because such a deed would not issue from the little world to which the dramatist had confined our attention.

4 Comedy stands in a different position. The tricks played by chance often form a principal part of the comic action.

5 It may be observed that the influence of the three elements just considered is to strengthen the tendency, produced by the sufferings considered first, to regard the tragic persons as passive rather than as agents.

6 An account of Hegel's view may be found in *Oxford Lectures on Poetry.*

7 The reader, however, will find considerable difficulty in placing some very important characters in these and other plays. I will give only two or three illustrations. Edgar is clearly not on the same side as Edmund, and yet it seems awkward to range him on Gloster's side when Gloster wishes to put him to death. Ophelia is in love with Hamlet, but how can she be said to be of Hamlet's party against the King and Polonius, or of their party against Hamlet? Desdemona worships Othello, yet it sounds odd to say that Othello is on the same side with a person whom he insults, strikes, and murders.

8 I have given names to the "spiritual forces" in *Macbeth* merely to illustrate the idea, and without any pretension to adequacy. Perhaps, in view of some interpretations of Shakespeare's plays, it will be as well to add that I do not dream of suggesting that in any of his dramas Shakespeare imagined two abstract principles or passions conflicting, and incorporated them in persons; or that there is any necessity for a reader to define for himself the particular forces which conflict in a given case.

9 Aristotle apparently would exclude them.

10 Richard II. is perhaps an exception, and I must confess that to me he is scarcely a tragic character, and that, if he is nevertheless a tragic figure, he is so only because his fall from prosperity to adversity is so great.

11 I say substantially; but the concluding remarks on *Hamlet* will modify a little the statements above.

12 I have raised no objection to the use of the idea of fate, because it occurs so often both in conversation and in books about Shakespeare's tragedies that I must suppose it to be natural to many readers. Yet I doubt whether it would be so if Greek tragedy had never been written; and I must in candour confess that to me it does not often occur while I am reading, or when I have just read, a tragedy of Shakespeare. Wordsworth's lines, for example, about

> *poor humanity's afflicted will*
> *Struggling in vain with ruthless destiny*

do not represent the impression I receive; much less do images which compare man to a puny creature helpless in the claws of a bird of prey. The reader should examine himself closely on this matter.

13 It is dangerous, I think, in reference to all really good tragedies, but I am dealing here only with Shakespeare's. In not a few Greek tragedies it is almost inevitable that we should think of justice and retribution, not only because the *dramatis personae* often speak of them, but also because there is something casuistical about the tragic problem itself. The poet treats the story in such a way that the question, Is the hero doing right or wrong? is almost forced upon us. But this is not so with Shakespeare. *Julius Caesar* is probably the only one of his tragedies in which the question suggests itself to us, and this is one of the reasons why that play has something of a classic air. Even here, if we ask the question, we have no doubt at all about the answer.

14 It is most essential to remember that an evil man is much more than the evil in him. I may add that in this paragraph I have, for the sake of clearness, considered evil in its most pronounced form; but what is said would apply, *mutatis mutandis,* to evil as imperfection, etc.

15 Partly in order not to anticipate later passages [in *Shakespearean Tragedy*], I abstained from treating fully here the question why we feel, at the death of the tragic hero, not only pain but also reconciliation and sometimes even exultation. . . . See . . . in *Oxford Lectures on Poetry, Hegel's Theory of Tragedy,* especially pp. 90, 91.

2

On the Principles
of Shakespeare Interpretation

G. WILSON KNIGHT

G. Wilson Knight has had three distinguished careers: he has taught since 1923 both in Canada and in England, where from 1956 to 1962 he was Professor of English Literature at Leeds University; he has produced and acted in a number of plays, many of them by Shakespeare; and he has written a score of books, of which seven are on Shakespeare. The present essay, the first chapter of his first book on Shakespeare, The Wheel of Fire *(1930), constitutes a virtual manifesto of Knight's brilliant, intensely personal, and highly controversial methodology. In what he calls his "spatial" approach, in his concern with organic unity as revealed through and controlled by "themes," and in his interest in "interpretation," Professor Knight shows himself heir to the tradition of Bradley (as he himself acknowledges), and behind Bradley of Coleridge; but in his refutation of "character" he declares his independence from Bradley. His interest in symbolism and in the relation of particular detail to the "visionary unit" which is his concept of the Shakespearean play associates him with the later work of the New Critics; it should be noted, however, that he has never belonged to any school of criticism, but has responded idiosyncratically to the same historical forces which were to shape their work.*

The following essays present an interpretation of Shakespeare's work which may tend at first to confuse and perhaps even repel the reader: therefore I here try to clarify the points at issue. In this essay I outline what I believe to be the main hindrances to a proper understanding of Shakespeare; I also suggest the path which I think a sound interpretation should pursue. My remarks are, however, to be read as a counsel of perfection. Yet, though I cannot claim to follow them throughout in practice, this . . . discussion, in showing what I have been at pains to do and to avoid, will serve to indicate the direction of my attempt.

At the start, I would draw a distinction between the terms "criticism" and "interpretation." It will be as well to define, purely for my immediate purpose, my personal uses of the words. "Criticism" to me suggests a certain process of deliberately objectifying the work under consideration; the comparison of it with other similar works in order especially to show in what respects it surpasses, or falls short of, those works; the dividing its "good" from its "bad"; and, finally, a formal judgement as to its lasting validity. "Interpretation," on the contrary, tends to merge into the work it analyses; it attempts, as far as possible, to understand its subject in the light of its own nature, employing external reference, if at all, only as a preliminary to understanding; it avoids discussion of merits, and, since its existence depends entirely on its original acceptance of the validity of the poetic unit which it claims, in some measure, to translate into discursive reasoning, it can recognize no division of "good" from "bad." Thus criticism is active and looks ahead, often treating past work as material on which to base future standards and canons of art; interpretation is passive, and looks back, regarding only the imperative challenge of a poetic vision. Criticism is a judgement of vision; interpretation a reconstruction of vision. In practice, it is probable that neither can exist, or at least has yet on any comprehensive scale existed, quite divorced from the other. The greater part of poetic commentary pursues a middle course between criticism and interpretation. But sometimes work is created of so resplendent a quality, so massive a solidity of imagination, that adverse criticism beats against it idly as the wind that flings its ineffectual force against a mountain-rock. Any profitable commentary on such work must necessarily tend towards a pure interpretation.

The work of Shakespeare is of this transcendent order. Though much has already been written on it, only that profitably survives which in its total effect tends to interpretation rather than criticism. Coleridge, repelled by one of the horrors in *King Lear*, admitted that the author's judgment, being so consistently faultless, was here probably superior to his own: and he was right. That is the interpretative approach. Hazlitt and A. C. Bradley both developed that approach: their work is primarily interpretative. But to-day there is a strong tendency to "criticize" Shakespeare, to select certain aspects of his mature works and point out faults. These faults are accounted for in various ways: it is said that Shakespeare, though a great genius, was yet a far from perfect artist; that certain elements were introduced solely to please a vulgar audience; or even, if the difficulty be extreme, that they are the work of another hand. Now it will generally be found that when a play is understood in its totality, these faults automatically vanish. For instance, Hamlet's slowness to avenge his father, the forgiveness of Angelo, Macbeth's vagueness of motive, Timon's universal hate—all these, which have continually baffled commentators, instead of projecting as ugly curiosities, will, when once we find the true focus demanded by the poet's work, appear not merely as relevant and even necessary, but as crucial, and themselves the very essence of the play concerned. It is, then, a matter of correct focal length; nor is it the poet's fault if our focus is wrong. For our imaginative focus is generally right enough. In reading, watching, or acting Shakespeare for pure enjoyment we accept everything. But when we think "critically" we see faults which are not implicit in the play or our enjoyment of it, but merely figments of our own minds. We should not, in fact, think critically at all: we should interpret our original imaginative experience into the slower consciousness of logic and intellect, preserving something of that child-like faith which we possess, or should possess, in the theatre. It is exactly this translation from one order of consciousness to another that interpretation claims to perform. Uncritically, and passively, it receives the whole of the poet's vision; it then proceeds to re-express this experience in its own terms.

But to receive the whole Shakespearian vision into the intellectual consciousness demands a certain and very definite act of mind. One must be prepared to see the whole play in space as well as in time. It is natural in analysis to pursue the steps of the

tale in sequence, noticing the logic that connects them, regarding
those essentials that Aristotle noted: the beginning, middle, and
end. But by giving supreme attention to this temporal nature of
drama we omit what, in Shakespeare, is at least of equivalent importance. A Shakespearian tragedy is set spatially as well as tem-
porally in the mind. By this I mean that there are throughout the
play a set of correspondences which relate to each other independently of the time-sequence which is the story: such are the
intuition-intelligence opposition active within and across *Troilus
and Cressida,* the death-theme in *Hamlet,* the nightmare evil of
Macbeth. This I have sometimes called the play's "atmosphere."
In interpretation of *Othello* it has to take the form of an essential
relation, abstracted from the story, existing between the Othello,
Desdemona, and Iago conceptions. Generally, however, there is
unity, not diversity. Perhaps it is what Aristotle meant by "unity
of idea." Now if we are prepared to see the whole play laid out,
so to speak, as an area, being simultaneously aware of these
thickly-scattered correspondences in a single view of the whole,
we possess the unique quality of the play in a new sense. "Faults"
begin to vanish into thin air. Immediately we begin to realize necessity where before we saw irrelevance and beauty dethroning
ugliness. For the Shakespearian person is intimately fused with
this atmospheric quality; he obeys a spatial as well as a temporal
necessity. Gloucester's mock-suicide, Malcolm's detailed confession of crimes, Ulysses' long speech on order, are cases in point.
But because we, in our own lives and those of our friends, see
events most strongly as a time-sequence—thereby blurring our vision of other significances—we next, quite arbitrarily and unjustly,
abstract from the Shakespearian drama that element which the
intellect most easily assimilates; and, finding it not to correspond
with our own life as we see it, begin to observe "faults." This,
however, is apparent only after we try to rationalize our impressions; what I have called the "spatial" approach is implicit in our
imaginative pleasure to a greater or a less degree always. It is,
probably, the ability to see larger and still larger areas of a great
work spatially with a continual widening of vision that causes us
to appreciate it more deeply, to own it with our minds more surely,
on every reading; whereas at first, knowing it only as a story,

much of it may have seemed sterile, and much of it irrelevant. A vivid analogy to this Shakespearian quality is provided by a fine modern play, *Journey's End*. Everything in the play gains tremendous significance from war. The story, which is slight, moves across a stationary background: if we forget that background for one instant parts of the dialogue fall limp; remember it, and the most ordinary remark is tense, poignant—often of shattering power. To study *Measure for Measure* or *Macbeth* without reference to their especial "atmospheres" is rather like forgetting the war as we read or witness *Journey's End;* or the cherry orchard in Tchehov's famous play. There is, however, a difference. In *Journey's End* the two elements, the dynamic and static, action and background, are each firmly actualized and separated except in so far as Stanhope, rather like Hamlet, bridges the two. In *The Cherry Orchard* there is the same division. But with Shakespeare a purely spiritual atmosphere interpenetrates the action, there is a fusing rather than a contrast; and where a direct personal symbol growing out of the dominating atmosphere is actualized, it may be a supernatural being, as the Ghost, symbol of the death-theme in *Hamlet,* or the Weird Sisters, symbols of the evil in *Macbeth.*

Since in Shakespeare there is this close fusion of the temporal, that is, the plot-chain of event following event, with the spatial, that is, the omnipresent and mysterious reality brooding motionless over and within the play's movement, it is evident that my two principles thus firmly divided in analysis are no more than provisional abstractions from the poetic unity. But since to make the first abstraction with especial crudity, that is, to analyse the sequence of events, the "causes" linking dramatic motive to action and action to result in time, is a blunder instinctive to the human intellect, I make no apology for restoring balance by insistence on the other. My emphasis is justified, in that it will be seen to clarify many difficulties. It throws neglected beauties into strong relief, and often resolves the whole play with a sudden revelation. For example, the ardour of Troilus in battle against the Greeks at the close of *Troilus and Cressida,* Mariana's lovely prayer for Angelo's life, the birth of love in Edmund at the close of *King Lear,* and the stately theme of Alcibiades' revenge in *Timon of*

Athens—all these cannot be properly understood without a clear knowledge of the general themes which vitalize the action of those plays.

These dual elements seem perfectly harmonized in *Troilus and Cressida, Measure for Measure, Macbeth,* and *King Lear.* In *Hamlet* the spatial element is mainly confined to the theme of Hamlet and the Ghost, both sharply contrasted with their environment: thus the play offers a less unified statement as a whole, and interpretation is rendered difficult and not wholly satisfactory. With *Othello,* too, there is difficulty. Unless the play is to be considered as purely a sequence of events, if we are to find a spatial reality, we must view the qualities of the three chief persons together and in their essential relation to each other expect to find the core of the metaphysical significance: for the primary fact of the play is not, as in *Macbeth* and *King Lear,* a blending, but rather a differentiating, a demarcation, and separation, of essence from essence. In *Timon of Athens* both elements appear, but the temporal predominates in that the imaginative atmosphere itself changes with the play's progress: which fact here seems to reflect the peculiar clarity and conscious mastery of the poet's mind. With the poet, as with the reader, the time-sequence will be uppermost in consciousness, the pervading atmosphere or static background tending to be unconsciously apprehended or created, a half-realized significance, a vague all-inclusive deity of the dramatic universe. In respect of this atmospheric suggestion we find a sense of mystery in *King Lear* which cannot be found in *Othello;* and, in so far as the Shakespearian play lacks mystery, it seems, as a rule, to lack profundity. But in *Timon of Athens* the mystery of *King Lear* is, as it were, mastered, and yet re-expressed with the clarity of *Othello.* Here the poet explicates the atmospheric quality of former plays in a philosophic tragedy whose dominant temporal quality thus mirrors the clarity, in no sense the sterility, of the poet's vision. The spatial, that is, the spiritual, quality uses the temporal, that is, the story, lending it dominance in order to express itself the more clearly: *Timon of Athens* is essentially an allegory or parable. My suggestion as to the poet's "consciousness" must, however, be considered as either pure hazard or useful metaphor, illuminating the play's nature and per-

haps hitting the truth of Shakespeare's mind in composition. Certainly Hazlitt thought that in *Timon of Athens* the poet was of all
his plays the most "in earnest." But elsewhere I am not concerned
with the poet's "consciousness," or "intentions." Nor need the
question arise; but, since a strong feeling exists that no subtlety
or profundity can be born from a mind itself partly unconscious
of such things, and since Shakespeare's life appears not to have
been mainly concerned with transcendental realities—except in
that he was born, loved, was ambitious, and died—it will be as
well to refer briefly to the matter of "intentions." This I shall do
next, and will afterwards deal with two other critical concepts
which, with "intentions," have helped to work chaos with our
understanding of poetry.

There is a maxim that a work of art should be criticized according to the artist's "intentions": than which no maxim could
be more false. The intentions of the artist are but clouded forms
which, if he attempt to crystallize them in consciousness, may prefigure a quite different reality from that which eventually emerges
in his work,

> *not answering the aim*
> *And that unbodied figure of the thought*
> *That gave't surmised shape.*

In those soliloquies where Brutus and Macbeth try to clarify
their own motives into clean-cut concepts, we may see good examples of the irrelevance borne by "intentions" to the instinctive
power which is bearing the man towards his fate: it is the same
with the poet. Milton's puritanical "intentions" bear little relevance to his Satan. "Intentions" belong to the plane of intellect
and memory: the swifter consciousness that awakens in poetic
composition touches subtleties and heights and depths unknow-
able by intellect and intractable to memory. That consciousness
we can enjoy at will when we submit ourselves with utmost passivity to the poet's work; but when the intellectual mode returns
it often brings with it a troop of concepts irrelevant to the nature
of the work it thinks to analyse, and, with its army of "intentions," "causes," "sources," and "characters," and its essentially

ethical outlook, works havoc with our minds, since it is trying to impose on the vivid reality of art a logic totally alien to its nature. In interpretation we must remember not the facts but the quality of the original poetic experience; and, in translating this into whatever concepts appear suitable, we find that the facts too fall into place automatically when once the qualitative focus is correct. Reference to the artist's "intentions" is usually a sign that the commentator—in so far as he is a commentator rather than a biographer—has lost touch with the essentials of the poetic work. He is thinking in terms of the time-sequence and causality, instead of allowing his mind to be purely receptive. It will be clear, then, that the following essays say nothing new as to Shakespeare's "intentions"; attempt to shed no light directly on Shakespeare the man; but claim rather to illuminate our own poetic experiences enjoyed whilst reading, or watching, the plays. In this sense, they are concerned only with realities, since they claim to interpret what is generally admitted to exist: the supreme quality of Shakespeare's work.

Next as to "sources." This concept is closely involved with that of "intentions." Both try to explain art in terms of causality, the most natural implement of intellect. Both fail empirically to explain any essential whatsoever. There is, clearly, a relation between Shakespeare's plays and the work of Plutarch, Holinshed, Vergil, Ovid, and the Bible; but not one of these, nor any number of them, can be considered a cause of Shakespeare's poetry and therefore the word "source," that is, the origin whence the poetic reality flows, is a false metaphor. In Shakespeare's best known passage of aesthetic philosophy we hear that the poet's eye glances "from heaven to earth, from earth to heaven," and that the poet's pen turns to "shapes" the "forms of things unknown." It "gives to airy nothing a local habitation and a name." That is, the source of poetry is rooted in the otherness of mental or spiritual realities; these, however, are a "nothing" until mated with earthly shapes. Creation is thus born of a union between "earth" and "heaven," the material and the spiritual. Without "shapes" the poet is speechless; he needs words, puppets of the drama, tales. But the unknown "forms" come first. In another profound but less known passage (Richard II, v. v. 6) we hear that in creation the brain is "the female to the soul." The spiritual then is the masculine, the material the feminine, agent in creation. The "source" of *Antony and Cleopatra,* if we must indeed have a "source" at all, is the transcendent erotic imagination of the poet which finds its worthy bride in an old-world romance. It seems, indeed, that the great poet must, if he is to forego nothing of concreteness and humanity, lose himself in contemplation of an actual tale or an actual event in order to find himself in supreme vision; otherwise he will tend to philosophy, to the divine element unmated to the earthly. Therefore "sources," as usually understood, have their use for the poet: they have little value for the interpreter. The tale of Cleopatra married to a Hardy's imagination would have given birth to a novel very different from Shakespeare's play: the final poetic result is always a mystery. That result, and not vague hazards as to its "source," must be the primary object of our attention. It should further be observed that, although the purely "temporal" element of Shakespearian drama may sometimes bear a close relation to a tale probably known by Shakespeare, what I have called the "spatial" reality is ever the unique child of his mind; therefore interpretation, concerned, as in the following essays, so largely with that reality, is clearly working outside and beyond the story alone. Now, whereas the spatial quality of these greater plays is different in each, they nearly all turn on the same plot. It is therefore reasonable to conclude that the poet has chosen a series of tales to whose life-rhythm he is spontaneously attracted, and has developed them in each instance according to his vision.

And finally, as to "character." In the following essays the term is refused, since it is so constantly entwined with a false and unduly ethical criticism. So often we hear that "in *Timon of Athens* it was Shakespeare's intention to show how a generous but weak character may come to ruin through an unwise use of his wealth"; that "Shakespeare wished in *Macbeth* to show how crime inevitably brings retribution"; that, "in *Antony and Cleopatra* Shakespeare has given us a lesson concerning the dangers of an uncontrolled passion." These are purely imaginary examples, coloured for my purpose, to indicate the type of ethical criticism to which I refer. It continually brings in the intention-concept, which our moral-philosophy, rightly or wrongly, involves. Hence, too, the constant and fruitless search for "motives" sufficient to account for Macbeth's and Iago's actions: since the moral critic feels he cannot blame a "character" until he understands his "intentions," and without the opportunity of praising and blaming he is dumb. It is not, indeed, possible to avoid ethical considerations; nor is it advisable. Where one person within the drama is immediately apparent as morally good and another as bad, we will note the difference: but we should follow our dramatic intuitions. A person in the drama may act in such a way that we are in no sense antagonized but are aware of beauty and supreme interest only; yet the analogy to that same action may well be intolerable to us in actual life. When such a divergence occurs the commentator must be true to his artistic, not his normal, ethic. Large quantities of Shakespeare criticism have wrecked themselves on the teeth of this dualism. In so far as moral values enter into our appreciation of the poetic work, they will tend to be instinctive to us: Shakespeare here, as in his other symbols, speaks our own language. I mean, it is as natural to us to like Cordelia better than Goneril with a liking which may be said to depend partly on moral values as it is for us to recognize the power of Shakespeare's tempest-symbol as suggesting human tragedy, or his use of jewel-metaphors to embody the costly riches of love. In ages hence, when perhaps tempests are controlled by science and communism has replaced wealth, then the point of Shakespeare's symbolism may need explanation; and then it may, from a new ethical view-point, be necessary to analyse at length the moral values implicit in the Cordelia and Edmund conceptions. But in these matters Shakespeare speaks almost the same language as we, and ethical terms, though they must frequently occur in interpretation, must only be allowed in so far as they are used in absolute obedience to the dramatic and aesthetic significance: in which case they cease to be ethical in the usual sense.

This false criticism is implied by the very use of the word "character." It is impossible to use the term without any tinge of a morality which blurs vision. The term, which in ordinary speech often denotes the degree of moral control exercised by the individual over his instinctive passions, is altogether unsuited to those persons of poetic drama whose life consists largely of passion unveiled. *Macbeth* and *King Lear* are created in a soul-dimension of primal feeling, of which in real life we may be only partly conscious or may be urged to control by a sense of right and wrong. In fact, it may well seem that the more we tend away from the passionate and curbless life of poetic drama, the stronger we shall be as "characters." And yet, in reading *Macbeth* or *King Lear* we are aware of strength, not weakness. We are not aware of failure: rather we "let determined things to destiny hold unbewailed their way." We must observe, then, this paradox: the strong protagonist of poetic drama would probably appear a weakling if he were a real man; and, indeed, the critic who notes primarily Macbeth's weakness is criticizing him as a man rather than a dramatic person. Ethics are essentially critical when applied to life; but if they hold any place at all in art, they will need to be modified into a new artistic ethic which obeys the peculiar nature of art as surely as a sound morality is based on the nature of man. From a true interpretation centred on the imaginative qualities of Shakespeare, certain facts will certainly emerge which bear relevance to human life, to human morals: but interpretation must come first. And interpretation must be metaphysical rather than ethical. We shall gain nothing by applying to the delicate symbols of the poet's imagination the rough machinery of an ethical philosophy created to control the turbulences of actual life. Thus when a critic adopts the ethical attitude, we shall generally find that he is unconsciously lifting the object of his attention from his setting and regarding him as actually alive. By noting "faults" in Timon's "character" we are in effect saying that he would not be a success in real life: which is beside the point, since he, and Macbeth, and Lear, are evidently dramatic successes. Now, whereas the moral attitude to life is positive and dynamic and tells us what we ought to do, that attitude applied to literature is invariably negative and destructive. It is continually thrusting on our attention a number of "failures," "mistakes," and "follies" in connexion with those dramatic persons from whom we have consistently derived delight and a sense of exultation. Even when terms of negation, such as "evil," necessarily appear—as with *Hamlet* and *Macbeth*—we should so employ them that the essence they express is felt to be something powerful, autonomous, and grand. Our reaction to great literature is a positive and dynamic experience. Crudely, sometimes ineffectually, interpretation will attempt to translate that experience in a spirit also positive and dynamic.

To do this we should regard each play as a visionary whole, close-knit in personification, atmospheric suggestion, and direct poetic-symbolism: three modes of transmission, equal in their importance. Too often the first of these alone receives attention: whereas, in truth, we should not be content even with all three, however clearly we have them in our minds, unless we can work back through them to the original vision they express. Each incident, each turn of thought, each suggestive symbol throughout *Macbeth* or *King Lear* radiates inwards from the play's circumference to the burning central core without knowledge of which we shall miss their relevance and necessity: they relate primarily, not directly to each other, nor to the normal appearances of human life, but to this central reality alone. The persons of Shakespeare have been analysed carefully in point of psychological realism. But in giving detailed and prolix attention to any one element of the poet's expression, the commentator, starting indeed from a point on the circumference, instead of working into the heart of the play, pursues a tangential course, riding, as it were, on his own life-experiences farther and farther from his proper goal. Such is the criticism that finds fault with the Duke's decisions at the close of *Measure for Measure*: if we are to understand the persons of Shakespeare we should consider always what they do rather than what they might have done. Each person, event, scene, is integral to the poetic statement: the removing, or blurring, of a single stone in the mosaic will clearly lessen our chance of visualizing the whole design.

Too often the commentator discusses Shakespeare's work without the requisite emotional sympathy and agility of intellect. Then the process of false criticism sets in: whatever elements lend themselves most readily to analysis on the analogy of actual life, these he selects, roots out, distorting their natural growth; he then praises or blames according to their measure of correspondence with his own life-experiences, and, creating the plaster figures of "character," searches everywhere for "causes" on the

analogy of human affairs, noting that Iago has no sufficient reason
for his villainy, executing some strange transference such as the
statement that Lady Macbeth would have done this or that in
Cordelia's position; observing that there appears to have been
dull weather on the occasion of Duncan's murder. But what he
will not do is recapture for analysis his own original experience,
concerned, as it was, purely with a dramatic and artistic reality:
with Iago the person of motiveless and instinctive villainy, with
Cordelia known only with reference to the *Lear* universe, with
the vivid extravagant symbolism of abnormal phenomena in beast
and element and the sun's eclipse which accompanies the unnatural act of murder. These, the true, the poetic, realities, the commentator too often passes over. He does not look straight at the
work he would interpret, is not true to his own imaginative reaction. My complaint is, not that such a commentator cannot appreciate the imaginative nature of Shakespeare—that would be
absurd and unjustifiable—but that he falsifies his own experience
when he begins to criticize. Part of the play—and that the less
important element of story—he tears out ruthlessly for detailed
analysis on the analogy of human life: with a word or two about
"the magic of poetry" or "the breath of genius" he dismisses the
rest. Hence the rich gems of Shakespeare's poetic symbolism have
been left untouched and unwanted, whilst Hamlet was being
treated in Harley Street. Hence arises the criticism discovering
faults in Shakespeare. But when a right interpretation is offered
it will generally be seen that both the fault and the criticism
which discovered it are without meaning. The older critics drove
psychological analysis to unnecessary lengths: the new school of
"realistic" criticism, in finding faults and explaining them with
regard to Shakespeare's purely practical and financial "intentions,"
is thus in reality following the wrong vision of its predecessors.
Both together trace the process of my imaginary critic, who,
thinking to have found an extreme degree of realism in one place,
ends by complaining that he finds too little in another. Neither
touch the heart of the Shakespearian play.

Nor will a sound knowledge of the stage and the especial
theatrical technique of Shakespeare's work render up its imaginative secret. True, the plays were written as plays, and meant to

be acted. But that tells us nothing relevant to our purpose. It explains why certain things cannot be found in Shakespeare: it does not explain why the finest things, the fascination of *Hamlet*, the rich music of *Othello*, the gripping evil of *Macbeth*, the pathos of *King Lear*, and the gigantic architecture of *Timon of Athens* came to birth. Shakespeare wrote in terms of drama, as he wrote in English. In the grammar of dramatic structure he expresses his vision: without that, or some other, structure he could not have expressed himself. But the dramatic nature of a play's origin cannot be adduced to disprove a quality implicit in the work itself. True, when there are any faults to be explained, this particular pursuit and aim of Shakespeare's poetry may well be noted to account for their presence. Interpretation, however, tends to resolve all but minor difficulties in connexion with the greater plays: therefore it is not necessary in the following essays to remember, or comment on, the dramatic structure of their expression, though from another point of view such comment and analysis may well be interesting. It illuminates one facet of their surface: but a true philosophic and imaginative interpretation will aim at cutting below the surface to reveal that burning core of mental or spiritual reality from which each play derives its nature and meaning.

That soul-life of the Shakespearian play is, indeed, a thing of divine worth. Its perennial fire is as mysterious, as near and yet as far, as that of the sun, and, like the sun, it burns on while generations pass. If interpretation attempts to split the original beam into different colours for inspection and analysis it does not claim, any more than will the scientist, that its spectroscope reveals the whole reality of its attention. It discovers something: exactly what it discovers, and whether that discovery be of ultimate value, cannot easily be demonstrated. But, though we know the sun better in the spring fields than in the laboratory, yet we might remember that the spectroscope discovered Helium first in the solar ray, which chemical was after sought and found on earth. So, too, the interpreation of poetic vision may have its use. And if it seems sometimes to bear little relevance to its original, if its mechanical joints creak and its philosophy lumber clumsily in attempt to follow the swift arrow-flight of poetry, it is, at least, no less rational a pursuit than that of the mathematician who writes a rhythmic curve in the stiff symbols of an algebraic equation.

I shall now shortly formulate what I take to be the main principles of right Shakespearian interpretation:

(i) Before noticing the presence of faults we should first regard each play as a visionary unit bound to obey none but its own self-imposed laws. To do this we should attempt to preserve absolute truth to our own imaginative reaction, whithersoever it may lead us in the way of paradox and unreason. We should at all costs avoid selecting what is easy to understand and forgetting the superlogical.

(ii) We should thus be prepared to recognize what I have called the "temporal" and the "spatial" elements: that is, to relate any given incident or speech either to the time-sequence of story or the peculiar atmosphere, intellectual or imaginative, which binds the play. Being aware of this new element we should not look for perfect verisimilitude to life, but rather see each play as an expanded metaphor, by means of which the original vision has been projected into forms roughly correspondent with actuality, conforming thereto with greater or less exactitude according to the demands of its own nature. It will then usually appear that many difficult actions and events become coherent and, within the scope of their universe, natural.

(iii) We should analyse the use and meaning of direct poetic symbolism—that is, events whose significance can hardly be related to the normal processes of actual life. Also the minor symbolic imagery of Shakespeare, which is extremely consistent, should receive careful attention. Where certain images continually recur in the same associative connexion, we can, if we have reason to believe that this associative force is strong enough, be ready to see the presence of the associative value when the images occur alone. Nor should we neglect the symbolic value of aural effects such as the discharge of cannon in *Hamlet* and *Othello* or the sound of trumpets in *Measure for Measure* and *King Lear*.

(iv) The plays from *Julius Caesar* (about 1599) to *The Tempest* (about 1611) when properly understood fall into a significant sequence. This I have called "the Shakespeare Progress." Therefore in detailed analysis of any one play it may sometimes be helpful to have regard to its place in the sequence, provided always that thought of this sequence be used to illuminate, and in no sense be allowed to distort, the view of the play under analysis. Particular notice should be given to what I have called the "hate-theme," which is turbulent throughout most of these plays: an especial mode of cynicism toward love, disgust at the physical body, and dismay at the thought of death; a revulsion from human life caused by a clear sight of its limitations—more especially limitations imposed by time. This progress I have outlined in *Myth and Miracle*, being concerned there especially with the Final Plays. The following essays are ordered according to the probable place in the Shakespeare Progress of the plays concerned. The order is that given by the late Professor Henry Norman Hudson in *The New Hudson Shakespeare*. Though I here compare one theme in *Julius Caesar* with *Macbeth*, I postpone a comprehensive analysis of the play, since its peculiar quality relates it more directly to the later tragedies than to those noticed in this treatment.

These arguments I have pursued at some length, since my interpretation reaches certain conclusions which may seem somewhat revolutionary. Especially will this be apparent in my reading of the Final Plays as mystical representations of a mystic vision. A first sketch of this reading I have already published in *Myth and Miracle*. Since the publication of my essay, my attention has been drawn to Mr. Colin Still's remarkable book *Shakespeare's Mystery Play: A Study of The Tempest* (Cecil Palmer, 1921). Mr. Still's interpretation of *The Tempest* is very similar to mine. His conclusions were reached by a detailed comparison of the play in its totality with other creations of literature, myth, and ritual throughout the ages; mine are reached solely through seeing *The Tempest* as the conclusion to the Shakespeare Progress. *The Tempest* is thus exactly located as a work of mystic insight with reference to the cross-axes of universal and Shakespearian vision. It would seem, therefore, that my method of interpretation as outlined in this essay has already met with some degree of empirical proof.

In conclusion, I would emphasize that I here lay down certain principles and make certain objections for my immediate purpose only. I would not be thought to level complaint against the value of "criticism" in general. My private and personal distinction between "criticism" and "interpretation" aims at no universal validity. It can hardly be absolute. No doubt I have narrowed the term "criticism" unjustly. Much of the critical work of to-day is, according to my distinction, work of a high interpretative order. Nor do I suggest that true "criticism" in the narrow sense I apply to it is of any lesser order than true interpretation: it may well be a higher pursuit, since it is, in a sense, the more creative and endures a greater burden of responsibility. The relative value of the two modes must vary in exact proportion to the greatness of the literature they analyse: that is why I believe the most profitable approach to Shakespeare to be interpretation rather than criticism.

✣ 3 ✣

The Question of Character in Shakespeare

L. C. KNIGHTS

As Professor Knights indicates at the outset, the title of his 1933 essay How Many Children Had Lady Macbeth? *is not, as has too often been assumed, a question A. C. Bradley asked. On the other hand, as a young member of a new intellectual generation that included F. R. Leavis and that was not characterized by reverence toward critics who had got themselves and their attitudes academically enshrined, Knights clearly aimed in his famous title at such Bradleyan questions as "Where was Hamlet at the time of his father's death?" and "Did Emilia suspect Iago?" and "Did Lady Macbeth really faint?" As he argues in the present essay, which is a lecture he delivered at the Summer School of the Shakespeare Memorial Theatre two decades later, his attack was and is more on a tendency in Bradley, exaggerated in his followers, than on the totality of Bradley's criticism. Though his argument bears strong resemblance to that of G. Wilson Knight, Knights' approach may suggest that the kind of reading suggested in the latter's work need not be entirely subjective. The response to the whole play which Knights advocates involves full and imaginative consciousness; but the very fullness of that consciousness necessarily involves, in addition to the "intuitive" skill on which he insists here, the kind of historical knowledge that Knights exemplified in one of his most notable books,* Drama and Society in the Age of Jonson *(1937). L. C. Knights has been Professor of English Literature at the University of Bristol since 1953.*

Let me begin with an unashamed bit of autobiography. In 1932
I was asked to give a paper to the Shakespeare Association in
London. I was a comparatively young man, dissatisfied with the
prevailing academic approach to Shakespeare, excited by the
glimpses I had obtained of new and, it seemed, more rewarding
approaches, and I welcomed the opportunity of proclaiming the
new principles in the very home of Shakespearian orthodoxy,
whilst at the same time having some fun with familiar irrele-
vancies of the kind parodied in my title, *How Many Children Had
Lady Macbeth?* I gave my paper and waited expectantly for the
lively discussion that would follow this rousing challenge to the
pundits. So far as I remember, nothing happened, except that
after a period of silence an elderly man got up at the back of the
room and said that he was very glad to hear Mr. Knights give this
paper because it was what he had always thought. The revolution
was over, and I went home. It was hardly a historic occasion, and
the only reason for mentioning it is that when my paper was published as one of Gordon Fraser's Minority Pamphlets it obtained
a certain mild notoriety that has never since entirely deserted it:
only a few years ago a writer in *The Listener* called it "the Com-
munist Manifesto of the new critical movement." Well of course
it was nothing of the kind. *How Many Children had Lady Macbeth?* has earned its footnote in the history of modern criticism
partly, I like to believe, because it says a few sensible things about
Macbeth, partly because of its sprightly title (which was suggested to me by F. R. Leavis), and partly because it reflected
the conviction of an increasing number of readers that the prevailing language of Shakespeare criticism didn't quite fit what
seemed to them of deepest importance in the experience of
Shakespeare's plays. In the last twenty-five or thirty years there
has certainly been a movement away from the older type of
"character" criticism which had for so long held the field and
which culminated in A. C. Bradley's *Shakespearean Tragedy*.[1]
But so far as any one book can be said to herald the new movement it was G. Wilson Knight's *The Wheel of Fire* (1930), shortly
to be followed by *The Imperial Theme* (1931).[2]

Now what I am here to do today is to try to get one aspect of that movement into perspective; more specifically I want to ask, after some twenty-five years of Shakespeare criticism that has not on the whole been on Bradleyean lines, what we now understand by the term "character" when we use it in giving an account of Shakespeare's plays, to what extent—and within what limitations—"character" can be a useful critical term when we set out to define the meaning—the living and life-nourishing significance—of a Shakespeare play.

I don't want to burden you with a history of Shakespeare criticism, ancient or modern, but a few historical reminders are necessary. Since Shakespeare criticism began, people have praised Shakespeare for the lifelikeness of his characters. But it was not until the end of the eighteenth century that Shakespeare's remarkable power to make his men and women convincing led to a more and more exclusive concentration on those features of the *dramatis personae* that could be defined in terms appropriate to characters in real life. The *locus classicus* is of course Maurice Morgann's *Essay on the Dramatic Character of Sir John Falstaff* (1777). Twelve years before, in 1765, Dr. Johnson, in his great Preface, had given the more traditional view:

> Nothing can please many, and please long, but just representations of general nature. . . . Shakespeare is above all writers, at least above all modern writers, the poet of nature. . . . His persons act and speak by the influence of those general passions and principles by which all minds are agitated, and the whole system of life is continued in motion. In the writings of other poets a character is too often an individual; in those of Shakespeare it is commonly a species.
>
> It is from this wide extension of design that so much instruction is derived. . . .[3]

Morgann, on the contrary, is interested in what is uniquely individual in the character he describes, and these individual traits, he affirms, can be elicited from the stage characters in much the same way as one builds up the character of an acquaintance in real life: "those characters in Shakespeare, which are seen only in part, are yet capable of being unfolded and understood in the whole."

> If the characters of Shakespeare [he goes on] are thus *whole,* as
> it were original, while those of almost all other writers are mere
> imitation, it may be fit to consider them rather as Historic than
> Dramatic beings; and, when occasion requires, to account for
> their conduct from the *whole* of character, from general prin-
> ciples, from latent motives, and from policies not avowed.

It is this principle that allows him to distinguished between
"the *real* character of Falstaff" and "his *apparent* one." What R.
W. Babcock, in his useful book, *The Genesis of Shakespeare
Idolatry, 1766–99,*[4] calls "the psychologizing of Shakespeare" was
well established even before Coleridge gave his lectures; and
Coleridge's influence, thought of course more subtly, worked in
the same direction. It seems true to say that in the nineteenth century Shakespeare's characters became "real people," and—with
varying degrees of relevance—the plays were discussed in terms
of the interaction of real people for whom sympathy or antipathy
was enlisted. Bradley's tremendously influential *Shakespearean
Tragedy* was published in 1904, and, for Bradley, "the centre of
the tragedy . . . may be said wtih equal truth to lie in action
issuing from character, or in character issuing in action": "action
is the centre of the story," but "this action is essentially the expression of character."

Now Bradley had the great virtue of being thoroughly immersed
in what he was talking about, and I am sure that his book has
helped very many people to make Shakespeare a present fact in
their lives. Also there is no need to make Bradley responsible for
all the vagaries of the how-many-children-had-Lady-Macbeth?
kind, which mostly lie on the fringes of criticism. But Bradley's
book did endorse a particular kind of preoccupation with "character," and once "character"-criticism became the dominant mode
of approach to Shakespeare, certain important matters were necessarily obscured, and people's experience of Shakespeare became
in some ways less rich and satisfying than it might have been.
For one thing genuine perceptions became entangled with irrelevant speculations—"How is it that Othello comes to be the companion of the one man in the world, who is at once able enough,
brave enough, and vile enough to ensnare him?"; Macbeth's

tendency to ambition "must have been greatly strengthened by his marriage." And if the critic who accepts too naïvely the character-in-action formula is liable to disappear down by-paths outside the play, he is almost equally likely to slight or ignore what is actually there if it does not minister to his particular preoccupation—witness the ease with which the old Arden edition of *Macbeth* dismissed as spurious scenes that do not contribute to the development of character or of a narrowly conceived dramatic action. Even at its best the focus is a narrow one. Shakespearian tragedy, says Bradley, "is pre-eminently the story of one person, the 'hero,' or at most of two, the 'hero' and 'heroine' "; and the mark of the tragic hero, besides his greatness, is that there is a "conflict of forces" in his soul. I suppose, if you look at matters in this way it doesn't necessarily mean that you idealize the hero as Bradley does Othello, missing the critical "placing" determined by the play as a whole. But it does mean that you are likely to ignore some important matters, such as the structure of ideas in *Macbeth*. After all, in his greater plays, Shakespeare was doing more than merely holding a mirror up to nature, more even than representing conflict in the souls of mighty characters: he was exploring the world and defining the values by which men live. In short, Shakespearian tragedy, any Shakespearian tragedy, is saying so much more than can be expressed in Bradleyean terms. It was some such perceptions as these—combined with an increasing knowledge of Elizabethan dramatic usage and convention—that prompted exploration of Shakespeare, not necessarily in opposition to Bradley, but to a large extent outside the Bradleyean frame of reference.

Simplifying for the sake of clarity, I would say that as a result of critical work done in the last quarter of a century, the approach to Shakespeare of an intelligent and informed reader to-day is likely to differ in three important respects from that of the intelligent and informed reader of a generation ago. To start with, he is likely to take it for granted that any one of Shakespeare's greater plays is very much more than a dramatized story; that it is, rather, a vision of life—more or less complex and inclusive—whose meaning is nothing less than *the play as a whole*. This is what Wilson Knight meant when he sometimes referred to his work in terms of "spatial analysis," as distinguished from the analysis of a series of steps in time. Ideally, we try to apprehend each play as though all its parts were simultaneously present: there is an obvious analogy with music, and criticism of this kind tends to describe Shakespeare's meanings in terms of "themes" rather than in terms of motive, character-development, and so on. Wilson Knight speaks of cutting below "the surface crust of plot and character," and remarks that in *Macbeth,* for example "the logic of imaginative correspondence is more significant and more exact than the logic of plot." He also, of course, told us that "we should not look for perfect verisimilitude to life, but rather see each play as an expanded metaphor, by means of which the original vision has been projected into forms roughly correspondent with actuality," and the fact that this remark has been quoted in innumerable examination papers shouldn't obscure its crucial importance in determining the kind of approach to Shakespeare that I am trying to define.[5] In the second place, our contemporary reader is likely to take for granted that the essential structure of the plays is to be sought in the poetry rather than in the more easily extractable elements of "plot" and "character." I think our age is more aware of the complex structure, of the depth of life, of Shakespeare's verse, than any of its predecessors. Critics have written at length about his imagery, his ambiguities and overlaying meanings, his word-play, and so on; and there is no doubt that such studies have sharpened our sense not only of the tremendous activity of Shakespeare's verse—its generative power —but of the strong and subtle interconnections of meaning within the imaginative structure of the plays. It is significant that "interpretation" relies heavily on extensive quotation and detailed analysis.[6] Finally—abandoning my hypothetical intelligent reader —I should say that our whole conception of Shakespeare's relation to his work, of what he was trying to do as an artist whilst at the same time satisfying the demands of the Elizabethan theatre, has undergone a very great change indeed. The "new" Shakespeare, I should say, is much less impersonal than the old. Whereas in the older view Shakespeare was the god-like creator of a peopled world, projecting—it is true—his own spirit into the inhabitants, but remaining essentially the analyst of "their" passions, he is now felt as much more immediately engaged in the action he puts before us. I don't of course mean that we have returned to Frank Harris's Shakespeare, engaged in drawing a succession of full-length portraits of himself, but that we feel the plays (in Mr. Eliot's words) "to be united by one significant, consistent, and developing personality": we feel that the plays, even if "in no obvious form," "are somehow dramatizing . . . an action or struggle for harmony in the soul of the poet." [7] We take it for granted that Shakespeare thought about the problems of life, and was at least as much interested in working towards an imaginative solution as he was in making a series of detached studies of different characters, their motives and their passions. Here again, specialist studies are indicative: we think it reasonable that a scholar should inquire what evidence there is that Shakespeare had read Hooker, and if so what effect it had on his plays; we inquire into Shakespeare's political ideas and their background; we are prepared to examine *Shakespeare's Philosophical Patterns* (which is the title of a book by the American scholar, W. C. Curry).[8] In short, we take seriously Coleridge's remark that Shakespeare was "a philosopher"; the vision of life that his plays express is, in a certain sense, a philosophic vision. But at the same time we remember— at least, I should like to be able to say we remember—that the plays are not dramatizations of abstract ideas, but imaginative constructions mediated through the poetry. If Shakespeare's verse has moved well into the centre of the picture, one reason is that linguistic vitality is now felt as the chief clue to the urgent personal themes that not only shape the poetic-dramatic structure of each play but form the figure in the carpet of the canon as a whole.[9]

This short and imperfect account may serve as an indication or reminder of the main lines of Shakespeare criticism since 1930, or thereabouts. Happily my job is not to award marks of merit to different critics, and I don't intend to offer a list of obligatory reading. We all have our own ideas about the recent critics who have helped us most in our understanding of Shakespeare, and I don't suppose that we should all agree about all of them. But I think we should agree that there have been some books offering genuinely new insights, and that where criticism has been most

illuminating it has usually been on quite non-Bradleyean lines.
At the same time let us recall certain facts. If "plot" and "character"—mere "precipitates from the memory"—sometimes seem to
be described in abstraction from the full living immediacy of our
direct experience of the plays, and therefore to lead away from
it, so too "themes" and "symbols" can be pursued mechanically
and, as it were, abstractly. Whereas it is equally obvious that
criticism in terms of "character" can be genuinely revealing; John
Palmer's *The Political Characters of Shakepeare* [10] is an example.
And of course you can't get away from the term. Not only does
the ordinary theatregoer or reader need it to explain his enjoyment, but even critics least in sympathy with Bradley at times
naturally and necessarily define their sense of significance in
terms appropriate to living people. Clearly the critical field has
not been given over to those whom J. I. M. Stewart calls "the new
Bowdlers, whom man delights not, no nor woman neither, and
who would give us not merely *Hamlet* without the Prince but the
Complete Works without their several *dramatis personae*." The
notion of "character," in some sense, has not disappeared, and is
not going to disappear, from Shakespeare criticism. What we
need to do is simply to clear up our minds about it, to make our
handling of the term both more flexible and more precise.

Before I go on to give my own simple summing up of things
as I see them I should like to mention two books that have a
direct bearing on the matters we are pursuing. The first is J. I. M.
Stewart's witty, entertaining and instructive *Character and Motive in Shakespeare*.[11] Stewart not only has some shrewd knocks
at those who over-play the element of Elizabethan dramatic convention in Shakespeare and those who would tailor the plays too
closely to the pattern of their own proprieties, he has some illuminating comments on particular plays. But his main interest,
in the present connexion, lies in the way he develops the conception of character-presentation beyond the bounds of natural-
ism. To the extent that Shakespeare is concerned with character
and motive—and he does "present 'man' and reveal psychological
truths"—he works not through realistic portrayal but through
poetry—that is, through symbolism and suggestion as well as by
more direct means; and in this way he makes us aware not—or

not only—of what we normally understand by character but of its hidden recesses.

> The characters, then (but I mean chiefly those major characters with whom the imagination of the dramatist is deeply engaged), have often the superior reality of individuals exposing the deepest springs of their action. But this superior reality is manifested through the medium of situations which are sometimes essentially symbolical; and these may be extravagant or merely fantastic when not interpreted by the quickened imagination, for it is only during the prevalence of a special mode of consciousness, the poetic, that the underlying significance of these situations is perceived. (pp. 9–10)

> Of just what Shakespeare brings from beyond this portal [of the depths of the mind], and how, we often can achieve little conceptual grasp; and often therefore the logical and unkindled mind finds difficulties which it labels as faults and attributes to the depravity of Shakespeare's audience or what it wills. But what the intellect finds arbitrary the imagination may accept and respond to, for when we read imaginatively or poetically we share the dramatist's penetration for a while and deep is calling to deep. (p. 30)[12]

The other book I want to refer to is *Character and Society in Shakespeare* [13] by Professor Arthur Sewell. It is a small book but, I think, an important one. Briefly, Mr. Sewell's contention is that the characters of a play only exist within the total vision that the play presents: "in Shakespeare's plays the essential process of character-creation is a prismatic breaking-up of the comprehensive vision of the play" (p. 19). There is, therefore, an absolute distinction between a dramatic character and a person in real life whose conduct can be accounted for "from general principles, from latent motives, and from policies not avowed." "We can only understand Shakespeare's characters so long as we agree that we cannot know all about them and are not supposed to know all about them" (p. 12). What is relevant for us is not an assumed hinterland of motives but simply the particular "address to the world" that is embodied, with different degrees of explicit-

ness, in the different characters. In the comedies the characters
tend to be static and, so to speak, socially conditioned: they
represent attitudes and modes of judgment that serve for the
presentation and critical inspection of our everyday world. In the
great tragedies the characters speak from out of a deeper level of
experience—"metaphysical" rather than social, though the distinction is not absolute; the vision they embody is transformed in the
full working out of the attitudes to which they are committed; and
their reality is established by our own active commitment to the
drama's dialectical play. Of both comedy and tragedy it can be
said that "unless Shakespeare had set our minds busy—and not
only our minds—on various kinds of evaluation, his characters
could never have engaged us and would have lacked all vitality"
(p. 18). And again, there is the suggestion "that character and
moral vision must be apprehended together, and that when character is understood separately from moral vision it is not in fact
understood at all" (p. 59).

Where, then, at the end of all this, do we come out? Perhaps
only among what many people will regard as a handful of commonplaces. Let me start with the most thumping platitude of all:
in Shakespeare's plays *some* impression of character is constantly
being made upon us. It is likely to begin as soon as a major
character is introduced.

> *Why, I, in this weak piping time of peace,*
> *Have no delight to pass away the time,*
> *Unless to see my shadow in the sun*
> *And descant on mine own deformity.*

> *Though yet of Hamlet our dear brother's death*
> *The memory be green, and that it us befitted*
> *To bear our hearts in grief and our whole kingdom*
> *To be contracted in one brow of woe,*
> *Yet so far hath discretion fought with nature. . . .*

> *I pray you, daughter, sing; or express yourself in a more comfortable*
> *sort.*

Here, and in innumerable other instances, we have what Mr.

Sewell calls the "distillation of personality into style." We know these people by the way they speak; as Mr. Stewart puts it, "In drama the voice *is* the character"—though we also have to add that often Shakespeare speaks *through* the person with a meaning different from, or even contrary to, that apparently intended by the character.

At the same time we have to admit that our sense of character —of a complex, unified tissue of thought and feeling from which a particular voice issues—varies enormously not only as between different plays, but as between the different figures within a single play. *All's Well That Ends Well* is nearer to a morality play, and is less concerned with characterization, in any sense, than is *Othello*. In *Measure for Measure* "analysis of character" may take us a long way with Angelo; it is utterly irrelevant as applied to the Duke.

Let me give another example—which will serve to illustrate Mr. Sewell's remark about the characters embodying "an address to the world," in case anyone should have been left uneasy with that phrase. Here is Don John introducing himself in conversation with Conrade in Act I of *Much Ado About Nothing*.

> I wonder that thou, being—as thou say'st thou art—born under Saturn, goest about to apply a moral medicine to a mortifying mischief. I cannot hide what I am: I must be sad when I have cause, and smile at no man's jests; eat when I have stomach, and wait for no man's leisure; sleep when I am drowsy, and tend no man's business; laugh when I am merry, and claw no man in his humour.

Conrade advises that he should apply himself to winning the good opinion of his brother the Duke, with whom he is lately reconciled, and Don John goes on:

> I had rather be a canker in a hedge than a rose in his grace; and it better fits my blood to be disdained of all than to fashion a carriage to rob love from any: in this, though I cannot be said to be a flattering honest man, it must not be denied but I am a plain-dealing villain. I am trusted with a muzzle and enfranchised with a clog; therefore I have decreed not to sing in my cage. If I had

my mouth, I would bite; if I had my liberty, I would do my
liking: in the meantime, let me be that I am, and seek not to
alter me.

A good many things are plain from this—Don John's exacerbated
sense of superiority ("I . . . I . . . I . . . ."), his particular kind of
"melancholy," and his affectation of a blunt, no-nonsense manner.
Clearly he is related to Richard of Gloucester and to Iago. Their
common characteristic is an egotism that clenches itself hard
against the claims of sympathy, and that is unwilling to change—
"I cannot hide what I am; I must be sad when I have cause . . .
let me be that I am, and seek not to alter me." It is, in short, the
opposite of a character "open" to others and to the real demands
of the present. That is all we know about Don John and all we
are required to know: we are not asked to consider his bastardy
or his other grievances. He is simply a perversely "melancholy"
man who serves as villain of the piece, the agent of an otherwise
unmotivated evil.

What is true of a minor figure like Don John is true of all the
characters of Shakespeare: we know about them only what the
play requires us to know. Even to put the matter in this way is—
as we shall see in a minute—over-simplified and misleading, but
it serves to remind us that however we define for ourselves a
character and his rôle, there is a strict criterion of relevance: he
belongs to his play, and his play is an art-form, not a slice of life.
The fact that this at least is now a commonplace is a guarantee
that we shall never again have to waste our time on the complete
irrelevance of some forms of character-analysis as applied to
Shakespeare's *dramatis personae*.

But we still haven't got to the heart of the matter. What is the
"play as a whole," to which we say the characters are subordinate?
To this question there is no simple answer, but we can at least
attempt an answer that will help our reading.

Poetic drama offers a vision of life, more or less complex, more
or less wide-embracing, as the case may be. Shakespeare's poetic
drama as a whole is different from Jonson's or Racine's; and
within Shakespeare's poetic drama as a whole there are many
different kinds. Even at its simplest there is some degree of com-

plexity, of dialectical play, as persons embodying different attitudes are set before us in action and interaction. Of course when
we are watching them we don't think of them as the embodiment
of attitudes—of different addresses to the world: we say simply,
Rosalind is in love with Orlando. Yet while we know that two addresses to the world can't fall in love, we also know—and this
knowledge moves from the back of our minds and comes into
action when, having seen or read the play several times, we try to
bring it into sharper focus—that Shakespeare is doing something
more significant with Rosalind and Orlando than showing us how
interesting it is when boy meets girl. *As You Like It*, which is a
fairly simple play, will help us here. *As You Like It* is of course a
romantic comedy, with its own interest and entertainment as such.
But the plot and the structure of the incidents point to an interest
in the meaning of a life lived "according to nature." Duke Senior's
idyllic picture ("Hath not old custom made this life more sweet
Than that of painted pomp?" etc.) is an over-simplification, as
the play makes plain; but it is a possible attitude, put forward for
inspection, and as the play goes on it is clear that we are meant
to take an intelligent interest in the varying degrees of naturalness
and sophistication—each playing off against the other—that are
put before us. *As You Like It*, in short, rings the changes on the
contrasting meanings of "natural" (either "human" or "close down
to the life of nature") and "civilized" (either "well nurtured" or
"artificial")—all especially pointed with reference to the passion
of love. It is largely an entertainment; but at the same time it is
a serious comedy of ideas—not abstract ideas to be debated, but
ideas as embodied in attitude and action. So that by playing off
against each other different attitudes to life, the play as a whole
offers a criticism of various forms of exaggeration and affection—
either "romantic" or professedly realistic—with Rosalind as arbiter,
although of course she is not above the action but involved in it
herself.[14]

What is true of *As You like It* is also true of greater plays, such
as *Measure for Measure, King Lear,* or *Antony and Cleopatra,*
though here of course the play of varied sympathies and anti-
pathies, of imaginative evaluation as different possibilities of living
are put before us, is more complex, and the experience handled

is more profound. But of all the greater plays it is true to say that *all* the characters are necessary to express the vision—the emergent "idea" or controlling preoccupation—and they are necessary only in so far as they do express it. Gloucester's part in *King Lear* is not to give additional human interest, but to enact and express a further aspect of the Lear experience; for with Gloucester, as with Lear, confident acceptance of an inadequate code gives place to humble acceptance of the human condition, and there are glimpses of a new wisdom:

> *I have no way, and therefore want no eyes;*
> *I stumbled when I saw.*

The striking parallels between the two men are proof enough of deliberate artistic intention in this respect.

What *King Lear* also forces on us, even when we are prepared to see the different characters as contributing to a pattern, is the inadequacy of terms relating to "character." What character has Edgar in his successive transformations? In the storm scenes, where Lear's vision of horror is built to a climax, we are acted on directly by the poetry, by what is said, in some respects independently of our sense of a particular person saying it. So too in the play as a whole, and in the other greater plays, our sense of the characters—of what the characters stand for in their "address to the world," their "moral encounter with the universe"—is inseparable from the more direct ways in which, by poetry and symbolism, our imaginations are called into play. To take one simple example. When Macbeth, on his first appearance, says, "So foul and fair a day I have not seen," he does far more than announce himself as a character—tired, collected, brooding; echoing the Witches' "Fair is foul, and foul is fair," he takes his place in the pattern of moral evaluations which make the play so much more than the story of a tragic hero, which makes it into a great vision of the unreality, the negative horror, that evil is. In reading Shakespeare our sense of "character," defined and limited as I have tried to define and limit it, is important; but so is our responsiveness to symbolism (the storm in *Othello* and Othello's trance, Lear's bare heath and Gloucester's Dover Cliff, Hermione's moving statue), and so is our responsiveness to imagery (the imagery of darkness conveying spiritual blindness in *Macbeth*), to verse rhythm, and to all the inter-acting elements of the poetry: it is from these that there emerges a controlling direction of exploratory and committed interests—of interests involving the personality as a whole—that we indicate by some such word as "themes."

Mr. John Holloway has recently objected to the use of "theme" in Shakespeare criticism[15]: it is a sign that the work in question is to be reduced to a generalized moral reflection, whereas literature does not provide us with general truths, only with particular instances. "What *Macbeth* does . . . is to depict for us, in great and remarkable detail, one imagined case and one only." "Narrative," he suggests, is "the fundamental quality of the full-length work," the essential principle of imaginative order. Now both these conceptions of the work of art as "one imagined case and one only," and of "narrative" as the controlling principle, seem to me to be, in their turn, open to objection. But I think we are dealing with something far greater than the particular question—Is Shakespeare most profitably discussed in terms of "character" or "theme" or "narrative"? What has come into sight, what we must take account of, is nothing less than the depth of life of any great work of art, its capacity to enter into our lives as power. What do we mean when we say that a great work of art has a universal appeal? Surely something more than that it tells a story likely to interest everybody. We mean that the special case (and I grant Mr. Holloway the artist's "passion for the special case") brings to a focus a whole range of awareness, that it generates an activity of imaginative apprehension that illuminates not only the "case" in question but life as we know it in our own experience: it can modify, or even transform, our whole way of seeing life and responding to it. It is this capacity to generate meanings that is the "universal" quality in the particular work of art. And it is the presence of the universal in the particular that compels the use of such generalizing terms as "themes" or "motifs." Of course, like other critical terms, they can be used mechanically or ineptly, can harden into counters pushed about in a critical game. But as simple pointers their function is to indicate the *direction* of interest that a play compels when we try to meet it with the whole of ourselves—to meet it, that is (using De Quincey's term), as literature of power.

To read Shakespeare, then (and in reading I include seeing his plays performed), we need to cultivate a complex skill. But there is no need to make heavy weather of this. That skill can be largely intuitive; we can reach it in many ways, and there is no need (especially if we are teachers) to be too insistent on any one approach. In "Demosius and Mystes," a dialogue appended to *Church and State,* Coleridge refers to a mighty conflict between two cats, "where one tail alone is said to have survived the battle." There is always a danger of critical squabbles becoming like that; and I for one would rather see among my pupils an honest and first-hand appreciation of what is offered by way of "character" than a merely mechanical working out of recurrent imagery and symbolic situations. We should remember also that the life of the imagination runs deeper than our conscious formulations. T. S. Eliot (in his Introduction to S. L. Bethell's book on Shakespeare), says of the persons of the play of a modern verse dramatist,

> they must on your stage be able to perform the same actions, and lead the same lives, as in the real world. But they must somehow disclose (not necessarily be aware of) a deeper reality than that of the plane of most of our conscious living; and what they disclose must be, not the psychologist's intellectualization of this reality, but the reality itself.

"They must somehow disclose (not necessarily be aware of) a deeper reality": I think that what Eliot says of the persons in verse plays like his own, applies—*mutatis mutandis*—to the spectators of poetic drama. To the extent that a Shakespeare tragedy truly enlists the imagination (and this means enlisting it for what is in the play, not for a display of virtuosity) it is precisely this deeper level of apprehension—the hidden potentialities, wishes, and fears of the individual spectator—that is being worked on, even though the spectator himself may not be conscious of it, and thinks that he is simply watching someone else's "character issuing in action."

All the same, even when this is admitted, there is no reason why the common reader should not be encouraged to see rather more. For it is in our imaginative response to *the whole play*—not simply to what can be extracted as "character," nor indeed to what can be simply extracted as "theme" or "symbol"—that the meaning lies; and Shakespeare calls on us to be as fully conscious as we can, even if consciousness includes relaxed enjoyment and absorption as well as, sometimes, more deliberate attention to this or that aspect of the whole experience.

¹ Macmillan, 1904.

² Methuen.

³ We may compare Johnson's characteristic comment on *Macbeth:* "The play is deservedly celebrated for the propriety of its fictions, and solemnity, grandeur, and variety of its action; but it has no nice discriminations of character, the events are too great to admit the influence of particular dispositions, and the course of the action necessarily determines the conduct of the agents. The danger of ambition is well desribed. . . ." Johnson, it is true, also says of Shakespeare, "Perhaps no poet ever kept his personages more distinct from each other."

⁴ University of North Carolina Press, 1931.

⁵ "And Shakespeare's was a mind that thought in images, so that metaphor packs into metaphor, producing the most surprising collocations of apparently diverse phenomena: he thought of time, and death, and eternity, in terms of a candle, a shadow, and an actor. Is it not likely that the large and composite image of the story as a whole would serve him as a metaphor or symbol for his attitudes to certain aspects of experience?"—S. L. Bethell, *Shakespeare and the Popular Dramatic Tradition* (Staples, 1948), p. 115.

⁶ A method that has its dangers, for we sometimes seem to run the risk of having the play read for us.

⁷ See T. S. Eliot's essay on John Ford.

⁸ Louisiana State University Press, 1937.

⁹ A few sentences in this paragraph are borrowed from my essay on the Tragedies in the Pelican Guide to English Literature (ed. Boris Ford), 2, *The Age of Shakespeare.*

¹⁰ Macmillan, 1945.

¹¹ Longmans, 1949.

¹² This insistence on the imaginative—on the non-rational but not therefore irrational—portrayal of character, and on the need to respond to it imaginatively, is important, and, as I have said, Mr. Stewart can be illuminating. But it also seems to me that his method, as he pursues it, can sometimes lead outside the play, as in his use of psycho-analytic concepts to define Leontes' jealousy. The main criticism of any psycho-

analytic account of Shakespeare's characters is not simply that it is irrelevant—though it may be—but that it reduces the material it works on to a category that can be known and docketed. To accept it is to feel that you know about a character something of importance that has been simply handed over, and that can be received alike by every reader, whatever the degree of his concern, the extent of his actual engagement, with the plays. It obscures not only the uniqueness but the *activity* of the work of art; whereas any play only exists for you to the extent that *you* have grappled with its meanings. Thus Mr. Stewart's account of Leontes' repressed homosexuality (reactivated by the presence of Polixenes, and then "projected" onto Hermione) is relevant inasmuch as it points to the presence in what Leontes stands for of unconscious motivations, of motives beyond conscious control. But within the context of the play as a whole their exact nature is irrelevant: they are simply an X within the equation which is the play. What the play gives us is the awakening of new life that can enlist the same impulses which, in the first part, have been shown as the material of an unruly aberration. All we need to know of the aberration is that it is a representative manifestation: to pin it down exactly as Mr. Stewart does, is to make Leontes' jealousy something that we *know about* instead of something we *respond to* as part of the total generative pattern of the play.

[13] Clarendon Press, 1951.

[14] See James Smith's excellent essay on *As You Like It* in *Scrutiny*, IX. i. June, 1940, reprinted in *The Importance of Scrutiny*, ed. Eric Bentley (Grove Press, New York, 1957).

[15] "The New 'Establishment' in Criticism," *The Listener*, September 20th and 27th, 1956.

❧ 4 ❧

The Naked Babe and the Cloak of Manliness

CLEANTH BROOKS

Cleanth Brooks, author of a number of influential books on litera-
ture and now Professor of English at Yale University, is among
the most talented and distinguished of the New Critics. He has
not shunned controversy, as the two essays following this one will
indicate, and he may not have won all the controversies he began.
But few will contest the assertion that, perhaps foremost among
his fellows, he taught a generation how to read. He argues in
The Well Wrought Urn *(1947) that "the language of poetry is the*
language of paradox," and in the present essay, taken from that
volume, he attempts to demonstrate that "paradox" is the prin-
ciple of unity not only in such poets as Donne, whose rediscovery
sparked the New Criticism, but also and above all in Shakespeare.
One may argue that his emphasis on imagery is too great, or
that "paradox," like the principle of "ambiguity" in the criticism
of William Empson, is too specialized a concept to make such
broad claims for. One should note, however, that Professor
Brooks is equally concerned with the problem of structure, and
even more with the problems of what and how literature means.
"The Naked Babe and the Cloak of Manliness" may be the most
brilliant Shakespearean essay the New Criticism has produced.

The debate about the proper limits of metaphor has perhaps
never been carried on in so spirited a fashion as it has been
within the last twenty-five years. The tendency has been to argue
for a much wider extension of those limits than critics like Dr.

Johnson, say, were willing to allow—one wider even than the Romantic poets were willing to allow. Indeed, some alarm has been expressed of late, in one quarter or another, lest John Donne's characteristic treatment of metaphor be taken as the type and norm, measured against which other poets must, of necessity, come off badly. Yet, on the whole, I think that it must be conceded that the debate on metaphor has been stimulating and illuminating—and not least so with reference to those poets who lie quite outside the tradition of metaphysical wit.

Since the "new criticism," so called, has tended to center around the rehabilitation of Donne, and the Donne tradition, the latter point, I believe, needs to be emphasized. Actually, it would be a poor rehabilitation which, if exalting Donne above all his fellow poets, in fact succeeded in leaving him quite as much isolated from the rest of them as he was before. What the new awareness of the importance of metaphor—if it is actually new, and if its character is really that of a freshened awareness—what this new awareness of metaphor results in when applied to poets other than Donne and his followers is therefore a matter of first importance. Shakepeare provides, of course, the supremely interesting case.

But there are some misapprehensions to be avoided at the outset. We tend to associate Donne with the self-conscious and witty figure—his comparison of the souls of the lovers to the two legs of the compass is the obvious example. Shakespeare's extended figures are elaborated in another fashion. They are, we are inclined to feel, spontaneous comparisons struck out in the heat of composition, and not carefully articulated, self-conscious conceits at all. Indeed, for the average reader the connection between spontaneity and seriously imaginative poetry is so strong that he will probably reject as preposterous any account of Shakespeare's poetry which sees an elaborate pattern in the imagery. He will reject it because to accept it means for him the assumption that the writer was not a fervent poet but a preternaturally cold and self-conscious monster.

Poems are certainly not made by formula and blueprint. One rightly holds suspect a critical interpretation that implies that they are. Shakespeare, we may be sure, was no such monster of calculation. But neither, for that matter, was Donne. Even in

Donne's poetry, the elaborated and logically developed comparisons are outnumbered by the abrupt and succinct comparisons —by what T. S. Eliot has called the "telescoped conceits." Moreover, the extended comparisons themselves are frequently knit together in the sudden and apparently uncalculated fashion of the telescoped images; and if one examines the way in which the famous compass comparison is related to the rest of the poem in which it occurs, he may feel that even this elaborately "logical" figure was probably the result of a happy accident.

The truth of the matter is that we know very little of the various poets' methods of composition, and that what may seem to us the product of deliberate choice may well have been as "spontaneous" as anything else in the poem. Certainly, the general vigor of metaphor in the Elizabethan period—as testified to by pamphlets, sermons, and plays—should warn us against putting the literature of that period at the mercy of our own personal theories of poetic composition. In any case, we shall probably speculate to better advantage—if speculate we must—on the possible significant interrelations of image with image rather than on the possible amount of pen-biting which the interrelations may have cost the author.

I do not intend, however, to beg the case by oversimplifying the relation between Shakespeare's intricate figures and Donne's. There are most important differences; and, indeed, Shakespeare's very similarities to the witty poets will, for many readers, tell against the thesis proposed here. For those instances in which Shakespeare most obviously resembles the witty poets occur in the earlier plays or in *Venus and Adonis* and *The Rape of Lucrece*; and these we are inclined to dismiss as early experiments—trial pieces from the Shakespearean workshop. We demand, quite properly, instances from the great style of the later plays.

Still, we will do well not to forget the witty examples in the poems and earlier plays. They indicate that Shakespeare is in the beginning not too far removed from Donne, and that, for certain effects at least, he was willing to play with the witty comparison. Dr. Johnson, in teasing the metaphysical poets for their fanciful conceits on the subject of tears, might well have added instances from Shakespeare. One remembers, for example, from *Venus and Adonis*:

> *O, how her eyes and tears did lend and borrow!*
> *Her eyes seen in her tears, tears in her eye;*
> *Both crystals, where they view'd each other's sorrow. . . .*

Or, that more exquisite instance which Shakespeare, perhaps half-smiling, provided for the King in *Love's Labor's Lost*:

> *So sweet a kiss the golden sun gives not*
> *To those fresh morning drops upon the rose,*
> *As thy eye-beams, when their fresh rays have smote*
> *The night of dew that on my cheeks down flows:*
> *Nor shines the silver moon one half so bright*
> *Through the transparent bosom of the deep,*
> *As does thy face through tears of mine give light:*
> *Thou shin'st in every tear that I do weep,*
> *No drop but as a coach doth carry thee:*
> *So ridest thou triumphing in my woe.*
> *Do but behold the tears that swell in me,*
> *And they thy glory through my grief will show:*
> *But do not love thyself—then thou wilt keep*
> *My tears for glasses, and still make me weep.*

But Berowne, we know, at the end of the play, foreswears all such

> *Taffeta phrases, silken terms precise,*
> *Three-piled hyperboles, spruce affectation,*
> *Figures pedantical*

in favor of "russet yeas and honest kersey noes." It is sometimes assumed that Shakespeare did the same thing in his later dramas, and certainly the epithet "taffeta phrases" does not describe the great style of *Macbeth* and *Lear*. Theirs is assuredly of a tougher fabric. But "russet" and "honest kersey" do not describe it either. The weaving was not so simple as that.

The weaving was very intricate indeed—if anything, *more* rather than *less* intricate than that of *Venus and Adonis*, though obviously the pattern was fashioned in accordance with other designs, and yielded other kinds of poetry. But in suggesting that there is a real continuity between the imagery of *Venus and Adonis*, say, and that of a play like *Macbeth*, I am glad to be able to avail myself of Coleridge's support. I refer to the remarkable fifteenth chapter of the *Biographia*.

There Coleridge stresses not the beautiful tapestry-work—the purely visual effect—of the images, but quite another quality. He suggests that Shakespeare was prompted by a secret dramatic instinct to realize, in the imagery itself, that "constant intervention and running comment by tone, look and gesture" ordinarily provided by the actor, and that Shakespeare's imagery becomes under this prompting "a series and never broken chain . . . always vivid and, because unbroken, often minute. . . ." Coleridge goes on, a few sentences later, to emphasize further "the perpetual activity of attention required on the part of the reader, . . . the rapid flow, the quick change, and the playful nature of the thoughts and images."

These characteristics, Coleridge hastens to say, are not in themselves enough to make superlative poetry. "They become proofs of original genius only as far as they are modified by a predominant passion; or by associated thoughts or images awakened by that passion; or when they have the effect of reducing multitude to unity, or succession to an instant; or lastly, when a human and intellectual life is transferred to them from the poet's own spirit."

Of the intellectual vigor which Shakespeare possessed, Coleridge then proceeds to speak—perhaps extravagantly. But he goes on to say: "In Shakespeare's *poems,* the creative power and the intellectual energy wrestle as in a war embrace. Each in its excess of strength seems to threaten the extinction of the other."

I am tempted to gloss Coleridge's comment here, perhaps too heavily, with remarks taken from Chapter XIII where he discusses the distinction between the Imagination and the Fancy—the modifying and creative power, on the one hand, and on the other, that "mode of Memory" . . . "blended with, and modified by . . . Choice." But if in *Venus and Adonis* and *The Rape of Lucrece* the powers grapple "in a war embrace," Coleridge goes on to pronounce: "At length, in the *Drama* they were reconciled, and fought each with its shield before the breast of the other."

It is a noble metaphor. I believe that it is also an accurate one, and that it comprises one of the most brilliant insights ever made into the nature of the dramatic poetry of Shakespeare's mature style. If it is accurate, we shall expect to find, even in the mature poetry, the "never broken chain" of images, "always vivid and, because unbroken, often minute," but we shall expect to find the individual images, not mechanically linked together in the mode of Fancy, but organically related, modified by "a predominant passion," and mutually modifying each other.

T. S. Eliot has remarked that "The difference between imagination and fancy, in view of [the] poetry of wit, is a very narrow one." If I have interpreted Coleridge correctly, he is saying that in Shakespeare's greatest work, the distinction lapses altogether —or rather, that one is caught up and merged in the other. As his latest champion, I. A. Richards, observes: "Coleridge often insisted—and would have insisted still more often had he been a better judge of his reader's capacity for misunderstanding—that Fancy and Imagination are not exclusive of, or inimical to, one another."

I began by suggesting that our reading of Donne might contribute something to our reading of Shakespeare, though I tried to make plain the fact that I had no design of trying to turn Shakespeare into Donne, or—what I regard as nonsense—of trying to exalt Donne above Shakespeare. I have in mind specifically some such matter as this: that since the *Songs and Sonnets* of Donne, no less than *Venus and Adonis*, requires a "perpetual activity of attention . . . on the part of the reader from the rapid flow, the quick change, and the playful nature of the thoughts and images," the discipline gained from reading Donne may allow us to see more clearly the survival of such qualities in the later style of Shakespeare. And, again, I have in mind some such matter as this: that if a reading of Donne has taught us that the "rapid flow, the quick change, and the playful nature of the thoughts and images"—qualities which we are all too prone to associate merely with the fancy—can, on occasion, take on imaginative power, we may, thus taught, better appreciate details in

Shakespeare which we shall otherwise dismiss as merely fanciful, or, what is more likely, which we shall simply ignore altogether.

With Donne, of course, the chains of imagery, "always vivid" and "often minute" are perfectly evident. For many readers they are all too evident. The difficulty is not to prove that they exist, but that, on occasion, they may subserve a more imaginative unity. With Shakespeare, the difficulty may well be to prove that the chains exist at all. In general, we may say, Shakespeare has made it relatively easy for his admirers to choose what they like and neglect what they like. What he gives on one or another level is usually so magnificent that the reader finds it easy to ignore other levels.

Yet there are passages not easy to ignore and on which even critics with the conventional interests have been forced to comment. One of these passages occurs in *Macbeth*, Act I, Scene vii, where Macbeth compares the pity for his victim-to-be, Duncan, to

> *a naked new-born babe,*
> *Striding the blast, or heaven's cherubim, hors'd*
> *Upon the sightless couriers of the air. . . .*

The comparison is odd, to say the least. Is the babe natural or supernatural—an ordinary, helpless baby, who, as newborn, could not, of course, even toddle, much less stride the blast? Or is it some infant Hercules, quite capable of striding the blast, but, since it is powerful and not helpless, hardly the typical pitiable object?

Shakespeare seems bent upon having it both ways—and, if we read on through the passage—bent upon having the best of both worlds; for he proceeds to give us the option: pity is like the babe "or heaven's cherubim" who quite appropriately, of course, do ride the blast. Yet, even if we waive the question of the legitimacy of the alternative (of which Shakespeare so promptly avails himself), is the cherubim comparison really any more successful than is the babe comparison? Would not one of the great warrior archangels be more appropriate to the scene than the cherub? Does Shakespeare mean for pity or for fear of retribution to be dominant in Macbeth's mind?

Or is it possible that Shakespeare could not make up his own mind? Was he merely writing hastily and loosely, letting the word "pity" suggest the typically pitiable object, the babe naked in the blast, and then, stirred by the vague notion that some threat to Macbeth should be hinted, using "heaven's cherubim"—already suggested by "babe"—to convey the hint? Is the passage vague or precise? Loosely or tightly organized? Comments upon the passage have ranged all the way from one critic's calling it "pure rant, and intended to be so" to another's laudation: "Either like a mortal babe, terrible in helplessness; or like heaven's angel-children, mighty in love and compassion. This magnificent passage. . . ."

An even more interesting, and perhaps more disturbing passage in the play is that in which Macbeth describes his discovery of the murder:

> *Here lay Duncan,*
> *His silver skin lac'd with his golden blood;*
> *And his gash'd stabs, look'd like a breach in nature*
> *For ruin's wasteful entrance: there, the murderers,*
> *Steep'd in the colours of their trade, their daggers*
> *Unmannerly breech'd with gore. . . .*

It is amusing to watch the textual critics, particularly those of the eighteenth century, fight a stubborn rear-guard action against the acceptance of "breech'd." Warburton emended "breech'd" to "reech'd"; Johnson, to "drench'd"; Seward, to "hatch'd." Other critics argued that the *breeches* implied were really the handles of the daggers, and that, accordingly, "breech'd" actually here meant "sheathed." The Variorum page witnesses the desperate character of the defense, but the position has had to be yielded, after all. *The Shakespeare Glossary* defines "breech'd" as meaning "covered as with breeches," and thus leaves the poet committed to a reading which must still shock the average reader as much as it shocked that nineteenth-century critic who pronounced upon it as follows: "A metaphor must not be far-fetched nor dwell upon the details of a disgusting picture, as in these lines. There is little, and that far-fetched, similarity between *gold lace* and *blood*, or between *bloody daggers* and *breech'd legs*. The slightness of the similarity, recalling the greatness of the dissimilarity, disgusts us with the attempted comparison."

The two passages are not of the utmost importance, I dare say, though the speeches (of which each is a part) are put in Macbeth's mouth and come at moments of great dramatic tension in the play. Yet, in neither case is there any warrant for thinking that Shakespeare was not trying to write as well as he could. Moreover, whether we like it or not, the imagery is fairly typical of Shakespeare's mature style. Either passage ought to raise some qualms among those who retreat to Shakespeare's authority when they seek to urge the claims of "noble simplicity." They are hardly simple. Yet it is possible that such passages as these may illustrate another poetic resource, another type of imagery which, even in spite of its apparent violence and complication, Shakespeare could absorb into the total structure of his work.

Shakespeare, I repeat, is not Donne—is a much greater poet than Donne; yet the example of his typical handling of imagery will scarcely render support to the usual attacks on Donne's imagery—for, with regard to the two passages in question, the second one, at any rate, is about as strained as Donne is at his most extreme pitch.

Yet I think that Shakespeare's daggers attired in their bloody breeches can be defended as poetry, and as characteristically Shakespearean poetry. Furthermore, both this passage and that about the newborn babe, it seems to me, are far more than excrescences, mere extravagances of detail: each, it seems to me, contains a central symbol of the play, and symbols which we must understand if we are to understand either the detailed passage or the play as a whole.

If this be true, then more is at stake than the merit of the quoted lines taken as lines. (The lines as constituting mere details of a larger structure could, of course, be omitted in the acting of the play without seriously damaging the total effect of the tragedy—though this argument obviously cuts two ways. Whole scenes, and admittedly fine scenes, might also be omitted —have in fact *been* omitted—without quite destroying the massive structure of the tragedy.) What is at stake is the whole matter of the relation of Shakespeare's imagery to the total structures of the plays themselves.

I should like to use the passages as convenient points of entry into the larger symbols which dominate the play. They *are* convenient because, even if we judge them to be faulty, they demonstrate how obsessive for Shakespeare the symbols were—they demonstrate how far the conscious (or unconscious) symbolism could take him.

If we see how the passages are related to these symbols, and they to the tragedy as a whole, the main matter is achieved; and having seen this, if we still prefer "to wish the lines away," that, of course, is our privilege. In the meantime, we may have learned something about Shakespeare's methods—not merely of building metaphors—but of encompassing his larger meanings.

One of the most startling things which has come out of Miss Spurgeon's book on Shakespeare's imagery is her discovery of the "old clothes" imagery in *Macbeth*. As she points out: "The idea constantly recurs that Macbeth's new honours sit ill upon him, like a loose and badly fitting garment, belonging to someone else." And she goes on to quote passage after passage in which the idea is expressed. But, though we are all in Miss Spurgeon's debt for having pointed this out, one has to observe that Miss Spurgeon has hardly explored the full implications of her discovery. Perhaps her interest in classifying and cataloguing the imagery of the plays has obscured for her some of the larger and more important relationships. At any rate, for reasons to be given below, she has realized only a part of the potentialities of her discovery.

Her comment on the clothes imagery reaches its climax with the following paragraphs:

> And, at the end, when the tyrant is at bay at Dunsinane, and the English troops are advancing, the Scottish lords still have this image in their minds. Caithness sees him as a man vainly trying to fasten a large garment on him with too small a belt:

> *He cannot buckle his distemper'd cause*
> *Within the belt of rule;*

while Angus, in a similar image, vividly sums up the essence of what they all have been thinking ever since Macbeth's accession to power:

> *now does he feel his title*
> *Hang loose about him, like a giant's robe*
> *Upon a dwarfish thief.*

This imaginative picture of a small, ignoble man encumbered and degraded by garments unsuited to him, should be put against the view emphasized by some critics (notably Coleridge and Bradley) of the likeness between Macbeth and Milton's Satan in grandeur and sublimity.

    Undoubtedly Macbeth . . . is great, magnificently great . . . But he could never be put beside, say, Hamlet or Othello, in nobility of nature; and there *is* an aspect in which he is but a poor, vain, cruel, treacherous creature, snatching ruthlessly over the dead bodies of kinsman and friend at place and power he is utterly unfitted to possess. It is worth remembering that it is thus that Shakespeare, with his unshrinking clarity of vision, repeatedly *sees* him.

But this is to make primary what is only one aspect of the old-clothes imagery! And there is no warrant for interpreting the garment imagery as used by Macbeth's enemies, Caithness and Angus, to mean that *Shakespeare* sees Macbeth as a poor and somewhat comic figure.

The crucial point of the comparison, it seems to me, lies not in the smallness of the man and the largeness of the robes, but rather in the fact that—whether the man be large or small—these are not *his* garments; in Macbeth's case they are actually stolen garments. Macbeth is uncomfortable in them because he is continually conscious of the fact that they do not belong to him. There is a further point, and it is one of the utmost importance; the oldest symbol for the hypocrite is that of the man who cloaks his true nature under a disguise. Macbeth loathes playing the part of the hypocrite—and actually does not play it too well. If we keep this in mind as we look back at the instances of the garment images which Miss Spurgeon has collected for us, we shall see that the pattern of imagery becomes very rich indeed. Macbeth says in Act I:

> *The Thane of Cawdor lives: why do you dress me*
> *In borrow'd robes?*

Macbeth at this point wants no honors that are not honestly his. Banquo says in Act I:

> *New honours come upon him,*
> *Like our strange garments, cleave not to their mould,*
> *But with the aid of use.*

But Banquo's remark, one must observe, is not censorious. It is indeed a compliment to say of one that he wears new honors with some awkwardness. The observation becomes ironical only in terms of what is to occur later.

Macbeth says in Act I:

> *He hath honour'd me of late; and I have bought*
> *Golden opinions from all sorts of people,*
> *Which would be worn now in their newest gloss,*
> *Not cast aside so soon.*

Macbeth here is proud of his new clothes: he is happy to wear what he has truly earned. It is the part of simple good husbandry not to throw aside these new garments and replace them with robes stolen from Duncan.

But Macbeth has already been wearing Duncan's garments in anticipation, as his wife implies in the metaphor with which she answers him:

> *Was the hope drunk,*
> *Wherein you dress'd yourself?*

(The metaphor may seem hopelessly mixed, and a full and accurate analysis of such mixed metaphors in terms of the premises of Shakespeare's style waits upon some critic who will have to consider not only this passage but many more like it in Shakespeare.) For our purposes here, however, one may observe that the psychological line, the line of the basic symbolism, runs on unbroken. A man dressed in a drunken hope is garbed in strange attire indeed—a ridiculous dress which accords thoroughly with the contemptuous picture that Lady Macbeth wishes to evoke. Macbeth's earlier dream of glory has been a drunken fantasy merely, if he flinches from action now.

But the series of garment metaphors which run through the play is paralleled by a series of masking or cloaking images which —if we free ourselves of Miss Spurgeon's rather mechanical scheme of classification—show themselves to be merely variants of the garments which hide none too well his disgraceful self. He is consciously hiding that self throughout the play.

"False face must hide what the false heart doth know," he counsels Lady Macbeth before the murder of Duncan; and later, just before the murder of Banquo, he invokes night to "Scarf up the eye of pitiful day."

One of the most powerful of these cloaking images is given to Lady Macbeth in the famous speech in Act I:

> *Come, thick night,*
> *And pall thee in the dunnest smoke of hell,*
> *That my keen knife see not the wound it makes,*
> *Nor heaven peep through the blanket of the dark,*
> *To cry, "Hold, Hold!"*

I suppose that it is natural to conceive the "keen knife" here as held in her own hand. Lady Macbeth is capable of wielding it. And in this interpretation, the imagery is thoroughly significant. Night is to be doubly black so that not even her knife may see the wound it makes. But I think that there is good warrant for regarding her "keen knife" as Macbeth himself. She has just, a few lines above, given her analysis of Macbeth's character as one who would "not play false,/ And yet [would] wrongly win." To bring him to the point of action, she will have to "chastise [him] with the valour of [her] tongue." There is good reason, then, for her to invoke night to become blacker still—to pall itself in the "dunnest smoke of hell." For night must not only screen the deed from the eye of heaven—conceal it at least until it is too late for heaven to call out to Macbeth "Hold, Hold!" Lady Macbeth would have night blanket the deed from the hesitant doer. The imagery thus repeats and reinforces the substance of Macbeth's anguished aside uttered in the preceding scene:

> *Let not light see my black and deep desires;*
> *The eye wink at the hand; yet let that be*
> *Which the eye fears, when it is done, to see.*

I do not know whether "blanket" and "pall" qualify as garment metaphors in Miss Spurgeon's classification: yet one is the clothing of sleep, and the other, the clothing of death—they are the appropriate garments of night; and they carry on an important aspect of the general clothes imagery. It is not necessary to attempt to give here an exhaustive list of instances of the garment metaphor; but one should say a word about the remarkable passage in II, iii.

Here, after the discovery of Duncan's murder, Banquo says

> *And when we have our naked frailties hid,*
> *That suffer in exposure, let us meet,*
> *And question this most bloody piece of work—*

that is, "When we have clothed ourselves against the chill morning air, let us meet to discuss this bloody piece of work." Macbeth answers, as if his subconscious mind were already taking Banquo's innocent phrase, "naked frailties," in a deeper, ironic sense:

> *Let's briefly put on manly readiness. . . .*

It is ironic; for the "manly readiness" which he urges the other lords to put on, is, in his own case, a hypocrite's garment: he can only pretend to be the loyal, grief-stricken liege who is almost unstrung by the horror of Duncan's murder.

But the word "manly" carries still a further ironic implication: earlier, Macbeth had told Lady Macbeth that he dared

> do all that may become a man;
> Who dares do more is none.

Under the weight of her reproaches of cowardice, however, he *has* dared do more, and has become less than a man, a beast. He has already laid aside, therefore, one kind of "manly readiness" and has assumed another: he has garbed himself in a sterner composure than that which he counsels to his fellows—the hard and inhuman "manly readiness" of the resolved murderer.

The clothes imagery, used sometimes with emphasis on one aspect of it, sometimes, on another, does pervade the play. And it should be evident that the daggers "breech'd with gore"—though Miss Spurgeon does not include the passage in her examples of clothes imagery—represent one more variant of this general symbol. Consider the passage once more:

> Here lay Duncan,
> *His silver skin lac'd with his golden blood;*
> *And his gash'd stabs look'd like a breach in nature*
> *For ruin's wasteful entrance: there, the murderers,*
> *Steep'd in the colours of their trade, their daggers*
> *Unmannerly breech'd with gore. . . .*

The clothes imagery runs throughout the passage; the body of the king is dressed in the most precious of garments, the blood royal itself; and the daggers too are dressed—in the same garment. The daggers, "naked" except for their lower parts which are reddened with blood, are like men in "unmannerly" dress—men, naked except for their red breeches, lying beside the red-handed grooms. The figure, though vivid, is fantastic; granted. But the basis for the comparison is *not* slight and adventitious. The metaphor fits the real situation on the deepest levels. As Macbeth and Lennox burst into the room, they find the daggers wearing, as Macbeth knows all too well, a horrible masquerade. They have been carefully "clothed" to play a part. They are not honest daggers, honorably naked in readiness to guard the king, or, "mannerly" clothed in their own sheaths. Yet the disguise which they wear will enable Macbeth to assume the robes of Duncan—

robes to which he is no more entitled than are the daggers to the royal garments which they now wear, grotesquely.

The reader will, of course, make up his own mind as to the value of the passage. But the metaphor in question, in the light of the other garment imagery, cannot be dismissed as merely a strained ingenuity, irrelevant to the play. And the reader who *does* accept it as poetry will probably be that reader who knows the play best, not the reader who knows it slightly and regards Shakespeare's poetry as a rhetoric more or less loosely draped over the "content" of the play.

And now what can be said of pity, the "naked new-born babe"? Though Miss Spurgeon does not note it (since the governing scheme of her book would have hardly allowed her to see it), there are, by the way, a great many references to babes in this play—references which occur on a number of levels. The babe appears sometimes as a character, such as Macduff's child; sometimes as a symbol, like the crowned babe and the bloody babe which are raised by the witches on the occasion of Macbeth's visit to them; sometimes, in a metaphor, as in the passage under discussion. The number of such references can hardly be accidental; and the babe turns out to be, as a matter of fact, perhaps the most powerful symbol in the tragedy.

But to see this fully, it will be necessary to review the motivation of the play. The stimulus to Duncan's murder, as we know, was the prophecy of the Weird Sisters. But Macbeth's subsequent career of bloodshed stems from the same prophecy. Macbeth was to have the crown, but the crown was to pass to Banquo's children. The second part of the prophecy troubles Macbeth from the start. It does not oppress him, however, until the crown has been won. But from this point on, the effect of the prophecy is to hurry Macbeth into action and more action until he is finally precipitated into ruin.

We need not spend much time in speculating on whether Macbeth, had he been content with Duncan's murder, had he tempted fate no further, had he been willing to court the favor of his nobles, might not have died peaceably in bed. We are dealing, not with history, but with a play. Yet, even in history the usurper sometimes succeeds; and he sometimes succeeds on the stage.

Shakespeare himself knew of, and wrote plays about, usurpers who successfully maintained possession of the crown. But, in any case, this much is plain: the train of murders into which Macbeth launches aggravates suspicions of his guilt and alienates the nobles.

Yet, a Macbeth who could act once, and then settle down to enjoy the fruits of this one attempt to meddle with the future would, of course, not be Macbeth. For it is not merely his great imagination and his warrior courage in defeat which redeem him for tragedy and place him beside the other great tragic protagonists: rather, it is his attempt to conquer the future, an attempt involving him, like Oedipus, in a desperate struggle with fate itself. It is this which holds our imaginative sympathy, even after he has degenerated into a bloody tyrant and has become the slayer of Macduff's wife and children.

To sum up, there can be no question that Macbeth stands at the height of his power after his murder of Duncan, and that the plan—as outlined by Lady Macbeth—has been relatively successful. The road turns toward disaster only when Macbeth decides to murder Banquo. Why does he make this decision? Shakespeare has pointed up the basic motivation very carefully:

> *Then prophet-like,*
> *They hail'd him father to a line of kings.*
> *Upon my head they plac'd a fruitless crown,*
> *And put a barren sceptre in my gripe,*
> *Thence to be wrench'd with a unlineal hand,*
> *No son of mine succeeding. If't be so,*
> *For Banquo's issue have I fil'd my mind;*
> *For them the gracious Duncan have I murder'd;*
> *Put rancours in the vessel of my peace*
> *Only for them; and mine eternal jewel*
> *Given to the common enemy of man,*
> *To make them kings, the seed of Banquo kings!*

Presumably, Macbeth had entered upon his course from sheer personal ambition. Ironically, it is the more human part of Macbeth—his desire to have more than a limited personal satisfaction, his desire to found a line, his wish to pass something on to later generations—which prompts him to dispose of Banquo. There is, of course, a resentment against Banquo, but that resentment is itself closely related to Macbeth's desire to found a dynasty. Banquo, who has risked nothing, who has remained upright, who has not defiled himself, will have kings for children; Macbeth, none. Again, ironically, the Weird Sisters who have given Macbeth, so he has thought, the priceless gift of knowledge of the future, have given the real future to Banquo.

So Banquo's murder is decided upon, and accomplished. But Banquo's son escapes, and once more, the future has eluded Macbeth. The murder of Banquo thus becomes almost meaningless. This general point may be obvious enough, but we shall do well to note some of the further ways in which Shakespeare has pointed up the significance of Macbeth's war with the future.

When Macbeth, at the beginning of Scene vii, Act I, contemplates Duncan's murder, it is the future over which he agonizes:

If it were done, when 'tis done, then 'twere well
It were done quickly; if the assassination
Could trammel up the consequence, and catch
With his surcease success; that but this blow
Might be the be-all and the end-all here. . . .

But the continuum of time cannot be partitioned off; the future is implicit in the present. There is no net strong enough to trammel up the consequence—not even in this world.

Lady Macbeth, of course, has fewer qualms. When Macbeth hesitates to repudiate the duties which he owes Duncan—duties which, by some accident of imagery perhaps—I hesitate to press the significance—he has earlier actually called "children"—Lady Macbeth cries out that she is willing to crush her own child in order to gain the crown:

I have given suck, and know
How tender 'tis to love the babe that milks me;
I would, while it was smiling in my face,
Have pluck'd my nipple from his boneless gums
And dash'd the brains out, had I so sworn as you
Have done to this.

Robert Penn Warren has made the penetrating observation that all of Shakespeare's villains are rationalists. Lady Macbeth is certainly of their company. She knows what she wants; and she is ruthless in her consideration of means. She will always "catch the nearest way." This is not to say that she ignores the problem of scruples, or that she is ready to oversimplify psychological complexities. But scruples are to be used to entangle one's enemies. One is not to become tangled in the mesh of scruples himself. Even though she loves her husband and though her ambition for herself is a part of her ambition for him, still she seems willing to consider even Macbeth at times as pure instrument, playing upon his hopes and fears and pride.

Her rationalism is quite sincere. She is apparently thoroughly honest in declaring that

> *The sleeping and the dead*
> *Are but as pictures; 'tis the eye of childhood*
> *That fears a painted devil. If he do bleed,*
> *I'll gild the faces of the grooms withal,*
> *For it must seem their guilt.*

For her, there is no moral order: *guilt* is something like *gilt*—one can wash it off or paint it on. Her pun is not frivolous and it is deeply expressive.

Lady Macbeth abjures all pity; she is willing to unsex herself; and her continual taunt to Macbeth, when he falters, is that he is acting like a baby—not like a man. This "manhood" Macbeth tries to learn. He is a dogged pupil. For that reason he is almost pathetic when the shallow rationalism which his wife urges upon him fails. His tone is almost one of puzzled bewilderment at nature's unfairness in failing to play the game according to the rules —the rules which have applied to other murders:

> *the time has been,*
> *That, when the brains were out, the man would die,*
> *And there an end; but now they rise again. . . .*

Yet, after the harrowing scene, Macbeth can say, with a sort of dogged weariness:

Come, we'll to sleep. My strange and self-abuse
Is the initiate fear that wants hard use:
We are yet but young in deed.

Ironically, Macbeth is still echoing the dominant metaphor of
Lady Macbeths' reproach. He has not yet attained to "manhood";
that *must* be the explanation. He has not yet succeeded in harden-
ing himself into something inhuman.

Tempted by the Weird Sisters and urged on by his wife, Macbeth is thus caught between the irrational and the rational. There
is a sense, of course, in which every man is caught between them.
Man must try to predict and plan and control his destiny. That
is man's fate; and the struggle, if he is to realize himself as a
man, cannot be avoided. The question, of course, which has always interested the tragic dramatist involves the terms on which
the struggle is accepted and the protagonist's attitude toward fate
and toward himself. Macbeth in his general concern for the future
is typical—is Every Man. He becomes the typical tragic protagonist when he yields to pride and *hybris*. The occasion for temptation is offered by the prophecy of the Weird Sisters. They offer
him knowledge which cannot be arrived at rationally. They offer
a key—if only a partial key—to what is otherwise unpredictable.
Lady Macbeth, on the other hand, by employing a ruthless clarity
of perception, by discounting all emotional claims, offers him the
promise of bringing about the course of events which he desires.

Now, in the middle of the play, though he has not lost confidence and though, as he himself says, there can be no turning
back, doubts have begun to arise; and he returns to the Weird
Sisters to secure unambiguous answers to his fears. But, pathetically and ironically for Macbeth, in returning to the Weird Sisters, he is really trying to impose rationality on what sets itself
forth plainly as irrational: that is, Macbeth would force a rigid
control on a future which, by definition—by the very fact that
the Weird Sisters already know it—stands beyond his manipulation.

It is because of his hopes for his own children and his fears of
Banquo's that he has returned to the witches for counsel. It is
altogether appropriate, therefore, that two of the apparitions by

which their counsel is revealed should be babes, the crowned babe and the bloody babe.

For the babe signifies the future which Macbeth would control and cannot control. It is the unpredictable thing itself—as Yeats has put it magnificently, "The uncontrollable mystery on the bestial floor." It is the one thing that can justify, even in Macbeth's mind, the murders which he has committed. Earlier in the play, Macbeth had declared that if the deed could "trammel up the consequence," he would be willing to "jump the life to come." But he cannot jump the life to come. In his own terms he is betrayed. For it is idle to speak of jumping the life to come if one yearns to found a line of kings. It is the babe that betrays Macbeth—his own babes, most of all.

The logic of Macbeth's distraught mind, thus, forces him to make war on children, a war which in itself reflects his desperation and is a confession of weakness. Macbeth's ruffians, for example, break into Macduff's castle and kill his wife and children. The scene in which the innocent child prattles with his mother about his absent father, and then is murdered, is typical Shakespearean "fourth act" pathos. But the pathos is not adventitious; the scene ties into the inner symbolism of the play. For the child, in its helplessness, defies the murderers. Its defiance testifies to the force which threatens Macbeth and which Macbeth cannot destroy.

But we are not, of course, to placard the child as The Future in a rather stiff and mechanical allegory. *Macbeth* is no such allegory. Shakespeare's symbols are richer and more flexible than that. The babe signifies not only the future; it symbolizes all those enlarging purposes which make life meaningful, and it symbolizes, furthermore, all those emotional and—to Lady Macbeth—irrational ties which make man more than a machine—which render him human. It signifies pre-eminently the pity which Macbeth, under Lady Macbeth's tutelage, would wean himself of as something "unmanly." Lady Macbeth's great speeches early in the play become brilliantly ironical when we realize that Shakespeare is using the same symbol for the unpredictable future that he uses for human compassion. Lady Macbeth is willing to go to any length to grasp the future: she would willingly dash out the brains of her own child if it stood in her way to that future. But this is to repudiate the future, for the child is its symbol.

Shakespeare does not, of course, limit himself to the symbolism of the child: he makes use of other symbols of growth and development, notably that of the plant. And this plant symbolism patterns itself to reflect the development of the play. For example, Banquo says to the Weird Sisters, early in the play:

> *If you can look into the seeds of time,*
> *And say which grain will grow and which will not,*
> *Speak then to me. . . .*

A little later, on welcoming Macbeth, Duncan says to him:

> *I have begun to plant thee, and will labour*
> *To make thee full of growing.*

After the murder of Duncan, Macbeth falls into the same metaphor when he comes to resolve on Banquo's death. The Weird Sisters, he reflects, had hailed Banquo as

> *. . . father to a line of kings.*
> *Upon my head they placed a fruitless crown,*
> *And put a barren sceptre in my gripe. . . .*

Late in the play, Macbeth sees himself as the winter-stricken tree:

> *I have liv'd long enough: my way of life*
> *Is fall'n into the sear, the yellow leaf. . . .*

The plant symbolism, then, supplements the child symbolism. At points it merges with it, as when Macbeth ponders bitterly that he has damned himself.

> *To make them kings, the seed of Banquo kings!*

And, in at least one brilliant example, the plant symbolism unites with the clothes symbolism. It is a crowning irony that one of the Weird Sisters' prophecies on which Macbeth has staked his hopes is fulfilled when Birnam Wood comes to Dunsinane. For, in a sense, Macbeth is here hoist on his own petard. Macbeth, who has invoked night to "Scarf up the tender eye of pitiful day," and who has, again and again, used the "false face" to "hide what the false heart doth know," here has the trick turned against him. But the garment which cloaks the avengers is the living green of nature itself, and nature seems, to the startled eyes of his sentinels, to be rising up against him.

But it is the babe, the child, that dominates the symbolism. Most fittingly, the last of the prophecies in which Macbeth has placed his confidence, concerns the child: and Macbeth comes to know the final worst when Macduff declares to him that he was not "born of woman" but was from his "mother's womb/ Untimely ripp'd." The babe here has defied even the thing which one feels may reasonably be predicted of him—his time of birth. With Macduff's pronouncement, the unpredictable has broken through the last shred of the net of calculation. The future cannot be trammelled up. The naked babe confronts Macbeth to pronounce his doom.

The passage with which we began this essay, then, is an integral part of a larger context, and of a very rich context:

> And pity, like a naked new-born babe,
> Striding the blast, or heaven's cherubim, hors'd
> Upon the sightless couriers of the air,
> Shall blow the horrid deed in every eye,
> That tears shall drown the wind.

Pity is like the naked babe, the most sensitive and helpless thing; yet, almost as soon as the comparison is announced, the symbol of weakness begins to turn into a symbol of strength; for the babe, though newborn, is pictured as "Striding the blast" like an elemental force—like "heaven's cherubim, hors'd/Upon the sightless couriers of the air." We can give an answer to the question put earlier: is Pity like the human and helpless babe, or powerful as the angel that rides the winds? It is both; and it is strong because of its very weakness. The paradox is inherent in the situation itself; and it is the paradox that will destroy the overbrittle rationalism on which Macbeth founds his career.

For what will it avail Macbeth to cover the deed with the blanket of the dark if the elemental forces that ride the winds will blow the horrid deed in every eye? And what will it avail Macbeth to clothe himself in "manliness"—to become bloody, bold, and resolute—if he is to find himself again and again, viewing his bloody work through the "eye of childhood/ That fears a painted devil"? Certainly, the final and climactic appearance of the babe symbol merges all the contradictory elements of the symbol. For, with Macduff's statement about his birth, the naked babe rises before Macbeth as not only the future that eludes calculation but as avenging angel as well.

The clothed daggers and the naked babe—mechanism and life —instrument and end—death and birth—that which should be left bare and clean and that which should be clothed and warmed— these are facets of two of the great symbols which run throughout the play. They are not the only symbols, to be sure; they are not the most obvious symbols: darkness and blood appear more often. But with a flexibility which must amaze the reader, the image of the garment and the image of the babe are so used as to encompass an astonishingly large area of the total situation. And between them—the naked babe, essential humanity, humanity stripped down to the naked thing itself, and yet as various as the future— and the various garbs which humanity assumes, the robes of honor, the hypocrite's disguise, the inhuman "manliness" with which Macbeth endeavors to cover up his essential humanity— between them, they furnish Shakespeare with his most subtle and ironically telling instruments.

5

A Reply to Cleanth Brooks

HELEN GARDNER

This essay, excerpted from a lecture given in 1953, illustrates one of the ways in which an interpretation by a New Critic can be contested. It is reprinted here not because it is necessarily right or wrong—that the reader must decide for himself—but because it illustrates so well the fruitfulness of an approach to Shakespeare which is concerned with the meaning of the whole and the relation to that whole of particular details. Perhaps the greatest compliment to a work of literary criticism is the recognition, implicit in such a reply as Helen Gardner's, that it is a statement in a dialogue; to bad criticism there is no answer beyond the gesture of rejection. Helen Gardner is Reader in Renaissance English Literature at Oxford. Her literary interests range from the Bible to mtaphysical poetry, from Renaissance drama and Milton to modern poetry; among her more important works are The Art of T. S. Eliot *(1949) and her authoritative edition of* The Divine Poems of John Donne *(1952). Miss Gardner's literary activities might suggest a kinship with the New Critics, but she is primarily a historical scholar and a member of no critical school. Her writing has long since won her a reputation for the depth of her perception, the clarity of her reason, the breadth of her learning, and the force of her common sense.*

The counterpoise to the necessity of "examining the genius of his age and the opinions of his contemporaries," if we are to arrive at "a just estimate" of a writer's quality and to understand his meaning, is the necessity of learning the author's own personal language, the idiom of his thought. The discipline of imaginative intercourse is not wholly different from the discipline of social intercourse. We learn to know our friends so that we do not misunderstand them, or put a wrong construction on their actions. We can say with certainty, "He can't have meant that," because we know the kind of person "he" is. In the same kind of way we can arrive at a similar conviction about a poem because we know the habit of an author's mind and are familiar with his associations of ideas and have come to sympathize with his moral temper. It is possible, in the light of this knowledge, to check our own habits and associations and feel some assurance that one interpretation is better, because more characteristic, than another.

Like the historical sense, this sense of a writer's individual habit of mind is no infallible guide. We cannot tie an author down to repeating himself any more than we can tie him to saying what his contemporaries say. Within the range of a temperament we often meet with surprises. If an author is prevailingly serious, we must not insist that he can never be jocose, and because we cannot find any parallel in his works we cannot, therefore, insist that he cannot mean in one work what he must mean there, if the work is to make sense. If it is a passage which we are interpreting; the final test is always the consistency of the interpretation of the passage with the interpretation of the work as a whole. If we are attempting the interpretation of a single complete work, the test is the reverse of this: does our interpretation of the whole make sense of all the parts?

A good example of the necessity of disciplining our imaginations and our responses by asking what associations the poet had in mind, rather than using the author's words as a starting-point for associations of our own, is a passage in *Macbeth* which was interpreted at some length by Professor Cleanth Brooks in *The Well Wrought Urn* (1947). It can be shown that the critic has distorted the sense of the passage to make it an example of his general theory of the nature of poetry as distinct from prose. The interpretation he gives is shallower and less in keeping with the play as a whole than the interpretation we can arrive at by using Shakespeare to comment on Shakespeare. He isolates for discussion the lines where Macbeth "compares the pity for his victim-to-be, Duncan," to

> *a naked new-born babe,*
> *Striding the blast, or heaven's cherubim, hors'd*
> *Upon the sightless couriers of the air. . . .*

and he comments as follows:

> The comparison is odd, to say the least. Is the babe natural or
> supernatural—an ordinary helpless baby, who, as newborn, could
> not, of course, even toddle, much less stride the blast? Or is it
> some infant Hercules, quite capable of striding the blast, but,
> since it is powerful and not helpless, hardly the typical pitiable
> object?
>
> Shakespeare seems bent upon having it both ways—and, if we
> read on through the passage—bent upon having the best of both
> worlds; for he proceeds to give us the option: pity is like the babe
> "or heaven's cherubim" who quite appropriately, of course, do
> ride the blast. Yet, even if we waive the question of the legitimacy
> of the alternative . . . is the cherubim comparison really any more
> successful than is the babe comparison? Would not one of the
> great warrior archangels be more appropriate to the scene than
> the cherub? Does Shakespeare mean for pity or for fear of retribu-
> tion to be dominant in Macbeth's mind?
>
> Or was it possible that Shakespeare could not make up his own
> mind? Was he merely writing hastily and loosely, letting the word
> "pity" suggest the typically pitiable object, the babe naked in the
> blast, and then, stirred by the vague notion that some threat to
> Macbeth should be hinted, using "heaven's cherubim"—already
> suggested by "babe"—to convey the hint?

We know what the answer will be to all this puzzlement.[1] Shakespeare "meant for both." The passage is an example of the ambiguity, irony, paradox—the terms are roughly interchangeable—
which Professor Brooks holds to be the differentiating quality
of poetic speech. Later in the same essay the meaning is revealed:

> Pity is like the naked babe, the most sensitive and helpless
> thing, yet almost as soon as the comparison is announced, the
> symbol of weakness begins to turn into a symbol of strength; for
> the babe, though newborn, is pictured as "Striding the blast" like
> an elemental force—like "heaven's cherubim". . . . We can give an

answer to the question put earlier: is Pity like the human and helpless babe, or powerful as the angel that rides the winds? It is both. . . . The final and climatic appearance of the babe symbol merges all the contradictory elements of the symbol. For, with Macduff's statement about his birth, the naked babe rises before Macbeth as not only the future that eludes calculation but as avenging angel as well.

But why does Professor Brooks think that "heaven's cherubim" "quite appropriately ride the blast"? Why are they any more suitably imagined as "horsed" than the naked babe as "striding"? Why is it to be assumed that they imply "some threat to Macbeth"? Are cherubin to be thought of as powerful? Have we any reason to suppose that they should at once suggest to us the cliché "avenging angel"?

Most editors rightly cite here Psalm xviii, where the Lord is described descending in judgement: "He bowed the heavens also and came down: and it was dark under his feet. He rode upon the cherubims and did fly: he came flying upon the wings of the wind." Similarly, in Ezekiel's vision the cherubim are between the wheels of the chariot of the Lord; for the cherubim, in the visions of the Old Testament, are the glory of the Lord, the signs of his presence. I do not doubt that the association "cherubims"— "wings of the wind" helped to create Shakespeare's lines. But there is no suggestion in the psalm, although it is a psalm of judgement, that cherubim are avenging angels. It is the Lord who is borne up by the cherubim; it is he that flies on the wings of the wind. The cherubim are among the higher orders of angels —the ministers who stand about the throne. They are not the executors of God's purposes. They are with the Lord, whether he comes in mercy or in judgement: "The Lord is King be the people never so unpatient; he sitteth between the cherubims be the earth never so unquiet." The cherubim, all gold and gilded over, carved at the two ends of the mercy-seat, in the description of the covenant in Exodus, are the tokens of the presence of the Lord among his people.

These are the cherubim of the Old Testament. Dionysius the Areopagite, who established the hierarchy of the angels, the source of the popular angelology of the Middle Ages, which the Elizabethans inherited, ranked the cherubim among the higher orders, as angels of the presence. They stood about the throne, contemplating the glory of God, not active, as were the lower orders, to fulfill his will on earth. The cherubim glowed with knowledge, as the seraphim burned with love. Hamlet, a scholarly character, glances at this learned conception of the cherubim in his retort to Claudius:

> *Claudius*. So is it, if thou knew'st our purposes.
> *Hamlet*. I see a cherub that sees them.

Elsewhere, apart from two references to the gilded carvings of cherubim, Shakespeare appears to use the word in its popular sense, to signify primarily beauty, particularly the radiant and innocent beauty of youth. Thus we may have the word used, as in Sonnet 114, for a simple opposite to the hideous:

> *To make of monsters and things indigest*
> *Such cherubins as your sweet self resemble.*

Or the idea of youthfulness is stressed, as in *The Merchant of Venice:*

> *Still quiring to the young-eyed cherubins*

or the idea of innocence, as in *Timon of Athens:*

> *This fell whore of thine*
> *Hath in her more destruction than thy sword*
> *For all her cherubin look.*

But in two plays, one written just before, the other some time after *Macbeth*, Shakespeare gives this innocent youthful beauty a certain moral colouring which is, as far as I know, his own; at least I have not met with it in another writer. In the late play, *The Tempest*, Prospero tells Miranda how he was set adrift with her when she was a baby, and she exclaims

> *Alack! what trouble*
> *Was I then to you.*

But he answers:

> *O, a cherubin*
> *Thou wast, that did preserve me! Thou didst smile,*
> *Infused with a fortitude from heaven,*
> *When I have deck'd the sea with drops full salt,*
> *Under my burden groan'd; which rais'd in me*
> *An undergoing stomach, to bear up*
> *Against what should ensue.*

Because Prospero sees the three-year-old Miranda as a cherub, smiling and giving him patience to bear up, I find no difficulty in taking Othello's cry "Patience, thou young and rose-lipped cherubin!" as an apostrophe to a virtue which Shakespeare elsewhere pictures as radiantly young and beautiful. In the recognition scene of *Pericles*, Pericles, gazing on his exquisite young daughter, who claims that she has endured "a grief might equal yours," wonders at her endurance, for, he exclaims,

> *thou dost look*
> *Like Patience gazing on kings' graves, and smiling*
> *Extremity out of act.*

Although Viola's description of her sister, "like Patience on a monument, smiling at grief," is often cited to prove that Shakespeare could not have thought of Patience as "young and rose-lipped," since Viola's sister had lost her damask cheek and had pined in thought,[2] the passage in *Pericles* admits of no doubt. It plainly implies a beauty untouched by care. In *Othello* then, written just before *Macbeth,* and in *The Tempest,* written some time after, a cherub is thought of as not only young, beautiful, and innocent, but as associated with the virtue of patience, conceived of as an endurance which is not grim, but heavenly, smiling, and serene. It could, however, be objected at this point that because Shakespeare elsewhere invariably sees the cherubim as young and beautiful, and conceives them as particularly asso-

ciated with the bearing of wrong rather than with the avenging
of it, we cannot assume that he never saw them otherwise. Although there is no support for the idea in Scripture or in popular
angelology, and no parallel elsewhere in his works, he might, in
this passage, because of a confused memory of Psalm xviii, conceive of cherubim as avengers threatening Macbeth; for there is
apocalyptic imagery just before in the simile of the accusing
"angels trumpet-tongu'd."

The context is our final test. Macbeth, having acknowledged
the certainty of retribution in this life, that "we still have judgement here," goes on to give the reasons which make the deed
which he is meditating peculiarly base. It is the murder of a kins-
man and a king, who is also a guest who trusts his host to protect
him:

> Besides, this Duncan
> Hath borne his faculties so meek, hath been
> So clear in his great office, that his virtues
> Will plead like angels trumpet-tongu'd against
> The deep damnation of his taking off;
> And pity, like a naked new-born babe,
> Striding the blast, or heaven's cherubin, hors'd
> Upon the sightless couriers of the air,
> Shall blow the horrid deed in every eye,
> That tears shall drown the wind.

The final image of the wind dropping as the rain begins is the
termination of the whole sequence of ideas and images. It is to
this close that they hurry. The passage ends with tears stilling
the blast. The final condemnation of the deed is not that it will
meet with punishment, not even that the doer of it will stand condemned; but that even indignation at the murder will be swal-
lowed up in universal pity for the victim. The whole world will
know, and knowing it will not curse but weep. The babe, naked
and new-born, the most helpless of all things, the cherubim, innocent and beautiful, call out the pity and the love by which
Macbeth is judged. It is not terror of heaven's vengeance which
makes him pause; but the terror of moral isolation. He ends by
seeing himself alone in a sudden silence, where nothing can be

heard but weeping, as, when a storm has blown itself out, the wind drops and we hear the steady falling of the rain, which sounds as if it would go on for ever. The naked babe "strides the blast" because pity is to Shakespeare the strongest and profoundest of human emotions, the distinctively human emotion. It rises above and masters indignation. The cherubim are borne with incredible swiftness about the world because the virtues of Duncan are of such heavenly beauty that they command universal love and reverence. He has "borne his faculties so meek" and been "so clear in his great office." The word "clear" is a radiant word, used by Shakespeare elsewhere of the Gods. The helplessness of the king who has trusted him, his gentle virtues, and patient goodness are transformed in Macbeth's mind into the most helpless of all things, what most demands our protection, and then into what awake tenderness, love, and reverence. The babe merges into the cherubim, not because Shakespeare means Macbeth to be feeling both pity and fear of retribution at the same time, but because Shakespeare, like Keats, believes in "the holiness of the heart's affections."

In a very early play, in a savage scene full of curses and cries for vengeance, Shakespeare uses the same natural image as he does here. In Henry VI, Part 3, Margaret, having crowned York with a paper crown, hands him a napkin dipped in his little son's blood, and York exclaims

> *Bidd'st thou me rage? why, now thou hast thy wish;*
> *Would'st have me weep? why, now thou hast thy will;*
> *For raging wind blows up incessant showers,*
> *And when the rage allays, the rain begins.*

And in his next speech he prophesies that Margaret's deed will have the same condemnation as Macbeth forsees for his:

> *Keep thou the napkin, and go boast of this;*
> *And if thou tell'st the heavy story right,*
> *Upon my soul, the hearers will shed tears;*
> *Yea, even my foes will shed fast-falling tears,*
> *And say, "Alas! it was a piteous deed."*

This seems feeble enough, and yet it holds the characteristic Shakespearian appeal to our deepest moral feelings. The worst suffering is to suffer alone; it is more comfort to York in his agony to think that common humanity will make even his enemies weep with him than to think of vengeance on the murderess of his son. Professor Brooks has sacrificed this Shakespearian depth of human feeling, visible even in this crude early play, by attempting to interpret an image by the aid of what associations it happens to arouse in him, and by being more interested in making symbols of babes fit each other than in listening to what Macbeth is saying. *Macbeth* is a tragedy and not a melodrama or a symbolic drama of retribution. The reappearance of "the babe symbol" in the apparition scene and in Macduff's revelation of his birth has distracted the critic's attention from what deeply moves the imagination and the conscience in this vision of a whole world weeping at the inhumanity of helplessness betrayed and innocence and beauty destroyed. It is the judgement of the human heart that Macbeth fears here, and the punishment which the speech foreshadows is not that he will be cut down by Macduff, but that having murdered his own humanity he will enter into a world of appalling loneliness, of meaningless activity, unloved himself, and unable to love.

1 It is a part of the game of "explication," as it has developed, to begin by expressing complete bafflement, as if the critic had never met a metaphor in his life. Then after every kind of obtuseness has been exhibited and all possible interpretations and misinterpretations have been considered, the true explication rises like the sun out of foggy mists.

2 This is absurdly supported by some commentators by reference to Nym's "Patience is a tired nag." There has been much discussion as to whether Shakespeare had a particular monument in mind. Although none has been discovered to fit the description, I think, in spite of their being far apart in time, we must take both Viola's and Pericles' words as referring to the same conception. Because Viola's sister lost her beauty, we need not take it that Shakespeare means us to think of the virtue which she exemplies as pale and worn. She is like Patience on a monument in that she "smiles at grief."

⚷⚶ 6 ⚶⚷

Monistic Criticism and the Structure of Shakespearean Drama

R. S. CRANE

R. S. Crane, Distinguished Service Professor of English, Emeritus, at the University of Chicago, has long been associated with the influential group of Chicago critics which includes, among others, Richard McKeon and Elder Olson, and which is best known for its use of Aristotle as a point of departure. Professor Crane is interested in critical theory and opposed to what he calls "the cult of the 'concrete'" in much modern criticism, that point of view which distrusts all but the practical and particular in writing about literature. He is a critical pluralist; following Aristotle's precept, he believes that "poetry exhibits a multiplicity of structures not capable of reduction to any single type." And this is the basis of his objection to the approach of the New Critics. Throughout The Languages of Criticism and the Structure of Poetry *(1953), from which this essay is excerpted, Professor Crane argues that a critic gets only the kind of answers that the terms of his questions permit. Cleanth Brooks' failure, from his point of view, is therefore the suggestion that the answers provided by a particular and limited methodology can state the whole truth about a work of art and constitute the "proper" way of approaching literature. "Our aim," Professor Crane asserts, "is an explanation and judgment of poetic works in terms of their structural causes," not the application to such works of a dogmatic hypothesis about the nature of all poetry. One may ask whether this approach imposes its own dogma, but one should note that Crane does not arbitrarily deny the value of the work of critics whose monism he attacks.*

The final test of any critical language is what its particular scheme of concepts permits or encourages us to say, in practical criticism, about individual works. And in the light of this test, it would seem that the critical revolution of the past three decades—the revolution that has given us the semantically oriented theories of poetry discussed in the last lecture—has been extraordinarily fruitful in concrete results. That at least has been the verdict of many of the writers who have committed themselves, more or less exclusively, to the new methods of interpreting literary works which the semantic movement has made available. "Critical writing like this," says Mr. Ransom, commenting on a page of subtle verbal analysis by R. P. Blackmur, "is done in our time. In depth and precision at once it is beyond all earlier criticism in our language." [1] The "only profitable approach to Shakespeare," Mr. Knights assures us, "is a consideration of his plays as dramatic poems" with close attention to the thematic structure most completely expressed in their imagery and diction; and of this approach it has remained for our generation, he says, after three centuries of criticism directed to less important things, to discover the proper technique. [2] "Our age," we are told in a recent essay on the movement as a whole, "is indeed an age of criticism. The structure of critical ideas and the practical criticism that British critics—Leavis, Turnell, Empson, Read—and American critics—Ransom, Tate, Brooks, Warren, Blackmur, Winters—have contrived upon the foundations of Eliot and Richards constitute an achievement in criticism the like of which has not been equaled in any previous period of our literary history." [3] And there would appear to be ample warrant for such enthusiasm not only in the many examples of "close readings" of texts but also in the large number of thorough-going "revaluations" of the great works and writers in our literary tradition which this school of critics has given us. The criticism of lyric poetry has been transformed; the criticism of the drama and the novel is in process of transformation; we now have a Shakespeare, or rather several Shakespeares, the existence of whom has been one of the startling discoveries of our time.

Let us suppose, at least for the duration of this lecture, that we have been convinced by these claims and these apparent evidences of progress in criticism and have resolved to deal with the problem of the structure of particular poetic works in the terms provided by the current view of poetic form as "meaning" and of literature as "ultimately metaphorical and symbolic." We should then have, as I suggested in the last lecture, the choice of two rather distinct approaches to the question, with the possibility that these might nevertheless be combined in a single more comprehensive view. In the first approach our concern would be with poetry considered as a special kind of language for the expression of meanings that cannot be expressed, or so accurately expressed, in other modes of discourse, and hence with the structures of meaning which poets themselves have devised; in the second approach, our emphasis would fall predominantly on the participation of poetry, certainly of great poetry, in the common symbolic operations of the human mind, and hence on the structures of meaning which, because they are basic and universal in man's experience, are in a sense given to poets rather than created by them. The first would be a kind of "Aristotelian" approach (though without Aristotle's devices for differentiating poetic forms) that would lead to a concentration on "symbolic structure"; the second would be a kind of "Platonic" approach (though with a dialectic moving in the opposite direction from Plato's) that would issue typically in a concentration on "archetypal patterns."

Let us imagine, to begin with, that we are critics of the first of these two types, for whom lyric poems, dramas, and works of fiction are semantic structures of a distinctive kind communicating, by symbolic devices peculiar to poetic or imaginative literature, a "total meaning" that is primarily of the poet's own making, however universally significant it may also be. Given such a work to be interpreted and judged in these terms, how can we proceed and what sort of results can we expect to get?

Our problem will be the same, let us remember, whether the work is lyric like *Lycidas,* a tragedy like *King Lear,* a comedy like *Much Ado about Nothing,* a tragicomedy like *Cymbeline,* a serious novel like *The Brothers Karamazov,* an allegory like *The Faerie Queene,* or a satire like *The Dunciad.* As poetic or imaginative works we shall not confuse these, in our readings, with scientific, philosophical, or rhetorical statements; but we shall not forget that poetic meaning or expression of meaning, wherever we find it, is one homogeneous kind of thing, in relation to which the formal or technical differences among poems are either irrelevant or have only a subordinate importance, as determining only the particular artistic means through which the writer's expressive intention or his insight into spiritual reality is made evident. The basic terms we shall use in our discussion will consequently be—and they can only be—the two terms that differentiate the elements present in all such works no matter of what specific kind. A poem, considered in this generalized way, in abstraction from the peculiar formal ends and effects at which different poems aim, is a composite of "meanings" or "themes" (in the sense of the ideas or attitudes or resolutions of opposed impulses which it symbolizes) and of the verbal and technical devices by which these are given concrete "poetic" embodiment in the poet's words. The "themes" will vary from poem to poem, and we shall see later how they may be identified or defined. All poems, novels, and dramas, we must insist, either have organizing themes or else are mere entertainments and hence not worthy of serious consideration; we must remember, as one of our contemporaries has insisted, that any poem, in so far as it is truly the poet's, "involves his own view of the world, his own values," and hence it will, "for better or worse, have relevance, by implication at least, to the world outside the poem" and be "not merely a device for creating an illusion." [4] And if it should be pointed out to us that to say this is to blur the old distinction between imitative and didactic works of literary art, or rather to make all good poems, in the sense of all poems that have "relevance to life," essentially didactic productions, our reply must be simply that we are not cutting our cake that way—that for our purposes the difference that matters is the difference between works in which we can find "themes" and works in which we cannot, and that there are no works, among those possessed of genuine poetic value, that do not fall in the first of these classes.

We shall accordingly not be content until we have discovered, for example, that the ballad of "The Three Ravens," through its contrasting symbols of the ravens and of the knight's hawks,

hound, and "fallow doe," represents two opposite ways of looking at life, the one in purely materialistic terms, the other in terms
that find "an importance in life beyond mere material circumstance";[5] or that Wordsworth's "Intimations" ode, through its imagery of light and darkness, explores "with some sensitiveness the
relation between the two modes of perception, that of the analytic
reason and that of the synthesizing imagination";[6] or that the central conflict in Joseph Conrad's *Victory* is between the forces of
Life, with their positive values of goodness, love, and faith, represented by Lena, and the forces of Death, with their negative
values of evil, hate, and skepticism, represented by Mr. Jones and
his companions, the contest centering upon Heyst, "who manifests
the pull of these two opposite poles of being." [7]

We must not give the impression, however, that such structures
of meaning are explicitly stated by the works in which we find
them or that they can ever be grasped, in their full emotional significance, except by sensitive study of the indirect poetic means
through which they are achieved. We shall need terms to discriminate and to talk about these; and we cannot do better, in this
respect, than to use the traditional names which older critics invented for very different rhetorical or poetic purposes: continuing
to speak, thus, with Aristotle and the later critics in his line, about
plot and characters, but treating these as "carriers" of meaning
rather than as structural parts; reviving, as Mr. Wimsatt and
others have done,[8] the ancient and Renaissance rhetoric of tropes
and figures, but giving a special importance—and an enlarged
definition—to such "figures of thought" as image, symbol, metaphor, paradox, irony, antithesis, synecdoche, allegory, pun, and
the like.

Such will be our not very complicated analytical apparatus for
reading poems of all kinds, and we can use it in two different but
complementary ways. We may want to put the emphasis, in our
writing or teaching, on the peculiar manner in which, in poetry
as distinct from other kinds of writing, meanings are apprehended
and expressed. We shall start, in that case, with the "theme," assuming that this is easily knowable and anyway, in our abstract
statement of it, not a primary cause of the poem's value, and our
attention will be concentrated on discriminating the various ele-

ments of rhythm, diction, statement, imagery, symbol, character, narrative, and so on, that cooperate, in a successful lyric, drama, or novel to give body, precision, and emotional force to what the poet is trying to say, our criteria being relative to the "form" rather than to the ideas of the poem and turning on such general qualities as concreteness, intensity, "organic unity," and dramatic rendering. The result will be the so-called "formal" criticism which has been made widely familiar, on this continent at least, in Brooks' and Warren's *Understanding Poetry,* and is practiced, with notable minuteness and ingenuity, by Mr. Blackmur.

We may prefer, however, to throw the emphasis on the meanings of poems rather than on their technique of meaningful expression; and in that case we shall tend to follow the more radical line taken by Brooks and Warren themselves in some of their later writings and by the many "new" critics of Shakespeare, from Wilson Knight to Harold Goddard and Robert Heilman, who have studied the plays for their poetic "meanings" rather than for their representations of characters and actions. We shall go in, that is to say, for what are called "interpretations," and more particularly for "interpretations" that will uncover deeper significances in well-known poems than they have usually been thought to contain. Our general procedure will consist, accordingly, in reducing the concrete elements of poems, plays, or novels to the underlying themes and interrelated patterns of themes which they embody, and our criteria of value, being relative to these rather than to the expression itself, will require statement in terms like "profundity," "maturity," "complexity," "universality," or "imaginative vision."

Let us follow, then, this second line and consider what equipment we need and what we have to do in order to reveal the "symbolic structures" or "thematic frameworks" that lie, as our method must suppose, beneath the surface of all serious poetic works, as the primary end of poets in writing or at any rate as our chief reward in contemplating their productions. What we shall want to be able to do can be gathered from what some of the critics whose example we are emulating have already done. It has been shown by one of them, for instance, that when Coleridge introduces the associated images of the Albatross, the moon,

and the wind into *The Rime of the Ancient Mariner,* he means
to tell us that the imagination, of which the moon is the symbol,
can be friendly to man but also inimical to him when its claims
as a source of knowledge are denied.[9] Another critic has brought
together in a similar fashion all the recurrent images in *Macbeth*
that relate to clothes on the one hand and to young and innocent
children on the other and, finding in these "the inner symbolism of
the play," has generalized from them a pervasive opposition between "the over-brittle rationalism on which Macbeth founds his
career" and the "irrational" forces in life which Macbeth and
Lady Macbeth have left out of account in their conspiracy to cap-
ture "the future" for themselves.[10] Another critic has applied the
same method, in a much more elaborate way, to *King Lear* and
has shown us how the many distinct "patterns" of imagery which
run through that play can be made to signify the terms of a complicated dialectic turning on the ways in which man must, and
must not, understand and assess the world of human experience
if he is to attain intellectual salvation: the play, in its ultimate
assertion, we are told, is "about" this problem, in all its many
ramifications, rather than about the tragic consequences, in a personal and merely human sense, of Lear's initial mistake.[11]

In all these instances, symbolic structure has been derived from
a consideration chiefly of imagery and diction, with the result
that dramas and novels are more or less completely assimilated
to lyric poems.[12] The more obvious structural elements of dramas
and novels, however—their characters and plots—may also be interpreted so as to yield meanings of the same sort. Thus the murder of Duncan, for one critic of *Macbeth,* symbolizes both the intrusion of political evil into the divinely ordered state and the
operation of evil desires in the individual soul;[13] and another
critic of the same play has seen in Macbeth's course of action after
Duncan's murder, and especially in the killing of Banquo and
the incidents of the feast in Act III, a parable of the failure—the
inevitable failure—of any one who attempts to restore the "natural
order" of society by "unnatural" means.[14] And similarly, in a recent book by a critic who holds that the "symbolic content" of
Shakespeare's plays finds "its most controlled expression in the
characters as people," the "ground-plan" of *King Lear* is reduced

to a scheme in which Edmund and Goneril and Regan represent the Flesh, Cordelia the Spirit, and Lear himself the Soul, which, because it occupies a middle place between the extremes of the Spirit and the Flesh, is capable of rejecting the Spirit but also "of being recalled and of turning again." [15] We need not assume that the characters and actions of drama and fiction are "symbolic" merely, as in allegory of the stricter type; we shall therefore find it convenient to make a distinction between the "symbolic" and the "realistic" in action and character, and to recognize that both modes of treatment may coexist in any work, the mark of the "symbolic" being that the character or action, however "realistically" handled, can be brought into significant relation, not merely with the plot, but also with the "theme" or "total meaning" we have attributed to the work as a whole; in that case it will be proper to speak of Othello, Desdemona, and Iago, for instance, not as persons simply, but, in the manner of Wilson Knight, as "the Othello, Desdemona and Iago conceptions." [16]

The general nature of our problem should be clear from these illustrations of the method in practice, as well as from those I mentioned earlier; and it really makes little difference, so far as our essential procedure is concerned, whether we seek the crucial meanings of poems in the subtleties of their verbal and imagistic expression, or in the "larger symbolisms" of their characters and plots, or in some combination of the two. For, irrespective of such distinctions, what we are committed to, if we want to write criticism of this kind at all, is the discovery of conceptual equivalents for the concrete relationships of elements discernible in poems—their contrasts of rhythmical movement, verbal tone, and imagery, their oppositions of characters, their conflicts of motives and actions. We want to be able to move—to give one more example—from a perception of the dramatic particularity of Lear's abdication as Shakespeare renders it in Act I of the play to a recognition that this decision of Lear's is something more than appears on the surface—that it really stands for "a kind of refusal of responsibility, a withdrawal from a necessary involvement in the world of action"; and having found in the scene this "meaning," we want to be able to relate it to the other particular "meanings" in this and later scenes and ultimately to the "total meaning" which constitutes the structure of the tragedy when viewed in these terms.[17] But how is this to be done? Not, certainly, by any such immediate grasp of meaning as gives us the import of any plain prose statement, or even of any ironical utterance in the usual sense, in a language we know, nor yet by the kind of quick inference from generally intelligible signs that allows us, when we witness a drama or read a novel, to gather what the characters are either doing or intending. It does not follow, because Lear abdicates, that he is refusing responsibility or disengaging himself from "a necessary involvement in the world of action"; it is indeed quite clear from the text that neither he nor anyone else in the play ever thinks of his action in any such abstract existentialist terms. Nor is there any natural or even conventionally constant connection between images of children and the idea of "the future" or between the moon and the imagination. Yet it is just such apparently arbitrary equivalences between poetic particulars (which in most poems have always been read as such) and general concepts that we have to assert if we are to pursue successfully this critical line.

Our problem bears this much resemblance to the problem of the scholarly interpretation of allegories like *Everyman* or *The Faerie Queene*, that the meanings we propose to attribute to poems must in some sense be better known to us than the poems themselves. It differs, however, in one all-important respect, namely, that whereas the most convincing interpretations of allegories have always started from a definite body of doctrinal propositions that con be shown to have been in the poet's mind when he wrote,[18] we, who have taken all serious imaginative literature as our province and are concerned besides with universal and poetic rather than with particular and historical meanings, have no such resource. Our problem is not to explain the allegories in allegorical poems, but to assert something akin to allegory of all "poetic" works that seem to us to have "relevance to life." We must attempt, therefore, to find a substitute for the historically known doctrines which have served the interpreters of Spenser and Dante; and this we can do only by providing ourselves with a set of reduction terms, as I shall call them, suitable for use in all cases—with a collection, that is, of preferred

general distinctions such as will enable us, when we come to
read particular works, to formulate and unify the complex oppositions and resolutions of "themes" in which, as embodied concretely
in the patterns of works, images, characters, or actions, we must
suppose that their "total meanings" consist.

These, along with a predisposition to look for symbolic relations everywhere and a certain facility in seeing affinities and
contrasts among the verbal and imaginative components of texts,
will form our essential equipment. And the distinctions we shall
need are not particularly hard to come by. The most useful distinctions, indeed, will be the most commonplace, in the double
sense of not being peculiar to any given science or system of
thought and of being applicable to the largest variety of contexts
in both literature and life; and it is noteworthy that the contemporary writers who have given us our most highly praised
models of this kind of interpretation have invariably used as reduction terms such familiar and all-embracing dichotomies as
life and death (or positive values and negative values), good and
evil, love and hate, harmony and strife, order and disorder,
eternity and time, reality and appearance, truth and falsity, certainty and doubt, true insight and false opinion, imagination and
intellect (as either sources of knowledge or guides in action),
emotion and reason, complexity and simplicity, nature and art,
the natural and the supernatural, nature as benignant and nature
as malignant, man as spirit and man as beast, the needs of society
and individual desires, internal states and outward acts, engagement and withdrawal. Of such universal contraries, not restricted
in their applicability to any kind of work, whether lyric, narrative, or dramatic, it will be easy enough for us to acquire an
adequate supply, and once we have them, or some selection of
them, in our minds as principles of interpretation, it will seldom
be hard to discover their presence in poems as organizing principles of symbolic content. It requires no great insight to find an
inner dialectic of order and disorder or a struggle of good and
evil forces in any serious plot; or a profound dialectic of appearance and reality in any plot in which the action turns on ignorance
or deception and discovery; or an intention to inculcate poetically
"the wholeness and complexity of things, in contrast with a partial

and simple view" (to quote a recent formula for *Romeo and Juliet*)[19] in any plot in which the characters become progressively aware that their enemies are not as bad or their friends as good as they had thought. And what is true of plots and characters is true also of language and imagery: perhaps the most striking thing about the essays on Shakespeare of Mr. Wilson Knight is the facility with which he has been able to subsume the wonderfully varied images of the plays under his favorite simple oppositions of "death themes" and "life themes," conflict and order, war and love, "tempests" and "music."

It would not, of course, be fair to say that our task of interpretation consists merely in imposing our preferred reduction terms arbitrarily on poems. The structure of meaning we are concerned to exhibit is one that we must suppose to be objectively in the poem by virtue of the poet's act of expression. It will be there, however, only indirectly, as what is symbolized by the totality of particular relationship and "tensions" observable in all the parts of the poem and on all the levels—from metaphors to plot or central image—on which meaning can be found; and in the best poems it will be identical with the one "theme" or "pattern of resolved stresses" which appears to harmonize most completely the many other "themes" or oppositions of values of which the poem consists. All of these, moreover, will be ambiguous, in the sense that they are embodied in symbols which permit, both in themselves and in correlation with other symbols, of a wide range of variant interpretations—at any rate when they are viewed as we have chosen to view them. Our problem, therefore, will be dual: to make sense, in the fashion already described, of all the particulars of the poem—to say, for instance, what, out of various possibilities, Cordelia stands for, or which of several possible meanings we ought to ascribe to the contrast of the sun and moon in *The Rime of the Ancient Mariner*—and, above all, to fix upon the one equally ambiguous opposition, among the many evident in the imagery or events of the work, which we are to regard as the "carrier" of the central meaning. The problem in both of its aspects is clearly insoluble unless we bring to it minds already prepared to look for one order of central meaning in the works we examine rather than any of

many other possible orders; and that this is precisely what the
critics whose procedure we are following have in fact done is
shown by the numerous incompatible semantic structures they
have attributed, for example, to plays like *Macbeth* or to lyrics
like the "Ode on a Grecian Urn." They are all selective interpretations, and the selection is governed in each case, though not
always crudely, by the favorite reduction terms the critic has
been able to find exemplified in the poem.

We shall have to be content, then, with a method of which the
essentially rhetorical character is perhaps evident from what I
have said. For the principles we must employ are not principles
of poetry as such, and still less of any of its kinds; they are rather
"topic" or "commonplaces" in the technical sense of the ancient,
medieval, and Renaissance writers on rhetoric—that is to say, convenient general distinctions or heads of interpretation that can
be made to fit without too much difficulty almost any poem we
have in hand, as the orator can use the *topoi* of honor and dishonor, praise and blame, to supply himself with predicates which
he will then attempt to make his hearers think are appropriate
to a given man. Or if they are not merely that, they will be at
best the contraries of a dialectic which is of our own making and
to which we are bent on assimilating the poetically expressed
thought or "vision" of the writers we are trying to interpret.

In either case we shall be engaged in imputing to our writers
a structure of meanings that is very different from the apparent
or (as we will prefer to say) superficial structures of any of
their poems; a structure, besides, that has hitherto escaped the
notice of readers and critics—or there would be no point in our
discovering it now. We cannot expect, therefore, that what we
say will at once command assent without a good deal of extra-
critical, and hence rhetorical, assistance on our part. Of the
various lines of persuasion open to us, I shall mention only a few
of those which have been most commonly used by critics of this
school. It can be urged that the interpretation we are proposing
for (say) *Macbeth*, though likely to seem radically disturbing
to traditional notions, does in fact succeed, as Roy Walker says
of his peculiarly ingenious interpretation of that play, in "illuminating the play in its entirety," that is, in subsuming all the details

under the construction we have put upon them.[20] And this will have considerable force so long as our readers fail to observe that the kind of construction placed on the details has already been determined, as in Mr. Walker's book, by the hypothesis which the details are said to support, or so long as they do not compare our account, as a scholar might do, point by point with alternative accounts by other critics that make similar claims to internal coherence and adequacy, and especially so long as they, or we, avoid bringing into the discussion the subversive principle of Occam's razor. Or we may concede that other formulae than our own have perhaps equal validity in their own terms, and then defend the validity of our own formula, as Mr. J. I. M. Stewart defends his version of Prince Hal's break with Falstaff, by insisting that on the deeper level poems may have multiple meanings, so that any plausible interpretation is correct.[21] Or, again, we may appeal to history: either in defense of a particular interpretation, as when Mr. Duthie supports his contention that the theme of Order and Disorder is a central organizing principle in most of Shakespeare by pointing to the very frequent occurrence of this antithesis in Elizabethan nondramatic writing;[22] or else in defense of the method of interpretation itself, as when Mr. Danby, presenting us with a highly allegorized *King Lear*, proceeds to urge the plausibility of this by reminding us that Shakespeare was a contemporary of Spenser and "stands closer than we do" to the morality plays and to the mental habits and the artistic attitudes of the Middle Ages, when "allegory-hunting was as exciting as motive-hunting is for us." [23] There is of course an unfortunate *non sequitur* in both of these historical arguments; and once we perceive this, we may well prefer to fall back, as many critics of this school have done, on still another topic of persuasion, and one excellently calculated to put both logic and history out of court. We can simply appeal to the doctrine—which has been explicitly stated, among others, by Wilson Knight and Harold Goddard [24]—that in poetic interpretation the ultimate authority is not historical fact or ordinary inference but the imagination or intuition of the critic himself, when he submits himself "with utmost passivity to the poet's work" undisturbed by analytical reason or historical method.[25] It is a truly powerful device, for of critical statements thus guaranteed the only possible refutation is one that convicts the objector in advance either of lacking the necessary spiritual equipment for reading poetry or of being misled by irrelevant intellectualism. And lastly, if this is not sufficient, there is always available to us the admirable topic which the older rhetoricians called "amplification." We can attempt to write so glowingly about the symbolic structures we find in poems that any literal-minded or skeptical reader will be made at least temporarily ashamed of his doubts (this is one of the great resources of Wilson Knight); or, short of this, we can advance our more difficult or novel points in sentences beginning with such phrases as "It is clear that" or "It is obvious that," etc., or, having stated a particularly daring interpretation, we can insist on its obviousness in the manner exemplified in Mr. Goddard's extremely original pages on the allegory in *Cymbeline*: "Does not the parabolic quality of all this," he asks, "fairly shout aloud and demand that we think of Imogen as the True England wedded secretly to the poor but genuinely gentle Posthumus Leonatus, English Manhood and Valor? . . . The moment we take the leading characters of the play in this way, numberless details rush forth to fit into what we can scarcely help calling the allegorical design." [26]

These, then, are the possibilities open to us, and the limits within which we must work, if we take the first of the two approaches to poetry as semantic structure: an approach in which we will tend to view poetry in all its varieties as a kind of dramatized dialectic, a form of discourse that uses "poetic" devices of imagery, metaphor, symbol, parable, and allegory as means of stating or resolving problems, exploring or bringing unity into large and complicated areas of experience, adjusting competing values, or reducing the chaos of life to a unified imaginative vision—and all this on the initial assumption that the significant patterns of meaning to be sought in poems, general as these will be in our statement of them, are patterns which poets themselves have constructed and which therefore have no existence or value apart from the "poetry" in which they inhere.

We must also distinguish between critical hypotheses in the

strict sense and interpretative hypotheses concerning the details
of literary works in their material aspects. It is not one of our
presuppositions that "form" in poetry is "meaning"; we should
hold, rather, that meaning is something involved in poems as a
necessary, but not sufficient, condition of the existence in them of
poetic form, and hence that the recovery of meaning is an essential prerequisite to the discovery of form though not in itself
such a discovery. Before we can understand a poem as an artistic
structure we must understand it as a grammatical structure made
up of successive words, sentences, paragraphs, and speeches
which give us both meanings in the ordinary sense of that term
and signs from which we may infer what the speakers, whether
characters or narrators, are like and what they are thinking, feeling, or doing. The great temptation for critics who are not trained
and practicing scholars is to take this understanding for granted
or to think that it may easily be obtained at second hand by
consulting the works of scholars. This is an illusion, just as it is
an illusion in scholars to suppose that they can see, without train-
ing in criticism, all the problems which their distinctive methods
are fitted to solve. The ideal would be that all critics should be
scholars and all scholars critics; but, although there ought to be
the closest correlation of the two functions in practice, they are
nevertheless distinct in nature and in the kinds of hypotheses to
which they lead. The hypotheses of interpretation are concerned
with the meanings and implications in texts that result from their
writers' expressive intentions in setting down particular words
and constructions and arranging these in particular sequences.
Such meanings and implications, indeed, are forms, of which
words and sentences are the matter; but they are forms of a kind
that can appear in any sort of discourse, however unpoetic. They
are to be interpreted by resolving the forms into the elements
which poems share with the common speech or writing and the
common thought and experience of the times when they were
written; and this requires the use of techniques and principles
quite different from any that poetic theory can afford: the techniques and principles of historical grammar, of the analysis and
history of ideals, of the history of literary conventions, manners,
and so on, and the still more general techniques and principles,

seldom methodized, by which we construe characters and actions in everyday life.

The hypotheses of criticism, on the contrary, are concerned with the shaping principles, peculiar to the poetic arts, which account in any work for the power of its grammatical materials, in the particular ordering given to these, to move our opinions and feelings in such-and-such a way. They will be of two sorts according as the questions to which they are answers relate to the principles by which poetic works have been constructed as wholes of certain definite kinds or to the reasons which connect a particular part of a given work, directly or indirectly, with such a principle by way of the poetic problems it set for the writer at this point. And there can be no good practical criticism in this mode in which both sorts are not present; for although the primary business of the critic is with the particulars of any work he studies down to its minuter details of diction and rhythm, he can never exhibit the artistic problems involved in these or find other than extrapoetic reasons for their solutions without the guidance of an explicit definition of the formal whole which they have made possible.

A single work will suffice to illustrate both kinds of critical hypotheses as well as the relation between them, and I will begin by considering what idea of the governing form of *Macbeth* appears to accord best with the facts of that play and the sequence of emotions it arouses in us. I need not say again why it seems to me futile to look for an adequate structural formula for *Macbeth* in any of the more "imaginative" directions commonly taken by recent criticism; I shall assume, therefore, without argument, that we have to do, not with a lyric "statement of evil" or an allegory of the workings of sin in the soul and the state or a metaphysical myth of destruction followed by recreation or a morality play with individualized characters rather than types, but simply with an imitative tragic drama based on historical materials. To call it an imitative tragic drama, however, does not carry us very far; it merely limits roughly the range of possible forms we have to consider. Among these are the contrasting plot-forms embodied respectively in *Othello* and in *Richard III*: the first a tragic plot-form in the classic sense of

Aristotle's analysis in *Poetics* 13; the second a plot-form which Aristotle rejected as nontragic but which appealed strongly to tragic poets in the Renaissance—a form of serious action designed to arouse moral indignation for the deliberately unjust and seemingly prospering acts of the protagonist and moral satisfaction at his subsequent ruin. The plot-form of *Macbeth* clearly involves elements which assimilate it now to the one and now to the other of both these kinds. The action of the play is twofold, and one of its aspects is the punitive action of Malcolm, Macduff, and their friends which in the end brings about the protagonist's downfall and death. The characters here are all good men, whom Macbeth has unforgivably wronged, and their cause is the unqualifiedly just cause of freeing Scotland from a bloody tyrant and restoring the rightful line of kings. All this is made clear in the representation not only directly through the speeches and acts of the avengers but indirectly by those wonderfully vivid devices of imagery and general thought in which modern critics have found the central value and meaning of the play as a whole; and our responses, when this part of the action is before us, are such as are clearly dictated by the immediate events and the poetic commentary: we desire, that is, the complete success of the counteraction and this as speedily as possible before Macbeth can commit further horrors. We desire this, however—and that is what at once takes the plot-form out of the merely retributive class—not only for the sake of humanity and Scotland but also for the sake of Macbeth himself. For what most sharply distinguishes our view of Macbeth from that of his victims and enemies is that, whereas they see him from the outside only, we see him also, throughout the other action of the play—the major action—from the inside, as he sees himself; and what we see thus is a moral spectacle the emotional quality of which, for the impartial observer, is not too far removed from the tragic *dynamis* specified in the *Poetics*. This is not to say that the main action of *Macbeth* is not significantly different, in several respects, from the kind of tragic action which Aristotle envisages. The change is not merely from good to bad fortune, but from a good state of character to a state in which the hero is almost, but not quite, transformed into a monster; and the tragic act which initiates the change, and still

more the subsequent unjust acts which this entails, are acts done—
unlike Othello's killing of Desdemona—in full knowledge of their
moral character. We cannot, therefore, state the form of this
action in strictly Aristotelian terms, but the form is none the less
one that involves, like tragedy in Aristotle's sense, the arousal and
catharsis of painful emotions for, and not merely with respect to,
the protagonist—emotions for which the terms pity and fear are
not entirely inapplicable.

Any adequate hypothesis about the structure of *Macbeth*, then,
would have to take both of these sets of facts into account. For
both of the views we are given of the hero are true: he is in fact,
in terms of the nature and objective consequences of his deeds,
what Macduff and Malcolm say he is throughout Acts IV and V,
but he is also—and the form of the play is really the interaction
of the two views in our opinions and emotions—what we ourselves see him to be as we witness the workings of his mind
before the murder of Duncan, then after the murder, and finally
when, at the end, all his illusions and hopes gone, he faces
Macduff. He is one who commits monstrous deeds without becoming wholly a monster, since his knowledge of the right principle is never altogether obscured, though it is almost so in Act
IV. We can understand such a person and hence feel fear and
pity of a kind for him because he is only doing upon a grander
scale and with deeper guilt and more terrifying consequences
for himself and others what we can, without too much difficulty,
imagine ourselves doing, however less extremely, in circumstances generally similar. For the essential story of *Macbeth* is
that of a man, not naturally depraved, who has fallen under the
compulsive power of an imagined better state for himself which
he can attain only by acting contrary to his normal habits and
feelings; who attains this state and then finds that he must continue to act thus, and even worse, in order to hold on to what
he has got; who persists and becomes progressively hardened
morally in the process; and who then, ultimately, when the once
alluring good is about to be taken away from him, faces the loss
in terms of what is left of his original character. It is something
like this moral universal that underlies, I think, and gives emotional form to the main action of *Macbeth*. It is a form that turns

upon the difference between what seemingly advantageous crime appears to be in advance to a basically good but incontinent man and what its moral consequences for such a man inevitably are; and the catharsis is effected not merely by the man's deserved overthrow but by his own inner suffering and by his discovery, before it is too late, of what he had not known before he began to act. If we are normal human beings we must abhor his crimes; yet we cannot completely abhor but must rather pity the man himself, and even when he seems most the monster (as Macbeth does in Act IV) we must still wish for such an outcome as will be best, under the circumstances, not merely for Scotland but for him.

But if this, or something close to it, is indeed the complex emotional structure intended in *Macbeth*, then we have a basis for defining with some precision the various problems of incident, character, thought, imagery, diction, and representation which confronted Shakespeare in writing the play, and hence a starting-point for discussing, in detail, the rationale of its parts.[27] Consider—to take only one instance—the final scene. In the light of the obvious consequences of the form I have attributed to the play as a whole, it is not difficult to state what the main problems at this point are. If the catharsis of the tragedy is to be complete, we must be made to feel both that Macbeth is being killed in a just cause and that his state of mind and the circumstances of his death are such as befit a man who, for all his crimes, has not altogether lost our pity and good will. We are of course prepared for this double response by all that has gone before, and, most immediately, in the earlier scenes of Act V, by the fresh glimpses we are given of the motivation of the avengers and by Macbeth's soliloquies. But it will clearly be better if the dual effect can be sustained until the very end; and this requires, on the one hand, that we should be vividly reminded once more of Macbeth's crimes and the justified hatred they have caused and of the prospect of a new and better time which his death holds out for Scotland, and, on the other hand, that we should be allowed to take satisfaction, at last, in the manner in which Macbeth himself behaves. The artistic triumph of the scene lies in the completeness with which both problems are solved: the first in the words and actions of Macduff, the speeches about young Siward, and Malcolm's closing address; the second by a variety of devices, both of invention and of representation, the appropriateness of which to the needed effect can be seen if we ask what we would not want Macbeth to do at this moment. We want him to be killed, as I have said, for his sake no less than that of Scotland; but we would not want him either to seek out Macduff or to flee the encounter when it comes or to "play the Roman fool"; we would not want him to show no recognition of the wrongs he has done Macduff or, when his last trust in the witches has gone, to continue to show fear or to yield or to fight with savage animosity; and he is made to do none of these things, but rather the contraries of all of them, so that he acts in the end as the Macbeth whose praises we have heard in the second scene of the play. And I would suggest that the cathartic effect of these words and acts is reinforced indirectly, in the representation, by the analogy we can hardly help drawing between his conduct now and the earlier conduct of young Siward, for of Macbeth too it can be said that "he parted well and paid his score"; the implication of this analogy is surely one of the functions, though not the only one, which the lines about Siward are intended to serve.

[1] *The New Criticism,* p. x. See also Ransom, *The World's Body,* p. 173; *The Kenyon Critics* (Cleveland and New York, 1951), pp. vii-viii.

[2] L. C. Knights, *Explorations,* p. 6.

[3] R. W. Stallman, *Critiques and Essays in Criticism,* p. 506.

[4] Robert Penn Warren, "A Poem of Pure Imagination: An Experiment in Reading," in *The Rime of the Ancient Mariner* (New York, 1946), pp. 63–64.

[5] Brooks and Warren, *Understanding Poetry,* pp. 118–21; rev. ed., pp. 41–48.

[6] Brooks, *The Well Wrought Urn,* p. 122.

[7] R. W. Stallman, "The Structure and Symbolism of Conrad's *Victory,*" *Western Review* (Spring, 1949), 149.

[8] See W. K. Wimsatt, Jr., "Verbal Style: Logical and Counterlogical," *PMLA,* LXV (1950), 5–20, and the other papers by the same writer mentioned therein. Cf. also Maynard Mack, " 'Wit and Poetry and Pope': Some Observations on His Imagery," in *Pope and His Contemporaries: Essays Presented to George Sherburn* (Oxford, 1949), pp. 20–40.

[9] Robert Penn Warren, *The Ancient Mariner,* pp. 87–93. Cf. E. E. Stoll, *PMLA,* LXIII (1948), 216–19, and Olson, in *Critics and Criticism,* pp. 138–44.

[10] Brooks, *The Well Wrought Urn,* pp. 27–46.

[11] Robert B. Heilman, *This Great Stage: Image and Structure in "King Lear"* (Baton Rouge, 1948). Cf. W. R. Keast, in *Critics and Criticism,* pp. 108–37.

[12] Cf. John Crowe Ransom, "The Understanding of Fiction," *Kenyon Review,* XII (1950), 189–218.

[13] Roy Walker, *The Time is Free,* esp. pp. xiv–xv, 64 ff.

[14] Knights, *Explorations,* p. 23.

[15] John F. Danby, *Shakespeare's Doctrine of Nature,* pp. 59, 174.

[16] G. Wilson Knight, *The Wheel of Fire* (London, 1949), pp. 3, 10, 119, 139. Cf. Tillyard, *Shakespeare's Last Plays*, pp. 27–40, 44–46, and Danby, *Shakespeare's Doctrine of Nature*, pp. 18–19.

[17] Heilman, *This Great Stage*, p. 35.

[18] An excellent recent example is Ernest Sirluck's "The *Faerie Queene*, Book II, and the *Nicomachean Ethics*," *Modern Philology*, XLIX (1951), 73–100.

[19] See Lawrence Edward Bowling, "The Thematic Framework of *Romeo and Juliet*," *PMLA*, LXIV (1949), 208.

[20] *The Time is Free*, pp. ix, 106–7.

[21] J. I. M. Stewart, *Character and Motive in Shakespeare* (London, 1949), p. 144. Cf. Hyman, *The Armed Vision*, pp. 405–7, and especially the following (p. 406): "Thus we could take, say, Eliot's symbol of the Waste Land in the poem of that name, a symbol of great depth and complexity, and read it at any level we cared to insert a vocabulary: at the most intimate level, to the Freudian, it would be castration and impotence; at a more conscious level, to a post-Freudian psychology, perhaps the fear of artistic sterility; on the daily-life level, in the biographical terms of Van Wyck Brooks, the symbol of Eliot's pre-conversion state; on a more social level, to a critic like Parrington, the empty life of the artist or the frustration of the upper class; to Eliot himself, the irreligion of the times; in broadly historical terms, to the Marxist, the decay of capitalism; in Jungian terms, the archetypal ritual of rebirth."

[22] George Ian Duthie, *Shakespeare* (London, 1951), especially pp. 39–56; see also his remarks in *Review of English Studies*, N.S., II (1951), 79–80.

[23] *Shakespeare's Doctrine of Nature*, pp. 121–23.

[24] Knight, *The Wheel of Fire*, pp. 2–9; Goddard, *The Meaning of Shakespeare*, pp. 8–13. Cf. also Walker, *The Time is Free*, pp. ix, 106–7.

[25] Knight, *The Wheel of Fire*, p. 7. See above, p. 34.

[26] *The Meaning of Shakespeare*, p. 642.

[27] See, in addition to what follows, Wayne C. Booth, *Journal of General Education*, VI (1951), 21–25. For a somewhat similar discussion of an episode in *King Lear*, cf. Maclean, in *Critics and Criticism*, pp. 595–615.

7

Macbeth *as the Imitation of an Action*

FRANCIS FERGUSSON

If Professor Crane suggests one way in which a consideration of
Macbeth *in the light of Aristotle may be fruitful, Professor Fergusson demonstrates that there are others. The present essay reflects its author's continuing interest in the work of art as an imitation (in Aristotle's sense) of an action, a motive, or, to use a Dantean phrase which Professor Fergusson characteristically employs, a "movement of spirit." The present essay reveals its author's lack of dogmatism, his awareness of the humane importance of art, his extraordinary perceptiveness, and again—as in the case of so many good critical essays—his common sense. Francis Fergusson, currently Professor of Comparative Literature at Rutgers, has studied and taught at a number of institutions, including the Institute for Advanced Study at Princeton. His* The Idea of a Theater *(1949) was almost beyond doubt the most influential critical work on the drama of a generation. The technique he here demonstrates is reflected in the earlier book in his famous essays on plays by Sophocles, Shakespeare, Racine, Wagner, and others; and it is reflected in other ways in an equally important study of the* Purgatorio *entitled* Dante's Drama of the Mind *(1953). Students of literature often find the concept of "structure" hardest to master and most likely to produce vague writing; Professor Fergusson's precise study of* Macbeth *is an instructive essay in the meaning and function of literary structure.*

I propose to attempt to illustrate the view that *Macbeth* may be understood as "the imitation of an action," in approximately Aristotle's sense of this phrase.

The word "action"—*praxis*—as Aristotle uses it in the *Poetics*, does not mean outward deeds or events, but something much more like "purpose" or "aim." Perhaps our word "motive" suggests most of its meaning. Dante (who in this respect is a sophisticated Aristotelian) uses the phrase *moto spiral*, spiritual movement, to indicate *praxis*. In Aristotle's own writings *praxis* is usually rational, a movement of the will in the light of the mind. But Dante's *moto spiral* refers to all modes of the spirit's life, all of its directions, or focuses, or motives, including those of childhood, dream, drunkenness, or passion, which are hardly rationalized at all. When using Aristotle's definition for the analysis of modern drama it is necessary to generalize his notion of action in this way, to include movements of the spirit in response to sensuous or emotionally charged images, as well as consciously willed purpose. But this seems to me a legitimate extension of the basic concept; and I do not think it does real violence to Aristotle's meaning.

Aristotle, in his *Psychology* and his *Ethics*, as well as in the *Poetics*, and Dante, in the *Divine Comedy*, seem to imagine the psyche much as an amoeba looks under the microscope: moving toward what attracts it, continually changing direction or aim, and taking its shape and color from the object to which it is attached at the moment. This movement is "action"; and so we see that while the psyche is alive it always has action; and that this changing action in pursuit of real or imagined objects defines its mode of being moment by moment.

When Aristotle says that a tragedy is the imitation of an action, he is thinking of an action, or motive, which governs the psyche's life for a considerable length of time. Such an action is the quest for Laius's slayer in *Oedipus Rex*, which persists through the changing circumstances of the play. In this period of time, it has a beginning, a middle, and an end, which comes when the slayer is at last identified.

I remarked that action is not outward deeds or events; but on the other hand, there can be no action without resulting deeds.

We guess at a man's action by way of what he does, his outward and visible deeds. We are aware that our own action, or motive, produces deeds of some sort as soon as it exists. Now the plot of a play is the arrangement of outward deeds or incidents, and the dramatist uses it, as Aristotle tells us, as the first means of imitating the action. He arranges a set of incidents which point to the action or motive from which they spring. You may say that the action is the spiritual content of the tragedy—the playwright's inspiration—and the plot defines its existence as an intelligible *play*. Thus, you cannot have a play without both plot and action; yet the distinction between plot and action is as fundamental as that between form and matter. The action is the matter; the plot is the "first form," or, as Aristotle puts it, the "soul," of the tragedy.

The dramatist imitates the action he has in mind, first by means of the plot, then in the characters, and finally in the media of language, music, and spectacle. In a well-written play, if we understood it thoroughly, we should perceive that plot, character, and diction, and the rest spring from the same source, or, in other words, realize the same action or motive in the forms appropriate to their various media.

You will notice that this is a diagrammatic description of the perfect play, perfectly understood. Therefore one cannot hope to illustrate it perfectly, even in the case of a play like *Macbeth*. *Macbeth*, however, does impress most of its readers as having a powerful and unmistakable unity of this kind: the plot, characters, and imagery all seem to spring from the one inspiration. It is that strong and immediately felt unity which I rely on—and upon your familiarity with the play. Not that I am so foolish as to suppose I grasp the play completely or that I could persuade you of my view of it in these few minutes. All I can attempt is to suggest the single action which seems to me to be the spiritual content of the play, and illustrate it, in only a few of its metaphors, plot devices, and characterizations.

The action of the play as a whole is best expressed in a phrase which Macbeth himself uses in Act II, scene 3, the aftermath of the murder. Macbeth is trying to appear innocent, but everything he says betrays his clear sense of his own evil motivation, or action. Trying to excuse his murder of Duncan's grooms, he says,

The expedition of my violent love [for Duncan, he means]
Outran the pauser, reason.

It is the phrase "to outrun the pauser, reason," which seems to me to describe the action, or motive, of the play as a whole. Macbeth, of course, literally means that his love for Duncan was so strong and swift that it got ahead of his reason, which would have counseled a pause. But in the same way we have seen his greed and ambition outrun his reason when he committed the murder; and in the same way all of the characters, in the irrational darkness of Scotland's evil hour, are compelled in their action to strive beyond what they can see by reason alone. Even Malcolm and Macduff, as we shall see, are compelled to go beyond reason in the action which destroys Macbeth and ends the play.

But let me consider the phrase itself for a moment. To "outrun" reason suggests an impossible stunt, like lifting oneself by one's own bootstraps. It also suggests a competition or race, like those of nightmare, which cannot be won. As for the word "reason," Shakespeare associates it with nature and nature's order, in the individual soul, in society, and in the cosmos. To outrun reason is thus to violate nature itself, to lose the bearings of common sense and of custom, and to move into a spiritual realm bounded by the irrational darkness of Hell one way, and the superrational grace of faith the other way. As the play develops before us, all the modes of this absurd, or evil, or supernatural, action are attempted, the last being Malcolm's and Macduff's acts of faith.

In the first part of the play Shakespeare, as is his custom, gives us the intimate feel of this paradoxical striving beyond reason in a series of echoing tropes and images. I remind you of some of them, as follows.

From the first Witches' scene:

When the battle's lost and won. . . .
Fair is foul and foul is fair.

From the "bleeding-sergeant" scene:

> *Doubtful it stood;*
> *As two spent swimmers that do cling together*
> *And choke their art. . . .*
> *So from that spring whence comfort seem'd to come*
> *Discomfort swells. . . .*
> *Confronted him with self-comparisons*
> *Point against point rebellious, arm 'gainst arm. . . .*
> *What he hath lost noble Macbeth hath won.*

From the second Witches' scene:

> *So fair and foul a day. . . .*
> *Lesser than Macbeth, and greater.*
> *His wonders and his praises do contend*
> *Which should be thine or his. . . .*
> *This supernatural soliciting*
> *Cannot be ill, cannot be good. . . .*
>   *. . . nothing is*
> *But what is not.*

These are only a few of the figures which suggest the desperate and paradoxical struggle. They are, of course, not identical with each other or with outrunning reason, which seems to me the most general of all. But they all point to the "action" I mean, and I present them as examples of the imitation of action by means of the arts of language.

But notice that though these images themselves suggest the action, they also confirm the actions of the characters as these are shown in the story. The bleeding sergeant, for instance, is striving beyond reason and nature in his effort to report the battle —itself a bewildering mixture of victory and defeat—in spite of his wounds. Even the old King Duncan, mild though he is, is caught in the race and sees his relation to Macbeth competitively. "Thou art so far before," he tells Macbeth in the next scene, "That swiftest wing of recompense is slow/To overtake thee." He then races Macbeth to his castle, whither the Messenger has outrun them both; and when he arrives, he is at once involved in a hollow competition with Lady Macbeth, to outdo her in ceremony.

I do not need to remind you of the great scenes preceding the murder, in which Macbeth and his Lady pull themselves together for their desperate effort. If you think over these scenes, you will notice that the Macbeths understand the action which begins here as a competition and a stunt, against reason and nature. Lady Macbeth fears her husband's human nature, as well as her own female nature, and therefore she fears the light of reason and the common daylight world. As for Macbeth, he knows from the first that he is engaged in an irrational stunt: "I have no spur/To prick the sides of my intent, but only/Vaulting ambition, which o'erleaps itself/And falls on the other." In this sequence there is also the theme of outwitting or transcending time, an aspect of nature's order as we know it: catching up the consequences, jumping the life to come, and the like. But this must suffice to remind you of the Macbeths' actions, which they paradoxically understand so well.

The Porter scene has been less thoroughly studied as a variation on the play's main action. But it is, in fact, a farcical and terrible version of "outrunning reason," a witty and very concentrated epitome of this absurd movement of spirit. The Porter first teases the knockers at the gate with a set of paradoxes, all of which present attempts to outrun reason; and he sees them all as ways into Hell. Henry N. Paul [1] has explained the contemporary references: the farmer who hanged himself on the expectation of plenty, the equivocator who swore both ways to commit treason for God's sake. When the Porter has admitted the knockers he ironically offers them lewd physical analogies for outrunning reason: drink as tempting lechery into a hopeless action; himself as wrestling with drink. The relation of the Porter to the knockers is like that of the Witches to Macbeth—he tempts them into Hell with ambiguities. And the inebriation of drink and lust, lewd and laughable as it is, is closely analogous to the more terrible and spiritual intoxication of the Macbeths.

Thus, in the first part of the play both the imagery and the actions of the various characters indicate or "imitate" the main action. Aristotle says the characters are imitated "with a view to the action"—and the Porter, who has little importance in the story—is presented to reveal the action of the play as a whole in the unexpected light of farcical analogies, contemporary or lewd and physical.

Before I leave this part of the play I wish to point out that the plot itself—"the arrangement or synthesis of the incidents"— also imitates a desperate race. This is partly a matter of the speed with which the main facts are presented, partly the effect of simultaneous movements like those of a race: Lady Macbeth is reading the letter at the same moment that her husband and Duncan are rushing toward her. And the facts in this part of the play are ambiguous in meaning and even as facts.

These few illustrations must serve to indicate how I understand the imitation of action in language, character, and plot in the first two acts of the play. Macbeth and his Lady are embarked on a race against reason itself; and all Scotland, the "many" whose lives depend upon the monarch, is precipitated into the same darkness and desperate strife. Shakespeare's monarchs do usually color the spiritual life of their realms. And we, who remember Hitlerite Germany, can understand that, I think. Even Hitler's exiles, like the refugees from Russian or Spanish tyranny, brought the shadow to this country with them.

I now wish to consider the action of the play at a later stage, in Act IV, scene 3. This is the moment which I mentioned before, the beginning of Malcolm's and Macduff's act of faith, which will constitute the final variation on "outrunning reason." The scene is laid in England, whither Malcolm and Macduff have fled, and it immediately follows the murder of Macduff's wife and child. Like the exiles we have known in this country, Macduff and Malcolm, though in England, have brought Scotland's darkness with them. They have lost all faith in reason, human nature, and common sense, and can therefore trust neither themselves nor each other. They are met in the hope of forming an alliance, in order to get rid of Macbeth; and yet under his shadow everything they do seems unreasonable, paradoxical, improbable.

In the first part of the scene, you remember, Malcolm and Macduff fail to find any basis for mutual trust. Malcolm mistrusts Macduff because he has left his wife and child behind; Macduff quickly learns to mistrust Malcolm, because he first protests that he is unworthy of the crown, to test Macduff, and then suddenly

reverses himself. The whole exchange is a tissue of falsity and
paradox, and it ends in a sort of nightmarish paralysis.

At this point there is the brief interlude with the Doctor. The
king's evil and its cure and the graces which hang about the
English throne are briefly described. Paul points out that this
interlude may have been introduced to flatter James I; but however that may be, it is appropriate in the build of the scene as a
whole. It marks the turning point, and it introduces the notion
of the appeal by faith to Divine Grace which will reverse the
evil course of the action when Malcolm and Macduff learn to
outrun reason in that way, instead of by responding to the
Witches' supernatural solicitations as Macbeth has done. Moreover, the Doctor in this scene, in whom religious and medical
healing are associated, foreshadows the Doctor who will note
Lady Macbeth's sleepwalking and describe it as a perturbation
in nature which requires a cure beyond nature.

But to return to the scene. After the Doctor's interlude, Ross
joins Malcolm and Macduff, bringing the latest news from Scotland. To greet him, Malcolm clearly states the action, or motive,
of the scene as a whole: "Good God, betimes remove/The means
that makes us strangers!" he says. Ross's chief news is, of course,
Lady Macduff's murder. When he has gradually revealed that,
and Macduff and Malcolm have taken it in, accepting some of the
guilt, they find that the means that made them strangers has in
fact been removed. They recognize themselves and each other
once more, in a sober, but not nightmarish, light. And at once they
join in faith in their cause and prepare to hazard all upon the
ordeal of battle, itself an appeal beyond reason. The scene, which
in its opening sections moved very slowly, reflecting the de-
moralization of Malcolm and Macduff, ends hopefully, with brisk
rhythms of speech which prepare the marching scenes to follow.

This tune goes manly. . . .

Receive what cheer you may:
The night is long that never finds the day.

The whole scene is often omitted or drastically cut in production, and many critics have objected to it. They complain of its

slowness, of the baroque overelaboration of Malcolm protests, and the fact that it is too long for what it tells us about the story. All we learn is that Malcolm and Macduff are joining the English army to attack Macbeth, and this information could have been conveyed much more quickly. In the first part of the play, and again after this scene, everything moves with the speed of a race; and one is tempted to say, at first, that in this scene Shakespeare lost the rhythm of his own play.

Now, one of the reasons I chose this scene to discuss is that it shows, as does the Porter scene, the necessity of distinguishing between plot and action. One cannot understand the function of the scene in the whole plot unless one remembers that the plot itself is there to imitate the action. It is then clear that this scene is the peripeteia, which is brought about by a series of recognitions. It starts with Malcolm and Macduff blind and impotent in Macbeth's shadow and ends when they have gradually learned to recognize themselves and each other even in that situation. "Outrunning reason" looks purely evil in the beginning, and at the end we see how it may be good, an act of faith beyond reason. The scene moves slowly at first because Shakespeare is imitating the action of groping in an atmosphere of the false and unnatural; yet we are aware all the while of continuing speed offstage, where

each new morn
New widows howl, new orphans cry, new sorrows
Strike heaven on the face....

The scene is thus (within the rhythmic scheme of the whole play) like a slow eddy on the edge of a swift current. After this turning, or peripeteia, the actions of Malcolm and Macduff join the rush of the main race, to win. I admit that these effects might be hard to achieve in production, but I believe that good actors could do it.

Shakespeare's tragedies usually have a peripeteia in the fourth act, with scenes of suffering and prophetic or symbolic recognitions and epiphanies. In the fourth act of *Macbeth* the Witches' scene reveals the coming end of the action in symbolic shows;

and this scene also, in another way, foretells the end. The last act, then, merely presents the literal facts, the windup of the plot, long felt as inevitable in principle. The fifth act of *Macbeth* shows the expected triumph of Malcolm's and Macduff's superrational faith. The wood does move; Macbeth does meet a man unborn of woman; and the paradoxical race against reason reaches its paradoxical end. The nightmare of Macbeth's evil version of the action is dissolved, and we are free to return to the familiar world, where reason, nature, and common sense still have their validity.

To sum up: my thesis is that *Macbeth* is the imitation of an action (or motive) which may be indicated by the phrase "to outrun the pauser, reason." I have tried to suggest how this action is presented in the metaphors, characters, and plot of the first two acts; and also in the peripeteia, with pathos and recognitions, the great scene between Malcolm, Macduff, and Ross.

I am painfully aware that these few illustrations are not enough to establish my thesis. Only a detailed analysis of the whole play might do that—and such an analysis would take hours of reading and discussion. But I think it would show that Aristotle was essentially right. He had never read *Macbeth*, and I suppose if he could he would find Shakespeare's Christian, or post-Christian, vision of evil hard to understand. But he saw that the art of drama is the art of imitating action; and this insight, confirmed and deepened by some of Aristotle's heirs, can still show us how to seek the unity of a play, even one which shows modes of the spirit's life undreamed of by Aristotle himself.

[1] See *The Royal Play of Macbeth*, Macmillan, 1950.

8

Ripeness Is All

J. V. CUNNINGHAM

"Ripeness Is All" is the introduction to J. V. Cunningham's Woe
or Wonder: The Emotional Effect of Shakespearean Tragedy,
*first published in 1951, and exemplifies his critical approach. Like
R. S. Crane, Professor Cunningham is distrustful of much contemporary literary criticism and acknowledges a debt to Aristotle.
The corrective he offers, however, is not a theory of critical
pluralism but a plea for and demonstration of literary scholarship. He argues that to understand a literary work we must understand it historically, and historical understanding involves both
the precise definition of words as the author and his audience
understood them and a knowledge of the literary, philosophical,
theological, and critical traditions which made the work possible
and made it comprehensible to its intended audience. The argument of the essay is characteristic of its author's concern that we
shed irrelevant and misleading modern preconceptions and his
faith that in so doing we rather enrich than impoverish our
literary experience. Like a number of other essays in* Approaches
to Shakespeare, *"Ripeness Is All" is essentially an attack on excessive subjectiveness; it is also the doorway to a large and rewarding area of inquiry. J. V. Cunningham is Professor of English
at Brandeis University.*

I am concerned in these essays with understanding precisely
what Shakespeare meant. It is true that "when we read Shakespeare's plays," as one scholar says, "we are always meeting our

own experiences and are constantly surprised by some phrase which expresses what we thought to be our own secret or our own discovery." [1] But the danger is that the meaning we find may really be our own secret, our own discovery, rather than Shakespeare's, and the more precious and beguiling for being our own. The danger I have in mind can be illustrated by our attitude toward one of the most famous of Shakespearean phrases, "Ripeness is all." It is a favorite quotation of Mr. Eliot's. "It seems to me," he says in discussing the question of truth and belief in poetry, "to have profound emotional meaning, with, at least, no literal fallacy." [2] He does not specify what this meaning is, but I take it that it is something not strictly denotative though emotionally compelling.

The phrase, indeed, has seemed to many to represent a profound intuition into reality and to sum up the essence of Shakespearean, or even of human, tragedy. It speaks quite nearly to us. What it means to each will perhaps depend on his own experience and his own way of relating the texture of experience to the insights of literature. Yet all would agree that "Ripeness is all" gathers into a phrase something of the ultimate value of this life; it reassures us that maturity of experience is a final good, and that there is a fullness of feeling, an inner and emotional completion in life that is attainable and that will resolve our tragedies. Such at least seems to be the interpretation of a recent critic. "After repeated disaster," he says of Gloucester in *King Lear*:

> he can assent, "And that's true too," to Edgar's "Ripeness is all."
> For man may ripen into fulness of being, which means, among other things, that one part of him does not rule all the rest and that one moment's mood does not close off all the perspectives available to him.[3]

In this way we discover in Shakespeare's phrase the secret morality of our own times. It is a meaning I can enter into quite as deeply as anyone, but it is not what Shakespeare meant.

Shakespeare meant something much more traditional. The phrase occurs in *King Lear*. In an earlier scene Edgar had prevented Gloucester from committing suicide, that act which consummates the sin of despair, and Gloucester had accepted the situation in the true spirit of Christian resignation:

> *henceforth I'll bear*
> *Affliction till it do cry out itself*
> *"Enough, enough," and die.*
> *(4.6.75–7)*

But now Gloucester seems to relapse for a moment, saying:

> *No further, sir; a man may rot even here.*

And Edgar stiffens his resolution with these words:

> *Men must endure*
> *Their going hence even as their coming hither:*
> *Ripeness is all.*
> *(5.2.9–11)*

The context is the desire for death. The conclusion is that as we were passive to the hour of our birth so we must be passive to the hour of our death. So far, surely, the speech is an affirmation of the spirit of resignation, and it would be reasonable to suppose that the summary clause at the end, "Ripeness is all," is but the final restatement of this attitude. It was certainly an available attitude. The experience of Christian resignation was dense with the history of the Western spirit, and that history was alive and present in Shakespeare's time; it spoke daily from the pulpit and in the private consolations of intimate friends. The theme, furthermore, was a favorite with Shakespeare. It had been fully explored in the Duke's great speech in *Measure for Measure*:

> *Be absolute for death. Either death or life*
> *Will thereby be the sweeter. Reason thus with life:*
> *If I do lose thee I do lose a thing*
> *That none but fools would keep. A breath thou art,*
> *Servile to all the skyey influences*

> *That do this habitation where thou keep'st*
> *Hourly afflict. Merely thou art death's fool;*
> *For him thou labour'st by the flight to shun,*
> *And yet runn'st toward him still. . . .*
>   *Yet in this life*
> *Lie hid moe thousand deaths; yet death we fear*
> *That makes these odds all even.*
>   *(3.1.5–13, 39–41)*

But the finest expression, other than in the passage from *Lear*, is
Hamlet's speech to Horatio as he goes to the catastrophe:

> *. . . we defy augury; there's a special providence in the fall of a*
> *sparrow. If it be now, 'tis not to come; if it be not to come, it will*
> *be now; if it be not now, yet it will come: the readiness is all.*
>   *(5.2.230–33)*

This is as much as to say that we must endure our going hence,
be it when it may, since the hour of our death is in the care of
Providence: *the readiness is all.*

It has been said that this is Stoic, and certainly *augury* hints
toward Antiquity. But he who speaks of a special providence
in the fall of a sparrow could trust an audience in the age of
Elizabeth to think of Christian theology and the New Testament:

> And fear not them which kill the body, but are not able to kill
> the soul: but rather fear him which is able to destroy both body
> and soul in hell. Are not two sparrows sold for a farthing? *And*
> *one of them shall not fall on the ground without your Father.*
> But the very hairs of your head are all numbered. Fear ye not
> therefore, ye are of more value than many sparrows.
> Watch therefore: for ye know not what hour your Lord doth
> come. But know this, that if the goodman of the house had known
> in what watch the thief would come, he would have watched,
> and would not have suffered his house to be broken up. *There-*
> *fore be ye also ready:* for in such hour as ye think not the Son of
> man cometh.

It was not only Seneca and his sons who could urge men to meet
death with equanimity. Bishop Latimer, the Protestant martyr,

in a sermon preached before King Edward VI speaks the thought
and almost the words of Hamlet:

> *Unusquisque enim certum tempus habet praedefinitum a Domino:*
> "For every man hath a certain time appointed him of God, and
> God hideth that same time from us." For some die in young age,
> some in old age, according as it pleaseth him. He hath not mani-
> fested to us the time because he would have us at all times ready;
> else if I knew the time, I would presume upon it, and so should
> be worse. But he would have us ready at all times, and there-
> fore he hideth the time of our death from us. . . . But of that we
> may be sure, there shall not fall one hair from our head without
> his will; and we shall not die before the time that God hath ap-
> pointed unto us: which is a comfortable thing, specially in time
> of sickness or wars. . . . There be some which say, when their
> friends are slain in battle, "Oh, if he had tarried at home, he
> should not have lost his life." These sayings are naught: for God
> hath appointed every man his time. To go to war in presump-
> tuousness, without an ordinary calling, such going to war I allow
> not: but when thou art called, go in the name of the Lord; and
> be well assured in thy heart that thou canst not shorten thy life
> with well-doing.[4]

The similarity of the phrase in *Hamlet* to the one in *Lear* is
so close that the first may be taken as the model and prototype
of the other. But in *Lear* the phrase has been transmuted, and
with it the idea and attitude. The deliberate and developed
rhetoric of *Measure for Measure* has served its purpose to explore the area of experience, and has been put aside. The riddling
logicality of Hamlet's speech has been simplified to the bare
utterance of:

> *Men must endure*
> *Their going hence even as their coming hither*

and the concept of the arbitrariness of birth has been introduced
to reinforce the arbitrariness of death. Finally, Hamlet's precise
and traditional statement, "the readiness is all," has been transformed into a metaphor.

What does the metaphor mean? There is no need for conjecture; it had already by the time of *Lear* become trite with use and with use in contexts closely related to this. In Thomas Wilson's *Art of Rhetoric* (1560) we read:

> Among fruit we see some apples are soon ripe and fall from the tree in the midst of summer; other be still green and tarry till winter, and hereupon are commonly called winter fruit: even so it is with man, some die young, some die old, and some die in their middle age.[5]

Shakespeare has Richard in *Richard II* comment on the death of John of Gaunt:

> *The ripest fruit first falls, and so doth he:*
> *His time is spent . . .*
>   *(2.1.153–54)*

That is, as fruit falls in the order of ripeness, so a man dies when his time is spent, at his due moment in the cosmic process. Again, Touchstone's dry summary of life and time in *As You Like It*:

> *And so, from hour to hour, we ripe and ripe,*
> *And then, from hour to hour, we rot and rot . . .*
>   *(2.7.26–27)*

does not mean that we ripen to maturity and then decline, but that we ripen toward death, and then quite simply and with no metaphors rot.

But death is not incidental to Shakespearean tragedy; it is rather the defining characteristic. Just as a Shakespearean comedy is a play that has a clown or two and ends in marriages, so a tragedy involves characters of high estate and concludes with violent deaths. The principle of its being is death, and when this is achieved the play is ended. In this sense, then, "Ripeness is all" is the structural principle of Shakespearean tragedy. Thus in *Richard III* the Cassandra-like chorus, the old Queen Margaret, enters alone as the play draws rapidly on to the final catastrophe and says:

> *So now prosperity begins to mellow*
> *And drop into the rotten mouth of death*
>   *(4.4.1–2)*

And in *Macbeth*, Malcolm says toward the close:

> *Macbeth*
> *Is ripe for shaking, and the pow'rs above*
> *Put on their instruments.*
>   *(4.3.237–39)*

In this passage the powers above, who are the agents of Providence, are associated with the ripened time. Providence is destiny, and in tragedy destiny is death.

By "Ripeness is all," then, Shakespeare means that the fruit will fall in its time, and man dies when God is ready. The phrase gathers into the simplest of sentences, the most final of linguistic patterns, a whole history of attempted formulations, and by the rhetorical device of a traditional metaphor transposes a state into a process. Furthermore, the metaphor shifts our point of view from a man's attitude toward death, from the "readiness" of Hamlet and the "Men must endure" of the first part of Edgar's speech, to the absoluteness of the external process of Providence on which the attitude depends.

But this is not what the phrase means to the uninstructed modern reader, and this poses a problem. The modern meaning is one that is dear to us and one that is rich and important in itself. It would be natural to ask, Need we give it up? I see no reason why we should give up the meaning: maturity of experience is certainly a good, and the phrase in a modern context is well enough fitted to convey this meaning. But it is our phrase now, and not Shakespeare's, and we should accept the responsibility for it. The difference in meaning is unmistakable: ours looks toward life and his toward death; ours finds its locus in modern psychology and his in Christian theology. If we are secure in our own feelings we will accept our own meanings as ours, and if we have any respect for the great we will penetrate and embrace Shakespeare's meaning as his. For our purpose in the study of literature, and particularly in the historical interpretation of texts, is not in the ordinary sense to further the understanding of ourselves. It is rather to enable us to see how we could think and feel otherwise than as we do. It is to erect a larger context of experience within which we may define and understand our own by attending to the disparity between it and the experience of others.

In fact, the problem that is here raised with respect to literature is really the problem of any human relationship: Shall we understand another on his terms or on ours? It is the problem of affection and truth, of appreciation and scholarship. Shakespeare has always been an object of affection and an object of study. Now, it is common experience that affection begins in misunderstanding. We see our own meanings in what we love and we misconstrue for our own purposes. But life will not leave us there, and not only because of external pressures. What concerns us is naturally an object of study. We sit across the room and trace the lineaments of experience on the face of concern, and we find it is not what we thought it was. We come to see that what Shakespeare is saying is not what we thought he was saying, and we come finally to appreciate it for what it is. Where before we had constructed the fact from our feeling, we now construct our feeling from the fact. The end of affection and concern is accuracy and truth, with an alteration but no diminution of feeling.

[1] G. B. Harrison, *Shakespeare: 23 Plays and the Sonnets* (New York, 1948), p. 3. Similarly O. J. Campbell, *The Living Shakespeare* (New York, 1949), p. 1: "In his plays we constantly meet our own experiences; in his poetry we constantly find our inmost thoughts and feelings expressed with an eloquence and a precision far beyond our reach."

[2] T. S. Eliot, *Selected Essays* (New York, 1932), p. 231.

[3] Robert Bechtold Heilman, *This Great Stage* (Baton Rouge, 1948), p. 112. The correct interpretation is given in passing by Alfred Harbage, *As They Liked It* (New York, 1947), p. 56.

[4] Hugh Latimore, *Sermons* ("Everyman's Library": London, 1906), pp. 352–53.

[5] G. H. Mair, ed. (Oxford, 1909), p. 83.
    John Bruce, ed., *Diary of John Manningham* ("Camden Society," XCIX: Westminster, 1868), under March 24, 1603: "This morning about three at clock her Majesty departed this life, mildly like a lamb, like a ripe apple from the tree."

9

The Cosmic Background

E. M. W. TILLYARD

This essay, the opening chapter of Professor Tillyard's Shakespeare's History Plays *(1944), is an extraordinarily compact summary of the complex and intricately interrelated notions of order shared in varying degrees by Shakespeare's audience. The author is interested, as are all who would like to know what can be known about Shakespeare's intellectual life, in discovering as precisely as possible the specific documents which can be demonstrated to have influenced the playwright. But here, as in* The Elizabethan World Picture *(1943), his major concern is in illuminating the assumptions so common in Shakespeare's time that the search for particular sources is virtually supererogatory. The view here presented is necessarily simplified and perhaps more optimistic than what the man in the Elizabethan street might have acknowledged if he could have articulated all his feelings, and Professor Tillyard's recreation of Shakespeare's intellectual environment must be taken with a bit of caution. It would be well to remember that certain intellectual tendencies threatened the age's sense of established order. As Theodore Spencer argues in* Shakespeare and the Nature of Man, *the pessimism always possible to a Christian culture that believes in the fact of the Fall was intensified by new doubts as assumptions about cosmological, natural, and political order were questioned by Copernicus, Montaigne, and Machiavelli; and doubt coexists with faith in Shakespeare. Nevertheless, "The Cosmic Background" exemplifies handsomely the value of intellectual history in understanding*

*Shakespeare. Master of Jesus College, Cambridge, E. M. W. Till-
yard, who died in 1962, occupied a central place in the histori-
ography and criticism of Renaissance English literature.*

1. INTRODUCTORY

Shakespeare's Histories have been associated with Holinshed's
chronicle and with the Chronicle Plays: and rightly. Holinshed is shorter than the more thoughtful Hall and he includes
more matter. Hall dealt with a single stretch of English history
from Richard II to Henry VIII; Holinshed goes back to the
very beginnings of British legend and includes the history of
Scotland. Shakespeare found Holinshed useful as an omnibus
volume.

Shakespeare's Histories belong to the class of English Chronicle Plays, and that class, like Holinshed, was practical and not
very thoughtful. It was rarely performed at the Inns of Court
and was enjoyed by the populace. It exploited the conscious
patriotism of the decade after the Armada and instructed an
inquisitive public in some of the facts and legends of English
history. In formal ingenuousness, it resembled the Miracle Plays.

It is easy, and up to a point true, to think of Shakespeare as
transforming by his genius the material of Holinshed and the
dramatic type of the Chronicle into something uniquely his
own. But to leave one's thought at that is a large error; for
what Shakespeare transformed was so much more than Holinshed and the Chronicle Play. If Shakespeare went to Holinshed
for many of his facts, he had meditated on the political philosophy of Hall and of his own day; and if he imparted much
historical information in the manner of the other Chronicle
Plays, he was not ignorant of the formal pattern of *Gorboduc.*
Shakespeare's Histories are more like his own Comedies and
Tragedies than like others' Histories, and they not so much try
out and discard a provincial mode as present one of his versions
of the whole contemporary pattern of culture. It was not his
completest version, but behind it, as behind the Tragedies, was
that pattern.

In this chapter I shall describe some parts of that pattern which have most to do with the Histories.

Now this pattern is complicated and was the possession only of the more learned part of society. It can be to the point only if Shakespeare too was learned. There is still a prejudice against thinking of him as such. That prejudice must be overcome if the substance of my first two chapters is to be relevant. To overcome it one can point out that a man can be learned in more ways than one and that at least one of those ways fitted Shakespeare; and then one can produce concrete examples of his learning.

For different ways of being learned, consider how Shakespeare might have dealt with the academic doctrine of the Three Dramatic Unities, which he respected in *The Tempest*. He might have studied it in Aristotle and in Aristotle's Italian commentators; he might have read of it in Sidney; he might have heard it discussed. If the first way is improbable, it is equally improbable that he could have avoided acquaintance with it in the other two ways. We may fairly conjecture that he was in fact learned; not in an academic way but in the way Johnson conjectured for Dryden:

> I rather believe that the knowledge of Dryden was gleaned from accidental intelligence and various conversation, by a quick apprehension, a judicious selection, and a happy memory, a keen appetite of knowledge, and a powerful digestion; by vigilance that permitted nothing to pass without notice, and a habit of reflection that suffered nothing useful to be lost. . . . I do not suppose that he despised books, or intentionally neglected them; but that he was carried out, by the impetuosity of his genius, to more vivid and speedy instructors; and that his studies were rather desultory and fortuitous than constant and systematical.

For proofs, take for example Lorenzo on music in the fifth act of the *Merchant of Venice*:

> Look how the floor of heaven
> Is thick inlaid with patines of bright gold:
> There's not the smallest orb which thou behold'st
> But in his motion like an angel sings,
> Still quiring to the young-eyed cherubins;

Such harmony is in immortal souls;
But whilst this muddy vesture of decay
Doth grossly close it in, we cannot hear it.

This has been called "an unlearned man's impression of Plato's sublime dream"; this dream being that "upon each of the heavenly spheres is a siren, who is borne round with the sphere uttering a single note; and the eight notes compose a single harmony." Shakespeare, it is alleged, gets Plato wrong in attributing song to the whole host of heaven instead of to the single spheres into which they were fitted. But more recently a specialist in Greek philosophy asserted that Shakespeare was in fact quite surprisingly knowledgeable and accurate. It is true that he garbled the above passage from the *Republic* by substituting cherubim for sirens and vastly enlarging the range of the heavenly music, but Lorenzo's general doctrine shows an accurate knowledge of a part of Plato's *Timaeus*. In that dialogue it is said that the planetary motions of the heavens have their counterpart in the immortal soul of man and that our souls would sound in accord with the grander music of the cosmos were it not for the earthy and perishable nature of the body. Shkespeare reproduces the gist of this doctrine.

Twice in the tragedies Shakespeare mentions the seeds or "germens" of nature: when Macbeth says to the Witches

        though the treasure
Of nature's germens tumble all together,

and when Lear, addressing the storm, bids it

Crack nature's moulds, all germens spill at once
That make ungrateful man.

It seems that behind these brief references is the whole doctrine of the λόγοι σπερματικοι or *rationes seminales:* the doctrine that God introduced into nature certain seminal principles that abide there waiting to be put into action. It is most apt to the passage in *Macbeth* because there was the further doctrine, found in Augustine and Aquinas, that angelic and demonic powers have the

gift, under God's permission, of speeding up these natural processes and producing apparently miraculous results.

If anything, we are apt to underestimate what such passing
references mean in a dramatist who (unlike Jonson) is not in the
least anxious to parade his learning. No one can doubt that Shakespeare knew the outlines of orthodox Christian theology. Yet how
few are the precise references to it in the plays. But what there
are become significant in inverse proportion to their brevity. Here
is one passage: Angelo and Isabella arguing about Claudio's condemnation in *Measure for Measure*—

> Ang. *Your brother is a forfeit of the law,*
>   *And you but waste your words.*
> Isab.   *Alas, alas!*
>   *Why all the souls that were were forfeit once;*
>   *And He that might the vantage best have took*
>   *Found out the remedy.*

The reference is of the slightest, yet it reveals and takes for
granted the total Pauline theology of Christ abrogating man's
enslavement to the old law incurred through the defection of
Adam. Now we can be certain that living in the age he did and
having the intelligence he had Shakespeare must have known
the outlines of orthodox Christian theology. To this theology
there are few references in the plays. Do not these two facts make
it *probable* that behind other correspondingly scanty references
there is a corresponding abundance of knowledge? When Brutus
talks of the state of man, like a little kingdom, suffering the nature of an insurrection, he implies not merely the bare commonplace analogy between the human body and the body politic but
the whole mass of traditional correspondences between the heavenly order, the macrocosm, the body politic, and the human body
or microcosm.

The argument gains in strength, if we compare the cases of
Shakespeare and of Montaigne. Montaigne, an expansive and discursive essayist, is free to give as much of his background and
derivation as he wishes. And he makes full use of this freedom
by constant quotation. His most famous essay takes off from and

partly denies the *Natural Theology* of Raymond de Sebonde. Before having his say about the state of man and his relation to the beasts, he tells how his father asked him to translate de Sebonde's book from the Latin and how gladly he complied. Had Montaigne been exclusively a dramatist, he might have given little or no sign of having read the Sebonde. His meditations on de Sebonde's material would certainly have got into his plays in some form or other. He would in fact have given us something not unlike Hamlet's pronouncements on the nature of man or Lear's and Timon's broken references to the relation of man and beast. Take in turn one of Hamlet's pronouncements:

> What a piece of work is a man: how noble in reason; how infinite in faculty; in form and moving how express and admirable; in action how like an angel; in apprehension how like a god; the beauty of the world, the paragon of animals.

This is Shakespeare's version of the very precise, traditional, orthodox encomia of what man was in his prelapsarian state and of what ideally he is still capable of being. Raymond de Sebonde himself, a mainly derivative writer, has such an encomium in the ninety-fifth to the ninety-ninth chapters of his *Natural Theology*. How Shakespeare got hold of this material matters little; he could have got it from plenty of places, the pulpit included. It is the stuff's somehow being there, behind Hamlet's sentences, that matters. The equivalent of Montaigne's discursiveness is implied.

Shakespeare, then, had much the same general equipment of learning as his more highly-educated contemporaries, Sidney and Spenser for instance, though it may have been less systematic, less detailed, and less derived from books. How does this equipment bear on the Histories?

2. THE CONTEXT OF HISTORY

The picture we get from Shakespeare's Histories is that of disorder. Unsuccessful war abroad and civil war at home are the large theme; victory abroad and harmony at home are the ex-

ceptions, and the fear of disorder is never absent. Henry V on the
eve of Agincourt prays that the ancestral curse may be suspended,
and the Bastard qualifies his patriotic epilogue in *King John* with
an *if*: if England to itself do rest but true. And by *resting true* he
meant not, displaying the English characteristic but avoiding internal treachery and contention. But to allow disorder to stand
as the unqualified description of Shakespeare's Histories would be
no truer than to call the *Fairy Queen* a study of mutability.
Throughout his poem Spenser shows the alertest sense of the in-
stability of earthly things. But as a non-dramatic, philosophical
poet Spenser has both the space and the obligation to make his
total doctrine clear. So, in the two cantos that survive from a
seventh book he turns Mutability into a goddess and makes Nature judge her claims to absolute domination. This is Nature's
pronouncement on the evidence:

> *I well consider all that ye have said*
> *And find that all things stedfastness do hate*
> *And changed be; yet, being rightly weigh'd,*
> *They are not changed from their first estate*
> *But by their change their being do dilate,*
> *And, turning to themselves at length again,*
> *Do work their own perfection so by fate.*
> *Then over them Change doth not rule and reign,*
> *But they reign over Change and do their states maintain.*

Even on earth then there is an order behind change, an order
which makes Spenser think of a heavenly order and

> *Of that same time when no more change shall be,*
> *But stedfast rest of all things, firmly stay'd*
> *Upon the pillars of Eternity,*
> *That is contrare of Mutability.*

The case is the same with Shakespeare. Behind disorder is some
sort of order or "degree" on earth, and that order has its counterpart in heaven. This assertion has nothing to do with the question
of Shakespeare's personal piety: it merely means that Shakespeare
used the thought-idiom of his age. The only way he could have
avoided that idiom in his picture of disorder was by not thinking

at all, like the authors of *Stukeley* or *Edward I*; for to go against the contemporary thought-idiom is to make it rather more than usually emphatic. Witness Marlowe's Tamburlaine, who, because he so very emphatically does *not* crash from Fortune's wheel, proclaims his affinity with all the traditional victims who lament their falls in the *Mirror for Magistrates*.

If a Spenserian analogy suggests that there is a general (and predominantly religious) doctrine behind the mass of particular events transacted in Shakespeare's Histories, the chronicles themselves point just the same way. Many of these kept to the religious setting which was common in medieval days. For instance, Grafton's *Chronicle at Large* (1569), though purporting to be British only, begins with the creation of the world and of paradise in the full medieval fashion. Now the medieval chronicler in writing of the creation habitually inserted the commonplaces of orthodox theology: the nature of the Trinity and of the Angels, the fall of Satan, the question of free will, and so on. Higden, for instance, writing in the first half of the fourteenth century, spends a large portion of the second book of *Polychronicon* on theology, before finally settling to chronicle the events of the world. History in fact grows quite naturally out of theology and is never separated from it. The connection was still flourishing after Shakespeare's death. A work that illustrates it to perfection is Raleigh's *History of the World*. The frontispiece shows History, a female figure, treading down Death and Oblivion, flanked by Truth and Experience, supporting the globe;; and over all is the eye of Providence.[1] And the first book deals with the creation and is as full of Augustinian theology as any medieval book of world history. Further, Raleigh's preface contains not only a disquisition on history but an account of English history from Edward II to Henry VII. This account is no mere summary but a view of this stretch of history in a definite pattern; and the pattern resembles Shakespeare's. Now, if these purely historical patterns are similar, it is most probable that behind both of them are similar philosophical or theological axioms, and that Raleigh's theological preface and first book instruct us in the commonplaces upon which not only his own but Shakespeare's historical writings were founded.

A sketch of English history very like Raleigh's occurs in a much less likely place, the *Microcosmos* of John Davies of Hereford. His chief poems, *Mirum in Modum, Summa Totalis,* and *Microcosmos* (written in the Spenserian stanza with a decasyllabic substituted for the final Alexandrine) are to the age of Shakespeare as the work of Soame Jenyns is to the mid-eighteenth century; they epitomise the commonplaces of the time's serious thought, all the better for being the product of a second-rate mind. Davies himself is especially to my purpose because he is Shakespeare's slightly younger contemporary, because his social status was almost identical with Shakespeare's, and because on the certain evidence of an epigram and the possible evidence of two marginal notes he knew Shakespeare personally. He came of middle-class parents, was educated at the local grammar school but did not attend the university, became a writing-master much patronised by the nobility, and ended by being writing-master to Prince Henry. He addressed short poems to most of the important and intelligent Englishmen of or near the court circle, and his serious poems epitomise just that knowledge the possession of which was taken for granted in that class of person. He writes of God and creation, the universe and the influence of the stars, the soul and body of man, man's mind and its passions. And from his repetitive and indifferently arranged stanzas as completely as from any single source I know of can be extracted the contemporary notion of order or degree which was never absent from Shakespeare's picture of disorder in the Histories. That Davies inserts his very Shakespearean version of English history into *Microcosmos* strongly confirms that belief.

3. THE ELIZABETHAN WORLD ORDER

Most readers of Shakespeare know that his own version of order or degree is in Ulysses's speech on the topic in *Troilus and Cressida*; not all would grant that it states the necessary setting of the Histories; and few realise how large a body of thought it epitomises or hints at. (May I here ask the reader to have before him a text of this speech?)

Its doctrine is primarily political but evidently goes far beyond mere practical politics. First, we learn that the order which prevails in the heavens is duplicated on earth, the king corresponding to the sun; then that disorder in the heavens breeds disorder on earth, both in the physical sublunary organisation and in the commonwealth of men. When Shakespeare calls degree the ladder to all high designs he probably has another correspondence in mind: that between the ascending grades of man in his social state and the ladder of creation or chain of being which stretched from the meanest piece of inanimate matter in unbroken ascent to the highest of the archangels. The musical metaphor in "Take but degree away, untune that string, and hark what discord follows" is far more than a metaphor; it implies the traditional Platonic doctrine that (in Dryden's words)

From harmony, from heavenly harmony
This universal frame began,

and that at the world's last hour

Music shall untune the sky.

Finally, when an Elizabethan audience heard the words "chaos, where degree is suffocate," the educated element at least would understand chaos in a more precise sense than we should naturally do. They would understand it as a parallel in the state to the primitive warring of the elements from which the universe was created and into which it would fall if the constant pressure of God's ordering and sustaining will were relaxed.

The above references are fragmentary but they show that Shakespeare had in mind a complete body of doctrine. Having made this the subject of another book, I need give no more than a short summary in this place.

The Elizabethan conception of world-order was in its outlines medieval although it had discarded much medieval detail. The universe was a unity, in which everything had its place, and it was the perfect work of God. Any imperfection was the work not of God but of man; for which the fall of man the universe underwent a sympathetic corruption. But for all the corruption the marks of God's perfection were still there, and one of the two great roads to salvation was through the study of created things. But though the idea of unity was basic, the actual order of the world presented itself to the Elizabethans under three different, though often related, appearances: a chain, a series of corresponding planes, and a dance to music.

As a chain, creation was a series of beings stretching from the lowest of inanimate objects up to the archangel nearest to the throne of God. The ascent was gradual, no step was missing; and on the borders of the great divisions between animate and inanimate, vegetative and sensitive, sensitive and rational, rational and angelic, there were the necessary transitions. One of the noblest accounts of the chain of being is by Sir John Fortescue, the fifteenth-century jurist:

> In this order hot things are in harmony with cold; dry with moist; heavy with light; great with little; high with low. In this order angel is set over angel, rank upon rank in the Kingdom of Heaven; man is set over man, beast over beast, bird over bird, and fish over fish, on the earth, in the air, and in the sea; so that there is no worm that crawls upon the ground, no bird that flies on high, no fish that swims in the depths, which the chain of this order binds not in most harmonious concord. God created as many different kinds of things as he did creatures, so that there is no creature which does not differ in some respect from all other creatures, and by which it is in some respect superior or inferior to all the rest. So that from the highest angel down to the lowest of his kind there is absolutely not found an angel that has not a superior and inferior; nor from man down to the meanest worm is there any creature which is not in some respect superior to one creature and inferior to another. So that there is nothing which the bond of order does not embrace. And since God has thus regulated all creatures, it is impious to think that he left unregulated the human race, which he made the highest of all earthly creatures.

The last sentence illustrates to perfection that same striving for unity and for correspondences that was so strong among the Elizabethans. Expediency was the last reason for justifying the laws of England: Fortescue justifies them because they are a necessary piece in the great jig-saw puzzle of the universe. For Shakespeare too the justification of that political order with which he is mainly concerned is the same.

For the way one large class is linked with another in the chain of being take a passage near the beginning of the second book of Higden's *Polychronicon*. Higden's evidence is of exactly the right kind. He can be trusted to give the perfect commonplace and he was extremely popular not only in his own day but well into the Tudor period. The opening of his second book is for a brief summary of "degree" as good as anything I know:

> In the universal order of things the top of an inferior class touches the bottom of a superior: as for instance oysters, which, occupying as it were the lowest position in the class of animals, scarcely rise above the life of plants, because they cling to the earth without motion and possess the sense of touch alone. The upper surface of the earth is in contact with the lowest surface of water; the highest part of the waters touches the lowest part of the air, and so by a ladder of ascent to the outermost sphere of the universe. So also the noblest entity in the category of bodies, the human body, when its humours are evenly balanced, touches the fringe of the next class above it, namely the human soul, which occupies the lowest rank in the spiritual order. For this reason the human soul is called the horizon or meeting-ground of corporeal and incorporeal; for in it begins the ascent from the lowest to the highest spiritual power. At times even, when it has been cleansed of earthly passions, it attains to the state of incorporeal beings.

It was this key-position in the chain of being, not the central position of the earth in the Ptolemaic astronomy, that made man so interesting among the objects of creation. Subject to lunar vicissitudes unknown in higher spheres and by its central position the repository of the dregs of things, the earth was not happily situated. But from before Plato till beyond Pope man's amazing position in creation—a kind of Clapham Junction where all the tracks converge and cross—exercised the human imagination and fostered the true humanist tradition; and at no period of English history so powerfully as in the age of Elizabeth. Here is a typical account of man's position between angel and beast, his high capacities and his proneness to fall, from Sir John Hayward, Shakespeare's contemporary:

> Thou art a man, endued with reason and understanding, wherein God hath engraven his lively image. In other creatures there is some likeness of him, some footsteps of his divine nature; but in man he hath stamped his image. Some things are like God in that they are; some in that they live; some in their excellent property and working. But this is not the image of God. His image is only in that we understand. Seeing then that thou art of so noble a nature and that thou bearest in thine understanding the image of God, so govern thyself as is fit for a creature of understanding. Be not like the brute beasts, which want understanding: either wild and unruly or else heavy and dull. . . . Certainly of all the creatures under heaven, which have received being from God, none degenerate, none forsake their natural dignity and being, but only man. Only man, abandoning the dignity of his proper nature, is changed like Proteus into divers forms. And this is occasioned by reason of the liberty of his will. And as every kind of beast is principally inclined to one sensuality more than to any other, so man transformeth himself into that beast to whose sensuality he principally declines.

But if man is allied to the beasts in sensuality and to God and the angels in understanding, he is most himself in being social. This passage, translated from the Italian about 1598, would have been accepted without question by every educated Elizabethan:

> Man, as he is in form from other creatures different, so is his end from theirs very diverse. The end of other creatures is no other thing but living, to generate those like themselves. Man, born in the kingdom of nature and fortune, is not only to live and generate but to live well and happily. Nature of herself provideth for other creatures things sufficient unto life: nature procureth man to live, but reason and fortune cause him to live well. Creatures live after the laws of nature man liveth by reason prudence and art. Living creatures may live a solitary life: man alone, being of himself insufficient and by nature an evil creature without domestical and civil conversation, cannot lead other than a miserable

and discontented life. And therefore, as the philosopher saith very well, that man which cannot live in civil company either he is a god or a beast, seeing only God is sufficient of himself, and a solitary life best agreeth with a beast.

It is with such a doctrine in mind that Shakespeare's Ulysses speaks of

> *communities,*
> *Degrees in schools and brotherhoods in cities,*
> *Peaceful commerce from dividable shores,*

standing by degree in authentic place. Such things are the organisations and activities proper to man in his place in the scale of being.

Although the Middle Ages found the doctrine of the chain of being useful they did not elaborate it. For the full exercise of medieval and Elizabethan ingenuity we must turn to the sets of correspondences worked out between the various planes of creation. These planes were God and the angels, the macrocosm or physical universe, the body politic or the state, and the microcosm or man. To a much smaller degree the animals and plants were included. The amount of intellectual and emotional satisfaction that these correspondences afforded is difficult both to picture and to overestimate. What to us is merely silly or trivial might for an Elizabethan be a solemn or joyful piece of evidence that he lived in an ordered universe, where there was no waste and where every detail was a part of nature's plan.

Shakespeare touches on one of the fundamental correspondences in Ulysses's speech on degree when he speaks of

> *the glorious planet Sol*
> *In noble eminence enthron'd and spher'd*
> *Amidst the other, whose medicinable eye*
> *Corrects the ill aspects of planets evil,*
> *And posts like the commandment of a king.*

But *le roi soleil* is only a part of a larger sequence of leadership, which included: God among the angels or all the works of crea-

tion, the sun among the stars, fire among the elements, the king in
the state, the head in the body, justice among the virtues, the lion
among the beasts, the eagle among the birds, the dolphin among
the fishes. It would be hard to find a single passage containing the
whole sequence (and there may be items I have not included),
but at the beginning of the *Complete Gentleman* Peacham gives
a very full list, itself intended to illustrate the universal principle
of order and hierarchy. To most of those already mentioned he
adds the oak, the rose, the pomeroy and queen-apple, gold and the
diamond.

For the general notion of correspondences I know of none better than a passage from an abridgement of de Sebonde's *Natural
Theology,* a passage quite valid for the Elizabethan age. It expresses admirably the cosmic order into which the human order
was always set. De Sebonde's theme here is the number and the
ordering of the angels.

> We must believe that the angels are there in marvellous and in-
> conceivable numbers, because the honour of a king consists in the
> great crowd of his vassals, while his disgrace or shame consists in
> their paucity. Therefore I say that thousands of thousands wait
> on the divine majesty and tenfold hundreds of millions join in his
> worship. Further, if in material nature there are numberless kinds
> of stones herbs trees fishes birds four-footed beasts and above
> these an infinitude of men, it must be said likewise that there are
> many kinds of angels. But remember that one must not conceive
> of their multitude as confused; on the contrary, among these
> spirits a lovely order is exquisitely maintained, an order more
> pleasing than can be expressed. That this is so we can see from
> the marvellous arrangement among material things, I mean that
> some of these are higher, others lower, and others in the middle.
> For instance the elements and all inanimate things are reckoned
> in the lowest grade, vegetative things in the second, sensitive in
> the third, and man in the fourth as sovereign. Within the human
> range are seen different states from the great to the least: such
> as labourers merchants burgesses knights barons counts dukes
> kings, and a single emperor as monarch. Similarly in the church
> there are curates deacons archdeacons deans priors abbots
> bishops archbishops patriarchs, and one Pope, who is their head.
> If then there is maintained such an order among low and earthly

things, the force of reason makes it necessary that among these most noble spirits there should be a marshalling unique, artistic, and beyond measure blessed. Further, beyond doubt, they are divided into three hierarchies or sacred principalities, in each of which there are the high middle and low. But this well-ordered multitude leads up to a single head: in precisely the same way as we see among the elements fire the first in dignity; among the fishes the dolphin; among the birds the eagle; among the beasts the lion; and among men the emperor.

Of all the correspondences between two planets that between the cosmic and the human was the commonest. Not only did man constitute in himself one of the planes of creation, but he was the microcosm, the sum in little of the great world itself. He was composed materially of the four elements and contained within himself, as well as his rational soul, vegetative and sensitive souls after the manners of plants and animals. The constitution of his body duplicated the constitution of the earth. His vital heat corresponded to the subterranean fire; his veins to rivers; his sighs to winds; the outbursts of his passions to storms and earthquakes. There is a whole complex body of doctrine behind the account of how Lear

> Strives in his little world of man to outscorn
> The to and fro conflicting wind and rain.

Storms were also frequent in another correspondence, that between macrocosm and body politic. Storms and perturbations in the heavens were duplicated by commotions and disasters in the state. The portents that marked the death of Caesar were more than portents; they were the heavenly enactment of the commotions that shook the Roman Empire after that event. Irregularities of the heavenly bodies duplicate the loss of order in the state. In the words of Ulysses,

> but when the planets
> In evil mixture to disorder wander,
> What plagues and what portents, what mutiny,
> What raging of the sea, shaking of earth,

Commotion in the winds, frights changes horrors,
Divert and crack, rend and deracinate
The unity and married calm of states
Quite from their fixture.

Last may be cited the correspondence between microcosm and body politic. It can take the form of Brutus in his agony of doubt comparing his own little world to a city in insurrection. But its most persistent form was an elaborate analogy between the various ranks in the state with different parts of the human body.

The picture of the universe as harmony or a dance to music is met with less often than the other two, but Shakespeare knew it as he shows by Ulysses's words once again:

Take but degree away, untune that string;
And hark what discord follows.

It was a notion that appealed especially to the more Platonic or mystically minded. It was dear to Milton, and in Elizabethan days it was the theme of Sir John Davies's *Orchestra*. This poem is a kind of academic disputation between Penelope and Antinous, most courtly of the Ithacan suitors, on the dance. Penelope will not dance, but Antinous seeks to persuade her that the universe and all it contains is one great dance-pattern and that she is going against the cosmic order by refraining. Finally he gives her a magic glass in which she sees Queen Elizabeth, the mortal moon, presiding over the dance-measures of her courtiers. Repeated at last in the polity, the dance-pattern, which has ranged through the whole order of nature, is complete. *Orchestra* is one of the most lovely and most typical of Elizabethan poems. It is also very apt to the present argument. Not only does it contain nearly every one of the commonplaces I have touched on, but it presents the cosmic as the background of the actual. The Elizabethan political order, the Golden Age brought in by the Tudors, is nothing apart from the cosmic order of which it is a part. If this is Davies's faith, is it not contrariwise the more likely that when Shakespeare deals with the concrete facts of English history he never forgets the principle of order behind all the terrible manifestations of dis-

order, a principle sometimes fulfilled, however imperfectly, even
in the kingdoms of this world?

4. SHAKESPEARE'S ACCESS TO THE DOCTRINE

If the total doctrine of order is indeed there behind Ulysses's
speech, what were the means by which Shakespeare came to learn
of it? Little can be said for certain, for we are now dealing with
a mass of material which was part of the collective consciousness
of the age, material so taken for granted that it appears more in
brief reference than in set exposition. The doctrine of the chain of
being was ignored by readers of Elizabethan literature till Love-
joy wrote his book on it; now, our eyes being open, we find it all
over the place. If Shakespeare knew it, there can be little question
of a single source. He could have got it from a hundred sources.
The fountain-heads of general cosmic doctrines were the *Book of
Genesis* and Plato; but the material derived thence is handled and
rehandled with infinite repetitions and small modifications till it
becomes a kind of impersonal ballad-lore, and the question of
sources is ridiculous. A book has been published in America on
the hexemeral literature, in other words, on the literature that
has accumulated round the account in *Genesis* of the six days of
creation. As there appears to be no copy of it in this country, I
have not read it; but it is said to imply that most of the alleged
sources of Milton, for instance in the Kabbala or Augustine, are
in fact doubtful because all the stuff is already there in the early
commentaries on *Genesis* and must have formed a body of oral
tradition that would have survived in sermon and talk independent of any written record. The theory is extremely plausible; and
to seek the exact sources of the Shakespearean doctrine of degree
is futile in just the same way. But there is one detail of derivation
which admits of greater certainty. Of all the passages I have read
dealing with "degree" one of the closest to Ulysses's speech is in
the original book of Homilies published in 1547 when Edward VI
was king. It is worth quoting, not only for its likeness to Shakespeare, but for its beauty, and for the greater amplitude with
which it states ideas that are only hinted at by the poet. Contrary

to my custom in this book I give the original spelling and punctuation; for the 1547 book of Homilies is a fine piece of printing and was produced with a care that earns the right of accurate transcription. The passage is the opening of the *Sermon of Obedience*, or *An Exhortation concerning good Ordre and Obedience to Rulers and Magistrates.*

Almightie God hath created and appoyncted all thynges, in heaven, yearth, and waters, in a moste excellent and perfect ordre. In heaven he hath appoynted distincte Orders and states of Archangelles and Angelles. In the yearth he hath assigned Kynges, princes, with other gouernors under them, all in good and necessarie ordre. The water aboue is kepte and raineth doune in dewe time and season. The Sonne, Moone, Sterres, Rainbowe, Thundre, Lightenyng, cloudes, and all birdes of the aire, do kepe their ordre. The Yearth, Trees, Seedes, Plantes, Herbes, and Corne, Grasse and all maner of beastes kepe theim in their ordre. All the partes of the whole yere, as Winter, Somer, Monethes, Nights and Daies, continue in their ordre. All kyndes of Fishes in the sea, Rivers and Waters, with all Fountaines, Sprynges, yea, the Seas themselves kepe their comely course and ordre. And Man himself also, hath all his partes, bothe within and without, as Soule, Harte, Mynd, Memory, Understandyng, Reason, speache, with all and syngular corporall membres of his body, in a profitable necessarie and pleasaunt ordre. Euery degree of people, in their vocacion, callyng, and office, hath appoyncted to them their duetie and ordre. Some are in high degree, some in lowe, some Kynges and Princes, some inferiors and subjectes, Priestes and Laymen, Masters and Servauntes, Fathers and Children, Husbandes and Lifes, Riche and Poore, and euery one haue nede of other, so that in all thynges is to bee lauded and praised the goodly ordre of God, without the whiche, no house, no citee, no common wealthe, can continue and endure. For where there is no right ordre, there reigneth all abuse, carnall libertie, enormitie, synne, and Babilonical confusion. Take awaie Kynges, Princes, Rulers, Magistrates, Judges, and suche states of God's ordre, no man shall ride or go by the high way unrobbed, no man shal slepe in his awne house or bed unkilled, no man shall kepe his wife, children, and possessions in quietnesse, all thynges shall be common, and there muste nedes folowe all mischief and utter destruccion, bothe of soules, bodies, goodes and common wealthes.

This passage and Ulysses's speech are close enough together to make it likely that at least an unconscious act of memory took place. It is also possible that it was first through this homily that Shakespeare had the idea of degree impressed on his mind. Alfred Hart has pointed out that Shakespeare was six years old when the great rebellion broke out in the north of England. His father as alderman would have shared responsibility for the local militia; Shakespeare himself would have seen the troops marching through Stratford to the north. The homily in question deals with civil obedience and was directed against civil war. At the time of the rebellion it must have had special point and been read with a special emphasis that Shakespeare, granted that he shared the precociousness of other Elizabethan children, was not likely to have missed. Four years later another and longer homily on the same topic, but with specific reference to the late rebellion, was added to the original collection. When Shakespeare was ten, he would have heard a part of a homily on order and civil obedience nine Sundays or holy-days in the year. Hart has added to the meagre stock of reasonable probabilities in the life of Shakespeare. Early experience of rebellion and of the detestation in which it was held may help to account both for his seriousness in speaking of order and for the attraction he felt towards the theme of civil war.

[1] To an Elizabethan a picture of the eye of Providence would first suggest, not, as to a Victorian, the eye remorselessly recording the minutest sin of the individual but the instrument of the power that sustained the world's vitality and prevented its slipping back into chaos.

❧ *10* ❧

Shakespeare:
A Marxist Interpretation

A. A. SMIRNOV

Marxist criticism represents another kind of response to the fact that Shakespeare's work is a historical phenomenon. Like Cunningham and Tillyard, Professor Smirnov insists that Shakespeare can be fully understood only in the context of the culture to which he preeminently gives voice. The Marxist differs from other historians, however, in his emphasis on social and economic process, and finds in Shakespeare a reflection of the changing values of a revolutionary period in European history. The brief discussion of Macbeth *at the end of this essay will give the reader some sense of the way in which a sensitive and knowledgeable critic committed to the Marxist view of history and of the nature and role of literature responds to a play we have already seen discussed by critics of different persuasions. Alexander Smirnov, Professor at Leningrad, has been the leading Soviet Shakespearean scholar since the mid-thirties. He has edited the text of the plays a number of times (and has now in progress an eight-volume, authoritative edition on which Alexander Anikst is collaborating), and has written a number of biographical and critical works on Shakespeare. The book from which the excerpts that follow are taken was published in Russia as* Shakespeare's Art *in 1934.*

We do not expect to find any specifically bourgeois content in Shakespeare which is normally absent from the works of the great humanists of the epoch. Marlowe and several other dramatists of his group exemplify this theory. This is also true of the humanist poets of other countries. The ordinary middle-class thematic material is completely alien to Petrarch, and if we do find some aspects of it in Boccaccio, in *The Decameron* and partly in the *Corbaccio*, we must not forget that this is but a small part of his inheritance. An equally significant aspect of his literary output, unjustly neglected in the popular evaluations because of his *Decameron,* is presented by a number of poetic romances on legendary themes of chivalry. These are *realistic in treatment and progressive in ideology.* This is also true of the splendid pastorals, *Ameto* and the *Ninfale Fiesolano,* so truly revolutionary in content, and *Fiammetta,* which laid the foundation of the new realistic and psychological novel. Bourgeois themes are not to be found in any of the books, nor in the work of the great painters of the time. Raphael, Michelangelo, Leonardo da Vinci carried out revolutionary ideas through aristocratic, mythological, and even religious, subject-matter. Middle-class themes would not have adequately expressed their ideas and would have restricted the depth and extent of their efforts.

Shakespeare, too, followed this trend. It was even more natural that he should have done so, because the circumstances attending the historical development of England—the fusion between the nobility and the middle classes—created conditions extremely favorable to such an art. In discussing the evolution of law, Engels says:

> The form in which this happens can, however, vary considerably. It is possible, as happened in England, in harmony with the whole national development, to retain in the main the forms of the old feudal laws while giving them a bourgeois content; in fact, directly giving a bourgeois meaning to the old feudal name.[1]

Is this not equally applicable to the literary scene? It is impossible, purely on the basis of the aristocratic nature of his characterizations and subject-matter, to draw the conclusion that Shakespeare was the ideologist of the new nobility which was fast acquiring bourgeois trappings. On the contrary, Shakespeare was strongly opposed to the attempt on the part of this new nobility to appropriate the fruits of primary accumulation and to monopolize all culture. However, Shakespeare found subject-

matter and imagery of a feudal character to be a convenient form
for the following reasons: the traditional dramatic plots, the blending of nobility and bourgeoisie, the avoidance of middle-class limitations. Since the substance was completely bourgeois, through
contact with the "new" content, the form was materially changed.

Shakespeare is *the humanist ideologist of the bourgeoisie of the
time,* for whom the source material of his plays had no importance, and which, as Engels has pointed out, he did not disdain
to borrow even from the Middle Ages. He was concerned only
with how he could adapt this material. It does not follow that
he denied the living present around him, or that he was but another of that group of "closet humanists" whom Engels characterized as "second or third-rate men, or cautious Philistines who
are afraid of burning their fingers (like Erasmus)."[2] His reactions
to the world around him, and to the changes in the political and
social currents of his time, were strong but complex. They found
expression not in impulsive outbursts or obvious allusions to the
evils of the times, but in profound internal upheavals and changed
evaluations of humanity and of the whole life process.

In view of this, Shakespeare's work, in spite of the internal
unity and the correctness of its basic ideology, falls into three
periods.

During the first period, until around 1601, there occurred the
coalescence of all the foremost forces of the country: upper middle-class, the monarchy, the gentry, and even a part of the landed
nobility. This process is reflected by the joyous optimism of Shakespeare's early work, which was filled with a bold and happy affirmation of life, and with obviously aristocratic elements. He has
two main themes—the assertion of the new absolutist national
state, and of the intoxicating joy of living now available to the individual, at last emancipated from feudal bondage. To the first
theme he dedicated the cycle of chronicle plays; to the second, the
series of enchanting, gay comedies. But the effects of the disintegration of the class alignment are already apparent in the plays
written towards the end of the period, around 1597. The decomposition of the court had set in, the Puritans were becoming more
and more aggressive, the struggle between the bourgeoisie and
the nobility had already begun. Hence, the tragic treatment of

royal power in *Julius Caesar* (1599), with its confused conclusions, its pessimism; and the gloomy overtones of the earlier *Much Ado about Nothing* (1598).

During the second period, to 1609—years which marked the decline of Elizabeth's reign and the advent, under James I, of feudal reaction—the process of disintegration was completed. The nobility, with the support of the monarchy, was preparing to defend its position against the imminent onslaught of the bourgeoisie and the gentry. Vacillation, evasion, compromise, were no longer possible; he who was not afraid to "burn his fingers" had to make a choice. Shakespeare made his. He broke through the circle of superficial, aristocratic emotions, discontinued the gay comedies and the idealized depiction of the past, written in celebration of that "glorious" present which was no more. With powerful tragedies, as well as sharply dramatic comedies, he entered the arena as champion of the heroic ideals of bourgeois humanism.

Shakespeare, however, was not destined to retain this position. Reality was against him. The age of humanism was at an end. Narrow, fanatical Puritanism began increasingly to permeate the bourgeoisie and this, in turn, affected Shakespeare. He was forced to choose between the degenerate royalists and the revolutionary, though sanctimonious, Puritan "hagglers." An additional factor entered the situation. By 1610, the London theatre had become very strongly aristocratic in flavor because of the growing royalist patronage and the irreconcilable hatred of the Puritans for the stage. The Beaumont and Fletcher type of play became the vogue. Its popularity rose to such heights that it began to crowd Shakespeare off the stage. Necessity forced the bourgeois dramatists to face the dilemma. Shakespeare, therefore, made a slight compromise. Without betraying either his basic principles, or his social, ethical, and political convictions, he made certain ideological concessions which affected even his style. During this third period (1609-1611) he wrote a series of tragicomedies in the manner of Fletcher. Psychological analysis and definitely motivated action then began to disappear; grim realism gave way to fairy tale and legend. Shakespeare became preoccupied with the complicated, cleverly constructed plots (*Cymbeline*) demanded by the public. His plays were once more filled with those purely decorative, esthetic elements—masques, pastorals, and fairy scenes—which abound in the plays of his first period, and are completely absent from those of his second. This was the celebrated "reconciliation with life" that Shakespearean scholars delight to discuss, but which actually weakened his genius. Shakespeare could not long endure such self-imposed violation of his artistic integrity. For the last time he gave full voice to his humanist credo in his swan-song, *The Tempest*. Five years before his death, at the height of his creative power, he stopped writing for the theatre (1611).

Nevertheless, in spite of the critical phases through which he passed, the basic characteristics of Shakespeare's point of view and style—his militant, revolutionary protests against feudal forms, conceptions, and institutions—remained unaffected throughout his life.

What were these characteristics? First of all—a new morality, based not on the authority of religion or of feudal tradition, but on the free will of man, on the voice of his conscience, on his sense of responsibility towards himself and the world. This called for the emancipation of the feelings and personality of the individual; in particular, this necessitated *individualism*, that most vital and typical characteristic of the Renaissance, which found its fullest expression in Shakespeare. This resulted in a new approach towards social relations, the organization of the state, the nature of authority. To Shakespeare, the highest authority was that of absolute monarchy, but his conception of this was not so much the authority of divine right as the authority of responsibility. The monarch justifies his rank and existence only when he expresses the collective will of the people and realizes their collective welfare.

Secondly—a *scientific* attitude towards the world, life, and reality, which, rejecting all metaphysical interpretations, demands a causal explanation of all natural, social, and psychological phenomena. The possibilities of such a scientific approach to reality were, to be sure, very limited in Shakespeare's day. Nevertheless, this is the essence and the basis of Shakespeare's creative method.

And, finally—the energy and optimism so characteristic of the Renaissance. Shakespeare did not permit resignation and apathy to enter the soul of man; struggle was to him the whole meaning and content of life—creative struggle for the realization, if not of the highest ideals, at least of the organic desires inherent in his individualistic character. Inactive natures, sunk in abstract dreaming or hedonism, or lacking in a sense of responsibility towards themselves and towards humanity, were destined by Shakespeare either for destruction (Richard II, Antony), or ridicule (Jaques in *As You Like It*). This approach is one of the most significant aspects of the new ethical philosophy of humanism as Shakespeare understood it.

Shakespeare was a humanist, a thorough representative of the epoch that Engels called "the greatest progressive revolution mankind had known up to that time." Inasmuch as he expounded the new morality, the new philosophy and ideology, which were about to supplant those of deteriorating feudalism, Shakespeare was an integral part of his *epoch* in the broadest sense of that word. But because a thousand threads bound him to the specific conditions which attended the development of capitalism in England, he also belonged to his *generation*.

The ideological contradictions and the extraordinary complexity of his work are due even more to the combination of these two factors than to the involved socio-economic conditions of his time, although these, too, were important. What Engels called "bourgeois content in feudal form" is always manifest in his works. Often in the same play, and even in the same act, there may be found conflicting ideas.

This complexity has so bewildered the bourgeois critics that they have gone so far as to maintain that Shakespeare was a genius who merely presented all the possibilities and tendencies of human thought with no consideration or awareness of world perspectives. Some of them have attempted to ascribe Shakespeare's work to an aristocratic author; others have advanced the hypothesis that Shakespeare's plays were written by several authors, differing in their ideological and class position, and that Shakespeare merely edited the entire collection. Even Soviet critics have at times formulated incorrect theories, which attempted to settle the question by dismissing it. There has appeared quite recently the thesis of the "three" Shakespeares: the political adapter, the tech-

nical formalist, and the philosophical poet. Such theories are eva-
sions. It is necessary not only to indicate the complexity of the
plays, but to determine its causes, the organic rather than the
formal unity.

The organic unity of Shakespeare's work emanates from his
striving to mirror objectively the life process, by distinguishing
the fundamental from the accidental, the permanent from the
transitory, and to interpret this process in the light of the new
world perspective.

The contradictions mentioned previously prevented Shakespeare's world perspective from fully crystallizing. This world
perspective is, therefore, revealed only as an aspiration and a
tendency, which, because of the nature of the class that had
championed it, could not be realized.

It would be futile to attempt to find a prescribed morality in
Shakespeare. His morality is of a general tenor, not consisting of
dogmatic tenets, but of broad rules of conduct. Such is the rule, or
principle, of *trust* in *Hamlet, King Lear,* and, to a lesser extent, in
Coriolanus; the principle of *conscience* in *Othello* and *Macbeth;*
the principle of *mercy* in *The Merchant of Venice* and *Measure
for Measure,* and so on. Even surpassing these is the principle of
the *creative love of life,* and the heroic *struggle for the preserva-
tion of its best aspects.*

From his own generation, Shakespeare drew the material for
the concrete expression of these abstract principles. It had either
been created by his own generation or had survived in tradition.
Together with a positive interpretation of royal power as the servant of the nation, his plays contain an apology for absolutism; together with a passionate plea for humanity, a relative exoneration
of murder; together with an unconditional recognition of equality,
a relative defense of hierarchy. Thus his vision of the present contained unerring intimation of the future.

Shakespeare does not sermonize; he is never didactic. The
moral aspects of each problem and each situation are revealed
so forcefully that the reader is inescapably compelled to draw his
own conclusions. In this light, it can be said that Shakespeare's
work abounds in moral elements. Accordingly, he elucidates the
problems of the individual: his rights, his relations to the family,

the state and society, and the race question. He always stresses the social roots of every problem. His conception of society is based on a broad and profound conception of the individual.

The tragic and comic elements are presented with equal force; however, they are not confined to tragedy and comedy respectively. A sense of the tragic permeates the gayest comedies, each of which contains socio-moral dramatic conflicts which bring the protagonists to the verge of ruin. Every tragedy is illuminated by an affirmation of life: Lear's suffering leads to a spiritual regeneration; Othello's, to a rebirth of faith in Desdemona's purity and in human nature at large; Antony's death, to an enlightening revelation of the universal historical process. Shakespeare unceasingly strove towards an understanding of the life process in all its extent and profundity. He explored the depths of human suffering, and through his understanding pointed the way to ethical and social values. Shakespeare rejected the medieval notion of "predestination" and man's "mission on earth." He recognized but one destiny; to exhaust all human creative possibilities. Having faith, like all the other great humanists, in the innate "goodness" of human nature, he believed that if man were allowed to develop naturally and fully in accordance with the needs and demands of society, he would achieve not only happiness, but social perfection.

As for the problem of "evil," Shakespeare's point of view is best summed up in *Romeo and Juliet* (II, 3):

Nor aught so good but, strain'd from that fair use,
Revolts from true birth, stumbling on abuse:
Virtue itself turns vice, being misapplied;
And vice sometimes by action dignified.

The whole meaning and content of the life process is man's unceasing struggle to achieve the "common good." It is a heroic struggle but there is no assurance of complete victory. Shakespeare's optimism is strengthened by this philosophy. The necessity for man's development thus becomes the unavoidable result of his nature, which in turn is determined by a series of causal relations.

Shakespeare's analysis of the life process leads to a disclosure of these interconnections. His method is scientific, combining as does Bacon's, the empirical and rational approach to an explanation of natural events and the spiritual activities of man. We are, therefore, justified in characterizing it as a *materialist* method. Objectively, Shakespeare does not accept the supernatural; religion is not an active factor in his work. Religious phraseology is seldom found; when it does appear, as in *Measure for Measure,* it merely reflects the language of his day. Not one of his thirty-seven plays, although written when England was torn by religious dissension, contains any evidence as to whether he was Catholic or Protestant. Shakespeare accepts only two forces: nature and man, the latter being the highest and most complex manifestation of the former. Shakespeare is essentially a *monist.*

That Shakespeare was not the ideologist of the feudal aristocracy is definitely established by his characters, in whom the aspects and forms of feudalism are subjected to the most merciless criticism. King Lear and Antony represent the glory and historical grandeur of feudalism; the feudal lords of the chronicles, its tottering but as yet unbroken power; the French knights in *Henry V,* its bankruptcy; Bertram in *All's Well that Ends Well,* its degeneration; the Montagues and Capulets, its pernicious remnants.

Nor is it possible to accept the thesis that Shakespeare was the ideologist of that section of the nobility which was acquiring bourgeois trappings. They, too, are subjected to the severest criticism: the courtiers in *Love's Labour's Lost,* Falstaff, Polonius and his family, Edmund in *King Lear,* the patricians in *Coriolanus.*

The conclusion that Shakespeare was the ideologist of the bourgeoisie is inescapable. It is impossible, however, to designate him as such without reservations. The rapacity, greed, cruelty, egoism, and philistinism so typical of the English bourgeoisie—embodied in Shylock, Malvolio, Iago—are no less scathingly denounced.

Shakespeare was the *humanist* ideologist of the bourgeoisie, the exponent of the program advanced by them when, in the name of humanity, they first challenged the feudal order, but which they later disavowed. This enabled Shakespeare to subject his class to keen and profound criticism, a criticism motivated by a definite, though not clearly formulated ideal. His strong sense of concrete reality deterred him from creating a utopia, yet he possessed utopian ideals.

At a later stage of bourgeois development Shakespeare became a threat to that class which had given him birth. *The bourgeoisie have never been able to understand or accept the revolutionary elements in Shakespeare's work,* because these immeasurably transcend the narrow confines of bourgeois thought. They have attempted, therefore, to transform his revolutionary humanism into specious philanthropy and to interpret his concepts of mercy and truth as "tenderness" and "righteousness"; his continued appeals for patience—perseverance in the struggle to attain the ideal —as "submissiveness"; his disregard for religion and metaphysics as "philosophical and religious tolerance." And so, the bourgeoisie have crowned him with the empty title: "The Universal Man."

In *Macbeth*, Shakespeare once more takes up the problem of royal power and usurpation.

Macbeth is, in a way, another Richard III, but more profoundly conceived. The tragedy develops rather in the consciousness of its chief characters than in their outward actions. Like Richard and Bolingbroke, Macbeth, with his bloody usurpation, paves the way for a counter-usurpation. But, unlike Richard and Bolingbroke, Macbeth is aware from the very beginning of the consequences attendant upon his action. Even before killing Duncan he states the iron law (I, 7):

> *. . . in these cases*
> *We still have judgment here; that we but teach*
> *Bloody instructions, which being taught return*
> *To plague the inventor: This even-handed justice*
> *Commends the ingredients of our poison'd chalice*
> *To our own lips.*

After the crime and his seizure of the throne, long before there are any indications of revolt, Macbeth, recognizing the inexorability of this iron law, begins to prepare his defenses by new murders and acts of violence, which only serve to hasten the inevitable counter-action. It may be said that having created the necessary conditions for counter-usurpation, Macbeth also supplied the immediate provocation.

In *Richard III*, some accident or other can always be adduced to explain any event—his enemies might have been frightened by Richard and might not have given him battle; Richmond might have been defeated; or, for that matter, there might have been no Richmond at all. In *Macbeth* similar alternatives are impossible. Macbeth himself creates his Richmond. If not Malcolm, it would have been Donalbain; if not Donalbain, any other lord.

No fear, except in the early scenes, or shadow of remorse is to be discerned in Macbeth and his wife. This is purely a struggle of active forces, developed in Macbeth's consciousness, which physically reflect that which must inevitably transpire in the socio-historical arena.

This transference of the basic action to the psychic plane explains the prevalence of the supernatural in the tragedy. Shakespearean scholars have pointed out that at the time of the writing of *Macbeth*, belief in spirits and witches was extremely widespread in England, even in the most cultivated circles of society. Shakespeare does not employ the supernatural in *Macbeth* as the creation of a deranged imagination. This is true, and it is possible that even Shakespeare, notwithstanding his enlightened mind, believed a little in the existence of spirits and witches. Vestiges of medieval superstitions are to be encountered in the works of the most brilliant scholars and philosophers of the Renaissance, and even in the works of Bacon, the creator of English materialism. Nevertheless, this bears no relation to Shakespeare's or Bacon's art and thought. For Shakespeare, the artist, the supernatural has no objective existence and no independent meaning, as for Calderón; nor does it even appear as a primary motivating force. As background and allegory, it serves only to emphasize the realistic elements which are the basic content of his plays. In *Macbeth*, which is utilized by some critics in their attempt to prove Shakespeare a symbolist and mystic, the supernatural as such is completely negated by the transference of the basic action to the psychic plane. The conversations of Macbeth with the witches and phantoms, like the famous dialogue of Ivan Karamazov with the devil, are but the inner dialectical struggle of Macbeth with himself. This struggle is projected on the supernatural plane, just as the socio-historical events arising from Macbeth's concrete actions are projected on the spiritual plane.

The lofty tragic pathos of this drama, one of the most profound and mature of Shakespeare's plays, has misled critics into emphasizing its gloominess. Such emphasis is correct insofar as it refers to the basic theme and situation. But on the periphery of the tragedy there move figures who relieve the gloom and prevent our accepting *Macbeth* as a picture of universal vileness. The chief protagonists, Macbeth and Lady Macbeth, are surrounded by wholesome, energetic individuals: Duncan, Malcolm, Donalbain, Macduff, Siward. Macbeth and his wife are a canker on the body of a society which, in contrast to that of Hamlet or Lear, is completely healthy.

The optimistic tone of the tragedy asserts itself especially in the figure of Malcolm. Fortinbras, who somewhat attenuates the pessimism of *Hamlet*, or Edgar, who partially dispels the gloom in *King Lear*, are vaguely outlined in their relationship to society. Malcolm's social relation, on the other hand, is fully revealed in the scene in which he and Macduff sound each other out before uniting against Macbeth (IV, 3). Malcolm, pretending he is unfit for the crown, mentions his fondness for women and his cupidity. Macduff is disturbed but is willing to overlook these defects. When, however, Malcolm announces that he is devoid of "justice, verity, temperance, stableness," Macduff recoils from him; he is placated only when he realizes that Malcolm has been subjecting him to a test. The advent of such a king augurs a beneficent reign.

---

1 *Ludwig Feuerbach and the Outcome of Classical German Philosophy* (N.Y.), p. 63, A[ngel] F[lores].

2 Alte Einleitung zur 'Naturdialektik'," in *Marx-Engels Archiv*, II, (Frankfurt, 1927), p. 240.—A.F.

11

Historical Criticism and the Interpretation of Shakespeare

ROBERT ORNSTEIN

The essays thus far have shared the unifying principle that modern criticism is a dialogue. One might assume that with the assertion that historical knowledge is valuable one section of the dialogue must come to a conclusion. One might disagree with this critic's assessment of the relative optimism or pessimism of a period, or with that critic's interpretation of its economic and political climate, but one might not expect any argument against historical criticism as a discipline. This essay demonstrates, however, that historical criticism is as vulnerable to objection as any other kind; and it demonstrates, as other essays in this volume do, that common sense is the critic's most valuable possession. Robert Ornstein, Professor of English at the University of Illinois, is the author of The Moral Vision of Jacobean Tragedy *(1960), a first-rate critical study which, it should be noted here, profits immeasurably by its author's ability to make intelligent use of his knowledge of intellectual and social history. Perhaps the most valuable dialogue is that which one conducts with oneself.*

There is no doubt that Shakespeare scholarship has advanced far beyond the Romantic criticism which confused literature and life. Yet it is possible that future generations will in their turn smile at the naïveté of some of our Shakespeare studies, particularly those concerned with the ethics of the plays. In recent decades the definition of Shakespeare's moral attitudes has been viewed as a problem in the history of ideas that can be solved by the accumulation of objective factual evidence. At best such an approach over-simplifies a complex aesthetic problem; at worst it ignores the essential realities of dramatic art. Professor E. E. Stoll suggested some years ago that we cannot intelligently discuss Shakespeare's characters unless we understand how the impression of character is created in poetic drama. I would suggest, in addition, that we cannot accurately interpret Shakespeare's moral intention unless we understand how moral judgments are translated into the artifice of poetic drama and apprehended by an audience.

It has been too frequently assumed that the moral interpretation of Shakespeare is the province of the scholarly researcher, who relates the thought and action of a play to the commonplace political, moral, and religious beliefs of the Elizabethan age. But the same assumptions about a dramatist and his cultural milieu which lead scholars to interpret Shakespeare by means of La Primaudaye, Charron, and Coeffeteau should lead us to interpret *A Streetcar Named Desire* by reference to Norman Vincent Peale, a latter-day ethical psychologist no less influential than his Renaissance counterparts. To be sure, Dr. Peale sheds some light on the tragedy of Blanche Du Bois: she has no mustard seeds, no "Attitude of Gratitude"; she might possibly have been saved had she been more of a positive thinker. We would not be surprised, moreover, to find striking similarities between Mitch's views on marriage and motherhood and those of Dr. Peale. Still we must insist that Tennessee Williams' view of life is not Dr. Peale's. We must distinguish between popular and intellectual levels of thought when discussing the cultural milieu of any dramatist. And we must recognize the difference between a moral intuition expressed in art and the traditional platitudes of systematized ethics.

That scholarly research enriches our understanding of Shakespeare is undeniable; that it affords a unique revelation of the meaning of the plays is debatable. The very nature of Elizabethan dramaturgy—the immediate plunge into dramatic action—demands that the moral apprehension of character be immediate. Motivation may be complex, subterranean, even inscrutable. The psychological depths of a character like Iago may be dark indeed; but we penetrate to that darkness in a very few moments. In their

moral natures the characters of Shakespearian tragedy are in-
finitely more transparent than the men and women we live
among.

The art that creates this moral transparency is not easily analyzed, but it is an art—a mastery of language and of living speech,
not a mastery of philosophy or theology. We apprehend a philosopher's moral vision intellectually, a dramatist's aesthetically.
In the most prurient love scenes of Fletcher's plays, for example,
there is no rational confusion of moral values. We do not accuse
Fletcher of tampering with moral categories but of failing to
translate a rhetorical morality into the presentation of character.
We are *told* that adultery is evil but it appears attractive; we
listen to moral sentiments even while our erotic impulses are
aroused. Fletcher illustrates (negatively, of course) the fact that
that moral apprehension of drama is an aesthetic experience
which depends upon the immediately created impression of character, thought, and action. In other words, the moral judgment
in art must be translated into qualitative, affective terms; it must
communicate an almost sensuous awareness of the beauty of
virtue and the sordidness of vice. Biblical and theological allusions may deepen this immediate "sensuous" impression of character in action, but they cannot substitute for it if the drama is
to live upon the stage.

The difference between Shakespeare and Fletcher is not that
between an objective and an objectional dramatist but between
one who appeals to and refines our deepest moral intuitions and
one who places theatrical effect above moral perception. Although
Shakespeare does not use his art to propagandize, although he
does not pattern experience according to rigid formulae, he nevertheless imposes immediately on his audience's sensibility a particular moral criticism of life. In the great tragedies almost every
line is calculated to elicit a specific emotional response—to shape
a particular moral judgment. But the art that elicits and shapes
that judgment is so sophisticated that it hides itself. We *seem* to
know the moral nature of Goneril or Iago intuitively. Moreover
Shakespeare's moral vision is so humane that it accords always
with the empirical truths of human experience; through his eyes
we see life clearly and whole.

If we turn to the Closet scene in *Hamlet*, we can see the extent to which Shakespeare's poetic and dramatic art shapes our moral responses. Consider the evidence objectively and rationally: An overwrought, passionate youth, bent upon revenge, strikes out in a blind fury at someone hidden behind the arras. He *hopes* that it will be the King, but he has no assurance that it will be, especially since he left Claudius at prayer in the preceding scene. Hamlet does not intend to kill Polonius, but at the moment he does not seem too much concerned about whom he may kill, and the preceding dialogue would lead us to believe that without Polonius' intervention he might possibly have killed his own mother. When he sees his error he is not stricken with remorse; instead he quips sardonically about Polonius' "policy," lectures to his mother on *her* guilt, and finally with a brutal callousness lugs the guts off the stage. Why do we not think of Hamlet then and thereafter as a murderer who, giving rein to his passions, dyed his hand indelibly in an innocent (or relatively innocent) man's blood? The answer is that the murder of Polonius does not disturb us because it does not disturb Hamlet; it is not near our conscience because it is not near his.

Here is a paradox that illuminates the difference between literature and life. In the ordinary world a criminal's remorse softens a spectator's condemnation while callousness and indifference to a criminal act seem chilling signs of unregeneracy. But in drama a guilty conscience may have an almost opposite effect on the spectator because conscience damns: it is the internalized moral chorus through which the dramatist and his audience contemplate the moral significance of a criminal act. It was convenient for Shakespeare that Elizabethans believed that most criminals suffer pangs of remorse, but that conventional belief does not explain the artistic function of conscience in Shakespearian tragedy. For example, the coldblooded treachery by which Richard III murders his brother should arouse a deeper moral revulsion than Macbeth's tormented and anguished decision to kill Duncan. However, just the reverse is true. The very loathing with which Macbeth contemplates his crime burns his guilt into our consciousness, while Richard's high-spirited lack of conscience temporarily suspends moral judgment and allows a moral holiday in which we can momentarily enjoy his outwitting of those who would play the same deadly, amoral game. When a pattern of retribution begins to impose itself on Richard's successes, then the signs of gnawing conscience in Richard and his henchmen dissipate the mood of melodramatic farce and engage a deeper moral response to Richard's villainy.

To return to the Closet scene, I would suggest that were Hamlet more sensitive about Polonius' death we would think the worse of him. The very accusation of his conscience would brand him a murderer in our eyes. But as the scene stands, instead of contemplating his guilt in killing Polonius, Hamlet shifts his mother's attention (and our own) away from his act to Gertrude's guilt in marrying Claudius. Because the moral significance of Hamlet's act is not contemplated, we feel no bizarre incongruity when he lectures to Gertrude on ethics while Polonius' body lies at his feet. Nor do we smile sardonically when in the midst of his moral exhortation Hamlet begs forgiveness for his virtue.

I do not mean that in this crucial scene Shakespeare juggles our moral responses or that he preserves our sympathy with Hamlet by avoiding condemnation of what should be condemned. I mean rather that our moral response to this scene is a complex aesthetic experience that is influenced by the total artifice of the play. What is not near Hamlet's conscience is not near our own because he is our moral interpreter. He is the voice of ethical sensibility in a sophisticated, courtly milieu; his bitter asides, which penetrate Claudius' façade of kingly virtue and propriety, initiate, so to speak, the moral action of the play. And throughout the play our identification with Hamlet's moral vision is such that we hate what he hates, admire what he admires. As centuries of Shakespeare criticism reveal, we accuse Hamlet primarily of what he accuses himself: namely, his slowness to revenge. And we accept the morality of blood revenge instantaneously and unquestioningly because Hamlet the idealist does. Indeed, nothing that we can learn about Renaissance attitudes towards revenge can alter that acceptance.

Our moral impression of Hamlet's character derives primarily from what he says rather than what he does. It is an almost intuitive awareness of the beauty, depth, and refinement of his

moral nature, upon which is thrust a savage burden of revenge
and of disillusion. If Shakespeare's characters are illusions created
by dramatic artifice, then what we love in Hamlet is an illusion
within an illusion: i.e., the suggestion of Hamlet's former self,
the Hamlet whom Ophelia remembers and who poignantly re-
appears in the conversations with Horatio, particularly those just
before the catastrophe. Through his consummate artistry Shakespeare creates within us a sympathy with Hamlet which becomes
almost an act of faith—a confidence in the untouched and un-
touchable core of his spiritual nature. This act of faith, renewed
by great speeches throughout the play, allows us to accept Hamlet's brutality towards Ophelia, his reaction to Polonius' death,
his savage refusal to kill Claudius at prayer, and his Machi-
avellian delight in disposing of Rosencrantz and Guildenstern.
Without the memory of the great soliloquies which preceded it,
our impression of the Closet scene would be vastly different. And,
in fact, to attempt to define Hamlet's character by weighing his
motives and actions against any system of Renaissance thought
is to stage *Hamlet* morally without the Prince of Denmark: i.e.,
without the felt impression of Hamlet's moral nature which is
created by poetic nuance.

Equally important in shaping our reaction to the Closet scene is
our response to Polonius. So far as a rational moral judgment of
Hamlet's "crime" is concerned, it does not matter who besides
Claudius was behind the arras. Yet the audience's reaction would
be vastly different if, let us say, Ophelia were the eavesdropper.
Believing the worst of her, Hamlet might as callously dismiss her
death, but from that moment the audience would part moral company with him. Polonius, is of course, more expendable. While
we may not share Hamlet's cynical contempt, we cannot escape
feeling that the foolish, doting, prying old man received the just
wages of a dupe and spy; he did find it dangerous to be too busy.

Even the moralistic critic derives some satisfaction in seeing
Polonius hoist with his own petard; and yet nothing which the
ancient Councilor does warrants death—indeed, if eavesdropping
be a mortal offense, God help the wicked! Although he snoops,
pries, and carries out Claudius' plans, it is without evil purpose;
there is absolutely no suggestion that he acts except for the gen-

eral (and his personal) good in discovering the cause of Hamlet's melancholy. He is as ignorant of Claudius' crimes as are the bystanders who are bewildered by the final slaughter. Our "satisfaction" with Polonius' death, then, must lie outside the realm of moral philosophy; and strictly speaking it is not moral at all. By legal obligation the good citizen must inform on his neighbors' misdemeanors, but who does not despise the informer whether he is outside or within the law? To society and even to the law, the devious means are repugnant, however moral the intention. A deeply engrained "folk" morality (built up, I imagine, through centuries of police oppression) cherishes openness, candor, and directness; we realize that no man is safe and no life secure in an atmosphere of mutual suspicion and distrust.

Thus the audience feels quite rightly that Polonius does not belong behind the arras. But one could quote a dozen Renaissance moral and political authorities who insist that a high Minister of State, entrusted with the security and well-being of a nation, has the right (nay, the duty) to go about the law, to spy and use suspect means to achieve a worthwhile end. Consider the long controversy over the Duke in *Measure for Measure*. The many essays on the play reveal that some very respectable critics see the Duke as a snooper, a meddler in other men's lives, a well-intentioned official who resorts to repugnant stratagems to achieve a moral goal. Scholars insist that this impression is mistaken and unhistorical; they quote Renaissance political, moral, and religious treatises to demonstrate that the Duke has a perfect justification for his deeds and that a Renaissance audience would not have been disturbed by what seems devious or sordid to a modern reader. Perhaps so, but let us be consistent in our criticism. If our moral judgment of the Duke is to be based, not on the immediate impression of his character but on the weight of Renaissance commonplace opinion, then the same should be true of our judgment of Polonius. Or, conversely, if a mass of carefully selected Renaissance opinions cannot obliterate our distaste for Polonius' policy, then it cannot obliterate a similar response to the Duke's policy.

I do not mean to identify Polonius and the Duke. Our response to Vincentio is far more complex because he plays a more significant and many-sided role. And if it is true, as critics argue, that the action of *Measure for Measure* proceeds on an allegorical as well as realistic level, then our apprehension of the Duke's dramatic role must be different from that of Polonius. But we cannot escape from the immediate impression of the Duke's character by defining his role analogically. The symbolic vision which allegory embodies in art cannot dictate our response to the immediate realities of life or to the image of life presented on a stage; it can only build upon that response, illuminating the shared qualities of "thing" and idea—the analogical relationships between character and concept—which allow the mind to move freely between the realistic and symbolic levels of action. When the mind of the audience cannot move freely in this way because the analogical relationships are obscurely, ingeniously, or casuistically contrived, then the allegory is decadent. When the symbolic vision seeks to identify the devious and the Divine, then the allegory is immoral.

Consider another instructive parallel, this time between Hamlet and Othello. We are told that Othello is damned to everlasting torments because he murdered innocence and did not according to strict theology, repent. If so, what shall we say of Hamlet? He does not strangle Ophelia, but he shocks and torments her, humiliates her before the Court, suggests that she is and treats her like a whore, murders her father and thus drives her insane. Othello's crimes against Desdemona have at least the extenuating circumstance of Iago's diabolical malice. Hamlet's brutality towards Ophelia is the product of his own hypersensitive imagination and the sexual nausea produced by the shock of his mother's infidelity. At her funeral he shouts melodramatically that he loved her but offers no apology for his treatment of her and recognizes no guilt. How shall Othello be damned and flights of angels sing Hamlet to his rest? [1]

Needless to say, we feel that the endings of *Hamlet* and *Othello* are inevitable and "right." This is so, not because we can by scholarly documentation "prove" that Hamlet was inspired always by moral or religious motives and that Othello fell beyond repentance, but because Shakespeare emphasizes the unsullied core of Hamlet's goodness (the exquisite moral sensibility tem-

porarily o'erthrown) while he emphasizes the degradation of
Othello's noble spirit. He shapes different judgments of character
by creating different artistic perspectives. Like Polonius, Ophelia
is a minor character; Hamlet's "crimes" against her are placed in
proportion and overshadowed by the larger moral action of the
play. Desdemona is the heroine; Othello's crime against her *is*
the moral action of the play.

To put it differently, in *Hamlet* and *Othello* as in *Lear* Shakespeare presents heroes who are sinned against as well as sinning,
who may be pitied as victims and condemned as wrongdoers.
He is interested in dramatic situations which although unambiguous admit diametrically opposite moral emphases. In *Othello*
his emphasis is upon the brutality of the destructive impulse. As
we watch the unsuspecting Desdemona prepare for bed, our
hearts steel against sympathy for the "abused" Othello. After this
knowledge of Desdemona's purity, innocence, and love, what
forgiveness for Othello? But without altering either his characterizations or the incidents of his fable, Shakespeare might have
created a very different judgment of Othello's deed. Were the
scene mentioned above eliminated, were the focus in the last
scenes shifted to Iago's sin (to the crime against Othello's innocence) we might accept as inevitable and "right" a very different final impression; we might look upon the tormented Othello
as one who deserves more pity than blame. A theological gloss of
Othello's last speeches cannot tell us how to judge Othello nor
can we discover by this means the particular moral emphasis
which Shakepeare creates through the total design of his play.
One doubts, moreover, that the mystery of Hamlet's "innocence"
can be solved either by Renaissance theology or moral philosophy.
The codes which govern society cannot easily admit what an
audience knows during a performance of *Hamlet*: namely, that a
man's spirit may be superior not only to his fate but even to his
own acts.

Thus while scholarship can make the interpretation of Shakespeare more scientific, it cannot make of interpretation a science
based upon factual information. The dichotomy of scholarly fact
and aesthetic impression is finally misleading because the refined,
disciplined aesthetic impression *is* the fact upon which the in-

terpretation of Shakespeare must ultimately rest; that is to say, all scholarly evidence outside the text of a play is related to it by inferences which must themselves be supported by aesthetic impressions.[2] The attempt of historical criticism to recapture (in so far as it is possible) Shakespeare's own artistic intention, is, or should be, the goal of all responsible criticism. But we must insist that that intention is fully realized in the play and can be grasped only from the play. A study of Renaissance thought may guide us to what is central in Shakespeare's drama; it may tell us why Shakespeare's vision of life is what it is. But we can apprehend his vision only as aesthetic experience. When the long history of Shakespeare studies indicates that certain characterizations are ambiguous, scholarly information cannot erase those ambiguities, for they arise either from detached, ironic, or ambivalent conceptions of character or from failures to translate univocal judgments into effective artifice. To announce that Ulysses' speech on order and degree is a great statement of Elizabethan commonplaces is merely to accent the irony of its dramatic context and to define more sharply the problem which the critical faculty alone can solve.

There will always be a welcome variety in the interpretation of Shakespeare. And there will always be eccentric interpretations, but they will not long withstand the assault of common sense, the sensitive and scrupulous examination of the text, and the insistence that Shakespeare's art is dramatic in intention— created for theatrical performance. Historical criticism has, of course, eliminated eccentric interpretations, but it has also, in some respects, fostered them by substituting completely unliterary standards for the traditional standards of critical perceptivity. We need now to redefine what is eccentric in interpretation by first redefining the legitimate criteria of critical judgment and the proper relationship between scholarship and criticism in Shakespeare studies. Only through the cooperation of scholarship and criticism will we arrive at an understanding of Shakespeare's art that precludes the dogmatism of the learned and the uninformed.

1 I do not argue that Horatio's exquisite farewell to his Prince proves the blessed state of Hamlet's immortal soul. On the contrary, unless a character were literally God's spy he would scarcely have authoritative knowledge of the Divine Judgment. We cannot dogmatize about the function of imagery drawn from popular religious beliefs in Shakespeare's plays, but we can demand consistency in critical methods. If the imagery of hell in Othello's last speeches indicates his damnation, then the apocalytic references at the end of *Lear* ("Is this the promised end? / Or image of that *horror?*" [my italics]) must indicate a failure of belief in Providential Order, a sense of cosmic dissolution and disillusion.

2 How shall we decide which of the Elizabethan views of melancholy are relevant to Shakespeare's portrait of Hamlet? Certainly not every obscure and contradictory Elizabethan opinion is part of the background of the play. If we are not to stress coincidental parallels or make erroneous assumptions about Shakespeare's beliefs, the selection of scholarly evidence must be an act of critical judgment. A scholar must begin with a conception of Hamlet's character if he is to find the contemporary thought which underlay Shakespeare's dramatic portrait. Thus while scholarly documentation validates a critical impression, that documentation will be apposite and illuminating only if based upon a sensitive and perceptive reading of the text.

Moreover, unless we are to assume that Shakespeare was incapable of original insights into human nature, we cannot say that an interpretation of character is mistaken because we cannot find sanction for it in Elizabethan treatises on moral philosophy or psychology. The Romantic notion that Hamlet loses his will to action in thought may be mistaken (I think it is mistaken), but it is not mistaken simply because Elizabethan courtiers were (or were supposed to be) men of action as well as thought. Beaumont and Fletcher's Amintor and Philaster are proof that the Romantic conception of Hamlet was plausible to the Elizabethan artistic mind, if not to the compiler of courtesy books.

꧁ 12 ꧂

Prince Hal's Conflict

ERNST KRIS

Unlike most of the other important approaches to Shakespeare, that taken by the Freudian critics has not yet found its theoretician. It may well be that the psychological view raises questions with which criticism is not yet fully prepared to deal: If Shakespeare creates in Hamlet a plot situation which can be explained only in psychoanalytic terms, how is the critic to account for the playwright's prescient acquaintance with Freudian principles? To what extent must a psychoanalytic inquiry into a work of art comprise an analysis, legitimate or illegitimate, of its usually unavailable author? Despite the difficulties of the problem it raises, however, the psychoanalytic approach has already produced significant work.* No critic of Hamlet, *for example, can afford to ignore Ernest Jones'* Hamlet and Oedipus *(1949), no matter how incompletely he may feel Freud's biographer has explored the assumptions on which he bases his essay or the totality of the play which he treats. Ernst Kris (1900–1957) was a leading psychoanalyst and one of the most brilliant innovators in twentieth-century esthetics. In this essay, which appeared first in* Psychoanalytic Quarterly *and later in the author's extraordinary book* Psychoanalytic Explorations in Art, *Dr. Kris demonstrates a way in which the Freudian approach can be combined with so traditional a* modus operandi *as source study to produce genuine literary criticism. His essay has the additional merit of its author's awareness of the theoretical implications of his approach to a single play.*

For well over a century some of Shakespeare's critics have
pointed to inconsistencies in the character of Henry, Prince of
Wales (later King Henry V), occasionally explained by the poet's
lack of interest, whose attention, it is said, was concentrated
mainly on the alternate but "true" hero, Falstaff. This seemed
the more plausible since most of the puzzling passages or incidents occur in King Henry IV, Parts I and II of the trilogy;
however, closer examination of three inconsistencies, to which
critics are wont to refer as typical of others, seems to throw new
light on the psychological conflict with which Sheakespeare has
invested the hero of the trilogy.[1]

Prince Hal's first appearance on the stage as Falstaff's friend
and Poins's companion is concluded by the soliloquy in which he
reveals his secret intentions. While he has just made plans to riot
with the gang and to rob the robbers, his mind turns to the future.

> I know you all, and will awhile uphold
> The unyok'd humour of your idleness:
> Yet herein will I imitate the sun,
> Who doth permit the base contagious clouds
> To smolder up his beauty from the world,
> That, when he please again to be himself,
> Being wanted, he may be more wonder'd at,
> By breaking through the foul and ugly mists
> Of vapours that did seem to strangle him.
> If all the year were playing holidays,
> To sport would be as tedious as to work;
> But when they seldom come, they wish'd-for come,
> And nothing pleaseth but rare accidents.
> So, when this loose behaviour I throw off,
> And pay the debt I never promised,
> By how much better than my word I am,
> By so much shall I falsify men's hopes,
> And, like bright metal on a sullen ground,
> My reformation, glittering o'er my fault,
> Shall show more goodly and attract more eyes
> Than that which hath no foil to set it off.
> I'll so offend, to make offence a skill;
> Redeeming time when men think least I will.[2]

Some critics feel that this announcement deprives the play of part of its dramatic effect: the change in the Prince's behavior should surprise the audience as it does the personages on the stage. The anticipation, we are told, was forced on the poet as a concession to the public. Henry V appeared to the Elizabethans as the incarnation of royal dignity and knightly valor. His early debauches had therefore to be made part of a morally oriented plan; but some critics find the price of justification too high, since it leaves a suspicion of hypocrisy on the Prince's character.

The second inconsistency is seen in the course of the Prince's reformation, which proceeds in two stages. In Part I, Prince Hal returns to his duties when the realm is endangered by rebels; at Shrewsbury, he saves the King's life and defeats Percy Hotspur in combat; but while the war against other rebels continues, we find him back in Eastcheap feasting with his companions. His final reformation takes place at the King's deathbed. Critics usually account for this protracted and repeated reformation by assuming that the success of the Falstaff episodes in Part I suggested their continuation in Part II, an argument supported by the widely accepted tradition that Falstaff's revival in *The Merry Wives of Windsor,* after the completion of the trilogy, was at the special request of Queen Elizabeth. It has nevertheless been emphasized that the concluding scenes of Part II follow in all essential details existing tradition.

The third and most frequently discussed inconsistency is King Henry V's treatment of his former companions with merciless severity. Falstaff, who waits to cheer the new King, is temporarily arrested and, while he hopes that Henry will revoke in private his public pronouncement, we later hear that he has hoped in vain. The King's harshness has broken his heart. In the "rejection of Falstaff," [3] who has won the audience's heart, the dramatist has "overshot his mark"; the King's reformation could have been illustrated by gentler means, and some critics suggest how this could have been achieved without offending the Old Knight. The formula of banishment, however, is only partly Shakespeare's invention since it paraphrases traditional accounts.

This tradition originated soon after Henry V suddenly died in Paris, at the age of thirty-five, crowned King of England and

France (1421). The tradition grew in chronicles and popular accounts, hesitantly at first, more rapidly later, when Henry's striving for European leadership and hegemony in the Channel appeared as an anticipation of the political goals of Tudor England. In Shakespeare's time, fact and legend had become firmly interwoven.[4]

Prince Henry (of Monmouth, born 1387) was early introduced to affairs of state. He was twelve years old when, in 1399, his father succeeded Richard II. At fifteen he took personal control of the administration of Wales and of the war against the Welsh. He had shared in this task since 1400, initially guided by Henry Percy, Hotspur, who at that time was thirty-nine, three years older than the Prince's father. In 1405 Hotspur led the rebellion of the Percies and attacked the Prince's forces at Shrewsbury. Supported by the King and his army, Henry of Monmouth carried the day. The rebellion and the pacification of Wales kept the Prince busy until 1408 or 1409. He then entered politics as leader of the parliamentary opposition against the King's council. Repeated illnesses complicated Henry IV's negotiations with Parliament that at the time of his uprising against Richard II had vested royal power in him. Since 1406 rumors concerning his abdication had been spreading. In 1408 he was thought to have died in an attack of seizures "but after some hours the vital spirits returned to him." From January, 1410 to November, 1411 the Prince governed England through the council, supported by the King's half-brothers, Henry and Thomas Beaufort. In November, 1411 Henry IV took over again and dismissed the Prince from the council. One of the reasons for the Prince's dismissal was his desire for an active policy in France. It seems that, initially without the King's consent, he had arranged for a small expeditionary force to be sent to the continent in support of Burgundy against the Royal House of France; later the King agreed to the expedition but the Prince had to renounce his intention to lead the forces.

The circumstances that led to Henry of Monmouth's removal from the council are not entirely clear. It seems that Henry IV was motivated by the suspicion that the Prince intended to depose him. The Prince issued public statements denying such intention, and demanded the punishment of those who had slandered him. He finally forced an interview on the King, during which a reconciliation took place. The struggle between father and son was terminated by Henry IV's death in 1413.

According to the chronicle of the fifteenth and sixteenth centuries, Henry of Monmouth's character changed after his accession to the throne. The early chronicles do not state in detail wherein the conversion consisted. They familiarize us, however, with two areas in which the Prince's attitude was different from that of the later King. The first of these areas is less well defined than the second: during the conflict with his father, the Prince appeared twice at court "with much peoples of lords and gentles." This show of strength was meant to exercise pressure on King and council. During his reign Henry V never used similar methods; no appeal to forces outside "government" is attributed to him, neither in his dealings with Parliament nor with the baronage. Within the framework of his age he was a rigorously constitutional monarch. Somewhat better defined is the change of the Prince's attitude to the Church. The noble leader of the Lollards, Sir John Oldcastle, was the Prince's personal friend, and at least by tolerance, the Prince seems vaguely to have favored the cause for which he stood. Shortly after Henry V's accession to the throne the persecution of the Lollards was intensified. Sir John was arrested and asked to abandon his error. He refused any compromise, succeeded twice in escaping, but he was finally, in 1417, executed after Parliament had determined on the extirpation of Lollardy as heresy.

The legendary versions of the Prince's reformation elaborated these incidents later on; in their earliest formulation they simply stated: "that the Prince was an assiduous center of lasciviousness and addicted exceedingly to instruments of music. Passing the bounds of modesty he was the fervent soldier of Venus as well as of Mars; youthlike, he was tired with her torches and in the midst of the worthy works of war found leisure for excess common to ungoverned age" (Kingsford, 1901, p. 12). Later sources place the Prince's reformation in relation to the conflict with his father: the baronage that had adopted the Prince as leader becomes a group of irresponsible delinquents. Among this group the name

of Sir John Oldcastle appears. The fanatic leader of a religious
sect thus underwent the transformation into Sir John Falstaff,
whose name was substituted by Shakespeare only after Oldcastle's descendants had complained of what seemed a vilification
of their ancestor; but various traces of the original name are extant in Shakespeare's text. The banishment of Falstaff then may
be considered as an elaboration of Henry's persecution of the
Lollards whom he once had favored. Other elements of the
legendary tradition are inserted with clearly moralistic intentions:
the Prince's reformation is used to exemplify the nature of royal
responsibility. Thus Sir Thomas Elliott in his treatise, *The Book
Called the Governor* (1536), introduced the tale of Prince and
Chiefjustice according to which the King confirms that Chiefjustice in office who, in the royal name, had once arrested the
riotous Prince. The image of Henry V was thus idealized into that
of the perfect Renaissance ruler (T. Spencer, 1942).

Shakespeare borrowed these and similar incidents of his trilogy
from a variety of sources, but mainly from the second edition of
Raphael Holinshed's *Chronicles of England, Scotland and Ireland*
(1587).[5] In addition to historical sources he relied upon a popular
play produced a few years earlier. So closely does he follow *The
Famous Victories of Henry V* that it seems as if he had set himself the task to retain as many as possible of the incidents familiar
to his audience in spite of the total transformation of the context.
Without commenting in detail upon this transformation—though
such a comparison would permit one to support the hypothesis
here to be proposed—it suffices to point to its general direction.
The historical facts concerning the conflict between Henry IV
and his son and "heir apparent," Henry of Monmouth, had been
blurred by legend. The conversion of the Prince became the dominant theme, a conversion modeled after that of the life of the
saints. Shakespeare returns to the core of this tradition, or rather
rediscovers that core, in the sources accessible to him. He centers
his attention on the conflict between father and son which is
made to account for both the Prince's debauchery and his reformation.

The conflict between father and son appears in Part I of Henry
IV in three versions, each time enacted by one central and two

related characters.[6] The theme is manifestly stated by the King in the introductory scene of the trilogy, when he compares Henry of Monmouth to Henry Percy.

> *Yea, there thou makest me sad and makest me sin*
> *In envy that my Lord Northumberland*
> *Should be the father to so blest a son,*
> *A son who is the theme of honour's tongue;*
> *Amongst a grove, the very straightest plant;*
> *Who is sweet fortune's minion and her pride:*
> *Whilst I, by looking on the praise of him,*
> *See riot and dishonour stain the brow*
> *Of my young Harry. O! that it could be prov'd*
> *That some night-tripping fairy had exchang'd*
> *In cradle-clothes our children where they lay,*
> *And called mine Percy, his Plantagenet!*
> *Then would I have his Harry, and he mine.[7]*

The position of the Prince between Falstaff and the King is almost as explicitly stated; he has two fathers, as the King has two sons. When he enacts with Falstaff his forthcoming interview with his father, the theme is brought into the open.[8] It is not limited to court and tavern, the centers of the "double plot," as W. Empson (1935) calls it, but extends to the rebel camp. Henry Percy stands between a weak father, Northumberland, who is prevented by illness from participating in the decisive battle, and a scheming uncle, Worcester, who plans the rebellion, conceals from Percy that the King offers reconciliation and drives him thus to battle and to death.

The three versions of the father-son conflict compelled Shakespeare to deviate from his sources and thereby to enrich the stage: he sharpened the report of the chronicles on the rebellion of the Percies in order to create the contrast of Worcester and Northumberland; he reduced Henry Percy's age from a slightly older contemporary of Henry IV to a somewhat older contemporary of the Prince—and he invented Falstaff.

The triangular relationships are not only similar to each other, since they all contain variations of the theme of good and bad fathers and sons, but within each triangle the parallel figures are closely interconnected; thus the two Harrys, whom Henry IV compares, form a unit; Hotspur's rebellion represents also Prince Hal's unconscious parricidal impulses.[9] Hotspur is the Prince's double. Impulses pertaining to one situation have thus been divided between two personages;[10] but though in the triangles the characters are paired and contrasted, each of the play's personages transcends the bondage to his function in this thematic configuration. They have all outgrown the symmetry which they serve, into the fullness of life.

To appraise Falstaff as a depreciated father figure is to grasp the superficial aspect of a character who, more than any other of Shakespeare, has enchanted readers and audiences since his creation. Franz Alexander (1933) finds two principal psychoanalytic explanations for this universal enchantment: Falstaff's hedonism, he says, represents the uninhibited gratification of an infantile and narcissistic quest for pleasure, a craving alive to some extent in every one of us; this hedonism, moreover, is made acceptable by contrast: one turns with relief from the court or the rebel camp to the tavern. In accordance with the last is the traditional antithesis of "tragic King and comic people" (Empson) used by Shakespeare to emphasize a moral antithesis. From Prince Hal's point of view, Falstaff is a contrast to the King, who represents another version of the unsatisfactory paternal image. Henry IV succeeded his cousin Richard II by rebellion and regicide. The feeling of guilt that overshadowed his life becomes manifest when on his deathbed, in addressing the Prince, he reviews the sorrows that the unlawfully acquired crown inflicted on him.

How I came by the crown, O God forgive;
And grant it may with thee in true peace live![11]

In this great scene Prince Henry's mood accords with his father's; he too is burdened with guilt. In the preceding scene he finds his father sleeping, and believes him to be dead. Shakespeare, adapting this scene from the chronicle play, has added a prop device: the crown which lies next to the King's bed.[12] The crown inspires the Prince with awe and apprehension. He longs to possess it, but "the best of gold" is "the worst of gold"; it endangers the bearer. He wages "the quarrel of a true inheritor," controls his desire and, in a mood of contemplation, concludes that royal responsibility is a heavy burden. He has overcome the hostile impulse, against the dying King and can now reply to his father:

> You won it, wore it, kept it, gave it me;
> Then plain and right must my possession be;[13]

It is an attempt to reassure: "Since I have come guiltless into the possession of the crown, since I refrained from regicide and parricide, I shall rightfully be King"; yet in the greatest crisis of his life, the Prince, now King Henry V, reveals that his apprehension has not been vanquished. The night before the battle of Agincourt, when his outnumbered army is weakened by disease, and confidence is more than ever required, he turns to prayer to avert divine retaliation for his father's crime that, with the crown, seems to have moved to his shoulders.

> O God of battles! steel my soldiers' hearts;
> Possess them not with fear; take from them now
> The sense of reckoning, if the opposed numbers
> Pluck their hearts from them! Not to-day, O Lord!
> O, not to-day, think not upon the fault
> My father made in compassing the crown!
> I Richard's body have interred anew;
> And on it have bestow'd more contrite tears
> Than from it issu'd forced drops of blood:
> Five hundred poor I have in yearly pay,
> Who twice a day their wither'd hands hold up
> Toward heaven, to pardon blood; and I have built
> Two chantries, where the sad and solemn priests
> Sing still for Richard's soul. More will I do;
> Though all that I can do is nothing worth,
> Since that my penitence comes after all,
> Imploring pardon.[14]

The essential passages of this prayer follow Holinshed's *Chronicles* wherein it is reported that after his succession to the throne

Henry V had King Richard's body ceremoniously interred in Westminster Abbey and made specified donations in commemoration. Reference to this incident and the place in which it is made invite comment. By reintroducing the theme of the tragic guilt attached to the House of Lancaster, Shakespeare establishes a link between Henry V and his older plays that dramatize the downfall of the Lancastrian Kings (Henry VI, Richard III). The victory of Agincourt and the life of Henry V are thus made to appear as a glorious interlude in a tragic tale of crime and doom; however, the King's prayer before the battle reveals the structure of the conflict which Shakespeare embodied in his character: the desire to avoid guilt and to keep himself pure of crime is paramount in Henry V. In one passage of the prayer the King recalls the tears he shed on Richard's coffin, a detail not recorded by Holinshed, and yet obviously suggested by other passages of the *Chronicle*. It may well be considered a hint—the only one we find in the trilogy—that there ever existed a personal relationship between Richard II and the son of his banished cousin Henry of Lancaster—Henry of Monmouth. During the last months of his rule King Richard II sailed for Ireland to quell a local rebellion and he took Henry of Monmouth with him. The young Prince seems to have attracted the King's attention. The Prince was knighted by Richard, Holinshed records, "for some valiant act that he did or some other favourable respect." Shakespeare was undoubtedly familiar with this account and very probably familiar with reports of the Prince's reaction to the news of his father's rebellion. Young Henry of Monmouth is said to have replied to a question of Richard's that he could not be held responsible for his father's deed.

In Shakespeare's *King Richard II* no direct reference is made to the relationship between Prince Hal and Richard,[15] but the theme to which we refer is present and clearly emphasized: one entire scene is devoted to it, the first in which the Prince is mentioned. Henry IV, newly enthroned, meets with his Lords—but his son is absent.

> *Can no man tell of my unthrifty son?*
> *'Tis full three months since I did see him last:*

If any plague hang over us, 'tis he.
I would to God, my lords, he might be found:
Inquire at London, 'mongst the taverns there,
For there, they say, he daily doth frequent,
With unrestrained loose companions,
Even such, they say, as stand in narrow lanes,
And beat our watch, and rob our passengers;[16]

The Prince has dissociated himself from the court that his father won by treason. In silent protest he has turned to the tavern rather than to participate in regicide.[17] Regicide dominates the scene that starts with Henry IV's quest for his absent son. The last of Richard's followers and the new King's cousin, the Duke of Aumerle, confesses to Henry IV that he has plotted against his life. Before Aumerle can complete his confession, the Duke of York, his father and the uncle of Henry IV, forces his way into their presence. He doubts whether the purpose of Aumerle's audience be murder or repentance and is prepared to surrender his son.[18] This is the environment from which the Prince withdraws, to which he prefers the vices of Eastcheap and the freedom of Falstaff's company.

In *King Henry IV*, Part II, the contrast between court and tavern is reëmphasized in a scene in which Falstaff's carefree vice is juxtaposed with John of Lancaster's virtuous villainy. This younger brother of Prince Hal is in command of the campaign against the still surviving rebels. Falstaff serves in his inglorious army. Lancaster promises the rebels pardon; they accept his offer and he breaks his word to send them to the gallows. We have just witnessed this monstrous performance—taken directly from Holinshed's *Chronicles*—when Lancaster and Falstaff meet. The "sober blooded youth" provokes Falstaff's soliloquy in praise of sherris sack and of Prince Hal, whose valor has not made him addicted to "thin potations."

Falstaff's loving praise of the Prince, and what others say when they refer to the Prince in the latter part of Part II of Henry IV remind us once more of how well he has succeeded in deceiving the world. His conversion upon his accession to the throne comes as a surprise to the court and to the tavern. Only the audience, having been in his confidence from his first soliloquy, are enabled to understand the contradictions in his behavior as being a part of his paramount conflict.

When Shakespeare familiarized himself with the youth of Henry V this conflict must have imposed itself upon his mind as one that would unify the various traits and incidents reported. The tendentious accounts in the *Chronicles* had not fully obliterated the traces of antagonism in the relationship between the Prince and the King. This antagonism, the legends of the Prince's debauchery and conversion, and other elements that the dramatist found in his sources, he wove into a plausible character. The Prince tries to dissociate himself from the crime his father had committed; he avoids contamination with regicide because the impulse to regicide (parricide) is alive in his unconscious. When the King's life is threatened he saves the King and kills the adversary, who is his alter ego. In shunning the court for the tavern he expresses his hostility to his father and escapes the temptation to parricide. He can permit himself to share Falstaff's vices because he does not condone the King's crime; but hostility to the father is only temporarily repressed. When finally he is in possession of the crown, he turns against the father substitute; hence the pointed cruelty of Falstaff's rejection. Both paternal figures between which the Prince oscillates have less meaning to him than appears at first. What he opposes to them is different and of an exalted nature: his ideals of kingship, royal duty and chivalry. These ideals are with him when he first appears on the stage; they grow in and with him throughout the tragedy, and they dominate throughout the five acts of *King Henry V*.

These ideals, one might speculate, may have been modeled on an idealization of Richard II, the murdered King, whom Prince Hal as a boy had accompanied to Ireland and whose favor he had won. Richard, however, was hardly fit to serve as model of a great king. Shakespeare has drawn him as a weak and irresponsible man, who depended presumptuously on the trappings of royalty for his kingship, on that ceremony that meant so little to Henry V and for which he substituted royal duty. One may conjecture this to have been a further reason why Shakespeare did not explicitly refer to the existence of a personal relationship between Prince Henry and King Richard. But all this is speculative. Opposed to it is solid evidence of the importance of moral conflicts in the personality of Henry V; it would be easy to demonstrate from metaphors and puns alone, with which the poet speaks through the hero, his proclivity to such conflicts. His major actions and interests all indicate too the Prince's search for moral justification.

While living the roistering life of the tavern, his thirst for glory won in battle—but only battle with a moral purpose—and chivalry was great; hence the Prince's bitter caricature of Hotspur.

> . . . I am not yet of Percy's mind, the Hotspur of the North; he that kills me some six or seven dozen of Scots at a breakfast, washes his hands, and says to his wife, "Fie upon this quiet life! I want work." "O my sweet Harry," says she; "how many hast thou killed to-day?" "Give my roan horse a drench," says he; and answers, "Some fourteen" an hour after; "a trifle, a trifle."[19]

There is jubilant relief when Percy turns to rebellion and the Prince can finally fight an envied rival, and in the service of a just cause liberate and use his own aggressive impulses; hence also, before the invasion of France, the preoccupation with legal points; and finally, on the night before Agincourt, the protracted debate with Williams, the soldier. Assuming that his partner in discussion is "Harry le Roy" an English commoner, the soldier argues

> . . . There are few die well that die in a battle; for how can they charitably dispose of anything, when blood is the argument? Now, if those men do not die well, it will be a black matter for the king that led them to it. . . .[20]

Henry goes to great lengths to refute this thesis. He contends that the King is answerable only for the justice of his cause and cannot be answerable for "the particular endings of his soldiers," since "every subject is the King's, but every subject's soul is his own." The moving subtleties of this theological discourse [21] lead to the King's soliloquy on ceremony and royal destiny:

Upon the king! let us our lives, our souls,
Our debts, our careful wives,
Our children, and our sins lay on the king!
We must bear all. O hard condition,
Twin-born with greatness, subject to the breath
Of every fool, whose sense no more can feel
But his own wringing! What infinite heart's-ease
Must kings neglect that private men enjoy!
And what have kings that privates have not too,
Save ceremony,—save general ceremony?
And what art thou, thou idol ceremony?[22]

Summoned to battle, the King kneels in prayer in which he dis-
claims any complicity in his father's crime; thus prepared, the
hero can conquer.

Henry V's preoccupation with morals is not glorified by Shakespeare nor presented as the dominant virtue of "a Christian
soldier"; it is shown in its dynamic interplay with opposite tendencies, and occasionally—with a slightly ironical smile—exposed
as a pretense. While the King is urging the clergy to establish
his claim to the throne of France, the audience knows that he has
forced the support of the Church by political pressure. The
bishops, who have accepted the deal and supplied the garbled
justification, are well aware of the King's burning desire for con-
quest. We are left in doubt as to whether it is political shrewdness
or self-deception which prompts the King to pose the question:[23]

May I with right and conscience make this claim?[24]

Ambiguities and schisms of motivation are characteristic of the
King. He flees to the tavern to escape from the evils of the court
—but he becomes a past master of licentious living. He strives for
humane warfare, and protects the citizens of conquered Harfleur;[25] but when the French break the laws of warfare in attacking the English encampment and killing the boys, Henry has
every French prisoner's throat cut. The "friction between flesh
and spirit" (Traversi), between impulse and inhibition, is fully
resolved only when from moral scrutiny Henry proceeds to
heroic venture, when as leader of men who are determined to

fight with a clear conscience against overwhelming odds, he feels himself one among peers;

We few, we happy few, we band of brothers.[26]

The inconsistencies in Prince Hal's character that some of Shakespeare's critics thought to have detected are not inconsistencies but attempts to resolve a conflict which is in some of its elements similar to Hamlet's. In Hamlet the oedipus is fully developed, centering around the queen. In Shakespeare's historical dramas women are absent or insignificant. Prince Hal's struggle against his father appears therefore in isolation, enacted in male society. Hamlet stands between a murdered father and a murderous uncle. Prince Hal's father murdered his second cousin—and predecessor—to whom the Prince had an attachment. Thus the crime is in both cases carried out by the father or by his substitute—the King in Hamlet—while both heroes are battling against the murderous impulse in their own hearts.

The psychological plausibility of Prince Hal as a dramatic character is not inferior to that of Hamlet, whatever the difference in depth and dramatic significance of the two plays may be. While only one part of the oedipal conflict is presented, the defenses which Prince Hal mobilizes in order to escape from his internal predicament are well known from the clinical study of male youths. In our analysis of the Prince's character we have implicitly referred mainly to two mechanisms: first, to the formation of the superego; second, the displacement of filial attachment onto a father substitute.

The Prince, in his thoughts, compares the King, his father, with an ideal of royal dignity far superior to the father himself. This ideal, derived from paternal figures but exalted and heightened, is his protection in the struggle against his parricidal impulses and against submission to the King. This mechanism operates in some form or other in every boy's development at the time of the resolution of the oedipal conflict. During this process the superego requires part of its severity and some of its autonomy. It is a process subject to many vicissitudes, as illustrated by a clinical example.

A boy of eight approached his father, a distinguished judge, with a request for advice. He held two one dollar bills and wanted to know whether he might keep them. They had been acquired by the sale to neighbors of pencils which a mail order house had sent him on his request. Upon the receipt of the two dollars he was to be sent a premium to which he now preferred the money. The judge asked to see the advertisement to which the boy had responded and the letter of the mail order house. After reading both he ruled: "You may keep the money; they have no right to make such contracts with minors."

When thirty-five years later the incident was recalled in analysis it appeared that he had not only lost confidence in all authority since that time, but also that when he had asked his father's advice he was testing him. He had grown suspicious that the father did not live up to the principles—sexual and moral—he advocated, and when in his own conflict he sought the father's advice, he had hoped that the father would support his own hesitant moral views. When this expectation was disappointed, he acquired a cynical independence. The compulsion to live up to his ideal became part of a complex neurotic symptomatology.

In one detail only did this patient resemble Prince Hal: his own moral standards assured his independence from all paternal figures and were used as aggressive reproach in every contact with them. Prince Hal uses not only his ideal of moral integrity as reproachful contrast against his father, but also his own playful depravity. The second mechanism of defense the Prince mobilizes is no less common than the first. He adopts an extrafamilial substitute who, true to a pattern frequently observed, is the antithesis of the father. Falstaff is closer to the Prince's heart than the King; he satisfies the libidinal demands in the father-son relation through his warmth and freedom. Yet the Prince proves superior to Falstaff in wit and royal reveling: he triumphs over both father and father substitute.[27] He is paramount in license as he will be paramount in royal dignity.

Literary critics seem of late weary of the intrusion of psychoanalysis. However politely, they assert—and rightly so—their independence.[28] This essay is a psychological analysis which attempts only to underline a few universal, unconscious mechanisms,

and is not intended as literary criticism. It suggests that Shakespeare had puzzled about the nature of Henry V's personality,
and that already, while writing the last act of *Richard II*, was
aware of the conflict on which he intended to center the character
development of the King. Shakespeare's plan, suggested in this
case by the nature of the tradition about the subject, must have
been one of the trends of thought that, on various levels of awareness, directed him in writing the trilogy. It is not suggested that
the plan was complete from the beginning; it might have mani-
fested itself to the poet during his work, i.e., it might have been
preconscious before. Moreover, some elements we here consider
part of this plan probably never reached consciousness. What
answer Shakespeare might have given if asked why Henry V kills
Falstaff by his harshness is comparatively irrelevant. What counts
is that he had the King do so, and he surely must have known
that this could hardly be popular with his audience. Such internal
consistency, the final parricide, can only have been conceived by
one who in creating had access to his own unconscious impulses.

If investigations similar to the one here attempted, but more
complete and authoritative, were carried out systematically; if
they were to comprehend all of Shakespeare's work and, at least
for purposes of comparison, the works of other Elizabethans; if
conflicts and their varied or preferred solutions, and those omitted
by one author, one group of authors, one period, or one cultural
area were collated—such an application of psychoanalysis might
be integrated with the work of the literary historian or critic.

Plot and character are clearly not the only, and not always the
most important, tools of the dramatic poet. Psychoanalysis suggests other approaches for the study of poetic language, its metaphors and hidden meaning.[29] Systematic investigation in this area
may lead to other types of integration than the study of plot or
character. The combination of various sequences of such systematic studies might finally lead to a topic in which critics and
psychoanalysts are equally interested and about which they are
both, each in his own field, almost equally ignorant: the nature of
the artist's personality, a question that must be studied in its cultural variations before generalizations can be made.

Psychoanalysis has frequently attempted short cuts, mostly by correlating one of the artist's works with an occurrence noted by his biographers,[30] assumptions that can rarely be verified.

Clinical analysis of creative artists suggests that the life experience of the artist is sometimes only in a limited sense the source of his vision; that his power to imagine conflicts may by far transcend the range of his own experience; or, to put it more accurately, that at least some artists possess the particular gift to generalize from whatever their own experience has been. One is always tempted to look for a cue that would link this or that character to its creator's personality. Falstaff, it has been said, is clearly Shakespeare himself. Why not Percy or Richard II? Are they not equally alive, equally consistent? Could not for each of these characters that very same psychological plausibility be claimed, that we here claim for Prince Hal? Such a quest seems futile and contrary to what clinical experience with artists as psychoanalytic subjects seems to indicate. Some great artists seem to be equally close to several of their characters, and may feel many of them as parts of themselves. The artist has created a world and not indulged in a daydream.

This writer is not exempt from the temptation to detect a neat connection between the artist and one of his characters. I therefore record my own venture in this direction, with appropriate reservations. At the time Shakespeare was working on Richard II, and studying the life of Prince Hal, he reëstablished the prestige of the Shakespeare family (which had been lost through his father's bankruptcy) by purchasing a coat of arms. The motto chosen is one that might well have been used to characterize Prince Hal's striving for the crown: "Non sanz droict."

* The best general discussion of the subject is Lionel Trilling's "Freud and Literature," reprinted in *The Liberal Imagination* (1950).

1 It is generally assumed that Part I of *King Henry IV* was written in 1596 or 1597, immediately or soon after the completion of King Richard II, and Part II in 1597 or 1598. *King Henry V* must have been completed shortly before or some time during 1599. See H. Spencer (1940).

2 *King Henry IV*, Part I, Act 1, Sc. 2.

3 See Bradley (1934), whose censure of Shakespeare is moderate compared to that of Hazlitt (1848).

4 For the legend of Prince Hal see especially Kabel (1936, pp. 363–416).

5 See Ax (1912).

6 That the repetition of one theme in various configurations indicates its central position was pointed out by Jekels (1933).

7 *King Henry IV*, Part I, Act 1, Sc. 1.

8 The idea of the travestied interview itself is borrowed from *The Famous Victories of Henry the Fifth*. There the Prince and his companions enact the Prince's subsequent interview with the Chiefjustice.

9 This point was made by Alexander (1933), and by Empson (1935, p. 43).

10 Ernest Jones (1911, 1949) speaks in a similar connection of decomposition.

11 *King Henry IV*, Part II, Act IV, Sc. 5.

12 The very crown that literally he had taken from Richard II. See *Richard II*, Act IV, Sc. 1.

13 *King Henry IV*, Part II, Act IV, Sc. 5.

14 *King Henry V*, Act IV, Sc. 1.

15 One might conjecture that Shakespeare preferred not to refer to the personal relationship between Prince Hal and King Richard since he needed a more mature Prince, not a boy of twelve.

16 *King Richard II*, Act V, Sc. 3.

[17] Only once Henry V states openly his disapproval of his father's actions, and then in a highly restrained fashion. When wooing, somewhat abruptly, Katherine of France he says
". . . I dare not swear thou lovest me; yet my blood begins to flatter me that thou dost, notwithstanding the poor and untempering effect of my visage. *Now beshrew my father's ambition! He was thinking of civil wars when he got me. . . .*" (Italics added.)

[18] York himself had plotted against Richard II and seeks his son's punishment out of a displaced feeling of guilt. Some of the complexities of this relationship were elucidated by Taylor (1927).

[19] *King Henry IV*, Part I, Act II, Sc. 4.

[20] *King Henry V*, Act IV, Sc. 1.

[21] Canterbury says of the newly enthroned Henry V (Act I, Sc. 1.):

Hear him but reason in divinity
And, all admiring, with an inward wish
You would desire the King were made a prelate.

[22] *King Henry V*, Act IV, Sc. 1.

[23] A somewhat similar analysis of this passage has been given by Traversi (1941), who in a remarkable essay stresses the importance of "cool reasoning" and "self-domination" in the King's character.

[24] *King Henry V*, Act I, Sc. 2.

[25] Traversi (1941) notes that when the King presents his ultimatum to Harfleur his passion rises, and that in accepting the surrender he regains self-control.

[26] *King Henry V*, Act IV, Sc. 3.

[27] The son's superiority over the father occurs also in other connections in the trilogy. Hotspur is superior to both Worcester and Northumberland and Aumerle is superior to his father, York, who first betrays King Richard before he betrays his own son.

[28] See Trilling's excellent essay, *Freud and Literature* (1947), or Knights' essay, *Prince Hamlet* (1946).

[29] See Sharpe (1946).

[30] This procedure was initiated in 1900 by a remark of Freud who envisaged the possibility that Shakespeare's choice of Hamlet as a topic and the treatment of the conflict might have to do with the death of Shakespeare's father and his son Hamnet.

13

Shakespearean Tragedy: A Christian Approach

ROY W. BATTENHOUSE

The question of how Christian Shakespeare's outlook is has pro-
duced a controversy which is being waged as vigorously as any
other critical battle now going on; from the intensity of the dis-
putation, one might infer that the stakes are somewhat higher
than in other academic debates. Interestingly enough, the ques-
tion is a product of the twentieth century. Those who see Shake-
speare as fundamentally a Christian often appeal to the Chris-
tianity of his age; but the historical argument is a two-edged
blade, and opponents of the Christian position can point to a
widespread skepticism in Shakespeare's own day in which they
argue he demonstrably participated and which adumbrates cur-
rents and habits of thought equally characteristic of our own day.
Responsible critics on both sides of this debate have in common
a concern for the truth. Moreover, they share an attitude which
as much as anything else has kept Shakespeare's work alive and
indispensable since the publication of the First Folio in 1623:
the belief that the plays constitute a complex and important
statement about the meaning of life. Professor Roy W. Batten-
house of Indiana University has devoted his life to the study of
Renaissance English literature and of Christian thought; charac-
teristic among his many publications are a learned and provoca-
tive study of Marlowe's Tamburlaine *and* A Companion to the
Study of St. Augustine, *and he has written Christian interpreta-*
tions of individual plays by Shakespeare as well as the more
general essay reprinted here.

In recent years a turning to Christian sources for perspective in reading Shakespeare has been developing markedly. Students of medieval thought, whether historical critics or followers of the so-called New Criticism, seem to be converging attention on patterns of Christian metaphysics and idiom imbedded in Shakespeare's logic and language. It has been argued, for example, that a profound Christian metaphysic is at work in Shakespeare's vision of justice;[1] that his whole theory of comedy is implicitly medieval in contrast to the neoclassical theory of his major contemporaries,[2] that several of the late comedies are parables of Christian doctrine,[3] that various of the major tragedies depend on the light of a Christian world-order for their delineation of the action,[4] and that Shakespeare's doctrine of love as set forth in his nondramatic *The Phoenix and the Turtle* mystically describes a love based on the analogy of the Persons of the Trinity.[5] So far these studies have been piecemeal in application, leaving much unexplored terrain and a good many unfinished edges. But together they reinforce the pertinence of the perspective they employ. The Christian perspective, moreover, being grounded initially in history and ritual rather than first of all in philosophy, is proving unusually congenial to our contemporary interest in anthropology on the one hand and the language of symbolism on the other. "Shakespeare's world," writes S. L. Bethell, "is the world of folk legend more profoundly understood—a development, in fact, of medieval Christianity"; and he goes on to point out that folk legend lies "beyond the neat categories of psychological motivation, in a world of signs and portents" in which the supernatural plays a controlling role.[6]

Critics such as Bethell are much indebted, of course, to the various books of G. Wilson Knight, who was the first to view drama as an expanded metaphor and to read Shakespeare in terms of a logic of symbol-patterns. Knight's own readings have been frequently brilliant. At other times his intuitionalism, while eclectically Christian, has seemed to lack discipline. Yet it is under his stimulus that studies in Shakespeare's imagery have taken hold and progressed beyond the techniques of counting and cataloguing to a search for thematic patterns as carriers of unrationalized yet logically shaped meanings. Knight is at his most challenging when he asserts that "each of Shakespeare's tragic heroes is a miniature Christ"; or, again, that since the Christian Mass is "at once a consummation and transcending of pagan ritual," the unique act of the Christian sacrifice "can, if we like, be felt as central" to the world of Shakespearean tragedy.[7] The danger I sense in a phrase such as "miniature Christ" is that the discontinuity of ethical dimension between pagan and Christian ritual, or between the tragic man's self-sacrifice and Christ's, may be blurred. Would not "miniature Adam" be a better phrase—especially if we add that Adam is related to Christ by inverse analogy, even as the Old Adam is related to the New Adam? Let us grant the insight of the Cambridge anthropologists that tragedy is related to ritual sacrifice; yet is not tragedy associated with a scapegoat-sacrifice, whereas the Mass substitutes for the scapegoat the lamb of God? If so, the Mass is a transfigured "fulfillment" of the tragedy, related to tragedy as type is related to antitype—by analogy but across a gulf of deadly irony. Or, to put the matter another way, the Mass is related to tragedy as Oblation is related to holocaust, both being a kind of pyre—as T. S. Eliot has so memorably written in *Little Gidding:*

> *The only hope, or else despair*
> *Lies in the choice of pyre or pyre—*
> *To be redeemed from fire by fire.*

For the fire of *cupiditas* which leads to destructive death (tragedy) is the antitype of the fire of *caritas* which leads to rebirth (comedy). They are analogous, but the transcendence of the latter may be said to "continue" the former by way of discontinuity: it fulfills love of self by recapitulating it under a higher principle. In this way tragedy can also prefigure comedy as its counterpart.

More recently it has been suggested by J. A. Bryant that any segment of story can be "placed" in relation to Christian story, finding there a center for the meaning of the located segment. He believes Shakespeare knew this—as, of course, Dante knew it and raised his *Divine Comedy* on this premise.

Fundamentally Shakespeare's plays are explorations of mythic fragments, whereby the movement of the fable at hand, whether from English history, Roman history, Italian novella, or English fabliau, is revealed as participating by analogy in an action which, from the poet's point of view, is Christian, divine, and eternal. *The Winter's Tale* is a case in point.[8]

This is a promising suggestion, worth pursuing. However, I should think we might expect *The Winter's Tale,* since it is a comedy or at least a tragicomedy, to carry an analogue somewhat differently placed from that of a play which is a tragedy principally. If the divine action of providence may be said to have in history its obverse and reverse turnings, its dispensations of death through the Old Adam and of life through the New, then tragedy might be said to be a segment of story related focally to the first of these two aspects.

There is space in the present essay only for trying out very briefly the kind of reading I believe this perspective can yield if elaborated. My efforts at illustration will necessarily be partial and tentative. I would suggest that in general Shakespeare's tragedies rehearse various segments of the Old Adam analogue. The segments can vary, according as particular historic cultures furnish us particular epochs in the analogue. But in each tragedy the hero of the action inclines toward some form of inordinate self-interest, an idolatry of some aspect of himself, and accordingly spends himself in destructive passion which ends in his own spiritual death, often concurrent with physical death. This is the essential tragic cycle, though Lear must represent somehow tragedy's extreme verge—an Old Adam in his old age, so to speak, who goes so far into and through death as to dream at the end of being taken "out of the grave" and beginning another life in a new order.

Lear's story seems to define an epoch in primitive paganism analogous to late Old Testament experience. That is, it is the tragedy of a trial-of-love adulterated by self-seeking, which betrays king and kingdom alike into self-division, with consequent alienations of affection and exiles of various kinds. At the same time the disastrous consequences of the king-father's self-centered love call forth a redemptive counteraction, stemming from his disinherited child. The kingdom's "saving remnant" is figured in

Cordelia, the one righteous shoot of the family stock, who, beginning with a Mosaic devotion to natural justice, develops into the gracious suffering servant of Isaiah and Jeremiah. Through her a divine comedy is progressively prepared for Lear and offered to him in foretaste by the end of Shakespeare's play. But first Lear's willful self must decompose (like Jonah's) in a whirlpool of thwarted endeavor, and the tragedy is a rehearsal of this discomposure. The fall is from willfulness to resignation, aided by self-mockery. Then to this wasteland of the self comes a visitation as by miracle, and Lear can depart in peace (like old Simeon of Luke 2), having caught a glimpse of the child who is to enlighten the Gentiles. This experience marks tragedy's untmost limit, at the very gates of comedy.

Or another way of viewing the logic of *Lear* would be to say that its hero is analogous to the prodigal son. He wastes his portion on harlots (which Goneril and Regan literally are in the play) and riotous living, until he is driven to eating husks with swine (as Lear does in feeding on empty memories in his hovel on the heath). As this prodigal begins to come to himself and look homeward, the father who comes out to meet and embrace him is, paradoxically, a daughter, Cordelia, who asks, "And wast thou fain, poor father, To hovel thee with swine" (IV.vii) and who says, "O dear father, It is thy business that I go about" (IV.iv). The latter statement allies her with the wise child of Luke 2:49, a status to which she has arrived after beginning the play with only a Mosaic bond of rational justice. Having begun with an initial attitude like that of the older brother in the prodigal son story, she has grown into the father of that story. Essentially, I suggest, her spiritual evolution is like that of the "younger" branch of the Bible's Old Adam (the branch whose mystical history unfolds from Abel to the child Jesus), providing at last a hinted redemption for the "abused nature" of Old Adam. In other words, *Lear* is an analogue of the Bible's story of mankind's journey toward revelation to a point as far as that journey can go short of the emergence of an adult New Adam.

Troilus and Cressida, by contrast, is a shorter segment. Its action carries us no further than a rehearsal of the logic of "vanity" spoken of in *Ecclesiastes*, culminating in evil days which have no pleasure in them. The golden bowl is broken and mourners go about the streets, as the curtain falls on Troy. The only comedy in this play is in the action of uncle Pandarus and his Greek complement Thersites; and their comic action is less a counteraction to the tragedy than a corroborative one, serving both to elicit and to scoff at the tragic action. Comedy here is related to the tragedy as a doubling of it rather than as a reversing of it. The comedy takes the form either of comedy-of-intrigue (typically Latin) or of satire (typically Greek); it is not romance comedy. Pandarus and Thersites are thus a saving-remnant only in the negative sense of dissolving by their cynicism of love-and-reason the hyphenated community of rationalism-and-chivalry which constitutes their civilization. A civilization whose official religion was humanism, a worship of man-made projections of reason and passion as if these were life's final order, directed its most characteristic action to winning or defending a supposed "immutability" of nature, only to find itself vanquished by mutability. Pandarus and Thersites are advance agents of this conclusion. All the characters in *Troilus and Cressida,* and especially its hero and heroine, come to rest in the vanity of human wishes.

Othello comes to an end in the suicide of its hero. This act exactly fulfills the merciless justice which has been Othello's trademark throughout the play. Toward flesh and blood he has no pity when an ideal of moral deserving is to be served. From the outset this has been so. When first he meets his own emotionally upset father-in-law, he shows him no pity or gratitude for past favors. Others with even closer bonds to Othello next come under his righteous indignation—Cassio for being tipsy, Desdemona for being forgetful—and finally his own flesh. He slays himself to vindicate his own sense of rectitude, which has been his particular idol since the play began. We are made aware of this idol in the first scene in which Othello appears, when he refers to "my perfect soul." His is a serene self-righteousness. By what analogue has Shakespeare patterned Othello's destiny? I have several to suggest, all of them perhaps cohering in the concept of "base Judean" (the F[1] reading of V.ii.347).

Let us look at the very center of Othello's first scene on stage. It is night, and Brabantio has come with armed men to seize

Othello. Othello says, "Put up your bright swords, for the dew will rust them," and adds a word of rebuke to Brabantio. Recall now, for a moment, Christ at Gethsemane and his words to Peter in John 18: "Put up your sword into the sheath; the cup which the Father hath given me, shall I not drink it?" The two scenes have a strange affinity, as if Othello were revealing to us a grotesque version of the biblical Christ: master of the night by scorn and rebuke instead of by humility and counsel. Another analogue is suggested in Act III, scene iii, when Desdemona, like Veronica of Christian legend, would soothe her lord's anguished face with a handkerchief. Othello brushes her off and the handkerchief is dropped and lost. Thus the episode is both like and unlike the Christian legend, a kind of antitype of it. Still another analogue, this time to Job, is apparent in Act IV, scene ii. Othello protests he could have had patience, had it pleased Heaven "To try me with affliction" and "all kinds of sores," but that he cannot bear to be discarded from "where I have garnered up my heart." But what an ironical version of Job we have here: Othello is suffering no sores other than of his own making; he is not disproving Satan's cynicism but getting his whole vision of life from a Satan-like Iago; he has garnered up his heart not in a trust in God's righteousness but in his own righteousness substituting as god. It is to this substitute god that Othello seems to cry out Job's celebrated words: "Though he slay me, yet will I trust him." Thus we have, as in the two examples above, an upside-down parallel of Christian story.

An analogue of another kind, however, comes at the play's end. Othello's words, "I kissed thee ere I killed thee," bring to mind Judas, as does also Othello's remorseful cry that "like the base Judean" he has thrown "a pearl away/Richer than all his tribe." Here we have a true parallel. Judas was the Judean who threw away the pearl-of-great-price (charity or Christ), and then committed suicide. Judas was the one disciple who was covetous and lacked charity.[9] He seems to have shared the idealism of the Pharisees for a religion of moral code rather than of forgiveness, for it was to these high priests of exterior righteousness that he betrayed Christ. Compare Othello's exterior righteousness, his confidence in his own "perfect soul," his inability to think of

Heaven as forgiving (it is "yon marble heaven"), the oath he
swears "by the worth of man's eternal soul," and the prayer he
addressed to this soul of his (like the Pharisee praying to himself
in Luke 18): "It is the cause, it is the cause, my soul." For this
"cause," Othello must "Put out the light, and then put out the
light," enacting unwittingly a kind of *tenebrae* service. No wonder
Othello slays himself at the end: he has had no good other than
his own soul or conscience, which is unable to forgive itself. So
despair leads to suicide. Is it true that he has "loved not wisely
but too well"? Yes; but what he has loved too well is his own will
and judgment. Augustine would call such a love a self-pleasing
love (*cupiditas*), whose final heroism (as in Cato) is suicide, a
violence against self in order to please the self-centered will. It
is a pagan "sacrifice"—related to Christian sacrifice in the way in
which Dante's bleeding wood-of-the-suicides is related to the
sacred wood of Calvary, by disjunctive analogy.

Finally, let us glance at a much earlier play of suicide, *Romeo
and Juliet*. A recent editor of this play, after debating whether the
lovers are "in any way responsible for their doom," concludes that
it is "not part of the basic design" that we should regard their
fate "as directly caused, even partly, by their own character
flaws." He believes there is "nothing we can hold against" Romeo,
unless we insist on "the (admitted) validity of moral conceptions
that have no meaning for Shakespeare in this play." How can we
blame Romeo, he asks, for killing himself on believing Juliet
dead, "since he has, from his first view of her, regarded her as his
whole life"? [10]

But perhaps this critic's own final clause can help us to an answer. Romeo does indeed imagine Juliet as his "whole life": he
imagines her as the light of his Heaven. Her lips, he says, bestow
an "immortal blessing" (as Helen's do for Faustus in Marlowe's
tragedy). To Romeo in the dark orchard, Juliet's beauty is his
"sun" in the East. To Romeo at the tomb, it is a "lanthorn" which
makes that vault a feast of light. Such language is glorious poetry;
but does it not imply an idolatry of the shadow-beauty of the
creature and thus an inordinate love? [11] In Sonnet 130, Shakespeare says, "My mistress' eyes are nothing like the sun," and she
is not a goddess. But in Romeo we have a lover whose mistress

is imagined as hardly walking the ground at all; she is a "bright angel" ministering to Romeo's passion for transcendence. The drama, of course, does not call on us to "blame" Romeo for his passion but simply to see it in its tragic potentialities, as we follow with pity and fear [12] the fate which that passion involves. It leads to violence toward neighbor and self, which we as spectators can recognize as moral disorder. But the essential flaw is anterior, a religious disorder. For does not Romeo have his religious stars crossed or confused when he makes of Juliet his dayspring from on high? His final visit to the churchyard with crowbar to force open the "jaws" of death is an action whose very shape makes it an antitype of the Bible's Easter story.

Let us note that Romeo speaks of "the devout religion of mine eye" as early as I.ii.91; the phrase perhaps signalizes his tragic flaw. He worships the idol of his eye—first Rosaline, whom he idealizes in the conventional language of the Petrarchan lover, and then Juliet, whom he hails as "true beauty," a jewel "too rich for use, for earth too dear." In the darkness of night (and night for Shakespeare is generally symbolic of a spiritual condition), Juliet is imagined as a "saint" and Romeo himself as a "pilgrim" to her "holy shrine," where "sin is purged" by a "faith" which her lips seal in answer to his "prayer." [13] Later he swears his love "by yonder moon," while Juliet asks him to swear rather by his "gracious self, the god of my idolatry." In the broad daylight of Verona's streets this religion of Romeo's wavers when tested against another idol of his heart, his reputation, and he gives way to fire-eyed fury. Juliet too, for the moment, calls her idol a "fiend angelical" and "damned saint." But neither lover can endure the thought of banishment from the other. For Romeo, "Heaven is here where Juliet lives" and

There is no world without Verona's walls
But purgatory, torture, hell itself.

Note that the earthly city is thus equated with paradise.

Both lovers now evidence a passion for death, which temporarily the Friar restrains by his rational counsels and plans. But the passion breaks out again in Juliet when confronted by her father's edict. She is but distracted from her distraction by the Friar's expedient for a mock-death. When that evasion fails, her passion fulfills itself in final self-slaying. Romeo, likewise, when again he thinks Juliet lost, can dream only of self-immolation at her tomb. There he drinks his cup of poison in a kind of *figura* of the Christian Mass. But his "obsequies and true love's rite," as he calls it, are a dark figure indeed of the Christian rite; his is a Thursday night last-supper, but the obverse of the Bible's. For Romeo it climaxes a religion of love which has transcended reason, only to lose itself not in God-the-Creator but in the creature and the creature's dream of self-transcendence. It is a religion of *eros* devoid of *agape*, like that of Dido or Cleopatra. It is natural love's dark analogue of a supernatural love—what Augustine would call the earthly city's highest glory. It is fittingly memorialized at the end by erecting a "statute in pure gold" to Juliet and also to Romeo. Verona's religion-of-the-eye now has its canonized household gods, potent images for resolving civil feuds and achieving a peace based on what Augustine would call concord or mutual agreement. This is the earthly city's highest peace.

A natural providence has been at work for the city, humbling hate by laying a "scourge" on it. Yet it is part of the tragedy of the story that the Friar's special providence for the lovers has miscarried. In them "grace" has not outgrown "rude will," but instead rude will has turned upon itself to devour the plant in death. As a gardener of his parish he has failed. Why? His natural fear for earthly reputation and safety is partly responsible. Like a hireling shepherd he flees. But also responsible is his reliance on nature's resources only—on moral philosophy and the natural magic of a drug. These are poor substitutes for grace and charity. He would correct Romeo's love-sickness with disputation ("Let me dispute with thee of thy estate") accompanied by exhortations to play the man. He would help Juliet evade suffering by giving her a cup analogous to Calvary's vinegar sponge. He is a kindly brother, who would restrain evil by natural means but has lost the secret of St. Francis for curing it. In this respect Brother Lawrence is a poor apothecary, related by polarity to the Mantuan apothecary of the play. Romeo receives from the Friar advice to "love moderately," whereas Romeo's basic need is to learn to love ordinately, giving to each object of his love its proper due. Again, Romeo is counseled to be "grateful" for the "mercy" of Verona's prince, but the Friar himself neglects the way of gratitude to which he has been ordained by his Savior-prince. Thus the star-crossed authority of the state, and nothing higher, opens and closes the play. Symbolically, perhaps, we are told it is not yet Lammastide, the time of St. Peter's release from prison. This spiritual situation is the fate which conditions the play's tragedy.

Verona's spiritual situation is defined in other ways too. The play opens, for example, with a servant Sampson saying: "Gregory, on my word we'll not carry coals." And presently we see that this Sampson is a firebrand, given to harlotry and feuding—in this respect like the biblical Samson during his unregenerate days. He and Gregory are interested, they tell us, in "flesh," not "fish." And Gregory, of course, is a delightful parody of the ideal his name connotes in Christian lore ("servant of the servants of God"). Such an opening scene is comedy, of course; but Shakespeare's comic scenes have a way of being integral with the theme of the play in which they are used. If read analogically, is not the play full of various Samsons feuding or marrying with their Philistine neighbors? Another passage integral to the play's theme, we may believe, is the set speech on Queen Mab, which Shakespeare assigns Mercutio in Scene iv. Surely it is more than decorative. It serves to define Verona's "courtly" atmosphere by telling us the nature of the "fairy" who captivates human beings to the service of *eros* in its many forms. She is a "hag," the midwife of earthly dreams. She elicits these dreams by a touch of moonshine, spider web, and film. Further interpretation is provided by the Chorus to Act II, which describes Romeo as "bewitched by the charm of looks" and Juliet as a stealer of "love's sweet bait from fearful hooks." Thus guidance for our understanding the tragedy has been given partly by folklore associations and partly by biblical ones.

Scholars have long been aware that Shakespeare's knowledge of the Bible was unusually extensive. From his plays have been garnered, at various times, hundreds of allusions or verbal echoes to "at least 42 books of the Bible" [14] and a tabulation of the 35 biblical characters whom Shakespeare names. But criticism has been slow to assimilate these facts to an over-all perspective on the plays. While the explication of individual passages has profited, the relation of these to the total action of a given play has scarcely begun. And the delay is understandable when the difficulty is considered. To begin with, there is the notable fact that where biblical reference is overt and on the surface, it comes generally from speakers who, like Satan, are citing Scripture for their own purposes—characters such as Shylock, Falstaff, Richard III, or Richard II. Is Shakespeare then using Scripture merely decoratively? Biblical echoes obviously lend poetic power to the talk of a given character. But how do they bear a relation to his action, or to the action of the play as a whole?

What I have suggested in my last few pages is that biblical allusion is less significant than biblical analogue. Analogue may be operating when allusion is not evident; and even when allusion is evident, it may be more important as signaling a dimension by which to read the play than it is as providing "thought" for the character whose speech contains it. A character in tragedy is, among other things, a victim of dramatic irony: his words and actions can mean something else to the spectator than they do to the character himself. Part of the artist's task is to implant this irony. It can be done by shaping an Othello who unwittingly parodies Job and resembles Judas: a Lear who unwittingly enacts the role of a prodigal son; a Romeo who unconsciously blasphemes Christian rites of pilgrimage and adoration of saints. Though few readers may at first discern this irony, dependent as it is on a theological order of fact in the drama, it would seem to be implicit in the shape of the tragic action and potentially apprenhendable. In any case, when a perspective grounded in Christian lore is brought to bear on a Shakespearean tragedy, meanings of a kind I have tried to sketch can arise. Their validity must be judged finally by their over-all fruitfulness in revealing the shaped logic of Shakespeare's art. We have, so far, only some first-fruits to judge by, yet enough to challenge further investigation.

[1] M. D. H. Parker, *The Slave of Life* (London: Chatto and Windus, 1955).

[2] Nevill Coghill, "The Basis of Shakespearean Comedy," *Essays and Studies: 1950*, Vol. III of the New Series of Essays and Studies Collected for the English Association, G. Rostrevor Hamilton, ed. (London: John Murray, 1950), pp. 1–28.

[3] For example: R. W. Battenhouse, "*Measure for Measure* and Christian Doctrine of the Atonement," *PMLA*, LXI (1946), pp. 1029–1059; and J. A. Bryant, "Shakespeare's Allegory: The Winter's Tale," *The Sewanee Review*, LXIII (1955), pp. 202–240.

[4] For example: S. L. Bethell, *Shakespeare and the Popular Dramatic Tradition* (London: King and Staples, 1944), esp. pp. 53–61 and 80–83; Francis Fergusson, "*Macbeth* as the Imitation of an Action," *English Institute Essays: 1951* (New York: Columbia University Press, 1952), pp. 31–43; Paul N. Siegel, "The Damnation of Othello," *PMLA*, LXVIII (1953), pp. 1068–1078; and R. W. Battenhouse, "Hamlet's Apostrophe on Man," *PMLA*, LXVI (1951) p. 1073–1113; "Shakespeare and the Tragedy of Our Time," *Theology Today*, VIII (1952), pp. 518–534; "Shakespeare and the Concept of Original Sin," *The Drew Gateway*, XXIV (1954), pp. 78-90.

[5] J. V. Cunningham, " 'Essence' and the *Phoenix and Turtle*," *ELH*, XIX (1952), pp. 265–276.

[6] S. L. Bethell, *Shakespeare and the Popular Dramatic Tradition*, p. 82.

[7] G. Wilson Knight, *Principles of Shakespearian Production* (Baltimore: Penguin Books, 1949), pp. 166–167.

[8] J. A. Bryant, "Shakespeare's Allegory," p. 211.

[9] According to Matthew 26 and John 12, Judas makes his final decision to betray when he covets to have given to his keeping alone the "alabaster cruse" of ointment which Mary of Bethany poured out on Jesus. There may be an analogue in Othello's coveting to have as his alone the "monumental alabaster" of Desdemona's body (V.ii.).

[10] G. I. Duthie, Introduction to *Romeo and Juliet* (Cambridge, Eng.: The University Press, 1955), pp. xix-xxi.

11 Ulrici has remarked of the lovers: "they mar their excellence by making idols of each other, and fanatically sacrificing all things to this idolatry." Quoted in the Variorum *Romeo and Juliet*, H. H. Furness, ed., p. 452.

12 And with awareness of the play's humor too. When Mercutio jests at Romeo's love as "like a great natural that runs lolling up and down to hide his bauble in a hole," there may well be beyond the sexual innuendo another truth: Shakespeare may be suggesting that Romeo's love is that of the "natural man," which attains its greatness in a dedication to the grave. By Act V, Romeo is ready to "set up my everlasting rest" at the grave.

13 The religiousness of the love here is typical of the ritual of Courtly Love, which Denis de Rougemont in his *Love in the Western World* (New York: Harcourt, Brace & Co., 1940) has traced to gnostic heresy. Note, however, that Juliet attempts to resist Romeo's making a shrine of her, as if she sensed heresy in it. But as the Friar elsewhere says, "Women may fall when there's no strength in men." She follows Romeo into idolatry and suicide.

14 Richmond Noble, *Shakespeare's Biblical Knowledge and Use of the Book of Common Prayer* (London: SPCK, 1935), p. 20.

14

Some Limitations of a Christian Approach to Shakespeare

SYLVAN BARNET

Professor Barnet's article is not a specific rejoinder to that of Professor Battenhouse, which in fact it antedates, but it exemplifies the kind of answer the pro-Christian argument arouses. In both essays, it will be noted, the writers involve in their presentations G. Wilson Knight and other critics represented in Approaches to Shakespeare. *The fact is, as both Professors Battenhouse and Barnet recognize, that the dispute began with Bradley and that it has engaged New Critics, historical scholars, and virtually everyone else who has written on Shakespeare in the twentieth century. Readers interested in following up the debate might want to consult a recent entry,* Hippolyta's View: Some Christian Aspects of Shakespeare's Plays, *by J. A. Bryant, Jr. Sylvan Barnet is Chairman of the Department of English at Tufts University.*

Broadly speaking, we can distinguish in our intellectual history two sharply opposed attitudes toward death: either it is an end, or it marks a beginning. "A man that is in his wits," writes Plutarch, "cannot be ignorant that he is . . . born to this very end that he must die." And to this pagan quotation we may contrast the message of Christ: "Verily, verily, I say unto you, Except a corn of wheat fall into the ground and die, it abideth alone: but if it die, it bringeth forth much fruit."

Eminent English and American scholars have, in the last few decades, emphasized the close relation of the Middle Ages to the Renaissance. The approach has yielded profitable results, but, like many theories, it has been overworked, and too often secular Elizabethan writings are analyzed against a religious medieval background. Tragic drama, and Shakespeare's work especially, has suffered from a subtle spiritualizing, and plays about fallible men are frequently studied as *exempla* in the sermon to which, it is implied, the Elizabethan was continually exposed, even when he deserted his shop for a visit to the theaters on the Bankside.

Shakespeare as Christian appears most subtly and most persuasively in the pages of Messrs. E. M. W. Tillyard and G. Wilson Knight, but he is also to be found in numerous books and articles by less sophisticated scholars and critics who have adopted the method, and lopped off or stretched out the tragedies to fit the Procrustean bed. Thus a recent contribution to Shakespearean scholarship sees God's love and mercy manifest throughout the tragedies, and asserts that Shakespeare's tragic heroes live in the most friendly of universes, for they act "within the boundaries of a beneficent and divine order," where "the wheels of retribution move irrevocably, quickly, impartially, but compassionately." [1] Knight and Tillyard look more closely at the plays and pay more attention to the characters in the dramas, but they, too, supply their own backdrop against which they examine the *dramatis personae*. Shakespeare, it is argued, was a Christian, and his audience thought in Christian terms. Now as St. Paul realized, the heart of Christianity is the resurrection, for if Christ is not risen, faith is a foolish hope, and death is not succeeded by life. The Christian pattern moves from weakness to strength, from death to life, from sin to bliss. Its form is therefore comic, and Dante writes a *Commedia* because he knows that a tragedy begins quietly and ends in horror, while a comedy begins harshly and concludes happily. Though Dante himself spoke of his poem merely as a comedy, the Tenth Epistle makes clear his view that a "divine" poem cannot be constructed in a tragic form. But Knight and Tillyard insist that Shakespeare's plays are written in accordance with Christian thinking, and that the tragedies no less than the comedies are sermons and moralities. The plays are seen to follow the Christian movement from death or catastrophe to regeneration, and Shakespeare's late romances are invoked to show the total structure of his dramatic thought is one of happiness following close upon disaster, with death turning into life. Knight suggests that the romances embody not Shakespeare's response to the demands of a new audience and a new (for Shakespeare) theater, but the dramatist's final vision of life. Shakespeare adds, Knight says in *The Crown of Life* (p. 30), his Paradiso to his other works.

Tillyard's theory runs close to Knight's: whatever tragedy is, it ultimately embodies the idea of regeneration, and the tragic hero quits the world a better man for his sufferings. Tillyard insists that *King Lear* and *Othello* follow this principle, and that the plays depict "through the hero not only the destruction of an established way of life, but the birth of a new order. Othello in his final soliloquy is a man of a more capacious mind than the Othello who first meets us." [2] Elsewhere Tillyard suggests that *Hamlet* is not a tragedy because the idea of regeneration is not present. The social order has been purged of its evil, and the hero has suffered greatly, but because his sufferings do not enlighten him and reorganize his personality, the play is not tragic.[3] Putting aside the problem of whether or not Hamlet becomes an enlightened avenger who is unsullied by base motives, we may for a moment inquire into the source and validity of Tillyard's definition of tragedy. He is, of course, influenced by traditional Christian teaching, but also by the anthropology of the last sixty years. Drawing chiefly upon the work of Maud Bodkin, he finds that ritual frequently enacts the idea of renewal through destruction. Primitive rituals (at least according to Frazer and Jung) thus parallel Christian beliefs, and since the drama had its beginnings in the church, what could be more natural than to examine tragedy in the light of its origins and analogues? But to do so, however methodically, is to engage in the reductive fallacy and to see the product as containing no more than the source. Furthermore, the claims of early anthropologists that the study of primitive (usually defined as non-literate) drama illuminates the drama of urban societies, we now realize, is ill-founded, for primitive people have their own history, and are not merely representatives of earlier stages of our past. Nor can we regard Elizabethan tragedies as ritual dramas. Though a study of early Christian rites sheds some light on the first stages of English drama, tragedy must be recognized as qualitatively different from ritual, containing themes not necessarily identical with those of its antece-

dents. Elizabethan drama can be traced back to church ceremonies, but only in a crude sense may we say that liturgy flowered
into tragedy. We can trace most of the steps in the secularization
of drama, but not even by hindsight can we detect the embryo
of tragedy in medieval plays. Elizabethan tragedies, then, are not
necessarily related to ritual dramas of other cultures; nor are they
merely artistic refinements of an earlier native ceremony.

Christianity is optimistic in its assertion that with God all things
are possible; and it is consummated in man's union with the love
that moves the sun and other stars, or with the affirmation of the
boys in *The Brothers Karamazov*. The crucifixion itself, viewed
properly, is an occasion for happiness, and St. Anselm wrote that
he felt joy when he thought of the benefits it brought.[4] But where
is the note of rejoicing in the tragedies of the master dramatists?
The Greeks, though deprived of Christianity, knew a good deal
about tragedy, and they seem not to have required the theme of
regeneration. Aristotle is silent on the subject, and though
Aeschylus sometimes ends his plays on a note of life, Sophocles
and Euripides are, for the most part, content to end merely with
a chronic summary of the catastrophe. The "quiet ending" of
Greek tragedy has helped to give rise to the belief that tragedy
ends happily, but the theme of renewal is, in fact, absent from
most of Sophocles and Euripides. *Oedipus the King* concludes
grimly enough, and where it not for *Oedipus at Colonus,* written
twenty years later, few critics would see in the exiled stumbling
hero the suggestion of a purified man beginning a new life.
Euripides' plays are even more clearly lacking in the idea of
renewal. Medea leaves Corinth, and Jason—about whom we are
not greatly concerned—is left to live out a barren life until the
day when a rotted timber will strike him dead. *Hippolytus* concludes with only the promise of more horror: Artemis will destroy
a favorite of Aphrodite's, and Theseus lives on futilely to lament
his error.[5]

A survey of the work of Shakespeare's contemporaries (playwrights and critics) reveals not that the Elizabethans demanded
that the final catastrophe be alleviated, but, on the contrary, that
they conceived of a tragedy as a play which concluded with the
death of the hero. A. C. Bradley, who generally interpreted Shake-

speare's tragedies without reference to Christianity, saw hints of regeneration in them and concluded, influenced probably by Hegel, that a tragedy suggests, among other ideas, that "if we could see the whole, and the tragic facts in their true place in it, we should find them, not abolished, of course, but so transmuted that they had ceased to be strictly tragic." [6] In a footnote to this passage he introduced the problem of the relevance of Christianity to the plays. He concluded that the idea that the tragic facts are not irreducible facts would, if too dominant, "confuse and even destroy the tragic impression. So would the constant presence of Christian beliefs. The reader most attached to these beliefs holds them in temporary suspension while he is immersed in a Shakespearean tragedy." [7] Now, Christianity is dramatic, but it is not tragic, for, as historians from Raleigh to Hegel have realized, Christian teleology robs death of its sting. The numerous scholars who compare tragedies to Elizabethan sermons invariably cramp the meanings of the great plays, and end with a saved hero or a damned villain, rather than a tragic man. We pick up Henry Hitch Adams' provocatively titled book, *English Domestic or Homiletic Tragedy*, only to find that Mr. Adams is not talking about tragedy at all, but about morality plays which show us adulterous wives who repent and are thus ensured of a place in heaven. In these plays the endings are frankly optimistic, for the women go and sin no more, and heaven is achieved. But advocates of Christian tragedy (if there is such a genre) assert that Shakespeare's dramas, too, have their note of regeneration. *Lear* and *Othello*, these critics suggest, follow the Christian pattern and portray divine justice dispensing new life to the heroes. De Quincey was correct in maintaining that *Paradise Lost* does not require *Paradise Regained*, for it contains within itself the note of rebirth, and, like *Samson Agonistes*, ends with nothing for tears. Milton scholars have agreed with his views, yet they have suggested that *Samson* is no less tragic than its Greek models or Elizabethan tragedies. But the choral comment at the end of *Samson* announces that all is well and fair,[8] while a typical choral comment in Shakespeare's tragedies emphasizes the picture of destruction, and the irreparable ruin. Horatio summarizes the happenings at Elsinore:

> *So shall you hear*
> *Of carnal, bloody, and unnatural acts,*
> *Of accidental judgments, casual slaughters;*
> *Of deaths put on by cunning and forc'd cause,*
> *And, in this upshot, purposes mistook*
> *Fall'n on the inventors' heads.*

Death stands at the end of each of Shakespeare's tragedies, and in none of these plays is death the beginning of life, for "the rest is silence." The point will be discussed below with the examination of Christian interpretations of *Lear* and *Othello,* but a few more general observations must first be made.

Shakespeare's plays have been analyzed not merely in ethical terms, but in terms of Christian theology. The procedure is harmful because the business of tragedy, unlike that of a religious system, is not to explain the world, but to portray an aspect of it. Tragedy does not claim to offer the whole truth, nor does it require an act of faith to be believed. It sets forth a kind of experience which every man knows, presenting suffering and death as the hard facts which most men feel them to be. If it presented the death of a good man in medieval Christian terms, i.e., the release of a man from this realm to his eternal reward, it would cease to be tragic.

Shakespeare was a writer of, among other things, tragedies, and his tragedies show the material fall of heroes. In the great plays this fall is generally accompanied by an increased awareness of the nature of life, but such profit is gained at the expense of life. Shakespeare had an Anglican education,[9] and the ethics in the plays partake of Christian ethics, but they are not based, as Christain ethics in fact are, upon the eschatology of the Christian system. Shakespeare finds such virtues as love and honor good, and such vices as hatred and cheating bad, but he does not concern himself with the fortunes of his lovers and haters in the next world, nor does he insist that the meek shall inherit the earth. Furthermore, his tragic heroes are heroic. Princes, kings, and generals, they are duly concerned about their strength and reputation, and have little in common with the heroes of Christianity, with Peter the fisherman, with Mary Magdalene, or with Jesus, the Son of God who humbled Himself. Altering Alcuin, we might well ask, "*Quid enim Othello cum Christo?*" Shakespeare employs, of course, Christian imagery and terminology, and presents ecclesiastical personages. *Romeo and Juliet* has a Friar Laurence, and the heroine is, in the hero's eyes, a "bright angel." But the play is not a Christian drama (although it might have been, had Shakespeare followed his source more closely), for the supernatural power seems to be not God but Fate, and though the lovers are rash and, more important, suicides, we cannot believe that Shakespeare sends them in a sixth unwritten but clearly imagined act to the seventh circle of Dante's Inferno.

Christian sentiments abound in Shakespeare's dramas, especially in the history plays, but when Guy Boas says that Desdemona is meek, and implies that the meek are assured of a Christian heaven,[10] he is reconstructing the play and shaping it into something with which Shakespeare probably would have agreed but did not himself write. Othello exclaims that Desdemona's look

> *will hurl my soul from Heaven,*
> *And fiends will snatch at it,*

but the ending of the play announces that Othello was "great of heart," and the bodies of Desdemona and the Moor are "the tragic loading of this bed." Othello is a great man, but he performs an abominable deed. Aware of his crime, he enjoins the public to remember his honorable deeds (an action which, from a Christian point of view, might seem to show undue pride), and then kills himself. What is the moral? Is the play merely a parable acted out? Does Shakespeare draw a simple moral? Does he even wish us to draw one?

The scholars who wish to apply Christian thinking to Shakespeare's plays insist that the dramas do not end with the heroes' death, but should be acted out to Judgment Day and for eternity. Mr. Kenneth Myrick, for example, asserts that Othello is not damned, for the Moor is repentant and contrite.[11] Othello's suicide, of course, presents a problem to the Christian interpreter, but Mr. Myrick nevertheless concludes that the hero

and heroine will join hands in the realm of the blessed. Othello
has, however, despaired of grace, and such a state of mind would
preclude salvation, though Myrick suggests that his last words
imply "repentance" and "contrition." But, as Dante points out
(Inferno XXVII), one cannot will a sin and simultaneously repent
it, and Othello's suicide must be viewed as a deadly sin. However, for Myrick an Elizabethan audience would be sure that
Hamlet is saved, Claudius damned, Laertes and the Queen
granted an audience before God, yet it would not regard
Ophelia as damned, though a *felo-de-se,* and would willingly
overlook Othello's self-slaughter. The latest study of *Othello,*
G. R. Elliott's *Flaming Minister,* interprets the play as a tragedy
of that deadly Christian sin, pride, but similarly suggests that
Othello, despite his suicide—which would not, according to Mr.
Elliott, be of great importance to the audience—is a worthy
tragic hero and is saved at last. But it is perfectly obvious that
if the spectators have been conscious of the play as a morality,
and regard the characters as figures or representations of hell,
various vices, Christ, and so forth, they will not suddenly transpose their thinking to a secular level merely in order to allow the
hero to escape the flames of hell. The truth is that Shakespeare
does not treat suicide in a consistent Christian manner. In the
Roman plays it is clearly not a sin, and these dramas are not outside the pattern of Shakespearean tragedy. We do not distinguish
between Shakespeare's pre-Christian and Christian plays, nor can
we separate the secular from the religious ones.

The Everlasting, as Hamlet knew, had fix'd his canon 'gainst
self-slaughter, and though a few suicides were traditionally num-
bered among the saints, these were very special persons whose
deaths had been dictated by God and redounded to His glory.
Obviously Othello is entitled to no special dispensation, and the
sanguine view of Myrick and Elliott runs contrary to the Christian
meaning which they have superimposed upon the first four acts.
Even G. Wilson Knight's more modest statement, that "the Iago
spirit never envelopes him, masters him, disintegrates his soul,"
is suspect, if the rest of the play is as theological as he suggests.[12]
A whole-hearted commitment to a Christian interpretation of
Shakespeare must insist, I should suppose, that Othello is damned,

and Paul Siegel and S. L. Bethell elect to sacrifice esthetics to theology.[13] Mr. Bethell damns Othello for his suicide, but Mr. Siegel insists that his fate is sealed even before he kills himself. Othello attacks Desdemona and "loses his own claim to God's mercy . . . Emilia pounds on the locked door to tell Othello of the attempted assassination of Cassio, who, escaped from death, can help the truth be revealed, but it is indeed too late: Othello's soul is lost." The truth is finally revealed to the Moor as "he realizes that he is indeed damned" and "knows his irrevocable fate." [14] But why, we may ask, is his fate irrevocable, and how has he forfeited his claim to God's mercy? The possibility of repentance yet remains, and Siegel is so anxious to interpret the tragedy as "The Damnation of Othello" that he prematurely introduces the Black Cherubim.

Having damned Othello, Siegel goes on to announce that Roderigo, too, will go down to the fiends' abode, though Desdemona will have the company of Emilia in heaven as on earth.[15] Here is the modern scholarly version of Mary Cowden Clark's *Girlhood of Shakespeare's Heroines.* Not the youth, however, but the second life of the characters is sketched according to the critic's fancies. Siegel cites not only the Christian references in the play, but Christianizes the action, so Desdemona, "reminiscent of Christ" (p. 1068), and a paragon of Christian ethics (here Mr. Boas anticipated him by a quarter of a century), will be saved, and when Othello's married life is cut short, "he loses an earthly paradise" (p. 1069). The Moor is damned, and we have witnessed God's justice, "terrible and pitiful" (p. 1077). In a footnote on the same page Siegel alludes to "the theology depicted in Dante and inherited by the Elizabethans," but he has apparently forgotten that, under the tutelage of Vergil, Dante learned that human pity for the damned is presumptuous and incompatible with Divine Justice:

> *Ancor sei tu de li altri sciocchi?*
> *Qui vive la pietà quan'd è ben morta.*
> *Chi è più scellerato che colui*
> *Che al giudicio divin passion comporta?*
> *(Inferno XX, 27–30)*

Bethell, who has made valuable contributions to the study of Elizabethan dramaturgy, and a less valuable one to the study of imagery, also interprets the tragedies (to say nothing of the last plays) in terms of Christian theology, although he concedes that *King Lear* portrays a world prior to Christian revelation.[16] Such a concession, however, does not prevent him from writing, in a more recent study, that "Lear, after being bound upon his fiery wheel in this life, attaining humility and patience, . . . is fit for heaven." [17]

Four years earlier Oscar James Campbell published an article entitled "The Salvation of Lear," [18] wherein he suggested that the drama was "a sublime morality play" which might be understood by reference to medieval and Elizabethan sermons about the road from sin to salvation. Because Mr. Campbell also discusses Lear as the tragedy of an unstoical man, his article is somewhat less theologically oriented than its title indicates, but on the whole he sees the play as a Christian picture of regeneration: "The real redemption of Lear comes when he awakens from the delusions of his frenzied mind to discover Cordelia and her unselfish enduring love. The mere sight of her 'kills the great rage' in him, the unstoical emotional turmoil from which all his sins and sufferings have sprung. Now he is calmly receptive to the healing power of Christian love." [19] Just why her love is specifically Christian, in a play set in pre-Christian days, is not explained, and the assertion that unstoical emotion causes sins would be, I think, acceptable neither to Stoics (who did not talk about sin) nor to Christians (who talk much about sin but not about the evils of unstoical emotion). Campbell continues, however, and suggests that Cordelia, like Christ, is hanged so that mankind might be saved, but he fails to explain just how her death saves the king, and why it is necessary when her mere presence had (as Campbell says) already restored health of soul to the king. Lear's agonized ravings over the dead Cordelia are explained away as mere preludes to his "blessed discovery that Cordelia is not dead after all, that the breath of life still trembles on her lips. . . . In the joy of this discovery the old man's heart breaks in a spasm of ecstasy. For only to earthbound intelligence is Lear pathetically deceived in thinking poor Cordelia alive.

Those familiar with the pattern of the morality play realize that Lear has discovered in her unselfish God-like love the one companion who is willing to go with him through Death up to the throne of the Everlasting Judge." [20]

But Cordelia is very dead, and Lear's discovery is a mistake, not the poet's allegorical statement that love is eternal. The king dies joyfully, as Bradley pointed out, but his joy is the product of an error, and the audience feels not merely relief for his death but also horror for his ultimate false perception. George Orwell refused to grant that Lear is a whit better at the end of the play than at the beginning,[21] but if this is too bold a conclusion, we can at least say that although Lear learns humility through suffering, at the conclusion he is still capable of the misconceptions and "unstoical emotion" which are the stuff of tragedy.

The rigidly Christian interpretation forces a tragedy to fit ideas which Shakespeare doubtless held but did not dramatize. It is of value in explicating some puzzling lines and in emphasizing the moral tone pervading the plays. But it turns Othello into a villain (at least in Bethell's and Siegel's view), and it gives a comic ending to every tragedy, for it insists that the good are rewarded and the bad are punished. It shifts the focus from this world to the next, muting the conflict of the tragic hero. It assumes that if he acted wrongly, he could have acted rightly or at least repented, and so is justly damned. Such interpretations are not based on a total appreciation of the tragedy, but on individual lines which are related to a preconceived context. Shakespeare presents such full worlds that it is possible, with a little ingenuity and effort, to find in him almost any theory which the researcher wishes to discover. It is perhaps better to accept the immediate impressions yielded by the plays, and to see in these dramas not explicit eternal theological verities, portrayed on a canvas stretching from hell-mouth to heaven, but a picture of man's achievements and failures, hopes and fears, life and death.

[1] Carmen Rogers, "Heavenly Justice in the Tragedies of Shakespeare," *Studies in Shakespeare*, ed. Arthur D. Matthews and Clark M. Emery (Coral Gables, Florida, 1953), pp. 117, 125.

[2] *Shakespeare's Last Plays* (London, 1938), p. 16.

[3] *Shakespeare's Problem Plays* (London, 1950), pp. 12–17.

[4] See Theodore Spencer, *Death and Elizabethan Tragedy* (Cambridge, Mass., 1936), p. 19.

[5] About one-third of the extant Greek tragedies do not end with death, and Aristotle, of course, recognized that many conclude with an "averted catastrophe"; but he clearly indicated his preference for the unhappy ending, and in chapter 13 of the *Poetics* he characterized it as the most truly tragic.

[6] *Shakespearean Tragedy* (London, 1950), p. 324.

[7] Twenty years later I. A. Richards recorded the same idea, and, like Bradley, seems to echo an aspect of Coleridge's esthetic. "Tragedy is only possible to a mind which is for the moment agnostic or Manichean. The least touch of any theology which has a compensating Heaven to offer the tragic hero is fatal" (*Principles of Literary Criticism* [London, 1925], p. 246).

[8] The concluding lines of *Samson Agonistes* are, I think, a poor summary of the play. The drama is tragic, but the chorus tries, at the end, to reconcile the action with Christian thinking, and thus insists that the piece is not really tragic. Milton is giving his version of Aristotle's doctrine of purgation, but it is one thing to say that *we* are purged, and quite another to suggest that the hero's death is a victory. Miltonists, including Tillyard, have tried to counteract Milton's chorus by insisting that we remember not the words of comfort, but the fallen hero. The choral comment, however, is clearly intended as a general summary and interpretation of the action.

[9] See T. W. Baldwin, *William Shakspere's Petty School* (Urbana, 1943).

[10] "Shakespeare and Christianity," *Shakespeare Review*, I (1928), 91.

[11] "The Theme of Damnation in Shakespearean Tragedy," *SP*, XXXVIII (1941), 244.

[12] *The Wheel of Fire* (London, 1949), p. 118.

[13] Paul N. Siegel, "The Damnation of Othello," *PMLA*, LXVIII (1953), 1068–78; S. L. Bethell, "Shakespeare's Imagery: The Diabolic Images in *Othello*," *Shakespeare Survey 5*, ed. Allardyce Nicoll (Cambridge, 1952), pp. 62–80.

[14] "The Damnation of Othello," pp. 1071–72.

[15] *Ibid.*, pp. 1074–77.

[16] *Shakespeare and the Popular Dramatic Tradition* (London, 1944), p. 54. Myrick, too, exempts *Lear* from his view of Shakespearean tragedy as Christian drama, as though *Lear* were an entirely different sort of play. Bethel suggests that Christianity enters at the end of the play. "The gods are often called on, but God only once ('God's spies' [*Lear*, v. iii.17]) when Lear's purgatorial struggle is completed" (*Shakespeare*, p. 54). But T. M. Parrott, in "God's or gods' in *King Lear*, V. iii. 17," *SQ*, IV (1953), 427–32, demonstrates that the correct reading is "gods'."

[17] "Shakespeare's Imagery," p. 78.

[18] *ELH*, XV (1948), 93–109.

[19] *Ibid*, 106.

[20] *Ibid*, 107.

[21] "Lear, Tolstoy and the Fool," *Shooting an Elephant and Other Essays* (New York, 1950), pp. 32–52.

♪ *15* ♪

The Saturnalian Pattern

C. L. BARBER

Only in very recent years has Shakespearean comedy begun to elicit from its critics the sort of provocative analysis writers have been performing on the tragedies since Bradley. The reasons for this are perplexing. It may be that comedy, often less overtly didactic than tragedy, is less available to the kind of formulation which in Bradley's work provided so stimulating a point of departure; it may be that critics, who tend to be moralists, have not considered comedy so much worth their serious attention; or it may simply be that the loss of Aristotle's essay on comedy set back the study of the latter while providing a language in which to discuss tragedy. Whatever the reasons, the balance is now well on the way to being redressed. One thinks immediately of John Russell Brown's Shakespeare and His Comedies *(1957), of Northrop Frye's pioneering essay "The Argument of Comedy" in* English Institute Essays *(1948), of Bertrand Evans'* Shakespeare's Comedies *(1960), and perhaps above all of C. L. Barber's* Shakespeare's Festive Comedy *(1959), of which the essay that follows is the introductory chapter. Like Professor Frye, but also like such historians of an earlier generation as E. K. Chambers and F. M. Cornford, Professor Barber has found it fruitful to explore the origins and the continuing involvement of comedy in festivals and other social customs.* Shakespeare's Festive Comedy *illustrates the way in which anthropology, responsibly employed, can enrich the study of literature. C. L. Barber is Chairman of the English Department at Indiana University.*

Messenger. Your honour's players, hearing your amendment,
    Are come to play a pleasant comedy . . .

Beggar. . . . Is not a comonty a Christian gambold or a tumbling
   trick?
Lady. No, my good lord; it is more pleasing stuff.
Beggar. What, household stuff?
Lady. It is a kind of history.
Beggar. Well, we'll see it. Come, madam wife, sit by my side
   and let the world slip. We shall ne'er be younger.
                              —Induction to *The Taming of the Shrew*

Much comedy is festive—all comedy, if the word *festive* is pressed
far enough. But much of Shakespeare's comedy is festive in a
quite special way which distinguishes it from the art of most of his
contemporaries and successors. The part of his work which I shall
be dealing with in this book, the merry comedy written up to the
period of *Hamlet* and the problem plays, is of course enormously
rich and wide in range; each new play, each new scene, does
something fresh, explores new possibilities. But the whole body of
this happy comic art is distinguished by the use it makes of forms
for experience which can be termed saturnalian. Once Shakespeare finds his own distinctive style, he is more Aristophanic
than any other great English comic dramatist, despite the fact
that the accepted educated models and theories when he started
to write were Terentian and Plautine. The Old Comedy cast of
his work results from his participation in native saturnalian traditions of the popular theater and the popular holidays. Not that he
"wanted art"—including Terentian art. But he used the resources
of a sophisticated theater to express, in his idyllic comedies and
in his clowns' ironic misrule, the experience of moving to humorous understanding through saturnalian release. "Festive" is usually an adjective for an atmosphere, and the word describes the
atmosphere of Shakespeare's comedy from *Love's Labour's Lost*
and *A Midsummer Night's Dream* through *Henry IV* and *Twelfth
Night*. But in exploring this work, "festive" can also be a term for
structure. I shall be trying to describe structure to get at the way
this comedy organizes experience. The saturnalian pattern appears in many variations, all of which involve inversion, statement and counterstatement, and a basic movement which can be
summarized in the formula, through release to clarification.

So much of the action in this comedy is random when looked at as intrigue, so many of the persons are neutral when regarded as character, so much of the wit is inapplicable when assessed as satire, that critics too often have fallen back on mere exclamations about poetry and mood. The criticism of the nineteenth century and after was particularly helpless, concerned as it was chiefly with character and story and moral quality. Recent criticism, concerned in a variety of ways with structure, has had much more to say. No figure in the carpet is the carpet. There is in the pointing out of patterns something that is opposed to life and art, an ungraciousness which artists in particular feel and resent. Readers feel it too, even critics: for every new moment, every new line or touch, is a triumph of opportunism, something snatched in from life beyond expectation and made design beyond design. And yet the fact remains that it is as we see the design that we see design outdone and brought alive.

O body swayed to music, O brightening glance,
How can we know the dancer from the dance?

To get at the form and meaning of the plays, which is my first and last interest, I have been led into an exploration of the way the social form of Elizabethan holidays contributed to the dramatic form of festive comedy. To relate this drama to holiday has proved to be the most effective way to describe its character. And this historical interplay between social and artistic form has an interest of its own: we can see here, with more clarity of outline and detail than is usually possible, how art develops underlying configurations in the social life of a culture. The saturnalian pattern came to Shakespeare from many sources, both in social and artistic tradition. It appeared in the theatrical institution of clowning: the clown or Vice, when Shakespeare started to write, was a recognized anarchist who made aberration obvious by carrying release to absurd extremes. The cult of fools and folly, half social and half literary, embodied a similar polarization of experience. One could formulate the saturnalian pattern effectively by referring first to these traditions: Shakespeare's first completely masterful comic scenes were written for the clowns.[1] But the festival occasion provides the clearest paradigm. It can illuminate not only those comedies where Shakespeare drew largely and directly on holiday motifs, like *Love's Labour Lost, A Midsummer Night's Dream,* and *Twelfth Night,* but also plays where there is relatively little direct use of holiday, notably *As You Like It* and *Henry IV.*

We can get hold of the spirit of Elizabethan holidays because they had form. "Merry England" was merry chiefly by virtue of its community observances of periodic sports and feast days. Mirth took form in morris-dances, sword-dances, wassailings, mock ceremonies of summer kings and queens and of lords of misrule, mummings, disguisings, masques—and a bewildering variety of sports, games, shows, and pageants improvised on traditional models. Such pastimes were a regular part of the celebration of a marriage, of the village wassail or wake, of Candlemas, Shrove Tuesday, Hocktide, May Day, Whitsuntide, Midsummer Eve, Harvest-home, Halloween, and the twelve days of the Christmas season ending with Twelfth Night. Custom prescribed, more or less definitely, some ways of making merry at each occasion. The seasonal feasts were not, as now, rare curiosities to be observed by folklorists in remote villages, but landmarks framing the cycle of the year, observed with varying degrees of sophistication by most elements in the society. Shakespeare's casual references to the holidays always assume that his audience is entirely familiar with them:

> *As fit as ten groats is for the hand of an attorney . . . as a pancake for Shrove Tuesday, a morris for May Day, as the nail to his hole. . . .*[2]

A great many detailed connections between the holidays and the comedies will claim our attention later, but what is most important is the correspondence between the whole festive occasion and the whole comedy. The underlying movement of attitude and awareness is not adequately expressed by any one thing in the day or the play, but is the day, is the play. Here one cannot say how far analogies between social rituals and dramatic forms show an influence, and how far they reflect the fact that the holiday occasion and the comedy are parallel manifestations of the same pattern of culture, of a way that men can cope with their life.

THROUGH RELEASE TO CLARIFICATION

Release, in the idyllic comedies, is expressed by making the whole experience of the play like that of a revel.

> *Come, woo me, woo me! for now I am in a holiday humour, and like enough to consent.*
>
> *(A.Y.L. IV.i.68–69)*

Such holiday humor is often abetted by directly staging pastimes, dances, songs, masques, plays extempore, etc. But the fundamental method is to shape the loose narrative so that "events" put its persons in the position of festive celebrants: if they do not seek holiday it happens to them. A tyrant duke forces Rosalind into disguise; but her mock wooing with Orlando amounts to a Disguising, with carnival freedom from the decorum of her identity and her sex. The misrule of Sir Toby is represented as personal idiosyncrasy, but it follows the pattern of the Twelfth Night occasion; the flyting match of Benedict and Beatrice, while appropriate to their special characters, suggests the customs of Easter Smacks and Hocktide abuse between the sexes. Much of the poetry and wit, however it may be occasioned by events, works in the economy of the whole play to promote the effect of a merry occasion where Nature reigns.

F. M. Cornford, in *The Origins of Attic Comedy*,[3] suggested that invocation and abuse were the basic gestures of a nature worship behind Aristophanes' union of poetry and railing. The two gestures were still practiced in the "folly" of Elizabethan Maygame, harvest-home, or winter revel: invocation, for example, in the manifold spring garlanding customs, "gathering for Robin Hood"; abuse, in the customary license to flout and fleer at what on other days commanded respect. The same double way of achieving release appears in Shakespeare's festive plays. There the poetry about the pleasures of nature and the naturalness of pleasure serves to evoke beneficent natural impulses; and much of the wit, mocking the good housewife Fortune from her wheel, acts to free the spirit as does the ritual abuse of hostile spirits. A saturnalian attitude, assumed by a clear-cut gesture toward liberty, brings mirth, an accession of wanton vitality. In the terms of Freud's analysis of wit, the energy normally occupied in maintaining inhibition is freed for celebration. The holidays in actual observance were built around the enjoyment of the vital pleasure of moments when nature and society are hospitable to life. In the summer, there was love in out-of-door idleness; in the winter, within-door warmth and food and drink. But the celebrants also got something for nothing from festive liberty—the vitality normally locked up in awe and respect. E. K. Chambers found among the visitation articles of Archbishop Grindal for the year 1576 instructions that the bishops determine

> Whether the ministers and churchwardens have suffered any lord of misrule or summer lords and ladies, or any disguised persons, or others, in Christmas or at May games, or any morris-dancers, or at any other times, to come unreverently into the church or churchyard, and there to dance, or play any unseemly parts, with scoffs, jests, wanton gestures, or ribald talk. . . .[4]

Shakespeare's gay comedy is like Aristophanes' because its expression of life is shaped by the form of feeling of such saturnalian occasions as these. The traditional Christian culture within which such holidays were celebrated in the Renaissance of course gave a very different emphasis and perspective to Shakespeare's art. But Dicaeopolis, worsting pompous Lamachus in *The Acharnians* by invoking the tangible benefits of Bacchus and Aphrodite, acts the same festive part as Sir Toby baffling Malvolio's visitation by an appeal to cakes and ale.

The *clarification* achieved by the festive comedies is concomitant to the release they dramatize: a heightened awareness of the relation between man and "nature"—the nature celebrated on holiday. The process of translating festive experience into drama involved extending the sort of awareness traditionally associated with holiday, and also becoming conscious of holiday itself in a new way. The plays present a mockery of what is unnatural which gives scope and point to the sort of scoffs and jests shouted by dancers in the churchyard or in "the quaint mazes in the wanton green." And they include another, complementary mockery of what is merely natural, a humor which puts holiday in perspective with life as a whole.

The butts in the festive plays consistently exhibit their unnaturalness by being kill-joys. On an occasion "full of warm blood, of mirth," they are too preoccupied with perverse satisfactions like pride or greed to "let the world slip" and join the dance. Satirical comedy tends to deal with relations between social classes and aberrations in movements between them. Saturanalian comedy is satiric only incidentally; its clarification comes with movement between poles of restraint and release in everybody's experience. Figures like Malvolio and Shylock embody the sort of kill-joy qualities which the "disguised persons" would find in any of Grindal's curates who would not suffer them to enter the churchyard. Craven or inadequate people appear, by virtue of the festive orientation, as would-be revellers, comically inadequate to hear the chimes at midnight. Pleasure thus becomes the touchstone for judgment of what bars it or is incapable of it. And though in Shakespeare the judgment is usually responsible—valid we feel for everyday as well as holiday—it is the whirligig of impulse that tries the characters. Behind the laughter at the butts there is always a sense of solidarity about pleasure, a communion embracing the merrymakers in the play and the audience, who have gone on holiday in going to a comedy.

While perverse hostility to pleasure is a subject for aggressive festive abuse, highflown idealism is mocked too, by a benevolent ridicule which sees it as a not unnatural attempt to be more than natural. It is unfortunate that Shakespeare's gay plays have come to be known as "the romantic comedies," for they almost always establish a humorous perspective about the vein of hyperbole they borrow from Renaissance romances. Wishful absolutes about love's finality, cultivated without reserve in conventional Arcadia, are made fun of by suggesting that love is not a matter of life and death, but of springtime, the only pretty ring time. The lover's conviction that he will love "for ever and a day" is seen as an illusion born of heady feeling, a symptom of the festive moment:

Say "a day" without the "ever." No, no, Orlando! Men are April
when they woo, December when they wed. Maids are May when
they are maids, but the sky changes when they are wives.
                                        (A.Y.L. IV.i.146–150)

This sort of clarification about love, a recognition of the seasons',
of nature's part in man, need not qualify the intensity of feeling
in the festive comedies: Rosalind when she says these lines is riding the full tide of her passionate gaiety. Where the conventional
romances tried to express intensity by elaborating hyperbole according to a pretty, pseudo-theological system, the comedies express the power of love as a compelling rhythm in man and nature.
So the term "romantic comedies" is misleading. Shakespeare, to
be sure, does not always transform his romantic plot materials. In
the Claudio-Hero business in *Much Ado*, for example, the borrowed plot involved negative behavior on the basis of romantic
absolutes which was not changed to carry festive feeling. Normally, however, as in *Twelfth Night*, he radically alters the emphasis when he employs romantic materials. Events which in his
source control the mood, and are drawn out to exhibit extremity
of devotion, producing now pathos, now anxiety, now sentiment,
are felt on his stage, in the rhythm of stage time, as incidents controlled by a prevailing mood of revel. What was sentimental extremity becomes impulsive extravagance. And judgment, not committed to systematic wishful distortion, can observe with Touchstone how

We that are true lovers run into strange capers; but as all is
mortal in nature, so is all nature in love mortal in folly.
                                        (A.Y.L. II.iv.53–56)

To turn on passionate experience and identify it with the holiday
moment, as Rosalind does in insisting that the sky will change,
puts the moment in perspective with life as a whole. Holiday, for
the Elizabethan sensibility, implied a contrast with "everyday,"
when "brightness falls from the air." Occasions like May day and

the Winter Revels, with their cult of natural vitality, were maintained within a civilization whose daily view of life focused on the mortality implicit in vitality. The tolerant disillusion of Anglican or Catholic culture allowed nature to have its day. But the release of that one day was understood to be a temporary license, a "misrule" which implied rule, so that the acceptance of nature was qualified. Holiday affirmations in praise of folly were limited by the underlying assumption that the natural in man is only one part of him, the part that will fade.

"How that a life was but a flower" (*A.Y.L.* V.iii.29) was a two-sided theme: it was usually a gesture preceding "And therefore take the present time"; but it could also lead to the recognition that

> *so, from hour to hour, we ripe and ripe,*
> *And then, from hour to hour, we rot and rot.*
> *(A.Y.L. II.vii.26–27)*

The second emphasis was implicit in the first; which attitude toward nature predominated depended, not on alternative "philosophies," but on where you were within a rhythm. And because the rhythm is recognized in the comedies, sentimental falsification is not necessary in expressing the ripening moment. It is indeed the present mirth and laughter of the festive plays—the immediate experience they give of nature's beneficence—which reconciles feeling, without recourse to sentimentality or cynicism, to the clarification conveyed about nature's limitations.

SHAKESPEARE'S ROUTE TO FESTIVE COMEDY

In drawing parallels between holiday and Shakespeare's comedy, it has been hard to avoid talking as though Shakespeare were a primitive who began with nothing but festival custom and invented a comedy to express it. Actually, of course, he started work with theatrical and literary resources already highly developed. This tradition was complex, and included folk themes and conventions along with the practice of classically trained innovators like Lyly, Kyd, and Marlowe. Shakespeare, though perfectly aware of unsophisticated forms like the morality and the jig, from the outset wrote plays which presented a narrative in three dimensions. In comedy, he began with cultivated models—Plautus for *The Comedy of Errors* and literary romance for *Two Gentlemen of Verona;* he worked out a consistently festive pattern for his comedy only after these preliminary experiments.

In his third early comedy, *Love's Labour's Lost,* instead of dramatizing a borrowed plot, he built his slight story around an elegant aristocratic entertainment. In doing so he worked out the holiday sequence of release and clarification which comes into its own in *A Midsummer Night's Dream.* This more serious play, his first comic masterpiece, has a crucial place in his development. To make a dramatic epithalamium, he expressed with full imaginative resonance the experience of the traditional summer holidays. He thus found his way back to a native festival tradition remarkably similar to that behind Aristophanes at the start of the literary tradition of comedy.[5] And in expressing the native holiday, he was in a position to use all the resources of a sophisticated dramatic art. So perfect an expression and understanding of folk cult was only possible in the moment when it was still in the blood but no longer in the brain.

Shakespeare never made another play from pastimes in the same direct fashion. But the pattern of feeling and awareness which he derived from the holiday occasion in *A Midsummer Night's Dream* becomes the dominant mode of organization in subsequent comedies until the period of the problem plays. The relation between his festive comedy and naive folk games is amusingly reflected in the passage from *The Taming of The Shrew* which I have used as an epigraph. When the bemused tinker Sly is asked with mock ceremony whether he will hear a comedy to "frame your mind to mirth and merriment," his response reflects his ignorant notion that a comedy is some sort of holiday game—"a Christmas gambold or a tumbling trick." He is corrected with: "it is more pleasing stuff . . . a kind of history." Shakespeare is neither primitive nor primitivist; he enjoys making game of the inadequacy of Sly's folk notions of entertainment. But folk attitudes and motifs are still present, as a matter of course, in the dramatist's cultivated work, so that even Sly is not entirely off the mark about comedy. Though it is a kind of history, it is the kind that frames the mind to mirth. So it functions like a Christmas gambol. It often includes gambols, and even, in the case of *As You Like It,* a tumbling trick. Though Sly has never seen a comedy, his holiday mottoes show that he knows in what spirit to take it: "let the world slip"; "we shall ne'er be younger." Prince Hal, in his festive youth, "daff'd the world aside / And bid it pass" (*1 H.IV* V.i.96). Feste sings that "Youth's a stuff will not endure" (*Twel.* II.iii.53).

The part of Shakespeare's earliest work where his mature patterns of comedy first appear clearly is, as I have suggested, the clowning. Although he did not find an entirely satisfactory comic form for the whole play until *A Midsummer Night's Dream,* the clown's part is satisfactory from the outset. Here the theatrical conventions with which he started writing already provided a congenial saturnalian organization of experience, and Shakespeare at once began working out its larger implications. It was of course a practice, going back beyond *The Second Shepherd's Play,* for the clowns to present a burlesque version of actions performed seriously by their betters. Wagner's conjuring in *Dr. Faustus* is an obvious example. In the drama just before Shakespeare began writing, there are a great many parallels of this sort between the low comedy and the main action.[6] One suspects that they often resulted from the initiative of the clown performer; he was, as Sidney said, thrust in "by head and shoulders to play a part in majestical matters"—and the handiest part to play was a low take-off of what the high people were doing. Though Sidney objected that the performances had "neither decency nor discretion," such burlesque, when properly controlled, had an artistic logic which Shakespeare was quick to develop.

At the simplest level, the clowns were foils, as one of the aristocrats remarks about the clown's show in *Love's Labour's Lost:*

> *'tis some policy*
> *To have one show worse than the King's and his company.*
> *(L.L.L. V.ii.513–514)*

But burlesque could also have a positive effect, as a vehicle for expressing aberrant impulse and thought. When the aberration was made relevant to the main action, clowning could provide both release for impulses which run counter to decency and decorum, and the clarification about limits which comes from going beyond the limit. Shakespeare used this movement from release to clarification with masterful control in clown episodes as early as 2 *Henry VI*. The scenes of the Jack Cade rebellion in that history are an astonishingly consistent expression of anarchy by clowning: the popular rising is presented throughout as a saturnalia, ignorantly undertaken in earnest; Cade's motto is: "then are we in order when we are most out of order" (IV.iii.199). In the early plays, the clown is usually represented as oblivious of what his burlesque implies. When he becomes the court fool, however, he can use his folly as a stalking horse, and his wit can express directly the function of his role as a dramatized commentary on the rest of the action.

In creating Falstaff, Shakespeare fused the clown's part with that of a festive celebrant, a Lord of Misrule, and worked out the saturnalian implications of both traditions more drastically and more complexly than anywhere else. If in the idyllic plays the humorous perspective can be described as looking past the reigning festive moment to the work-a-day world beyond, in 1 *Henry IV*, the relation of comic and serious action can be described by saying that holiday is balanced against everyday and the doomsday of battle. The comedy expresses impulses and awareness inhibited by the urgency and decorum of political life, so that the comic and serious strains are contrapuntal, each conveying the ironies limiting the other. Then in 2 *Henry IV* Shakespeare confronts the anarchic potentialities of misrule when it seeks to become not a holiday extravagance but an everyday racket.

It might be logical to start where Shakespeare started, by considering first the festive elements present in the imitative comedies and the early clowns and in the literary and theatrical traditions of comedy into which he entered as an apprentice. Instead, because Shakespeare's development followed the route I have sketched, I start with three chapters dealing with the Elizabethan tradition of holiday and with two examples of holiday shows, then enter Shakespeare's work at *Love's Labour's Lost*, where he first makes use of festivity in a large way. To begin with the apprenticeship would involve saying over again a great deal that has been said before in order to separate out the festive elements with which I am properly concerned. It is important to recognize, however, here at the outset, that the order of my discussion brings out the social origins of the festive mode of comedy at the expense of literary and theatrical origins. It would be possible to start with festive affinities of the comic plots Shakespeare found at hand. One could go on to notice how Shakespeare tends to bring out this potential in the way he shapes his early comedies. And one could say a great deal about the way he uses his early clowns to extrapolate the follies of their masters, notably about Launce's romance with his dog Crab as a burlesque of the extravagant romantic postures of the two gentlemen of Verona. Much of this "apprentice" work is wonderful. And it is wonderful what powers are in the comic machine itself, in the literary-theatrical resource for organizing experience which was there for the young Shakespeare to appropriate. But by looking first at the social resource of holiday customs, and then at the early masterpieces where he first fully uses this resource on the stage, we shall be able to bring into focus an influence from the life of his time which shaped his comic art profoundly.

The sort of interpretation I have proposed in outline here does not center on the way the comedies imitate characteristics of actual men and manners; but this neglect of the social observation in the plays does not imply that the way they handle social materials is unimportant. Comedy is not, obviously enough, the same thing as ritual; if it were, it would not perform its function. To express the underlying rhythm his comedy had in common with holiday, Shakespeare did not simply stage mummings; he found in the social life of his time the stuff for "a kind of history." We can see in the Saint George plays how cryptic and arbitrary action derived from ritual becomes when it is merely a fossil remnant. In a self-conscious culture, the heritage of cult is kept alive by art which makes it relevant as a mode of perception and expression. The artist gives the ritual pattern aesthetic actuality by discovering expressions of it in the fragmentary and incomplete gestures of daily life. He fulfills these gestures by making them moments in the complete action which is the art form. The form finds meaning in life.

This process of translation from social into artistic form has great historical as well as literary interest. Shakespeare's theater was taking over on a professional and everyday basis functions which until his time had largely been performed by amateurs on holiday. And he wrote at a moment when the educated part of society was modifying a ceremonial, ritualistic conception of human life to create a historical, psychological conception. His drama, indeed, was an important agency in this transformation: it provided a "theater" where the failures of ceremony could be looked at in a place apart and understood as history; it provided new ways of representing relations between language and action so as to express personality. In making drama out of rituals of state, Shakespeare makes clear their meaning as social and psychological conflict, as history. So too with the rituals of pleasure, of misrule, as against rule: his comedy presents holiday magic as imagination, games as expressive gestures. At high moments it brings into focus, as part of the play, the significance of the saturnalian form itself as a paradoxical human need, problem and resource.

¹ Miss Enid Welsford includes perceptive treatment of Shakespeare's fools in relation to tradition in her fine study, *The Fool: His Social and Literary History* (New York, n.d. [1935]). Professor Willard Farnham characterizes Shakespeare's grotesque or fool comedy in relation to Erasmus and More and the mediaeval feeling for man's natural imperfection in "The Mediaeval Comic Spirit in the English Renaissance," *Joseph Quincy Adams Memorial Studies*, ed. James G. McManaway *et al.* (Washington, D.C., 1948), pp. 429–39. The use of mediaeval elements for comic counterstatement is described in C. L. Barber, "The Use of Comedy in *As You Like It*," *PQ*, XXI (1942), 353–67.

² *All's W.* II.ii.22. Citations of Shakespeare are to *The Complete Works*, ed. George Lyman Kittredge (Boston, 1936). Abbreviations of titles follow the usage recommended by the *Shakespearean Quarterly*.

³ London, 1914.

⁴ *The Mediaeval Stage* (Oxford, 1903), I, 181, n. I.

⁵ Mr. Northrup Frye has formulated a similar view of Shakespeare's development in a brilliant, compressed summary of the whole tradition of literary comedy and Shakespeare's relation to it, "The Argument of Comedy," *English Institute Essays, 1948*, ed. D. A. Robertson, Jr. (New York, 1949).

⁶ William Empson discusses the effects achieved by such double plots in *English Pastoral Poetry* (New York, 1938; originally printed with the better title, *Some Versions of Pastoral*, London, 1935), pp. 27–86. I am much indebted to Mr. Empson's work: festive comedy, as I discuss it here, is a "version of pastoral."

16

Shakespeare's Prose

JONAS A. BARISH

Every essay up to this point in Approaches to Shakespeare *has been concerned, in one way or another, with the problem of meaning: of a passage in its context, of a whole play, or of all the plays. Even such essays as deal in detail with imagery and thus with Shakespeare's technique—and this is true as well of Caroline Spurgeon's and Wolfgang Clemen's books on Shakespeare's imagery—chiefly address the problem of ascertaining what a play says. Interestingly enough, though Shakespeare's own education was based in large part on the study of literary masterpieces, the meaning of those works, on which modern education spends so much time and energy, was pretty much taken for granted. Shakespeare's study of Ovid or Terence was primarily rhetorical; his teachers would have asked him not to point out an image cluster or formulate a theme, but to identify a rhetorical trope or analyze the structure of a phrase. Few would question the legitimacy or value of the kinds of criticism developed in recent decades, but all of us can profit from an increased awareness of and sensitivity to the sort of problem with which Shakespeare and educated members of his audience might have been most familiar. Several important rhetorical studies of Shakespeare have appeared in recent years. Some of them, like Sister Miriam Joseph's invaluable* Shakespeare's Use of the Arts of Language *(1947), are primarily concerned with the analysis of the playwright's rhetoric in the terms he would have known himself. Professor Barish's essay, which is excerpted from* Ben Jonson and the Language of Prose Comedy *(1960), is an equally valuable exploration of Shakespeare's prose style which profits by the*

*discoveries of modern students of prose. Jonas A. Barish teaches
at the University of California, Berkeley.*

Shakespeare starts with the highly specialized set of expressive devices worked out by Lyly, inflects them variously, fills
them with nuance, widens their range, and so finally transcends
them, but without departing from the structural principles on
which they are based. One tends not to notice the logicality of
Shakespeare's prose because it is managed with such virtuosity
as to seem as natural as breathing. But by his constant invention
of fresh logical formulas, his endless improvising of new patterns,
Shakespeare, if anything, carries logical syntax even further than
Lyly.

The term logicality, here, refers not merely to the use of syl-
logisms, and other formal schemes, though these are numerous
enough,[1] but to a stylistic habit that includes these and goes
deeper: the habit, first, of treating a piece of discourse as argument, of tracking effects back to causes, discovering consequences
from antecedents, elucidating premises, proposing hypotheses,
and the like; and second, more important, the habit of proceeding
disjunctively, of splitting every idea into its component elements
and then symmetrizing the elements so as to sharpen the sense
of division between them.

Shakespeare's early plays tinker inventively, but perhaps also
a bit facilely, with the kind of formal Euphuism in which pages
pick apart each other's language and match wits with their masters. It is in the great middle comedies, as Bond has shown (I,
150–154), that Euphuism has been assimilated into the marrow
of the language and reigns as the undisputed expressive principle. Somewhat less absolutely, it dominates the prose of the
Lancastrian histories, and it continues to supply the chief structural basis for the prose of the tragedies and late romances, while
gradually being absorbed and transformed into a style greater
than itself.

A general discussion of Shakespeare's prose being clearly out
of the question here,[2] the following pages will try to sketch out
a glossary of some of his logical tactics in order to indicate their
radical importance in his language. Examples from the tragedies

and late romances will be included to support the contention that the logicality, though it evolves, remains an essential stylistic principle even in the final phase.

Like Lodge, Shakespeare makes a heavy-duty particle of the conjunction "for"—the "cause-renderer," as Jonson calls it in his *English Grammar* (Herford and Simpson, VIII, 550). Examples are legion, and citation would be useless. One point, however, seems worth noting: despite the frequency of the word in Shakespeare—he probably uses it oftener than any other playwright of the period, Lodge included—it never comes to sound like a nervous tic, because Shakespeare, unlike Lodge, is not enslaved to it. It forms only one of a variety of logical hinges that by their constant interchange maintain the syntactic sequence. A few specimens of the logical linchpin "therefore" may be given; the following are all from *Much Ado about Nothing.*

> *There is no measure in the occasion that breeds, therefore the sadnesse is without limit.*[3] (L.121; I.iii.3–4)
>
> *I am trusted with a mussell, and enfranchised with a clog, therefore I haue decreed, not to sing in my cage.* (L.122; I.iii.34–36)
>
> *. . . marry once before he wonne it of mee, with false dice, therefore your Grace may well say I haue lost it.* (L.124; II.i.289–291)
>
> *I cannot be a man with wishing, therefore I will die a woman with grieuing.* (L.134; IV.i.324–326)
>
> *Foule words is but foule wind, and foule wind is but foule breath, and foule breath is noisome, therefore I will depart vnkist.*
> (L.138; V.ii.52–54)

Instances of the numerous substitutes for "therefore"—"hence," "ergo," "thus," "so," and the like—may be omitted, as may the occasional "because" or "the reason is" that doubles for "for."[4]

It is well to remember, when discussing such humdrum phenomena as the use of "for," "therefore," and conjunctions and correlatives, that they are not mere inert forms just because they are common.

The greatest obstacle to recognizing the expressive value of rhetorical devices is the fact that they recur. One notices that

Cicero uses a *litotes* or a *praeteritio* several times in a few pages, or so many hundreds of balances are counted in the *Ramblers* of Johnson. . . . The so-called "devices," really no more devices than a sentence is a device, express more special forms of meaning, not so common to thinking that they cannot be avoided, like the sentence, but common enough to reappear frequently in certain types of thinking and hence to characterize the thinking, or the style.[5]

What applies to "the so-called 'devices'" applies to sentence types and syntactic formulas. They are significant, indeed, in proportion to their frequency; if the following pages tax the patience of the reader, it is because one must demonstrate, if only in a limited fashion, that certain kinds of construction appear *often* in Shakespeare, often enough "to characterize the thinking, or the style."

The cause-and-effect relation that Shakespeare indicates rather formally with such conjunctions as "for" and "therefore" he may suggest more unobtrusively by such formulas as "so . . . that," where "so" indicates the way a thing is done and "that" describes its effect.

> *O she did so course o're my exteriors with such a greedy intention that the appetite of her eye, did seeme to scorch me vp like a burning-glasse.*   (*L.160; MW I.iii.72–75*)
>
> *Hee must fight singly to morrow with* Hector, *and is so prophetically proud of an heroicall cudgelling, that he raues in saying nothing.*   (*L.604; Troil. III.iii.248–249*)
>
> *For the Nobles receyue so to heart, the Banishment of that worthy* Coriolanus, *that they are in a ripe aptnesse, to take al power from the people, and to plucke from them their Tribunes for euer.*
>   (*L.637; Cor. IV.iii.20–26*)

A related strategy, suppressing the "so," foretells the effect one hopes will follow a given cause. The "that" here is roughly equivalent to "in order that":

> *Let vs sit and mocke the good housewife* Fortune *from her wheele, that her gifts may henceforth bee bestowed equally.*
>   (*L.204; AYL I.ii.34–36*)

> . . . *therefore I shall craue of you your leaue, that I may beare*
> *my euils alone.*   *(L.278; TN II.i.5–7)*
>
> *Why I haue often wisht my selfe poorer, that I might come*
> *neerer to you.*   *(L.697; Tim. I.ii.103–105)*
>
> *Wee will giue you sleepie Drinkes, that your Sences (vn-intelli-*
> *gent of our insufficience) may, though they cannot prayse vs, as*
> *little accuse vs.*   *(L.295; WT I.i.14–17)*

One may also reach a conclusion by way of a qualification,
first stating some real or imagined difficulty in a "though" clause,
then overriding it in the main clause.

> . . . *though honestie be no Puritan, yet it will doe no hurt* . . .
>   *(L.251; Alls W I.iii.97–98)*
>
> . . . *though you change your place, you neede not change your*
> *Trade.*   *(L.80; MM I.ii.110–111)*
>
> . . . *though patience be a tyred [mare], yet shee will plodde* . . .
>   *(L.427; HV I.ii.25–26)*
>
> *Though this be madnesse, / Yet there is Method in't.*
>   *(L.769; Ham. II.ii.208–209)*
>
> . . . *though the wisedome of Nature can reason it thus, and thus,*
> *yet Nature finds it selfe scourg'd by the sequent effects.*
>   *(L.794; Lear I.ii.113–115)*
>
> *Though I am not bookish, yet I can reade Waiting-Gentlewoman*
> *in the scape.*   *(L.306–307; WT III.iii.73–75)*
>
> *Though thou canst swim like a Ducke, thou art made like a*
> *Goose.*   *(L.28; Temp. II.ii.134–135)*

There is no reason why the "though" clause must precede the
main clause in such cases, but Shakespeare, with his penchant
for strongly marked disjunctions, usually makes it do so, and by
adding the antithetic particle "yet" at the head of the main clause,
he fences the two halves of the statement even more rigidly off
from each other.

One of the hallmarks, indeed, of a logical style is its taste for
disjunction. Needless to say, all language depends on disjunction,
on separating strips of words into intelligible units, and—to speak
not very paradoxically—every conjunction occurs at a point of

disjunction. "Sir Cranberry stalked his prey waited" does not become coherent discourse until some division is made between the two halves, either with a vocal pattern that we may represent by a semicolon ("Sir Cranberry stalked; his prey waited") or a comma ("Sir Cranberry stalked his prey, waited . . ."), or else with some word like "while," "but," or "and," which cuts apart the two elements at the same time that it establishes some kind of relation between them. What we find in Shakespeare and in writers like him is a tendency to insist on the points of disjunction, to hold up the two pieces of the sentence side by side, in full view, to symmetrize them and brandish them in their matched antagonism. "The dragon bellows if attacked" contains an unobtrusive disjunction marked by the "if." "If attacked, the dragon bellows" walls the two elements more firmly off from each other by making a heavier vocal suspension. A writer like Shakespeare will tend to prefer the second pattern, and in fact Shakespeare's prose is honeycombed with sentences of this type.

> . . . if a Trassel sing, he fals straight a capring, he will fence with his own shadow. If I should marry him, I should marry twentie husbands: if hee would despise me, I would forgiue him, for if he loue me to madnesse, I should neuer requite him.
> (L.183; Merch. I.iii.65–70)

> If you head, and hang all that offend that way but for ten yeare together; you'll be glad to giue out a Commission for more heads: if this law hold in Vienna ten yeare, ile rent the fairest house in it after three pence a Bay: if you liue to see this come to passe, say Pompey told you so. (L.84; MM II.i.251–257)

By placing the dependent clause before the major clause, Shakespeare achieves the maximum effect of climax, balance, and strong demarcation between the two halves. When the simple "if" formation is expanded by being doubled with its own antithesis ("If attacked, the dragon bellows; if ignored, he preens his scales"), we move into the domain of the highly disjunctive style, which pits each element rigidly against its opposite and matches it fiercely with its partner, dividing and binding in the same moment. "If thou beest a man, shew they selfe in thy like-

ness: If thou beest a diuell, take't as thou list" (L. 30; *Temp.*
III.ii.137–139); or, more elaborately:

> ... *if you pricke vs doe we not bleede? If you tickle vs, doe we
> not laugh? if you poison vs doe we not die? and if you wrong vs
> shall we not reuenge? if we are like you in the rest, we will
> resemble you in that. If a* Iew *wrong a* Christian, *what is his
> humility, reuenge? If a* Christian *wrong a* Iew, *what should his
> sufferance be by Christian example, why reuenge?*
>   (L.191; Merch. III.i.67–74)

A related discoupling mechanism, highly characteristic of
Shakespeare, is the "if . . . if not" formula. This stakes out logical
alternatives and specifies the possible consequences of each.

> *Ile go sleepe if I can: if I cannot, Ile raile against all the first
> borne of Egypt.*   (L.210; AYL II.v.62–63)
> *If it bee worth stooping for, there it lies, in your eye: if not, bee it
> his that findes it.*   (L.278; TN II.ii.15–17)
> ... *if your Father will do me any Honor, so: if not, let him kill
> the next* Percie *himselfe.*   (L.392; IHIV V.iv.143–145)
> *When thou has[t] leysure, say thy praiers: when thou hast none,
> remember thy Friends.*   (L.249; Alls W I.i.227–229)
> *If it be now, 'tis not to come: if it bee not to come, it will bee
> now: if it be not now; yet it will come . . .*
>   (L.788; Ham. V.ii.231–233)
> *If she will returne me my Iewels, I will giue ouer my Suit, and
> repent my vnlawfull solicitation. If not, assure your selfe, I will
> seeke satisfaction of you.*   (L.841; Oth. IV.ii.200–202)
> ... *if you will take it on you to assist him, it shall redeeme you
> from your Gyues: if not, you shall haue your full time of im-
> prisonment . . .*   (L.93; MM IV.ii.10–13)

It is worth noticing here, as with most of Shakespeare's logical
schemes, that though the pattern itself is highly formulaic, the
completion of it is anything but predictable. "Ile go sleepe if I
can" may prompt us to suspect an antithesis; "if I cannot" confirms the suspicion. But who could have foreseen the bizarre
outcome, "Ile raile against all the first borne of Egypt"? Unlike

Lyly, Shakespeare is never rigid. He achieves the maximum amount of syntactic lucidity without sacrificing his privilege of surprising us; he lures us into unexpected marshes or drops us into brambles with comical thud, or else conforms to expectation so generously and graciously that even this comes as a surprise.

Another way of splitting things into antithetic alternatives is to group them under opposed headings like "the one . . . the other." This frequently produces even more strict patterning than the "if . . . if not" scheme.

> . . . the one is too like an image and saies nothing, and the other too like my Ladies eldest sonne, euermore tatling.
>
> (L.122; Much Ado II.i.9–11)
>
> —Who ambles Time withal?
> —With a Priest that lacks Latine, and a rich man that hath not the Gowt: for the one sleepes easily because he cannot study, and the other liues merrily, because he feels no paine: the one lacking the burthen of leane and waistful Learning; the other knowing no burthen of heauie tedious penurie.
>
> (L.215; AYL III.ii.337–343)
>
> Out vpon thee knaue, doest thou put vpon mee at once both the office of God and the diuel: one brings thee in grace, and the other brings thee out.   (L.269; Alls W V.ii.51–54)
>
> Prethee peace: pay her the debt you owe her, and vnpay the villany you haue done her: the one you may do with sterling mony, & the other with currant repentance.
>
> (L.399; IIHIV II.i.129–132)
>
> You are mistaken: the one may be solde or giuen, or if there were wealth enough for the purchases, or merite for the guift. The other is not a thing for sale, and onely the guift of the Gods.
>
> (L.880; Cymb. I.iv.89–93)
>
> Shee had one Eye declin'd for the losse of her Husband, another eleuated, that the Oracle was fulfill'd.
>
> (L.319; WT V.ii.80–82)

Again one may notice the richness and variety that Shakespeare packs into his logical schemes, the colloquial sting of Beatrice's "euermore tatling" in contrast to the more matter-of-fact "like an image"; the complex crisscross between the ignorant priest and the gouty rich man in Rosalind's lecture, which ends by making them sound like twins; the concise pun on "sterling mony" and "currant repentance" with which the Lord Chief Justice concludes his judgment on Falstaff; the surprising and affecting Latinisms —"declin'd" and "eleuated"—that portray the mingle of feelings in Paulina. Far from lending itself to stiffness, as it does in Lyly's romances, logical syntax in Shakespeare produces the utmost freedom and flexibility, like a ground bass on which an infinite number of variations may be played.

Schematic pointers such as "the one . . . the other" may of course be replaced by the nouns or pronouns to which they refer:

Yet it had not beene amisse the rod had beene made, and the garland too, for the garland he might haue worne himselfe, and the rod hee might haue bestowed on you, who (as I take it) haue stolne his birds nest. (L.124; Much Ado II.ii.235–238)

For the boxe of th'eare that the Prince gaue you, he gaue it like a rude Prince, and you tooke it like a sensible Lord.
(L.397; IIHIV I.ii.217–219)

Now blesse thy selfe: thou met'st with things dying, I with things new borne. (L.307; WT III.iii.115–116)

Nor is there any reason why the two alternatives cannot be expanded to include a third:

I maruell what kin thou and thy daughters are, they'l haue me whipt for speaking true: thou'l haue me whipt for lying, and sometimes I am whipt for holding my peace.
(L. 796; Lear I.iv.200–203)

Less fully developed alternatives may be expressed by the formula "either X or Y":

. . . in the managing of quarrels you may see hee is wise, for either hee auoydes them with great discretion, or vndertakes them with a Christian-like feare.
(L.127; Much Ado II.iii.197–200)

If this vncouth Forrest yeeld any thing sauage, I wil either be food for it, or bring it for foode to thee.
(L.210; AYL II.vi.6–8)

*. . . there is eyther liquor in his pate, or mony in his purse, when
hee lookes so merrily.*   *(L.62; MW II.i.197–198)*

*. . . thou hauing made me Businesses, (which none (without
thee) can sufficiently manage) must either stay to execute them
thy selfe, or take away with thee the very seruices thou hast done.*
       (L.307; WT IV.ii.15–19)

For he does neither affect companies, / Nor is he fit for't indeed.
       (L. 697; Tim. I.ii.30–31)

And if one of the alternatives is asserted over the other, the
pattern may run, "not X but Y":

. . . the commendation is not in his witte, but in his villanie . . .
       (L.123; Much Ado II.i.146)

*. . . the yong Lion repents: Marry not in ashes and sacke-cloath,
but in new Silke, and old Sacke.*   *(L.397; IIHIV I.ii.220–222)*

*For the Gods know, I speake this in hunger for Bread, not in
thirst for Reuenge.*   *(L.617; Cor. I.i.24–25)*

Expressions of choice, where the speaker asserts a preference
for one thing over another, lend themselves naturally to antithetic
formulation. The commonest disjunctive strategy here is the
arrangement "rather X than Y."

*I had rather (forsooth) go before you like a man, then follow him
like a dwarfe.*   *(L.67; MW III.ii.5–6)*

*I had rather my brother die by the Law, then my sonne should be
vnlawfullie borne.*   *(L.90; MM III.i.194–195)*

I had rather be a Ticke in a Sheepe, then such a valiant ignorance.
       (L.604; Troil. III.iii.313–315)

*. . . I had rather had eleuen dye Nobly for their Countrey, then
one voluptuously surfet out of Action.*   *(L.620; Cor. I.iii.26–28)*

*You had rather be at a breakefast of Enemies, then a dinner of
Friends.*   *(L.697; Tim. I.ii.78–79)*

The antithetic halves, obviously, follow a variety of patterns.
They may observe strict parison ("breakefast of Enemies," "dinner
of Friends"), or exact antithesis without parison ("by the Law,"
"vnlawfullie"), or they may have no relation whatever outside

the pattern in which they are set ("a Ticke in a Sheepe," "such a valiant ignorance"). And the same is true of such expressions of preference, or comparative judgments, cast in the form "more X than Y":

> *You haue Witch-craft in your Lippes,* Kate: *there is more eloquence in a Sugar touch of them, then in the Tongues of the French Councell; and they should sooner perswade* Harry *of* England, *then a generall Petition of Monarchs.*
> *(L.448; HV V.ii.302–305)*

> *I will no more trust him when hee leeres, then I will a Serpent when he hisses.* *(L.610; Troil. V.i.95–97)*

> *The Swallow followes not Summer more willing, then we your Lordship.* *(L.705; Tim. III.vi.33–34)*

> *If my Sonne were my Husband, I should freelier reioyce in that absence wherein he wonne Honor, then in the embracements of his Bed, where he would shew most loue.* *(L.620; Cor. I.iii.2–6)*

> *Kings are no lesse vnhappy, their issue, not being gracious, then they are in loosing them, when they haue approued their Vertues.* *(L.308; WT IV.ii.30–32)*

Preference may be expressed more modestly, or with a tinge of irony, by disposing the antithetic choices under the formula "as . . . as."

> *I had as liefe they would put Rats-bane in my mouth, as offer to stoppe it with Security.* *(L.396; IIHIV I.ii.47–49)*

> *I had as lief haue the foppery of freedome, as the mortality of imprisonment.* *(L.81; MM I.ii.136–138)*

> *I had as liue haue a Reede that will doe me no seruice, as a Partizan I could not heaue.* *(L.858; Ant. II.vii.13–15)*

But the "as . . . as" disjunction may serve to affirm any kind of equivalence, literal or metaphoric:

> *It is as easie to count Atomies as to resolue the propositions of a Louer.* *(L.214; AYL III.ii.245–246)*

> *. . . they are as sicke that surfet with too much, as they that starue with nothing.* *(L.182; Merch. I.ii.6–7)*

> . . . *thou art as ful of enuy at his greatnes, as* Cerberus *is at*
> Proserpina's *beauty.*   (*L.594;* Troil. *II.i.36–37*)

> . . . *it is as dangerous to be aged in any kinde of course, as it is*
> *vertuous to be constant in any vndertaking.*
>   (*L.92;* MM *III.ii.237–239*)

A more emphatic equation results from the pattern "as X,
so Y," where "so" not merely insists on the identity between the
two elements, but insinuates as causal relation between them.

> . . . *as* Alexander *kild his friend* Clytus, *being in his Ales and his*
> *Cuppes; so also* Harry Monmouth *being in his right wittes, and*
> *his good iudgements, turn'd away the fat Knight with the great*
> *belly doublet.*   (*L.443;* HV *IV.vii.47–51*)

> . . . *but as all is mortall in nature, so is all nature in loue, mortall*
> *in folly.*   (*L.209;* AYL *II.iv.55–56*)

> . . . *but as she spit in his face, so she defide him.*
>   (*L.83;* MM *II.i.86*)

> *For, as it is a heart-breaking to see a handsome man loose-Wiu'd,*
> *so it is a deadly sorrow, to beholde a foule Knaue vncuckolded.*
>   (*L.894;* Ant. *I.ii.74–77*)

One may observe that in the first example here, Captain Fluel-
len's Welsh dialect does not obscure the logicality of his syntax,
just as, in the last example, Egyptian disorder and promiscuous
living are suggested in the highly logical analogy of Iras. And
so with virtually all the extracts so far cited. They are, at the
same time, precise logical mechanisms, and completely appropriate to their speakers. The logical mechanism itself is an
instrument that can be used in limitless ways. And there is hence
no special moment or purpose for which Shakespeare employs it;
rather, there are special moments and special purposes for which
he deliberately discards it.[6]

When the two matching elements are to be semantically com-
pounded rather than disjoined, Shakespeare still often contrives
to emphasize the juncture, and hence the opposition between
them, by some such device as the scheme "not only . . . but also."

. . . I shall not onely receiue this villanous wrong, but stand vnder
the adoption of abhominable termes, and by him that does mee
this wrong.   *(L.65; MW II.ii.307–310)*

. . . and the cure of it not onely saues your brother, but keepes
you from dishonor in doing it.   *(L.90; MM III.i.244–246)*

. . . then must we looke from his age, to receiue not alone the
imperfections of long ingraffed condition, but therewithall the
vnruly way-wardnesse, that infirme and cholericke yeares bring
with them.   *(L.793; Lear I.i.299–303)*

There is not onely disgrace and dishonor in that Monster, but an
infinite losse.   *(L.33; Temp. IV.i.209–210)*

But Shakespeare's fertility in the invention and use of disjunctive devices is almost limitless, and it would be as pointless as
as it would be vain to try to classify them all. If the reader's
patience is not quite exhausted, we may cite a few instances that
do not conform exactly to any of the categories so far discussed,
merely to illustrate the freedom with which he improvises.

O powerfull Loue, that in some respects makes a Beast a Man: in
som other, a Man a beast.   *(L.76; MW V.v.4–6)*

. . . where they feared the death, they haue borne life away;
and where they would bee safe, they perish.
                                        (L.438; HV IV.i.181–183)

What a merit were it in death to take this poore maid from the
world? what corruption in this life, that it will let this man liue?
                                        (L.90; MM III.i.240–242)

The Food that to him now is as lushious as Locusts, shalbe to him
shortly, as bitter as Coloquintida.   *(L.823; Oth. I.iii.354–356)*

Not so young Sir to loue a woman for singing, nor so old to dote
on her for any thing.   *(L.795; Lear I.iv.40–41)*

— He's a Lambe indeed, that baes like a Beare.
— Hee's a Beare indeede, that liues like a Lambe.
                                        (L.624; Cor. II.i.12–14)

The foregoing tabulation makes no claim to completeness; it is
intended only to be suggestive. (No mention has been made,
for example, of the parisonic series, a logical formation on which

Shakespeare relies throughout his career.) The cited extracts
have been chosen partly for their brevity, so as to isolate the
figures in question. But it goes without saying that Shakespeare
is as versatile in combining them as he is resourceful in unearthing
them in the first place. As we proceed from the simple schemes
described above, we encounter more complex sentence structures,
much less easy to classify, but often clearly reducible to com-
posites of the simple figures, and hence stamped with the same
logical clarity.

> 2. *Off.* 'Faith, there hath beene many great men that haue flat-
> ter'd the people, who ne're loued them; and there be many that
> they haue loued, they know not wherefore: so that if they loue
> they know not why, they hate vpon no better a ground. There-
> fore, for *Coriolanus* neyther to care whether they loue, or hate
> him, manifests the true knowledge he ha's in their disposition, and
> out of his Noble carelesnesse lets them plainely see't.
> 1. *Off.* If he did not care whether he had their loue, or no, hee
> waued indifferently, 'twixt doing them neyther good, nor harme:
> but he seekes their hate with greater deuotion, then they can
> render it him; and leaues nothing vndone, that may fully dis-
> couer him their opposite. Now to seeme to affect the mallice and
> displeasure of the People, is as bad, as that which he dislikes, to
> flatter them for their loue.   (L.626; *Cor.* II.ii.7–26)

It needs no tedious explication to demonstrate that such a
passage consists of an intricate interlocking of many of the
rudimentary analytic schemes, and that despite its greater in-
tricacy, it displays the same clean edges and precision grinding
that characterize its inner parts. Nothing floats ambiguously or
tangentially from its reference; every element is locked firmly in
place by the logic of the syntax.

Shakespeare's prose, of course, encompasses enormous range
and variety, and one neither hopes nor wishes to classify it under
a single rubric. With his prodigious mimetic powers, he could
virtually erase his own voice and become his own linguistic
antiself. Nevertheless, he does have a voice, and that voice
emerges in the kind of passage we have been discussing. When
Shakespeare mimics the polysyndetic gabble of Pompey or Shal-

low, or the gasping phrases of Mistress Quickly, or the slovenly jawing of the carriers at Gadshill, his control of decorum is so absolute that incoherence itself never falters. But no tragic hero talks like Pompey; no romantic heroine sounds like Mistress Quickly; no villain reminds us of Shallow. Whereas the language of heroes, fools, and villains alike—of Hamlet and the gravedigger, Falstaff and the Lord Chief Justice, Rosalind and Touchstone, Don John and Dogberry, Edmund and Lear's Fool, Autolycus and Polixenes—if we track it back to its syntactic skeleton, shares the same basic analytic structure, the logicality that in turn is traceable to Euphuism. The logical style, in Shakespeare, represents a norm from which the special idioms of Pompey or Shallow are purposeful departures. In Jonson, to anticipate, and to speak even more roughly, it is the other way around.

To the question of how these stylistic habits correspond to other aspects of Shakespearean drama, one can offer only hesitant answers. The argumentative character of the prose, its tendency to stick close to its syllogistic basis and to acknowledge this openly through the abundance of logical links—these one might relate to the network of causality that composes the intrigue plot. The intrigue plot depends on a multitude of chain reactions in which events spring out of other events and in their turn precipitate others. Lyly, who carries his own kind of logicality to extremes, tends to lay parallel or antithetic elements side by side without stressing the nexus between them. To speak more simply, he uses fewer connectives, and his plots display an analogous tendency to juxtapose scenes without binding them to each other in causal sequence. Shakespeare, in this respect, resembles more closely the popular playwrights with their "for's" and "therefore's," with the difference that he works with a fuller magazine of logical links; what in the plays of his contemporaries often reduces itself to a linear arrangement of "A leads to B leads to C," becomes in Shakespeare a dense tissue of inner relations, complexly interdependent on one another.

The symmetry and exact balance in Shakespeare's prose, on the other hand, form one aspect of the ceremoniousness of Shakespearean theater. In the prose as in the verse, we feel that we are never far from incantation or ritual. Even when the characters speak with the astounding lifelikeness that Shakespeare seems to command so effortlessly, we rarely lose the sense that they are talking a language superior to ours, more incisively rhythmical, more spacious, and more ordered. With the balanced, analytic syntax constantly feeding this sense even in moments of low tension, it requires only a slight tightening of the screws to bring us into the great formal harmonies of Falstaff's praise of sack, or Henry V's meditation on kingship, or Edmund's rejection of astrology. At such moments, even when the speaker himself is a spokesman for disorder, the resonant symmetries in the language seem to be reflecting a larger concord on which the plays repose as on a quiet.

Shakespeare's logicality, in any case, contributes to a prose style that—far from being "ungrammatical, perplexed and obscure," as Dr. Johnson complained[7]—is close to a model of clarity. And its clarity probably accounts in part for the unique hold its author's plays have maintained in the theater. Jonson's dramatic prose, winding and knotty, probably did not disturb an Elizabethan audience, but is likely to baffle a contemporary ear, which cannot predict where a sentence will go until it has already reached its destination. But Shakespeare maintains a balance between suspense and resolution just sufficient to satisfy the ear without taxing it. When we hear that "A good Sherris-Sack hath a two-fold operation in it" (L.412; *IIHIV* IV.iii.103–104), we have an advance blueprint of the discourse to be unfolded, and if Falstaff lingers over the description of Operation Number One, we wait expectantly but without irritation for Operation Number Two. When we hear that of two things, "the one" does such and such, we expect shortly to learn that "the other" does thus and so. When we hear "either," we know we shall soon confront the antithetic "or"; when we discover that someone would "rather" do something, we await the inevitable "than." And so with the dozens of other ways in which Shakespeare carves out divisions of thought. They not only foster clarity of exposition, they affect gesture and delivery, dictating antithetic or contrasting motion, and suggesting the proper weight for pauses and accents, enabling a speech to be heard slowly without fatigue or swiftly without bewilderment.[8] They form the building blocks of a speech that even today compensates for changes in the language, and carries an audience securely through any involutions of thought or plot. If these stylistic virtues play only a secondary role in the continuous presence of Shakespeare in the theater, their opposite (which is not a vice), a more irregular and captious syntax, may be held partly responsible for the unjust neglect of Jonson's great comedies.

[1] See Hardin Craig, "Shakespeare and Formal Logic," in *Studies in English Philology, A Miscellany in Honor of Frederick Klaeber,* ed. Kemp Malone and Martin B. Ruud (Minneapolis, 1929), pp. 380–396; Sister Miriam Joseph, *Shakespeare's Use of the Arts of Language* (New York, 1947), *passim;* and, for specimens of formal logic in the Elizabethan drama at large, Allan H. Gilbert, "Logic in the Elizabethan Drama," *Studies in Philology,* XXXII (1935), 527–545.

[2] One approaches the subject with more than usual diffidence because of the beating it has taken at the hands of other critics. Setting aside the various attempts to discover a principle governing the shifts between verse and prose, for which (most of them absurd) see the critical bibliography in Milton Crane, *Shakespeare's Prose* (Chicago, 1951), pp. 214–216, one finds mainly a highly charged impressionism combined with a spurious classificationism, as in J. Churton Collins, "Shakespeare as a Prose Writer," *Studies in Shakespeare* (New York, 1904), or Henry W. Wells, "The Continuity of Shaksperian Prose," *Shakespeare Association Bulletin,* XV (July 1940), 175–183. For an up-to-date bibliography see M. C. Bradbrook, "Fifty Years of the Criticism of Shakespeare's Style: A Retrospect," *Shakespeare Survey,* VII (1954), 1–11. Miss Bradbrook's suspicion (p. 4) that the study of Euphuism and related traditional topics has by now exhausted its usefulness is perhaps a wholesome caution; nevertheless only Bond, it seems to me, has fully grasped the importance of Euphuism in Shakespeare, and his documentation remains to be interpreted.

[3] Quotations will be from the Folio facsimile edited by Sir Sidney Lee (Oxford, 1902). Each extract is followed by the page number in Lee, then by the corresponding act, scene, and line number in the edition of George Lyman Kittredge (New York, 1936). The following abbreviations are used:

IHIV: Henry the Fourth, Part One	Troil: Troilus and Cressida
IIHIV: Henry the Fourth, Part Two	MW: The Merry Wives of Windsor
HV: Henry the Fifth	Ham.: Hamlet
Much Ado: Much Ado about Nothing	Oth.: Othello
Merch.: The Merchant of Venice	Lear: King Lear
TN: Twelfth Night	Tim.: Timon of Athens
AYL: As You Like It	Cor.: Coriolanus
Alls W: All's Well that Ends Well	Ant.: Antony and Cleopatra
MM: Measure for Measure	Cymb.: Cymbeline
	WT: The Winter's Tale
	Temp.: The Tempest

[4] E. A. Abbott, *A Shakespearian Grammar,* 3d ed. (London, 1897), pp. 101–102, cites a few appearances of the conjunction "for," but

without giving any inkling of its frequency. Abbott, interested primarily in irregularities, i.e., in points of difference between Elizabethan and modern grammar, also ignores causal connectives such as "hence" and "therefore" whose usage remains unchanged in the modern language. Wilhelm Franz's exhaustive and imposing *Die Sprache Shakespeares*, 4th ed. of *Shakespeare Grammatik* (Halle, 1939), tabulates many of the logical devices, the correlatives, etc., discussed below, especially in pp. 427–473 ("Die Konjunktion"), but, again, chiefly in order to define the limits of Shakespearean grammar, the range of its possibilities, without concerning himself with whether such-and-such a syntactic scheme occurs once or a hundred times in Shakespeare.

[5] W. K. Wimsatt, Jr., *The Prose Style of Samuel Johnson* (New Haven, 1941), p. 12.

[6] With the following observation of Kenneth Muir I naturally find myself in hearty accord: "Shakespeare was in no danger of becoming too colloquial in his dialogue. Even his apparently colloquial prose is a good deal further from actual Elizabethan speech than the dialogue of Middleton or Jonson; and when in his verse he uses language of extraordinary simplicity the powerful effect is obtained largely by contrast with the more complex language used elsewhere" ("Shakespeare and Rhetoric," *Shakespeare Jahrbuch*, XC [1954], 60).

[7] *Johnson on Shakspeare*, ed. Walter Raleigh (London, 1908), p. 42—speaking, evidently, of Shakespeare's prose and verse alike.

[8] Surprisingly, something like the same point was made by Ralph Waldo Emerson, in "Shakespeare, or The Poet," *Complete Works*, ed. Edward Waldo Emerson, 12 vols. (Boston, 1903), IV, 214: "Though the speeches in the plays, and single lines, have a beauty which tempts the ear to pause on them for their euphuism, yet the sentence is so loaded with meaning and so linked with its foregoers and followers, that the logician is satisfied."

✍ 17 ✍

What Shakespeare Wrote

FREDSON BOWERS

To the layman, nothing in the scholarly study of literature might seem to promise less scope for intellection or opportunity for excitement than editing. It should take little reflection, however, to realize the significance of certain facts. The only way we have of knowing what Shakespeare wrote is the text of his works; and that text, in the printing of which the author seems to have taken no part, has been transmitted to us by printers who knew nothing of modern standards (incidentally, the trusting layman might be surprised to learn how many errors creep into modern texts and become enshrined as if the author had intended them in the first place). One might respond to the realization that Shakespeare's manuscripts are irrecoverably lost (did Hamlet say "sullied" or "solid" flesh?) in one of two ways: one might decide that such a problem is insoluble (and a modern text would have to provide both alternatives, one in a footnote perhaps) or that the question can only be decided on esthetic grounds ("solid" is more consistent with the imagery of the passage). Recently, however, a new science of bibliography has been developing which makes it possible to recover most of what Shakespeare wrote by a close study of the text in the light of Elizabethan printing practices. Foremost in the new movement has been Professor Fredson Bowers of the University of Virginia, who is an eminent literary critic and historian of Elizabethan dramatic convention as well as an authoritative editor. Readers interested in the fuller development of the ideas presented here should consult Professor Bowers's Textual and Literary Criticism *(1959). Professor Bowers has demonstrated, by the way, that Shakespeare wrote "sallied"—that is,* sullied.

Although Sir Laurence Olivier may assert of *Hamlet* in a se-
pulchral voice, "This is a play about a man who could not make
up his mind," the editor of *Hamlet* cannot afford a corresponding
luxury. Faced with two variant words in two early texts, he cannot
say to the reader, "Well, maybe this one is what Shakespeare
meant; or, maybe, now I think of it, the other one." And then,
with an air of pleased surprise, "But after all, may we not think
that perhaps he meant them both!" An editor, in fact, must
engage himself to that most difficult of all human problems—making up his mind. Only thus can he give us the complete and
coherent result of his labors in an established text of Shakespeare.

The concern of this paper is to try to sketch in non-technical
language what the difficulties are in the recovery of Shakespeare's
true text from the imperfect witnesses of the past, and something
of the methods and the textual logic that are being used in the
more recent attacks on these problems. Of only one thing can we
all be assured. Outside of the original documents, whatever text
of Shakespeare we pick up to read, whether a popular paperback
or a scholarly production festooned with footnotes and commentary, this text reflects, in general, only what some editor thought—
or hoped—that Shakespeare wrote.

I am not referring to questions of whether Shakespeare was
Shakespeare and wrote his own plays, or whether he was
the Earl of Oxford or Sir Edward Dyer. My old teacher, George
Lyman Kittredge, had a perfectly good answer to that one. Putting a sweetly reasonable expression on his face, he declared himself well prepared to accept Francis Bacon as the author of
Shakespeare—provided that someone would tell him who wrote
Bacon. Let us accept "that man from Stratford" (as the lunatic
fringe like to call him), and worry only about what he wrote.

By what he wrote, I am not referring (either) to just what
plays he wrote. There are some grounds for believing that not all
of Shakespeare's plays have been preserved; in addition, critics
are still worrying about whether he wrote *The Two Noble Kins-
men* and *Henry VIII* all by himself, whether he wrote them at all
or whether he collaborated in writing them with John Fletcher.
By what he wrote, I am referring to his exact words, down to the
smallest detail. Sometimes this passion for truth may seem nig-

gling; but if one is doing a job, one might as well do a good job while one is about it. The cumulative effect of accepting error after error in Shakespeare (as we do, for example, in all but one modern edition of *Richard III*) can lead in the long run to a vitiated text that is an insult to a great writer. Admittedly, if we follow one editor's version of *Hamlet* rather than another's, we shall not discover Claudius emerging as the hero, nor will Hamlet suddenly be exposed as a woman in disguise. Beside these scary possibilities it may seem rather trivial to worry whether Hamlet's father's bones were *interred* or *enurned;* whether the *safety, sanity* or the *sanctity* of the Danish state is involved; or, indeed, whether Hamlet's flesh, he regrets, is *too, too solid* or *too, too sullied.* These choices that beset an editor are only a few of the hundreds that appear in the early texts of *Hamlet* and have some claim to authority. The problem is, how do editors—or, rather, how should editors—go about deciding which one Shakespeare wrote.

No Shakespeare manuscript is in existence. This is not surprising: they were not collectors' items. Printers would have thrown them away after setting type from them; almost twenty years passed in the Commonwealth with no public performances of plays, and the manuscripts of the disbanded theatrical companies were completely dispersed; the Great Fire of London must have destroyed some. Indeed, only a relative handful of the hundreds and hundreds of Elizabethan plays have come down to us in manuscript form, and it is our bad luck that so few of these are by major dramatists. None is Shakespeare's, if we except the good possibility that one scene in the manuscript of the unacted *Sir Thomas More* is in his hand. However, unless such a manuscript were in autograph, we should not be much the wiser about Shakespearian text in general if one turned up tomorrow.

To see the problem, let us start with a reconstruction of what happened when Shakespeare wrote a play. Heming and Condell, the actors who seem to have taken responsibility for getting the First Folio into print, speak admiringly of the cleanness of Shakespeare's manuscripts delivered to the company, and how he seldom "blotted" a line; that is, he had made few alterations. This is no doubt literary hyperbole by two men who had little occasion to distinguish a Shakespeare autograph from a copy. The evidence is strongly against the accuracy of the picture. We know that most dramatists were required to submit to the theatrical companies a fair copy of their plays—this was the ordinary procedure. But Shakespeare was in an unusual position, almost unique in his time. He was not a dramatist writing for any company that would buy his plays. On the contrary, he had been made a part-owner in his company in return for his talents, and he wrote for one company alone, of which he was a member. Under these circumstances, it has been conjectured, he could turn in rather messy papers, rewritten drafts, almost anything, no matter how badly written and difficult to read, since he could look over and correct the copy made by the theater's scribe. This carelessness may well have been permitted, if we do not suppose that it happened with every play. At any rate, on what evidence we have it would seem that Shakespeare submitted a manuscript that was not always copied out fair but was sometimes composed of his hastily written sheets, known technically as "foul papers." A scribe then copied this manuscript either directly into promptbook form or, sometimes, into an intermediate form that would in turn be the basis for a promptbook to be made later.

That Shakespeare did not always read over with complete attention the theatrical copy may be shown by small pieces of evidence scattered through the plays. For instance, in *The Merry Wives of Windsor* Corporal Nym is remarking to Falstaff that Bardolph is not an expert thief. He is too slow and clumsy. The trick is—Nym says—to steal "at a minutes rest." At least that is what the text of the First Folio prints. And, curiously, an earlier (quite bad) text has the same phrase. This bad text seems to have been cobbled up from the memory of one or more persons who had acted in the play. Here, at least, we know that the actor had recited "at a minute's rest," which is the very phrase found in the Folio version.

Does this mean it must be right? A few editors, like Sisson, have argued so; but most have preferred a phrase that has a great deal more meaning, and, moreover, one used by Mercutio in *Romeo and Juliet*: "at a minim's rest." A *minim* is the smallest interval in music. Thus a minim's rest is the shortest pause that can be perceived between two musical notes played one after the other. It is a vivid phrase, and almost certainly it is right. But the actor did not say it so in *The Merry Wives* at the Globe, nor did the manuscript have it so that was sent to the printer. The only explanation is that both texts were based on the promptbook, that the promptbook made the error of *minutes* for *minims* when it was being copied from Shakespeare's papers, or an intermediate manuscript, and that Shakespeare never caught the error in the promptbook or by hearing the mistake repeated on the stage.

This little story is salutary in several respects. First, it shows that from documents that are all in error, informed criticism can recover what Shakespeare actually wrote. Second, it shows that the documentary sources for Shakespeare's text can make mistakes if they were not in his own handwriting. The minute a copy is made of anything, whether by an Elizabethan scribe or a modern typist, errors will creep in. Moreover, this is as true in Shakespeare's day whether a scribe is copying out his manuscript to make up a promptbook, or a compositor is setting type in a printing-house from Shakespeare's own papers.

However, if a compositor is setting type from Shakespeare's manuscript, only one intermediary comes between us and Shakespeare's words in his own hand. But if the compositor is given a manuscript made by a scribe, then two intermediaries appear, and the chances for error are doubled. This is true for *The Merry Wives of Windsor*, except here we can be sure that at least three intermediaries intervened. From certain unusual characteristics we recognize that the two Folio compositors concerned with this play worked from a manuscript copied out for them by the theatrical scribe Ralph Crane. If we are right in asserting that the correct phrase is "at a minim's rest," then other evidence joins to indicate that Crane was copying from a promptbook. This, in turn, would have been transcribed from Shakespeare's papers or from some intermediate manuscript made from them. When we get a chain of transmission like this, the end result is still recognizably Shakespeare, but we can be positive that it is not exact Shakespeare in every detail. And, indeed, all editors of *The Merry Wives* have recognized that, here and there, at least five or six phrases or lines have demonstrably been omitted in the Folio text.

How many have been unwittingly altered without our knowledge is troublesome to think of.

How did Shakespeare's manuscripts get to the printers? There is not the slightest evidence that Shakespeare ever concerned himself in the least with the printing of any of his plays. Moreover, almost half were not put into print until after his death. Indeed, on the evidence, Shakespeare felt little incentive to worry about the form of his plays in print. Plays were not regarded as "literature"; when Shakespeare in his early days wrote two narrative poems that were respectable literary forms, he seems to have taken some care to assure himself that they were carefully printed. But not the plays on which—at the time—anything that could be called a literary reputation could rest.

Moreover, there is some evidence that by and large Shakespeare's company was not anxious to have his plays printed lest this interfere with the gate receipts. Hence, not all of his plays that got into print were from the manuscripts that were authorized by his company. On two occasions—*Romeo and Juliet* and *Hamlet*—when a very corrupt piratical text was printed first, the company took care to put a better text before the public, but it did not do so for *King Lear* or for *Henry V* or for *Richard III*.

When Shakespeare's company allowed one of his plays to be printed, the evidence suggests that they sent to the printer the manuscript that was most convenient for them to part with. What they would not do, under any circumstances, would be to send the promptbook itself, for this was a precious and irreplaceable piece of property. If the promptbook were the only manuscript the company had, it would be copied out for the printer, as happened with *The Merry Wives*. But if some other manuscript were available, the expense of copying could be saved; and the evidence suggests the company thought that any spare manuscript would do for printing.

By our good luck, this spare manuscript often proved to be Shakespeare's foul papers, or his own writing-out of the play. When such a manuscript was given to the printer, we may have numerous compositorial errors that stem from the difficulty of reading the handwriting, as in *Hamlet*. But these errors we have some chance of recognizing and correcting, since they will at least slightly approximate the correct words. The errors any editor learns to fear are those, he suspects, that arose during the transmission of a text from copyist to copyist. These errors are seldom obvious and often make perfectly good sense. The only difficulty is the obvious one: they simply do not happen to be the words that Shakespeare wrote.

One of the first tasks of the editor, therefore, is to try to identify the kind of manuscript that served as printer's copy for a Shakespeare first edition and for any other later authoritative form of the text. Indeed, his editorial practice will be largely dictated by what he finds in this enquiry. If the manuscript, he thinks, was a Shakespeare autograph, the printer's errors will often be simple ones of misreading the handwriting, mixed with some amount of memorial error. The editor will be inclined to give the benefit of the doubt to difficult words or phrases, less likely to be the invention of the compositor than of the author, and he will feel that they can represent Shakespeare's own, or else in some recoverable form a recognizably corrupt version of what Shakespeare wrote. But although the printed text will be superficially cleaner and more correct if the printer's copy were a scribal transcript, the editor will know that it is sure to harbor concealed corruptions of a different sort from the first, and he will incline to be much bolder in his emendation of passable but not entirely characteristic readings.

When more than one edition of a play was printed, the editor must compare the text of the later against the earlier to discover whether the later is a simple reprint, in which case although some errors in the first may be corrected by good guesswork, no change can actually be authoritative, and most variants will be out-and-out corruptions. Or else, as happened with some Shakespeare plays, the printer of a later edition may have had access to another manuscript. When this occurs, all variants between the two editions must be scrutinized with the greatest care, since ordinarily one will be an error and the other will be what Shakespeare wrote, except for some instances when both may be right if the variant represents a Shakespeare revision of an earlier form. No edition later than the Shakespeare First Folio has ever been found to contain any possibility of such authoritative texts. But, even so, some quite complex situations develop before the First Folio.

Let us take the most prominent textual situations in respect to Shakespeare's plays and see how they affect our knowledge of what Shakespeare wrote.

Number 1. The simplest case. Here there is only one edition that was set from any manuscript, and all later editions are simple reprints without authority. The purest examples come in plays first printed in the 1623 First Folio. (The Second, Third, and Fourth Folios, we have had demonstrated to us, tried to correct the First Folio text but only by editorial or compositorial guesswork, and always without authority.) *The Two Gentlemen of Verona* is such a play, and so is *Macbeth*, or *Antony and Cleopatra*.

I pick these three plays advisedly because they represent different textual situations. The *Two Gentlemen* was printed from a scribal copy, made by Ralph Crane, from some manuscript whose nature we do not know. *Macbeth* is a scribal copy made from a promptbook. It represents what seems to be a severely cut version for the stage made up at a date much later than the original writing and containing some parts written by another dramatist, Thomas Middleton. Serious as are its deficiencies, it is the only text we have. *Antony and Cleopatra* may well have been set from the most authoritative possible source, Shakespeare's own manuscript, probably without cutting for the stage representation.

What can an editor do about these situations? First, he can find out as much as he can about the probable nature of the manuscript that served as printer's copy. His finds will have a great deal to do with his conservatism or his boldness in treating the text, and indeed with his assessment of the kinds of error that, he suspects, lurk in the printed version.

Second, regardless of his suspicions, what can he do about knowing what Shakespeare wrote when, according to the play, he has only what a compositor made out of a manuscript that may be Shakespeare's (if he is lucky) or (if he is unlucky) what a compositor made out of what a scribe made out of what a scribe made out of a theatrically cut and patched version of what Shakespeare once had written. Well, he can try to see what discoverable effect the printing process may have had upon the transmission of the text from manuscript to print. Whether the type-pages were set in regular order will prove to be important, or whether the manuscript copy was marked off according to an estimate and the pages were set in irregular order according to the sequence that would be laid on the press to print one side of a sheet of paper.

Moreover, we are beginning to find out something about the general habits and relative accuracy of some of the compositors who set various Shakespearian texts. If it is the workman in the Folio known as Compositor A, we know that most of his departures from copy will be rather literal misreadings that can often be recognized and the true reading recovered, whereas his fellow, Compositor B, who set all of *Antony and Cleopatra*, is more likely to crowd his memory with too much manuscript material before he turns to his cases to set type, and therefore serious errors will result from his memorial failure that causes paraphrases and substitutions. Moreover, Compositor B is inclined to tinker with the metre of verse and sometimes to change words that he thinks are not quite right. Thus the incidence of error in B's work will be higher than in A's, and an editor must judge the text accordingly.

Sometimes one compositor can be played off against another. For instance, it is one of our strongest proofs that in *Hamlet* "too too sallied flesh" is what Shakespeare wrote, because his "sallied" (meaning "sullied") was set by one compositor in Q2 whereas when the same word appears again, in a Polonius speech to Reynaldo, this "sally" (meaning "sully") was set by a different workman. On the contrary, changes in the characteristics of the text when they occur, not after one compositor has taken over from another, but instead within the work of a single identified compositor, can be assigned with confidence to a change in the characteristics of the manuscript that was the printer's copy. An editor of *1 Henry VI* must be prepared to find that about one-half of the manuscript was written out in a different hand (with different spelling characteristics in the print) from the other half, and therefore the reliability of the text in both parts may not be equal. A plausible theory has been contrived on such evidence for the Second Quarto of *Romeo and Juliet;* that is, that the latter third of the play was set from an earlier and rougher state of the manuscript than the authorial fair copy of the first two-thirds.

It may happen during the course of printing that the printing-house proofreader will stop the press and change some readings in the type that had been set by the compositor from manuscript. If this happened, an editor wants to know the evidence, for the corrector seldom read proof back against copy, and his changes were usually his own ideas and not always good ones. An excellent example occurs in the Second Quarto of *Hamlet.* Originally, the compositor set "An houre of quiet thirtie shall we see," which makes nonsense. The proofreader saw that an error had occurred but he did not bother to consult the manuscript before (as a bad guess) he altered "thirtie" to "thereby," a word that makes fair sense and seems to be close in its shape to "thirtie." However, on the evidence of the Folio what Shakespeare wrote was "An hour of quiet shortly shall we see." The moral here is this: if the Folio text with its obviously correct reading had not existed, and so if an editor had known only the proofreader's corruption "thereby," we should be reading today what Shakespeare did *not* write. But if the editor had compared all known copies of *Hamlet* in the Second Quarto form to discover what changes had been made during the course of printing, he would have found that "thereby" was not what the compositor had originally set. Alerted to the possibility that "thereby" was a proofreader's corruption, thus, he might have been able to reconstruct "shortlie" as a palaeographical possibility from "thirtie," superior to "thereby" and so to recover independently what Shakespeare actually wrote.

An editor can sometimes know what Shakespeare must have written in one place by utilizing the evidence of what he wrote somewhere else. In *The Merry Wives of Windsor* the clinching evidence for *minim's,* not *minute's,* comes when something like the same joke is made in *Romeo and Juliet.* When Cleopatra in the Folio text bids the Messenger from Antony, "Ram thou thy fruitful tidings in mine ears," some editors—doubtless led astray by "fruitful" and the easy handwriting confusion between *in* and *m*—have emended to "Rain thou thy fruitful tidings." But that Shakespeare wrote "Ram" as in the printed text is almost certainly indicated by such parallels as "thrusting this report into his ears" from *Julius Caesar*, or "You cram these words into my ears" in *The Tempest*. On the other hand, analogies must be used with some caution. The Ghost, approving of Hamlet's resolution, remarks in the Second Quarto that if Hamlet had behaved otherwise he would have been duller than "the fat weed that roots on Lethe wharf." Misled by a quotation from *Antony and Cleopatra* about the vagabond flag that moves back and forth with the current and so "rots itself in motion," some editors have decided that the Folio was correct when it printed "the fat weed that rots on Lethe wharf." But a "wharf" is a bank, and the *Antony and Cleopatra* water image has no application to the *Hamlet* word, for the waters of the river of forgetfulness merely flow past the "fat weed" above them on the bank and therefore can have nothing to do with its rooting or rotting. The true odds are that Shakespeare wrote *roots*.

Sometimes an inspired guess gives us with absolute conviction of rightness what Shakespeare must have written, even though we rely on faith and not on concrete evidence. When the old critic Theobald emended the death of Falstaff in *Henry V* from the nonsense "a Table of green fields" to "a babbl'd of green fields," he had what was surely a real meeting of minds with Shakespeare. Thus an editor can recover what Shakespeare wrote sometimes by the use of bibliographical evidence, but sometimes by the use of linguistic or purely critical. But in his assumptions he is ultimately dependent upon what he thinks was the manuscript that underlay the printed copy with which he must work. If this manuscript were a cut version for the stage, no power on earth can recover what is missing from Shakespeare's full original, unless fresh authority is to intervene in some other edition. If we had only the Folio text of *Hamlet*, we should never have known of the existence of the soliloquy, "How all occasions do inform against me," lines that were cut in the version of the manuscript behind the Folio text but that are preserved, fortunately, in the Second Quarto version.

Number 2. A slightly more complex case. There is only one edition of a play printed from manuscript, always one before the

Folio, but the editors of the Folio made a very quick comparison of the early quarto with their playhouse copy and wrote in minor changes before sending the marked printed edition to Jaggard's shop. Usually these alterations do not affect the text but reflect the Folio editors' concern for such theatrical matters as the stage directions or speech prefixes. This happened to a few plays like *The Merchant of Venice,* and the editor must come to some conclusions about the accuracy of the alterations. In *Titus Andronicus* the Folio editors did not touch any details of the printed quarto text, but from their playhouse manuscript they did add a new scene not present in the early editions.

Number 3. A much more troublesome case. Here the earliest edition of a play in print is what is known technically as a "bad quarto." In the details of their origin these bad quartos no doubt vary widely, but they all have one point in common; that is, there is no transcriptional link with any Shakespeare manuscript. The most popular theory, and one that (for some plays at least) seems to be demonstrable, is that these texts were attempts by one or more actors to reconstruct the plays in which they had performed.

This desire is quite understandable. A number of touring companies acted in the provinces, and these travelling players had to have plays. Since there was no such thing as copyright, they usually seemed to have taken over any play they liked that was in print. But a new and popular London play might not see print for years. Hence an attempt, it seems, was occasionally made to secure the text in some form so that it could be acted in the country. If one of the actors had performed in the play on the London stage, he could attempt a reconstruction of what he remembered from it.

The first edition of *Hamlet,* in 1603, for instance, was a Bad Quarto. Every critic has noticed that in the scenes in Act I in which Marcellus participates, the bad text is noticeably better than elsewhere in its correspondence to the good text—evidence that a reporting actor's memory was adequate for what he had played and what he would have had occasion to overhear. Also, the speech of Voltemand, a part that this Marcellus-actor seems to have doubled, is almost perfect. Thereafter, when this actor no longer appears, the text degenerates remarkably. Indeed, even in Act I the reporting is noticeably poor in the scenes in which he did not participate and thus had no occasion to remember with any distinctness. Hence it seems that this 1603 text originated with the actor who had played both Marcellus and Voltemand, and that he wrote out or recited to a scribe as much of the play as he could recall. It is no marvel that the actor's uncertain memory produced lines that are often perilously close to nonsense. Here, for instance, is his garbled recollection of Hamlet's "To be or not to be" soliloquy:

> To be, or not to be, I there's the point,
> To Die, to sleepe, is that all? I all:
> No, to sleepe, to dreame, I mary there it goes,
> For in that dreame of death, when wee awake,
> And borne before an euerlasting Iudge,
> From whence no passenger euer retur'ned,
> The vndiscouered country, at whose sight
> The happy smile, and the accursed damn'd.
> But for this, the ioyfull hope of this,
> Whol'd beare the scornes and flattery of the world,
> Scorned by the right rich, the rich curssed of the poore?
> The widow being oppressed, the orphan wrong'd,
> The taste of hunger, or a tirants raigne,
> And thousand more calamities besides,
> To grunt and sweate vnder this weary life,
> When that he may his full Quietus make,
> With a bare bodkin, who would this indure,
> But for a hope of something after death?
> Which pusles the braine, and doth confound the sence,
> Which makes vs rather beare those euilles we haue,
> Than flie to others that we know not of.
> I that, O this conscience makes cowardes of vs all,
> Lady in thy orizons, be all my sinnes remembred.

Some of Shakespeare's most popular plays were pirated in this manner: *Hamlet, King Lear, Henry V, Richard III, Romeo and Juliet, The Merry Wives of Windsor,* for example. For some of these, like *Romeo and Juliet* and *Hamlet,* Shakespeare's company seems to have issued a better text within a few years of the publication of the bad quarto, perhaps because the garbled version was no very good advertisement for the play. Yet other dramas, like *King Lear* and *Richard III*, or *The Merry Wives*, had to wait for the Folio for an improved version. It is worthy of note that *Pericles* was the only bad quarto that was not replaced by a good text at some period.

We now find ourselves in a most interesting question about textual transmission that has important consequences for our knowledge of what Shakespeare really wrote. In a very few instances, as with *The Merry Wives of Windsor*, when a new text was issued, this good text was typeset directly from the manuscript that the company furnished. Since this line of transmission gives us our best texts, at least in theory, we may regret that it is found in relatively few plays, chiefly in *The Merry Wives*, in the Second Quarto *Hamlet*, and in some major part in the Second Quarto *Romeo and Juliet*.

Yet even here a critic can feel most uneasy that in every play for which there is a bad quarto and a good text, editors have felt it necessary on some occasions to go back to the bad version to find what they think Shakespeare really wrote. This process began in the eighteenth century when the nature of the bad texts was not known and they were thought on the whole to be Shakespearian first drafts, a view that Hardin Craig, unfortunately, still holds today. Modern editors make much less use of the bad texts, but they cannot escape sometimes preferring these to the readings in the good editions.

For some readings there is no excuse for the choice of the bad over the good text. *Romeo and Juliet* furnishes us with a particularly egregious example. Because early editors thought that the bad First Quarto's "a rose by any other name would smell as sweet" was superior in some unspecified literary way to the good Second Quarto's "a rose by any other word," this *name* got put into the received texts in early days when no distinction was made between bad and good authority, and it has remained ever since, although it is completely wrong.

As an object lesson let us pause to see what the implications of this choice are. In the first place, to read *name* one must believe that the actor's memory was more trustworthy than the com-

positor's setting *word* from the good manuscript. It might be possible to conjecture—if this manuscript had been a scribal transcript—that somehow Shakespeare's *name* got changed to *word*
by a careless scribe. But there is no evidence that it did, nor is
word so inferior a reading as to lead one to suppose it a corruption. On the other hand, if the printer's copy for the good quarto
was Shakespeare's own manuscript, as is usually believed, then
this line of conjecture becomes impossible. An editor who chose
name would need to believe that *name* was also the reading in
the manuscript for the good quarto, but the compositor made a
memorial error and set *word* by mistake. Here one must recall
the golden platitude that a possibility is not a probability, a point
that is often overlooked by textual critics. If we are to believe
this for *name* and *word*, we have just as much right to believe it
for hundreds of other variant readings in the bad and good texts.
Nor will the hypothesis do that Shakespeare originally wrote
word, as found in his manuscript, but later changed it to *name*
in the promptbook, whence the actor derived his memory. Such
a theory is completely undemonstrable and is not supported by
any evidence for other promptbook revision. Again, it could be
held about any of hundreds of other readings in the play, and we
should have chaos.

Tradition, alone, can account for the presentday editions still
printing "a rose by any other name would smell as sweet." No
editor can have logically thought through the reasons for his
choice, or he would reject the bad text forthwith. In these cases,
conventional editors, who do not know their business, get between us and what Shakespeare actually wrote.

I once read a musical criticism in which Winthrop Sargeant
used the violinist's treatment of a single phrase in the opening of
Beethoven's Violin Concerto as a touchstone to show whether the
violinist really understood the Concerto throughout. In somewhat
similar manner, I use this choice in *Romeo and Juliet* of *name* for
word as a touchstone to distinguish a textually untrained editor
from a good one.

Nevertheless, there is no Shakespeare text where once in a
while an editor quite legitimately is not forced back to the bad
text for the right reading. When in *The Merry Wives* we can

satisfactorily conjecture at least three transcriptions between us and Shakespeare's manuscript, it may not be astonishing that even the most conservative editors (and here I include myself) have been forced to revert to the bad quarto to repair some quite clear cut accidental omissions in the good Folio text. One line is commonly accepted on the somewhat dangerous grounds that it seems to have the true Shakespearian ring: this is Pistol's answer to Falstaff when he is attempting to borrow money from the knight. "I will retort the sum in equipage." On the other hand, there are obvious omissions in the good text that can be repaired only by taking over the wording of the bad quarto. For example, when the Host is reconciling Sir Hugh and Doctor Caius, he speaks as follows in the Folio: "Shall I lose my doctor? no; he gives me the potions and the motions. Shall I lose my parson, my priest, my Sir Hugh? no; he gives me the proverbs and the no-verbs. Give me thy hand, celestial; so. Boys of art, I have deceived you both" and so on. Here the text fairly cries out for the Host to grasp Doctor Caius's hand as well, and any editor may feel confident that he is recovering what Shakespeare actually wrote when he takes over from the bad quarto, "Give me thy hand, terrestrial; so" addressed to Caius, before proceeding, as in the Folio, to the parson and "Give me thy hand, celestial; so." The necessary action, and the equation of *terrestrial* and *celestial* for the arts of medicine and divinity, are irresistible.

The situation grows more complex when the manuscript that stands behind the good text was not itself used as printer's copy; but, instead, the printer's copy was made up from the earlier printed bad quarto corrected by comparison with the manuscript. It is quite demonstrable that the good Folio text of such plays as *King Lear* and *Richard III* was typeset from a copy of the printed bad quarto that had been interlined, marginally annotated, and very likely even festooned with slips of paper, all the work of some scribe consulting a manuscript and collating it against the printed text. It seems to be a fact, curious though it may be, that a printer preferred even such extraordinarily marked-up printed copy to setting throughout from a manuscript.

Four particular problems arise when the transmission of the text is established through such a marked-up copy.

First, the compositor may have had more than usual difficulty in reading some of the insertions, and errors may creep in from this source.

Second, the scribe is in some sense copying out the manuscript again, and is therefore liable to error. It is quite possible for him to change a correct reading in the printed copy to an incorrect one under the illusion that he is making a required alteration. Or, an incorrect reading may be altered, not to a correct but to another error.

Third, depending upon the nature of the manuscript, it may be (especially if the manuscript is at some remove from Shakespeare's autograph) that it will contain errors that are found in their correct form in the actor's memory as reflected in the bad quarto.

Fourth, the scribe may miss some differences between print and manuscript and fail to correct errors in the printed copy, in which case we are stuck with the reading of the bad quarto and can never know what was Shakespeare's reading in the manuscript; indeed, in many cases we shall not know even that the scribe failed to alter his printed copy and thus that we are reading what Shakespeare did *not* write.

King Lear went through two bad-quarto editions before the corrected Folio text, but the Folio version, in considerable part, seems to have been set from a marked-up copy of the first edition, even though some leaves from the second edition may also have served as copy. In this case the editor has considerable difficulty in deciding how much error there may be in the Folio as against many readings in the bad quarto. He also finds that he has particular difficulty with the problem of transmitted error in readings that the scribe may have failed to alter.

As always when the transmission of a text is in question, the exact details—insofar as they can be recovered—are most important guides to editorial theory. For instance, some editors have explained error in the corrected Folio text as the result of the theater's prompter having made up the printer's copy. Wrong alterations, they speculate, could have come about if this book-keeper relied on his memory from time to time instead of always carefully comparing his manuscript against the printed copy.

This absurd notion, fortunately, is not so popular now as it was once; and the odds are being recognized that most annotated copy probably originated not in the theater but instead with the printer, who had been given a manuscript but preferred to save compositorial time by preparing marked-up printed copy for his workmen.

Several important consequences follow on this change of hypothesis. For instance, the book-keeper and his faulty memory vanish as a corrupting influence, and instead we have a more naïve, and therefore objective, transcript made by someone in the printing-house who had no prior acquaintance with the text. Second, since we can be sure that the company would not send to the printer its good promptbook, we can expect that the manuscript would sometimes be the most readily spared of all, that is, Shakespeare's own foul papers, or some prepromptbook manuscript close to the autograph. Only in cases of necessity would the company copy out the promptbook or send to the printing-house a worn-out promptbook that was no longer needed, either of which may have happened with *Hamlet* in the Folio version. Some more precise assumptions about the nature of the underlying manuscript can be made, therefore. It is most important to recognize the impact of the possibility that the manuscript may have been in Shakespeare's own hand; whereas if the company had made up an annotated quarto to send to the printer, almost inevitably the promptbook, with its lesser authority from our point of view, would have served as the manuscript source of the comparison.

One can scarcely question the seriousness of the problems when the good text has been printed not from a manuscript direct, but from a bad quarto brought into some conformity with the manuscript by annotation, and this worked-over print given the compositor to set in type. Yet despite all the various sources of error in the resulting good text, there is usually a strong presumption that most of the variants between the good and bad texts result from the correction of the bad. Thus any individual reading can be assessed against the background of the whole, with the odds favoring the accuracy of the good text even though in some few readings the bad quarto may be thought to retain Shakespeare's authentic words.

However, for our final category, *Number 4,* the situation may be very much more complex. Such plays as *Othello, Troilus and Cressida, Hamlet,* and perhaps *2 Henry IV,* were originally printed in quarto in good texts that certainly were Shakespeare autographs or else were derived from the original papers at only a short remove. Yet when these plays came to be printed in the Folio, we find there another good text although one of a different tradition. The reason for the rejection of the earlier printed good texts can be most obscure. Copyright problems just possibly may have dictated the shift in *Troilus and Cressida,* but certainly not in *Hamlet* or *2 Henry IV.* Whatever the cause, the editor may view with some mixed feelings the embarrassment of riches thereby thrust upon him.

If both texts are authoritative, the choice is often not a clear-cut one between corruption and correction such as is found in the bad-quarto revisions in the Folio, where the weight on correction is manifestly in favor of the altered good text. Instead, the variant may represent, just about as often, correctness in the original good edition, and corruption in the altered Folio version, if the manuscript used for the Folio, though authoritative, were farther removed in its line of transmission from Shakespeare's original than the manuscript used as printer's copy for the earlier quarto.

This state of affairs seems to be present in *Hamlet,* which runs the gamut of modes of textual transmission. *Hamlet* was first printed in 1603 in a bad-quarto text. In 1604-5 a revised good quarto was issued, generally thought to have been printed from a very ill-written manuscript in Shakespeare's own hand. In 1623 the Folio printed a version that seems to have a theatrical origin and this to have passed through the hands of several scribes, with ensuing corruptions. Ordinarily, the more literary version of the Second Quarto, the one printed from a manuscript closest to Shakespeare, would have pre-eminent authority, and any Folio variant would need to show cause why it should be accepted as a substitute. For many readings this state of affairs is quite accurate. We know, for example, that the Folio version toned down some oaths to conform to laws passed after the original writing. Thus when the Folio reads, "Oh good Horatio," and the Second Quarto "Oh God, Horatio," we can be certain that the Folio is altering what Shakespeare wrote; and for this particular reading we can demonstrate the sophistication by referring to the Bad Quarto's "Oh fie, Horatio." "Fie" was a strong word of reproof in Shakespeare's day, not a slightly comic slap on the wrist, as we have come to think of it. Hence its appearance shows that the actor remembered some strong ejaculation here, as in the Second Quarto, even though he did not get it quite right. In my view, the Folio's "too too solid flesh" is also a sophistication of the bad and good Second Quarto's "sallied" (i. e., sullied) flesh, and there are dozens and dozens of other examples.

On the other hand, an editor in his thinking must balance two additional factors. First, the compositors of the Second Quarto *Hamlet* had serious trouble reading a difficult manuscript. For Act I it is clear that the first compositor frequently referred for assistance to a copy of the Bad Quarto, and thus that some readings in the Second Quarto may not represent what were in Shakespeare's manuscript but instead may derive from an actor's faulty memory as reproduced in the 1603 printed text. Second, even so, many errors were made when the Bad Quarto was no longer of assistance, and we must presume that the Folio manuscript in a number of cases had these words right and hence that the Folio can often correct a real compositorial error in the good Second Quarto.

When in the second scene of Act I Hamlet addresses the Queen, "Tis not alone my inky cloak, good mother, Nor customary suits of solemn black," we read the Folio version, for editors unite in rejecting the Quarto line, "Tis not alone my inky cloak, cold mother." But all examples are not so clear-cut as this. Did Shakespeare write with the Second Quarto, "What we have two nights seen," or with the Folio, "What we two nights have seen"? With the Quarto, "jump at this dead hour," or with the Folio, "just at this dead hour"? Did Old Hamlet and Old Fortinbras before their duel sign a "comart" or a "covenant"? Were young Fortinbras's mercenary soldiers "lawless" or "landless" men? Is the cock "the trumpet to the morn" or "to the day"? When just before Christmas the cock sings all night long, is it "no spirit dare stir abroad" or "no spirit can walk abroad"? Does Polonius warn Laertes against buying drinks for "each new hatch'd unfledg'd

courage" or "each unhatch'd, unfledg'd comrade," or—as some
editors would have it—"each new hatch'd, unfledg'd comrague"?
Did Ophelia, as she floated to her death, sing snatches of "old
lauds" or of "old tunes"?

Of one thing we may be certain. When two words are so close
in their shapes as *comart* and *covenant*, *lawless* and *landless*, or
jump and *just*, one or other must be an error. The problem is: is
the Second Quarto word the result of the compositor misreading
the handwriting and getting the wrong word? Or is the Second
Quarto word the right one, and the Folio word a scribal mistake
or normalization somewhere in the course of transmission?

In the few places where the First Quarto can act as a witness,
it can tell us what the actor remembered that Shakespeare wrote.
That is, in ordinary circumstances when the Bad Quarto agrees
with the Second Quarto against the Folio, we seem to be in possession of what Shakespeare wrote in his own papers and what
was transferred accurately to the promptbook. Thus if the Folio
text varies, it is logical to take it that the theatrical text from
which it derives has been altered, wittingly or unwittingly, at
some later point in its transmission. For instance, when the two
quartos read "jump at this dead hour," and the Folio "just at this
dead hour," we not only suspect the Folio substitution of a color-
less normal word for a vigorous unusual one, but we have the
evidence that the actor remembered "jump," and that Shakespeare's manuscript seems to have read "jump."

There is, unfortunately, one difficulty with this textual logic.
We know that the compositor of the Second Quarto relied to some
extent on the Bad Quarto when he was typesetting Act I. Hence
there is always the possibility to be considered that a word like
"jump" was an actor's error for "just," and that "jump" appears
in the Second Quarto only because it was taken over from the Bad
Quarto. Shakespeare's manuscript may have read "just," as does
the Folio. That this is no idle objection may be shown in Marcellus' query to Horatio. "Why such daily cast of brazen cannon?"
This is undoubtedly correct reading of the Folio, whereas both
the First and Second Quartos read "cost," a word making little
sense.

From another point of view, the agreement of Folio and Bad Quarto against the Second Quarto may be significant, as in the assignment to Marcellus instead of to Horatio of "What, has this thing appeared again tonight?" Yet concurrence of Folio and Bad Quarto may be less weighty than concurrence of Bad and Good Quartos: we must not forget that both the Bad Quarto and the Folio ultimately go back to the same promptbook, and this may have contained an error not present in Shakespeare's own papers. An example may occur in Act I, scene 5 of *Hamlet,* where the Second Quarto reads, correctly, "Haste me to know't, that I, with wings as swift as Meditation or the thoughts of love, May sweep to my revenge." Curiously, both the Bad Quarto and the Folio omit the necessary "I" and read, "Haste me to know it that with wings," etc.

The editor's troubles in determining what Shakespeare actually wrote do not end merely with variants between two texts, as in these examples. It may be that he will be dissatisfied with what is a common reading, as I am dissatisfied with Polonius telling Ophelia that Hamlet's words are "mere implorators of unholy suits, Breathing like sanctified and pious bonds, The better to beguile." The real Shakespearian reading, as the sense of the whole passage requires, is not *pious bonds* but *pious bawds.* Yet both the Second Quarto and the Folio read *bonds,* just as they agree that a dead dog is a "good kissing carrion" whereas most editors prefer to emend that the sun shining on the dog is a "god kissing carrion."

Here we revert once more to the always crucial question of the physical transmission of the text. Was the Folio set from a new manuscript, or was a copy of the Second Quarto compared with such a manuscript, marked up with alterations, and turned over to the compositor? If a fresh manuscript were itself used as the printer's copy, the agreement of two such independent witnesses should be the strongest guarantee of authenticity, and *bonds* or *good kissing* ought to be correct. To believe otherwise would be to take it that Shakespeare's handwriting in the word *b-a-u-d-s* and *g-o-d* was so ambiguous that, quite separately, the compositor of the Second Quarto and the scribe making up the theater's promptbook each misread these words in the same way as *bonds* and *good.* This is possible, but one would not like to take such a bucket to the well too often, especially twice in the same play.

Hence the editorial emendation of *bonds* to *bawds* and the *good* to *god* would offer serious difficulty if one believed that Shakespeare's own manuscript was the printer's copy for the Second Quarto, and a theatrical manuscript was the copy for the Folio. (Of course, as in *minim's rest* in *The Merry Wives,* if we were to suppose that the printer's copy for the Second Quarto were itself a theatrical manuscript, the authenticity of *bonds* and *good* would be much less certain, since common errors in two manuscripts in the same tradition are to be expected.)

On the other hand, if one could be sure that (as seems actually to be the case) the Folio printer's copy was a marked-up, annotated exemplar of the Second Quarto, then the emendations present no difficulty at all. The editor need only assume that the scribe who was making up the Folio printer's copy overlooked the fact that his manuscript read *bauds* and *god,* and so (in error) failed to alter either word in the Second Quarto that he was preparing for the press.

Editorial theory, and the recovery of Shakespeare's true words, we may see once again, rest very substantially upon establishing the exact physical relationship between any two authoritative documents, and from bibliographical fact evolving a logical basis for editorial action.

Occasionally a Shakespeare play permits us to establish certain controls that are the most valuable. In *Hamlet* a copy of the Second Quarto, not of the Third or Fourth, was interlined and marginally annotated to form the Folio printer's copy. But in *Richard III* either the third or the sixth edition, or some leaves of both (the exact facts are still in dispute), was marked up for the Folio printer. Here the first edition was a bad quarto; all later editions before the Folio were simple reprints that soon corrupted the text still further. No change in any edition between the first and the sixth can have any authority. Thus when the Folio follows a reading that was altered in a later quarto, instead of its reproducing the word found in the first edition, we have postive evidence that the scribe overlooked the difference between his manuscript and the printed copy he was marking up. On the other hand, when the Folio prints a word that does not appear in any earlier edition, this is presumptive evidence that it came from the manuscript and is therefore more likely to be Shakespeare's than the word the actor remembered, as found in the First Quarto.

Most interestingly, when (say) a word is changed in the second and all later editions from the reading of the first, and the Folio forsakes its printed copy to revert to the original word of the first edition, then we have proof positive that the change was made by the scribe from the reading of his manuscript. If in this manner the actor's memory and the scribe's manuscript agree, we ought to feel that we know what Shakespeare wrote, for sure, barring the odd chance that the promptbook behind the actor's memory and the manuscript behind the Folio text might have had a common error. (If there may be degrees of desirability in error, it could even be argued that, if so, it is better to follow the error of the promptbook than the compositor's error of a late and authoritative reprint. The first will surely be closer to Shakespeare's intention than the second.)

It is time to sum up, even though several situations involving Shakespeare's text deserve mention. A most humbling thought is our recognition that a great deal of what we suppose Shakespeare wrote must rest on our ignorance. By this I mean: when only one authoritative text exists, as for all plays first printed in the Folio, or for plays first printed in an earlier quarto but simply reprinted in the Folio without any editorial attention, no opportunity can exist to know more. On the other hand, every single time that more than one good authority appears for a Shakespeare play, as with *Troilus and Cressida*, or *Hamlet*, or *Othello*, where we have two authoritative but different texts in the quartos and Folio, we see that an astonishing amount of variation occurs between the two versions.[1]

Some of these differences must no doubt be imputed to Shakespeare revising his own work, but some are manifestly to be laid at the door of theatrical or other agents who are altering Shakespeare's plays, occasionally inadvertently but occasionally on purpose. For the single-text plays we can never know what other lost forms may have existed that would have given us the opportunity to test what is our only extant authority, as we can in some part test *Othello* or *Hamlet,* or even (with the uncertain help of the Bad Quartos) such plays as *The Merry Wives* and *King Lear.* When we have a play like *Macbeth,* with a text based on an abbreviated theatrical copy, we can never recover the full original form that Shakespeare wrote, as (except for one line or so) we have a very good chance of doing with *Hamlet.*

Our knowledge of what Shakespeare wrote can go no further than the original documents that have been preserved, wherein we are more fortunate than for any other Elizabethan dramatist except Ben Jonson, and Beaumont and Fletcher. Yet we have by no means reached a dead end in the exhaustion of the evidence of these documents. The early editors trusted to little else than their literary judgment both for independent emendation and for the choice of readings among various texts, whether authoritative or unauthoritative. Little by little, however, an increasing logical rigor has entered Shakespeare textual criticism, and at the present day new techniques are just being developed that in future years will carry the refining process still further.

Of these, the most prominent is the bibliographical analysis of the text based on a study of the compositors who put the Shakespeare plays into type. These workmen were individuals, each with different characteristics not only of spelling and punctuation but also of carefulness in the matter of reading the manuscripts and transferring the exact words into print. A considerable difference can be detected, for example, in the work of a thoroughly experienced compositor of some years' standing, like A in the First Folio, and the workman we call E, but whose name was John Leason, an apprentice who had joined Jaggard's printing-house only a few months before he learned how to set type and was put to work on the Folio.

Shakespeare's words passed through the minds, and then through the fingers, of such men with varying degrees of accuracy. The more we know about these workmen, the better we can assess what we know about Shakespeare's text.

In this process I have some hopes that electronic computers can be put to work to digest and to analyze much information that at present we do not have. It will be a blessed day in the future when one can press a button and give such a lordly command as "List for me every time Compositor B follows his copy in spelling *win* as *win* or *winne*, every time he changes a copy spelling *win* to *winne*, or *winne* to *win*, and distinguish in each case between what he does in setting prose and in setting verse. Then give me all the occurrences of *win* and *winne* in texts that he set from manuscript."

When that day comes, we shall be on the New Frontier of Shakespearian textual criticism, and if we cannot do better than in the past in deciding what Shakespeare wrote, then we have no place in an age where science is supposed to be our servant; and we had better turn to some other line of business. Selling insurance, perhaps; at any rate, not selling textual criticism of Shakespeare.

---

[1] We must except such cases as the introduction of a new scene in *Titus Andronicus* or of revised speech prefixes and stage directions in *The Merchant of Venice.* That in *The Merchant* little else was altered, whereas much was changed between Quarto and Folio *Othello,* does not necessarily mean that the theater's manuscripts for plays like *The Merchant* coincided with the printed quarto texts any more than we may presume that the theater's manuscript of *Romeo and Juliet* coincided with the text for the third quarto that was used as copy for the Folio reprint, apparently with no alteration of any kind. The reason for the highly variable editorial attention given to the Folio must remain quite speculative.

Shakespeare's Laundry Bills: The Rationale of External Evidence

F. W. BATESON

F. W. Bateson, University Lecturer in English Literature at Oxford since 1946 and founder and editor of Essays in Criticism, *has achieved a formidable reputation. Like Fredson Bowers he has explored the history of the drama* (English Comic Drama, 1700–1750); *like him again, he has written on a range of literary topics, from Shakespeare to Pope to Blake and Wordsworth; among his books is* English Poetry and the English Language. *Once again we see the vitality of contemporary criticism as we observe that not even so definitive a statement as Professor Bowers's is accepted by all intelligent men as the last word on a given subject. The reader will have to ask himself whether Professor Bowers dispenses with conventional techniques of literary judgment so fully as Dr. Bateson implies, but he should note that even what we might call the bibliographical approach to Shakespeare, rather than constituting an end to discussion, takes an active part in the dialogue to which other kinds of criticism contribute.*

Shakespearian scholarship is entitled, like any other reputable human activity, to its own comic mythology. The laundry bills —they are entirely hypothetical objects, of course—are a nice *reductio ad absurdum* of external evidence pursued for its own sake, a sort of *ne plus ultra* of "pure" literary research. I believe Leslie Stephen was the inventor of this particular conceit. "It does not follow," Stephen wrote in a review of the Brownings' letters that is reprinted in *Studies of a Biographer,* "that because I want fact not fiction I therefore want all the facts, big and small; the poet's washing bills, as well as his early drafts of great works." [1] The mythic figure was revived, or concocted independently, by T. S. Eliot in the penultimate paragraph of "The Function of Criticism," one of his early essays Dr. Leavis most admires. Eliot's central theme is that the critical gift *par excellence* is "a very highly developed sense of fact":

> And any book, any essay, any note in *Notes and Queries,* which produces a fact even of the lowest order about a work of art is a better piece of work than nine-tenths of the most pretentious critical journalism, in journals or in books. We assume, of course, that we are masters and not servants of facts, and that we know that the discovery of Shakespeare's laundry bills would not be of much use to us; but we must always reserve final judgment as to the futility of the research which has discovered them, in the possibility that some genius will appear who will know of a use to which to put them.[2]

Since Mr. Eliot began a recent lecture ("The Frontiers of Criticism") by reaffirming the doctrines of "The Function of Criticism"—"I was glad to find nothing positively to contradict my present opinions" [3]—I suppose he sticks to the laundry bills. It may be useful therefore to take up the argument where he has left it. Some issues of considerable practical and contemporary importance are involved.

Opposed to "fact" in the Eliot schema is "opinion." There is a hierarchy of facts, though what distinguishes a fact "of the lowest order" from one of a higher order is not explained; but opinion, apparently, is always vicious:

> *fact* cannot corrupt taste; it can at worst gratify one taste—a taste for history, let us say, or antiquities or biography—under the illusion that it is assisting another. The real corrupters are those who supply opinion or fancy; and Goethe and Coleridge are not guiltless—for what is Coleridge's *Hamlet:* is it an honest inquiry as far as the data permit, or is it an attempt to present Coleridge in an attractive costume?[4]

I do not propose to attempt a defence of Goethe and Coleridge here; the Romantic interpretation of *Hamlet* is not likely to corrupt much taste in the 1960s that would not be corrupted anyway. It is the status of Shakespearian "fact" in general that needs investigation and perhaps deflation. The monuments of scholarship raised by McKerrow, Greg and Chambers—are they in retrospect more than impeccable works of reference for the books those intellectual giants never wrote—perhaps, their premises being what they were, never could have written?

The laundry bills' claim to scholarly attention is presumably based on the critical doctrine that a poet's style is, or ought to be, the man. It seems to follow, then, that every aspect of Shakespeare the man must connect in some way with Shakespeare the writer. The exact connection awaits that critical genius with the supremely developed sense of fact of Eliot's hypothetical future, but we can guess how the laundry bills might be used if they were ever discovered. They might demonstrate, for example, that Shakespeare changed his linen every day. I do not deny that such biographical minutiae have a certain interest.

What porridge had John Keats? The difficulty is to connect them, directly or even indirectly, with the actual words and word-orders of Shakespeare's or Keats's plays and poems. If it is claimed, for example, that the passion for clean linen would corroborate the absence of sexual cynicism in Shakespearian drama, are we not back in the proscribed area of "opinion"?

The relationship between external evidence (fact) and internal evidence (opinion) needs re-statement. As against the Eliot antithesis between the two procedures the formula I prefer is an interdependence of *relevant* fact and *relevant* opinion. The definition of relevance will vary with the scholarly context, but in Shakespearian studies it seems reasonable to posit as our central criterion a relevance to the meaning of Shakespeare's text. The kind of antiquarianism, therefore, that is symbolized by the laundry bills must prove its right of entry by a demonstration of its textual relevance; equally a Shakespearean critical opinion must survive exactly the same test. Coleridge's interpretation of *Hamlet* on this basis is erroneous, in so far as it is erroneous, not because it is disguised autobiography but because it does not make sense when confronted with the play's text; it is *irrelevant* to it.

But if textual relevance is the criterion that we must apply both to Shakespearian "fact" and to Shakespearian "opinion or fancy," this is not to say that relevant textual fact is the same thing as relevant textual opinion. Rather they are two stages, both equally indispensable, in a single process. It might be put this way: an elementary understanding of the separate words, images, theatrical situations, modes of characterisation, etc., has to precede an appreciation of the combinations or sequences of such dramatic constituents. In other words, to a greater or less degree Shakespeare, or indeed any other writer, is for all of us a sort of foreign language that has just to be learnt. First of all, then, in the order of logic, we need the facts (external evidence); the relevant opinions (internal evidence) come later. If the logical order of these events is reversed or confused, error or irrelevance is likely to break in.

Suppose, for example, I am challenged to make out a case for the emendation "a' talked of green fields" (which was proposed by Theobald's "Gentleman sometime deceas'd" [5] and was supported by Tennyson's friend Spedding, the editor of Bacon) against the Folio's "a Table of greene fields" and Theobald's own "a' babbled of green fields." What evidence am I likely to use? What would the order be in which I ought to call my witnesses?

I shall obviously be well advised to begin with the kind of evidence that would be acceptable in a court of law. My first witness, then, would probably be Hand D's scene in *Sir Thomas More*, which is approximately contemporary with *Henry V* and provides four items of palaeographical relevance:

(i) Doll Williamson, a character of the same general type as the Hostess, uses "a" (so spelled) for the unemphatic form of "he" ("a keepes a plentyfull shrevaltry, and a made my Brother Arther watchin Serjant Safes yeoman").

(ii) Commas, like the other stops, are rare in D and always introduce a new clause; the comma in Doll's "shrevaltry, and a made" would be an exact parallel to the Folio's "for his Nose was as sharp as a Pen, and a Table of greene fields," if "Table" is a misprint for a verb like *talked* or *babbled.*

(iii) Since D reserves its initial capitals for the beginnings of sentences or proper names, the *T* in the Folio's "Table" must be the compositor's contribution.

(iv) Theobald's reading assumes that Shakespeare wrote "babld" which was mis-read "table." D's *d* is certainly almost indistinguishable from its *e*, but its initial *ba* is always easily legible (e. g., 1.75, "their babyes at their backes") and is not at all likely to be confused with its initial *ta* (e. g., l. 80, "taught"), which is also easily legible. On the other hand, D's *k* might be confused with a *b*. A compositor meeting what looked like *talbe* (but was really *talkd*) may be excused for emending it to *table.* (John Munro points out that there are two *b* for *k* misprints in *King Lear.*[6])

My second witness might well be this Folio compositor—who in this passage, to judge by the spellings, is apparently Jaggard's Compositor A. The obvious objection to "a Table of greene fields" is that it does not seem to make sense. But sentences that do not make sense are the characteristic failing of Compositor A. Whereas his fellows tended, even in their most careless moments, to look beyond the word to its immediate context, A (a simple-minded man) was content if each word made sense by itself. Provided each separate word that he set was a real English word A was satisfied. A specimen of his handiwork is to be found at the end of the Hostess's speech:

> *then I felt to his knees, and so up-pear'd, and upward, and all was as cold as any stone.*

The quartos, F3 and modern editions correct "up-pear'd" to "upward," which is obviously the right reading. But for A, proceeding word by word instead of clause by clause, "up-pear'd" was good enough; it was after all a possible English word. A's methods, half-baked though they may seem, have the great virtue of approximate fidelity to the copy. What he has mis-read was really there; he does not insert words of his own to try and make sense of a passage that has defeated him. We may be certain, then, that something that looked like *a table* was actually in the manuscript from which A was working. Our range of possible emendation is therefore greatly narrowed. Indeed, to the best of my knowledge, *babbled* and *talked* are so far the only alternatives to *table* that have ever been proposed. To those editors, then, who struggle desperately to coax some meaning from the Folio text A's frequent contentment with meaningless *is*, I should say, a sufficient rejoinder.

My third witness is the "bad" or "reported" quarto of 1600. Q omits the crucial phrase altogether, rearranging the passage as follows:

> *His nose was as sharpe as a pen: For when I saw him fumble with the sheetes, And talk of floures, and smile upon his fingers ends I knew there was no way but one.*

It is worth noticing that F's "play with Flowers" is corrupted in Q to "talk of floures": the verb may well be a relic from the lost clause. Now *babble* is a more memorable word than *talk*. If the words omitted had been *babbled of green fields*, would not Q have preferred *babble of flowers* to *talk of flowers?* A significant feature of the passage in Q is that, apart from omissions and changes of word-order, Q's deviations from F are all trivial, such as "when" instead of "after." The one exception is "talk"—an exception that would prove the rule if F's "Table" is indeed a misprint of *talkd*.

The three witnesses hitherto called all belong to the honourable department of external evidence known as textual criticism. And the points that have emerged in the analysis of their evidence are certainly relevant to the problem to which I am committed, which *is* a controversial detail of Shakespeare's text. The embarrassing thing, though, about them is the disproportion between the two short disputed words and the hundreds and hundreds that my commentary, which is far from complete, seems to require. A mountain of disquisition and the molehill of *a' talked!* Unlike the work of the detective in real life, which is normally the bringing to justice of serious crime, textual criticism does not carry its own justification with it. After all, what was Compositor A really

guilty of? The peccadillo of momentary carelessness! All this fuss
over two words seems to verge on pedantry.

But I have two more witnesses to call—the dramatic critic and
the literary critic. With them a more humane series of values
enters into the argument. To the dramatic critic the Hostess (Mrs.
Quickly in *2 Henry IV* and *The Merry Wives*) is a masterpiece
of comic characterisation, but a masterpiece in virtue of what she
says rather than what she does. It is her mode of speech—brilliantly breathless, touchingly domestic and comically malapropist
—that enchants him. She has an idiom of her own that is maintained with extraordinary consistency throughout the three plays.
It is the positiveness of this idiom that is fatal, I believe, to all
the various attempts that have been made to retain the Folio's
"and a Table" unemended, or with "on" substituted for "and."
These emendations generally consist in an extension and elaboration of the Hostess's simile: Falstaff's nose is as sharp as a pen
on a table covered with the green cloth usual in counting-houses
(Henry Bradley), *and a memorial tablet pointed in Gothic fashion in the green fields of a cemetery* (Percival R. Cole), *in an
engraving of Sir Richard Grenville* (Leslie Hotson).[7] The pen
in these examples has been the ordinary quill-pen, but it too can
be reinterpreted and for Hilda Hulme it is *a device on a coat-of-
arms, the field vert,* and for John S. Tuckey *a mountain-peak
rising steeply from a tableland consisting of green fields.*[8] The
game will no doubt continue. As ways of making some sort of
sense of the Folio reading such interpretations deserve, I suppose,
their modicum of praise. But they lose all their plausibility once
they are put side by side with the Hostess's other similes. Compare these elaborate and sophisticated analogies with those of
2 Henry IV (IV ii): *red as any rose, rheumatic as two dry toasts,
and 'twere on aspen leaf.* Or those of *Henry V* (apart from the
pen): *honey-sweet, as any christom child, as any stone.* The
Hostess's metaphors and similes are always short, colloquial, traditional. She has only one simile in all her appearances that she may
be supposed to have made up herself, and that, significantly, is in
The Merry Wives: "a great round Beard, like a Glovers pairing-
knife." That paring-knife does not ring quite true to me, but it is
naïve compared to the elaborate Wycherley-type witticisms at-

tributed to her by Henry Bradley and the others. She just doesn't talk like that.

The dramatic critic's testimony can be put in peremptory terms: such interpretations have only one defect—*they ruin the Hostess's part.* It would be far better to leave the whole clause out, as Q does, than to spoil her best speech with this sort of laboured and quite uncharacteristic rubbish. No such objection can be riased to *babbled* or *talked.* Both words are probably within the range of the Hostess's vocabulary, though *babbled* (unlike *talked*) does not appear elsewhere in her part. The word may well have been a bit beyond her; it only occurs nine times in Shakespeare, six of these being *babbling,* and it is usually confined to the upper-class characters. (But Dogberry uses it once: "for the Watch to babble and to talke, is not tollerable.")

I have one more witness to call—the literary critic. As between *babbled* and *talked,* the first question the critic will want to ask is the exact difference in meaning between the two words at the end of the sixteenth century. The quick answer is that *talk* had much the same range of meanings as to-day, but that *babble* in all the Shakespearian passages—including two from *Titus Andronicus* which may be pseudo-Shakespearian—meant only one thing, viz., "to talk excessively or inopportunely, to chatter" (*O. E. D.*). Whereas to *talk* is neutral, the speech may be either silly or sensible, to *babble,* as Shakespeare uses the word, always carries a dyslogistic sense of silly speech. The critical or stylistic problem, then, is whether a neutral meaning or a dyslogistic meaning is more appropriate in the context of this passage. The sentences concerned could, I suggest, be summarized as follows:

> *When I saw him fumbling* (foolishly) *with the sheets, and playing* (foolishly) *with flowers, and smiling* (foolishly) *at his fingertips, I knew he would soon be dead. His nose looked* (ridiculously) *pointed, and he talked* (foolishly) *about green fields.*

The object of this summary is twofold: (i) to make it clear that the five traditional symptoms of approaching death form a continuous series of parallel items; (ii) to show that the five symptoms are all to some degree grotesque and even absurd. And by

adding the italicized adverbs in brackets I have tried to bring
out the *implicit* character of the absurdities. The Hostess does
not say in so many words that the first four symptoms are foolish
or ridiculous, but we certainly respond to them as such; to maintain the continuity of the imagery therefore the fifth symptom
must also be only implicitly absurd. To read *babbled* (= talked
foolishly) is to break the semantic series by making the comment
explicit; no such objection can be made to the apparently neutral
talked.

I shall rest the case for *a' talked* at this point. My immediate
concern is not with the superior plausibility of the Deceased Gentleman's emendation so much as with the general character of
the items of evidence on which an emendation such as his must
depend. The evidence has been reasonably representative, I think,
if by no means complete. One very significant point that emerges
in analysis is a difference of objectives in the external evidence
(Hand D, Compositor A, and the "reported" quarto) and the internal evidence (the consistency of dramatic idiom, the stylistics
of serial imagery). They cannot be used to prove the same thing.
The external evidence has combined to demonstrate *what Shakespeare probably wrote*; namely *talkd*, in the minuscules of the sec-
retary hand; in the other hand, the internal evidence has been
concerned to show *what Shakespeare must have meant;* namely
a popular and "neutral" kind of talk that is not brought out satisfactorily in the other interpretations or emendations.

In this instance what was probably written and what must have
been meant overlap; they will normally do so. But they do not
necessarily coincide, and if a divergence can be established what
Shakespeare wrote will have to be corrected, so far as that is
possible, by what he must be presumed to have meant.

The point is easily demonstrated. Heminge's and Condell's testimony that "what he thought, he uttered with that easinesse that
wee have scarce received from him a blot in his papers" must
mean that Shakespeare's manuscripts showed little sign of revision. But anyone writing *currente calamo* is bound to have some
words that have been miswritten, or even left out altogether, and
the punctuation is sure to be more or less imperfect. Some revision, however slight, some final tidying-up, is always necessary.

Hand D's scene is typical. The number of minims in sequences like *in* or *un* is incorrect seven times in the 147 lines, and there are also, according to Greg, "slips," "errors," malformed letters, a word the writer "forgot to cross out" and another in which "the writer's intention is quite obscure." [9] Finally D's punctuation, or absence of punctuation, is wildly erratic and inconsistent. If this scene is typical one must agree with Ben Jonson: "would he had blotted a thousand." I do not mean that the scene in *Sir Thomas More* is riddled with textual cruxes. This is not so. The errors and omissions are most of them easily corrected. But it remains true that what Shakespeare meant in this scene has to be recovered from what he wrote by the application of exactly the same methods that editors use with the printed texts of the early editions. An autograph differs only in degree, not in kind, from other texts.

Greg's first editorial rule—"The aim of a critical edition should be to present the text, so far as the available evidence permits, in the form in which we may suppose that it would have stood in a fair copy, made by the author himself, of the work as he finally intended it" [10]—stems from the Eliot illusion that "fact" (external evidence) must be preserved at any cost from the corrupting influence of "opinion." An author's final intentions are buried with him and will never be known in their entirety, but even between his penultimate or antepenultimate intentions and the fairest fair copy in which they are written down there is always the possibility of accidental error. The last editorial word must still be with *what Shakespeare must have meant*; it is the final criterion between what is and is not error in *what Shakespeare wrote*. A reading only proves its correctness by its coherence with the context of meaning preceding it. It is true that the point of departure here is external evidence—the letters on the printed page or manuscript that present themselves to the reader as Shakespeare's play. But at this point a two-way process is necessarily started— first from the external text to the internal meanings it communicates to the reader, and then, as the meanings form themselves internally into a coherent aesthetic body, a reversal of direction from the reader's mind to the text, either confirming it or correcting it. A common or garden misprint is a simple example of the process: we correct a misprint because it doesn't make sense in its context.

The dead-end into which textual criticism is driven if it ignores the stylistic core at the heart of every literary problem may be illustrated by a passage from the trumpet-call against the critics recently blown by Professor Fredson Bowers of the University of Virginia:

> not much is changed whether Hamlet's father's bones were *interred* as in Q 2, or *inurned* as in the Folio (I iv 49). Yet I hold it to be an occupation eminently worth while, warranting any number of hours, to determine whether Shakespeare wrote one, or the other, or both. The decision, if clear-cut, might be crucial in the accumulation of evidence whether on the whole the Folio variants from the quarto *Hamlet* are corruptions, corrections, or revisions. If this is a problem no editor has fairly faced, neither should a literary critic be indifferent to the question. Depending upon what can be proved, some hundreds of readings will be affected if an editor decides that Shakespeare revised the text after its second quarto form; for in that case the Folio variants should be chosen in all but the most obvious cases of sophistication. Or he might decide that in only a few cases, where the second quarto compositors have corrupted the text, should the Folio readings take precedence over the generally authoritative second quarto.[11]

It is impossible not to warm to that "occupation eminently worth while, warranting any number of hours." This is the heroic spirit of scholarship. But an examination of the problem soon shows that the respective status of *interred* and *inurned* can only be finally determined from the internal evidence of style. The bibliographical evidence is quite indecisive. No doubt Q2 does derive more or less directly from Shakespeare's autograph, but its Act I was set up, as Bowers agrees, either from a copy of the "reported" Q1 partly corrected from the autograph, or (more probably) from a special printing-house transcript of this corrected copy. Now Q1 also reads "interr'd" here, and the possibility must be faced that the reading is simply a mistake of the reporter's carelessly carried over into Q2. The Folio "enurn'd" is certainly the *difficilior lectio:* whereas *inter* is a common Eliza-

bethan word, *inurn* has not been traced, I believe, before its occurrence here and the word is probably a coinage of Shakespeare's. He was fond of words of this type; the following verbs
are not found before Shakespeare according to the *O. E. D.*:
*emball, embound, enclog, endart, enrank, enridge, enschedule,
entreasure, illume, immask, impaint, impleach, impress, inclip, in-
corpse, inhearse, injoint, inscroll, inship, insinew.* In other words,
on the textual evidence both readings are just about equally
plausible. No more and no less.

Well, even the most cursory stylistic analysis can do better
than that. It is clear from the preceding and succeeding lines
that the elder Hamlet was buried and not cremated. "Why thy
Canoniz'd bones Hearsed in death, / Have hurst their cerments,
why the Sepulcher / ... Hath op'd his ponderous and Marble
jawes, / To cast thee up againe?" (F text, but Q1 and Q2 are in
substantial agreement with it) can mean nothing else. In the face
of these direct references to burial *inurn* can only be defended as
a dead metaphor. But to impute to Shakespeare of all people an
unconsciousness of the cremation-image latent in the word is
indeed a desperate conjecture. When the play was originally
written the line must surely have read, as in Q2,

> *Wherein we saw thee quietly interr'd*

Nevertheless *quietly inurned* has a very Shakespearian ring. I
suspect it is the product of a later revision. It is a characteristic
of authorial revision, especially of poetry, that it improves the
immediate meaning at the cost of that of the wider context. The
ashes implied by *in-urn,* though nonsense in the passage as a
whole, do go very nicely with *quietly.* This urn too is a bride of
quietness, whereas the corpse that has been merely buried carries
with it the faint suggestion of movement—the body disintegrates,
the flesh decays, the worms enter on their grisly feast—and even
a slight movement is surely incompatible with poetic quietness.
Another stylistic consideration also points to *inurned* as a later
revision by Shakespeare himself. In terms of style the original
passage was not in Shakespeare's best manner. Like so much of
his blank verse at this period (*Henry V* is the notorious exam-

ple) it is "Parnassian" in Hopkins's sense of the word: the words
and images have come rather too easily; Shakespeare is relying
too much on a rhetoric that resounds a little mechanically. If we
can feel this, Shakespeare must have been aware of it too, and it
is at least possible that he tried later on, when his blank verse
had recovered from its "Parnassian" phase, to touch the passage
up. Word for word, just as pure poetry, *quietly inurned* is an improvement on *quietly interred,* as it certainly is on *canonized
bones,* and even on *ponderous and marble jaws.* Unfortunately
however they make dramatic sense, and it doesn't.

I may be wrong. Even if I am right and *inurned* is a case of
revision, that is still no guarantee, of course, as Professor Bowers
would like us to believe, that the other Folio variants, apart from
the "obvious" corruptions, are also revisions by Shakespeare. They
may be revisions by somebody else, Burbage, for example. Each
reading must be considered on its merits, external and internal,
and both kinds of evidence must be used together, one as the corrective or supplement of the other. Our external-internal dialogue
may often be prolonged and sometimes indecisive. That is the
nature of most literary problems. But one thing is certain. Whether
the enquiry is decisive or indecisive the last word in it must
always be allowed to "meaning" or "style," not to Mr. Eliot's
"fact" or Professor Bowers's "bibliography." Inconvenient though
it may be for research purposes, the literary artifact remains obsti-
nately in the last resort "an intellectual thing," which cannot be
pinned down on the laboratory bench. With that proviso we need
not reject as points of critical departure even the laundry bills
themselves.

[1] Ser. 2, III (1902), 30.

[2] *Selected Essays* (1932), p. 33.

[3] *On Poetry and Poets* (1957), p. 103.

[4] *Selected Essays*, p. 33.

[5] *Shakespeare Restored* (1926), p. 138.

[6] *The London Shakespeare* (1958), IV, 1055n.

[7] See *London Shakespeare* as above, and *TLS* 6 April 1956.

[8] *Essays in Criticism*, VI (1956), 117–19, 486–91.

[9] *Shakespeare's Hand in the Play of Sir Thomas More* (1923), pp. 230-43.

[10] *The Editorial Problem in Shakespeare*, 2nd ed. (1951), p. x.

[11] *Textual and Literary Criticism* (1959), pp. 7–8.

১৯ ১৯

Theatrical Research and the
Criticism of Shakespeare
and His Contemporaries*

JOHN RUSSELL BROWN

*Certainly no sensible Shakespearean critic ever forgets that the
works he studies were written for the theater by a man so little
concerned with their life outside that theater that he apparently
made no efforts to get them published. On the other hand, dealing with Shakespeare as a literary artist, we sometimes forget how
much theatrical exigencies—the possibilities of the stage, the
nature of the audience, the conventions of the drama in which
they were written—dictate what the plays actually are. John
Russell Brown, who teaches at Birmingham University, has written on Shakespearean comedy and has edited plays by Shakespeare and his contemporaries. His essay outlines the ways in
which theater research can constitute an approach to Shakespeare.
He has published articles along the lines of the present essay, and
in other branches of theatrical criticism, in* Stratford-upon-Avon
Studies, Tulane Drama Review, *and* Shakespeare Survey *and
hopes to collect and add to these in a volume to be called*
Shakespeare's Plays in Performance.

My approach to playwriting and the drama itself is organic; and
to make this glaringly evident at once it is necessary to separate
drama from what we think of today as literature. A drama ought
not be looked at first and foremost from literary perspectives
merely because it uses words, verbal rhythm, and poetic image.
These can be its most memorable parts, it is true, but they are
not its inevitable accompaniments.

So Mr. Arthur Miller introduces his *Collected Plays*,[1] and proceeds to demonstrate that we must think of his development as a
dramatist in terms of a full theatrical experience, including the
management of time, visual backgrounds and relationships, and

the kind of "questions" which are asked and answered each time
an actor walks on to the stage. He convinces us that his plays need
a theatrical criticism, not a mere adaptation of literary criticism.

There are many reasons for believing that the same is true of
Shakespeare's plays. Clearly he was a man of the theater, more
so than Mr. Miller: he was actor, "instructor" of actors, manager
and theater-owner, as well as author, and he never took the trouble
to publish his plays with notes, special stage-directions, preface or
dedication as most of his contemporaries did on occasion, the
more literary ones many times. He surely cultivated "literary"
qualities in his writing, but the experience of watching one of
his plays in rehearsal demonstrates forcibly how the text is awakened, colored, emphasized, extended in performance, in relation
to visual and temporal elements inherent in it. The need for a theatrical criticism of Shakespeare seems self-evident, for even the
consciously literary dramatists of the present century, as Yeats or
Mr. Eliot, have obviously modified their writing in response to the
experience of seeing their works in performance; a critic of plays
must understand and account for such things.

Yet it is said on all sides that Shakespeare is an exception to
this rule. In his latest and most perceptive book, Professor L. C.
Knights has claimed that:

> in recent Shakespeare criticism, the *verse* has moved well into the
> centre of the picture, . . . because linguistic vitality is now felt as
> the *chief* clue to the urgent personal themes that not only shape
> the poetic-dramatic structure of each play but form the figure in
> the carpet of the canon as a whole.[2]

For our greatest dramatist, so this theory goes, words are the
heart of the matter, and many critics have followed this literary
lead. The result is that books are written about Shakespeare's doctrine, themes, ethic, philosophical patterns, images, moral ideas,
and fewer and fewer about his dramas, plays, varieties of theatrical experiences. And the chief clues to this philosophic Shakespeare lie, necessarily, in the variety of his verbal images, the
structure of his complex words, his "linguistic vitality," rather than
in his theatrical technique, his use of time, movement or isolation.
Almost all the criticism of Shakespeare—and the criticism of lesser
writers tends to follow suit—uses specifically literary techniques

and terminology, is based on literary perceptions, and leads to literary definition.

There are many reasons for this attitude. Critics, trained in literary disciplines, are apt to think that theatrical experience is coarse and vulgar, to be measured only in terms of popular appeal—as if the brave color of Van Gogh's sunflowers were all the finesse of which the visual arts were capable. More informed is the belief that theatrical experience is too complex and unmanageable to be talked about profitably: among its obvious difficulties are antiquarian considerations, the lack of terminology, diversity and conflict of opinion, and dispersal of interest among many trivial phenomena. Professor Wilson Knight, a critic who has himself acted, produced plays and attended many performances, has averred after much study:

> my experience . . . leaves me uncompromising in my assertion that the literary analysis of great drama in terms of theatrical technique accomplishes singularly little. . . .

Professor Knight believes that it is necessary to "write of Shakespeare . . . as a philosophic poet rather than a man of the stage." [3] And the majority of twentieth-century critics agree with him, when judging Shakespeare's plays or those of his contemporaries.

In this situation in the play of criticism it seems appropriate for theater research to make an entrance. There are many ways in which it can help to define the theatrical experience provided by the text of a play, to remind the critic of its visual and temporal elements as well as the verbal, and so to lead towards a full theatrical criticism. Literary criticism has set the pace and revealed the subtlety and range of one part of Shakespeare's imagination; theater research can help to reveal and define other parts.

In a simple and obvious way it can sharpen the critic's eye. By recovering, ordering and assessing the records and reviews of past performances, theater research can help the critic to see what stage actions, movements and visual relationships are implied by the author's text. For instance. Mr. Gordon Crosse's *Shakespearean Playgoing, 1890-1952* (1953) by describing past productions shows the potential force of Banquo "keenly" watching Macbeth in Act II during the discovery of Duncan's murder (p. 64). This is an important fact, critically. Banquo's silent watch can make an audience aware of Macbeth's equivocations—his concern to make his foul seem fair—throughout the scene in which he appears most successfully to cast his guilt on others; it adds force to Banquo's "In the great hand of God I stand" with which he rejoins the general dialogue; and its immobility contrasts with Macbeth's new rapidity, with his actions implied in "Let's briefly put on manly readiness." In short, the theatrical effectiveness of Banquo's silent presence, which in reading the play it is easy to forget, is an important indication of the design of the tragedy, showing how continuous was Shakespeare's concern with the responsible, theocentric world against which, and over against which, Macbeth is shown living and fighting. The same record of past performances can again act as visual prompter in describing the force of Macduff's standing apart in Act V, Scene vi, when the other characters talk stirringly of imminent battle:[4] the fact that he breaks a conspicuous silence to say:

Make all our trumpets speak: give them all breath,
Those clamorous harbingers of blood and death.

shows that he, unlike the others, has been thinking of the cost of battle in terms of "blood and death"; and that Shakespeare was still, as in the earlier scene in England, concerned to show the particular, personal loss which Macduff alone has sustained in the death of his wife and children, to remind the audience here, at the last moment, that Macbeth has broken bonds of private affection as well as those of social, political and religious order.

The usefulness of research into theater records in serving as a prompter to those who try to understand the full theatrical implications of a dramatic text could be illustrated in thousands of instances. Two more may suffice here. A review [5] after the performance of *The White Devil* in London on March 6, 1947, points to the importance of a one-line part in this play which many have read, but few have been able to see. It describes the sense of embarrassment which Webster achieved by introducing a young, anonymous page to contradict Cornelia's attempt to shield her son from Bracciano's anger, with a simple "This is not true, madam"; attention is thus drawn away, rapidly and without warning, from the center of a very "dramatic" situation, and a silence follows. This is not a trivial point, though it might easily be overlooked in reading: it illustrates Webster's power of using violent and crowded scenes for sudden, and, therefore, striking, manifestations of an individual's lies or hypocrisy, the "variety" of a "busy trade of life"; and it prepares the audience for another young, unsubtle voice at the end of the play, that of Giovanni, meting out justice without knowing the full complexity and danger of his task.

A further example of theatrical prompting is one which does not depend on the record of a single review. Almost any production of *Much Ado about Nothing* will furnish reviews commenting upon the speaking of Beatrice's words "Kill Claudio," and they will often be contradictory. Read together, as they may be by a theatrical researcher, they show how precarious the comic and sentimental issues are at just this point in the play; how, in performance, these two words can trigger off great and opposing reactions, sometimes causing laughter, sometimes concern. Again this is of more than incidental significance: it marks how powerful the "covered fire" of passion is, beneath the easy wit and rapid movement of Benedick and Beatrice; it shows that Shakespeare was concerned with the danger and the absurdity of the way in which they love while refusing to say they love.

Sometimes the reviews and accounts of past productions can clarify the balance of a whole play. A reading of *Measure for Measure*, for example, may suggest that little importance attaches to Lucio; his jokes seem stale or obscure, his part in the development of the action slight. There are several well-known criticisms of this play which barely mention him: H. B. Charlton's chapter in his *Shakespearian Comedy* (1938) refers to him briefly on two occasions only, once calling him a "most fallible mortal," and once dismissing him as "sewage." But accounts of performances show again and again that the actor of Lucio attracts considerable attention. *The London Chronicle* of 1758 testifies fully:

> The part of Lucio . . . is, as far as I can judge, both for humour and nature, by many degrees superior to any character of the same stamp, introduced upon the stage since. And notwithstand-

ing the audience have seen it so often inimitably performed by Mr. Woodward, the unanimous applause they gave to Mr. Obrien, who appeared in it the above night [October 10], was a convincing argument that they thought he displayed very great theatrical talents.

Theater research can tell the critic, at least, that Lucio is a fine opportunity for an actor, and a full criticism of the play must take this into account: his dismissal in the last scene is not an easy or slight incident.

The study of cast-lists and playbills—now greatly simplified for the eighteenth century by Mr. C. B. Hogan's *Shakespeare in the Theater* (1952, 1957) [6]—can in itself serve the literary critic by indicating the range of interpretation a part or a play has received, and how it has found favor in one century as opposed to another. While modern literary critics extol *Antony and Cleopatra,* and place it among the finest of Shakespeare's works, it will sharpen our comprehension of the nature of Shakespeare's achievement in this tragedy to know that in the eighteenth century it was in the repertory only for one year, 1759, and not revived. Similarly the critic may be given a useful train of inquiry when he has to explain to himself why *Richard II*, displacing Theobald's version of the play in 1738 and 1739, was not revised again in that century. When it is argued, as by Dr. Leslie Hotson,[7] that Shakespeare intended Malvolio to be a laughing-stock or comic gull, or that a modern, sentimental concern for the underdog is alone responsible for the more sympathetic, or "straight," interpretation of the role, a consultation of theatrical records can show that two comics, Charles Macklin and Thomas King, were succeeded as Malvolio at Drury Lane in 1777 by a "straight" actor, Robert Bensley: King played mayor roles in the company for twenty years after this time, but he never took back Malvolio from Bensley; so the player of the Gravedigger, Stephano and Touchstone was replaced by the player of Antonio (in *The Merchant of Venice*), of Banquo, the Ghost in *Hamlet*, Henry IV, Prospero, and Wolsey. Malvolio was more than a comic butt, long before the contemporary cult of the misunderstood. Feste's thrusts at him

. . . with dagger of lath,
In his rage and his wrath

are not, necessarily, a duel with a character who has a comic's
resilience; it may well be a real storm among the "matter for a
May morning." And Malvolio's final appearance, baited before
his mistress and his fellows, may be meant for laughter only after
it has been, as Fabian says, "justly weighed"; it may be a sober
moment before "golden time convents" and "fancy's queen" happily entertained. Theater research shows that this is an old, as
well as a modern, interpretation.

Cast-lists, reviews, illustrations, prompt-books, memoirs, can all,
together or separately, show the range of possible interpretations
of dramatic texts, and also help the critic to discriminate between
them. Mr. Michael Langham's production of *Hamlet* at Stratford-
upon-Avon, with Mr. Alan Badel as the prince, is fully documented
in the Memorial Theatre Library, with press-cuttings, photographs, and prompt-book. For this production, the reviews were
in notable accord: it was a careful, responsible presentation of an
anti-romantic, unglamorous prince who has "of late lost all his
mirth," who pities and sometimes hates himself; it showed, with
much imaginative detail, a man in a situation stronger than his
power to comprehend, who cannot communicate easily until he
loses himself in action. The interpretation has some support from
modern literary criticism, so that the reviews and prompt-book
make particularly fascinating reading. First, all reviewers—even
the favorable ones—agree that interest was not always sustained;
this might be due in part to the actor rather than the interpretation, but further reading can prove that the charge was a new
one against Mr. Badel. Photographs and prompt-book show, moreover, that the stage was particularly bare, the action continuous
and swift; several reviewers noticed this, but nevertheless still insisted on the incomplete hold of the play. Reading further it is
clear that in order to keep the pace rapid, or because the passage
did not seem necessary to this interpretation, the dialogue between Hamlet and Horatio at the beginning of Act V, Scene ii,
was completely cut; there was nothing of Rosencrantz and Guildenstern "going to't" and not lying near Hamlet's conscience, nothing

of the question "is't not perfect conscience" to requite Claudius; the last scene started with Hamlet's regret that he had forgotten himself towards Laertes. These adjustments, necessary for Mr. Langham's interpretation of the play, and the strangely unanimous verdict of the reviewers, academic as well as journalistic, can help the critic to judge this reading of the play in its full theatrical life.

Few theaters performing the plays of Shakespeare and his contemporaries in English maintain comprehensive archives like the Shakespeare Memorial Theatre, but nevertheless persistent research can often bring the consequences of any particular interpretation into vivid light. Mr. Moelwyn Merchant's discussion of illustrations and settings for *Henry VIII* and *Coriolanus* in his pioneering and perceptive book, *Shakespeare and the Artist* (1959), shows the varying visual emphases of different readings of these plays. Professor Sprague's description of the stage business as various Falstaffs have tried to lift the dead Hotspur on to their backs draws attention to the picture which Shakespeare has contrived, in which the Spirit of Comedy, with difficulty, carries the Spirit of Heroism from the field of battle; a literary critic might never guess from a reading of the play that the sheer physical difficulty of a fat man lifting a "dead" weight necessarily holds this picture for the audience's attention, nor how some interpretations used it purely for low comedy while others strove to avoid laughter.[8] Occasionally a single piece of evidence will, luckily, suggest the theatrical consequences of a particular interpretation. For example, *Twelfth Night* was presented by Daly in high romantic style, heartfelt and tender, and a delighted description of one scene in the *New York Herald Tribune* of November 28, 1894, illustrates how much against the quick-moving and complicated action of Shakespeare's play this one-sided reading can be:

> The scene is Olivia's garden. The time is evening. Viola, disguised as the minstrel Cesario, having received an intimation that perhaps her brother, Sebastian, has not been drowned, has spoken her joyous soliloquy upon that auspicious thought, and has sunk into a seat, in meditation. The moon is rising over the

distant sea, and in the fancied freshness of the balmy rising breeze
you can almost hear the ripple of the leaves. The lovelorn
Orsino enters, with many musicians, and they sing a serenade,
beneath the windows of Olivia's palace. The proud beauty comes
forth upon her balcony, and, parting her veil, looks down upon
Viola. . . . Not a word is spoken and not a word is needed. The
garden is all in moonlight; the delicious music flows on; and
. . . the curtain slowly falls. It was a perfect triumph of art, in
the highest and best vein.

So much for the romantic opportunities Shakespeare missed in
his "romantic comedy," as it is often called. "Not a word is
spoken and not a word is needed"—this, with the contrived en-
trances, marks the distance from Shakespeare's text that a sentimental interpretation can stray.

Sometimes it is possible to go, with book in hand, to theatrical
records to test a new interpretation. Mr. Derek Traversi in his
recent book, *Shakespeare From 'Richard II' to 'Henry V'* (1958),
has searched for what he calls "meanings" in the "language and
verse" of these plays, and has pronounced (pp. 49 and 107) that
Prince Hal is "the central figure" of *Henry IV, Part 1*, and that
"the last word of the play has really been spoken" with the end
of the penultimate scene. "Are these things true in the theater?,"
we may ask the theater researcher: "is the last scene often cut,
or does it pass unnoticed by reviewers and actors?," "do surviving
illustrations or stage-directions in prompt-books give Hal, and not
Falstaff or Hotspur, the central place?" Theater research cannot
always answer such questions unequivocally, but it can always
insure that our search for answers is not exclusively literary. It
can extend the critic's response towards the visual and temporal
elements of a drama, and give hints of its form and pressure in
performance in varying ages, under varying stage-conditions and
according to a wide range of interpretations. Experience is of
course needed to read the records: stage conditions and audiences and actors are never similar to those of the first performances of plays; good reviewers must be distinguished from those
who are prejudiced or inefficient; evidence is never complete.
But the records are responses to the essential fact of dramatic illusion, and so, even when clear information is denied, the critic

from reading them may grow in perception of theatrical experience, and in power to describe the theatrical possibilities of any particular play, or scene, or word, or silence.

If this recourse is available, it seems unfortunate and inexplicable that it is so little used, and that critics are content to write of Shakespeare as a "philosophic poet *rather than* a man of the stage." Why is criticism so consistently literary, so seldom theatrical?

The main reason is probably that the evidence for theater research is so dispersed. There are collections like those at the New York Public Library and the Birmingham Reference Library, and some private collections to which a student may have access. But it is not easy to attempt complete surveys, and easy to fall into error. Consequently potential theater researchers are often discouraged. The Arden Shakespeare has a tradition of including stage histories in each volume, but in the last four years the editors of *Richard II, Henry VI, Part Two, Othello,* and *All's Well* have all shrunk from this responsibility, their volumes appearing without this customary aid to the student. When stage histories do appear they are often erratic and sometimes absurd. That in the Variorum Edition of *Troilus and Cressida,* published in 1953, is a bad example: divergent opinions on a production are quoted without comment; other productions are represented by a part of a single review; an amateur *reading* one evening at University College, London, of an *abbreviated* version under the auspices of the British Empire Shakespeare Society is noticed, while two major full-scale productions (involving Sir Donald Wolfit, Miss Pamela Brown and Mr. Paul Scofield) are not even listed; and all is presented in a "take-it-or-leave-it" manner, which transcribes comments on little local difficulties (like the late arrival of helmets for an amateur production in Boston, Mass.), and sometimes relies wholly on statistics, sometimes on worn-out journalese.

It is easy to see the compilers' difficulties. And one must recognize the diverse claims that are made upon them: they try to satisfy readers interested in the personality and art of great actors, those interested in the development of taste or scenic design, of lighting techniques, or of acting techniques, those following the stories of theater buildings, of dramatists, of managers, of directors. Because the literary critic may not be aware of all these demands, he may become impatient of even the best among stage-histories, and find theater research a discipline too bewildering for use. Mr. Herbert Marshall's introduction to the "pictorial record" of *Hamlet through the Ages* (1952) lists some of the questions which prompted the compilation and editing of this book, unfortunately still unique:

> What would we not give to know really how Duse acted, or Irving produced or how Shakespeare's company played at the Globe? How did an Antoine production compare with Molière? Or Saxe-Meiningen with Reinhardt or Piscator? How did Gordon Craig's Shakespeare production compare with Granville-Barker's? (P. xi.)

and in all this conjecture, the literary critic will not find one of his own questions explicitly stated: theater research can seem oblivious to his needs. Professor Sprague is a literary critic as well as an original theater scholar, yet his list of criteria for considering pieces of stage business in his book on *Shakespeare and the Actors* would not reassure another literary critic turning to theater research for the first time:

> in deciding to include rather than reject a piece of business, I have usually been guided by one or more of the following considerations: that it possessed artistic merit in itself; or served to illustrate, or to enforce, the meaning of the lines; that it was early in time; that it had a place in the acting tradition of the play. (P. xvii)

The phrase "meaning of the lines" will sound familiar to the literary scholar, but it will not sound adventurous or likely to tell him anything he could not discover for himself; and little else in this list seems to be connected with his particular interest in the plays themselves.

These are considerable difficulties preventing a fuller use of theater research. There is little need to spend time denouncing shoddy stage histories, inaccurate and unhelpful, but new ones should be encouraged and steps must be taken to insure that they answer the questions of the literary critic more fully, or, perhaps, more obviously, than is the custom. Among all the various and important demands made upon the theater researcher, those of the critic need to be attended to more closely. He is, in a word, interested in the play itself, the play which the author wrote and its inherent theatrical life. Of course, details about Forbes-Robinson or Irving acting Hamlet can tell an experienced reader about the play itself; but there are other facts which speak more directly and with less chance of misinterpretation. These could, and should, be found in stage histories and other works of theatrical research, and given some prominence.

Four precise suggestions may clarify the needs of a literary critic. The first is very simple, and could be followed almost mechanically. It is that the theater researcher should always record those occasions when he comes across a group of unconnected reviews or accounts of performances which concur in remarking upon any one particular detail of a play. The concern of many reviewers and actors, over many years, with the words "Kill Claudio" is an example of such a fact: that this crisis (seldom mentioned in books of criticism) has great difficulty and ambiguity in the theater should be clearly recorded by theater historians, for the literary critic will never learn the fact by a rigorous analysis of its not very complex words. There is a somewhat similar concurrence of interest upon a few lines in Webster's *The White Devil*. This play has been given three professional productions in London in the present century, in 1925, 1935 and 1947; each production gave a different emphasis, and yet after each of them a number of reviewers independently noted the deep impression made by a few of Flamineo's words:

> *I have a strange thing in me, to th'which*
> *I cannot give a name, without it be*
> *Compassion.*

The reviewers spoke of "human feeling" or "imaginative agony," and, although one of them considered it an "irrelevant" moment, they all testified to its power.[9] Now this is a most important fact for the critic, for these lines provide an excentric moment in the presentation of Flamineo and so, in reading, they might be passed over lightly, or judged to be due to forgetfulness on Webster's part of the sort of character he had created. Nor does their theatrical power influence only our "reading" of Flamineo's role; it can modify our view of the play as a whole. Clearly the heroine, Vittoria Corrambona, is committed to a life of pleasure, passion and courage, instigates two murders, and pleads not guilty to her evident adultery; she has some moments of alarm, when she cries "O me accurst" or "O me! this place is hell," but it seems, in her own words, that "nothing but blood could allay" the demands of life as she found it. Only at the very end does she suggest that she could imagine any other way of life; then, in her dying words, she gives a quite contrary impression:

> O happy they that never saw the court,
> Nor ever knew great man but by report.

This sentiment is so out of key with the rest of her part, that a responsible and imaginative editor, M. W. Sampson, has suggested that the two lines belong to Zanche, the waiting-woman, and not to Webster's heroine. But if Flamineo's single and brief recognition of compassion is clearly of great power in the theater, perhaps Webster intended Vittoria's single regret to have a similar power. Another character in the play says that

> ... affliction
> Expresseth virtue, fully, whether true,
> Or else adulterate,

and in *The Duchess of Malfi* Webster has alluded to the commonplace that at death a man speaks truly, like a Hotspur or Laertes. So perhaps Flamineo, witnessing the winding of his brother's corpse, and Vittoria facing death itself are both meant to "come to themselves" (the phrase is Webster's), and speak their inmost, truest, thoughts and feelings. Theater history, if it records the simple fact of the reviewers' concurrence of interest in Flamineo's speech, can give notable support to such an interpretation, a view of Webster possessed, not so much with death, as with an inescapable, inward guilt and compassion.

It might also be worthwhile to record remarkable agreements

among accounts of even a single production. For example, when *Henry IV, Part 1* was performed at Stratford-upon-Avon in 1951, at least two reviewers agreed that the short episode presenting Glendower, and Mortimer and Hotspur with their wives, was the "most moving scene" in the whole play (they used, independently, the same words);[10] and almost every other reviewer paid special attention to this scene. Now in critical accounts of *Henry IV*, the so-called Welsh Scene often goes entirely unnoticed—as in Professor Harold Jenkins' consideration of the play's *Structural Problem* (1956) or in Professor L. C. Knights' investigation into its "themes" [11]—or else the scene is mentioned briefly for its incidental satire—as by Mr. Traversi. The fact is that most literary critics cannot hear the music called for by the text, nor observe the new restfulness of the characters, relaxing to listen to that music; and so they have missed the visual and temporal stillness of this scene (the more impressive since it is in contrast with the movement and tensions of the rest of the play), and hence they have also missed its potential importance in the dramatic whole. The unanimity of the reviewers in paying tribute to the playing of this scene in the 1951 production should be recorded in order to direct the literary critic's attention towards a significant feature of the play's theatrical life, a scene which gives a still center in personal affection, to the round of wars, distrust and self-aggrandisement.

A second suggestion is of more general implication: theater historians should not restrict their attention to performances of major characters. The effectiveness of the page in *The White Devil* is an example of the interest, for a literary critic, of a one-line part. A reader researching for information about great acting, or stage business, or theater fashions may pass by such a detail without thought, but whenever such a small character gains apparently incommensurate attention, the literary critic can use the information; it tells him about a detail of the play's theatrical life which a reading of its text can seldom indicate.

A third suggestion is linked to this: a critic is especially interested in impressions arising from a character's silence, and in visual and temporal effects. None of the examples in this present discussion has involved a famous and lengthy speech: the various and sometimes contradictory meanings of the actual lines of a play, the literary critic can tease out for himself—indeed he is often over-cunning in this respect. But he does need visual prompting, and a way of measuring tension and relaxation in time. So it is especially important for theater historians to record visual relationships between characters (irrespective of invented background or business), and unambiguous impressions of haste, slowness, boredom and expectation. Interest in the silent presences of Banquo and Macduff are examples of the value of such detail.

The last of these suggestions may be that theater historians should pay special regard to the effect of plays seldom performed but of obvious literary and theatrical importance, and to those parts of famous plays which can seldom be seen in the theater. An instance of the latter is the scenes depicting Aumerle's rebellion and discovery in the last act of *Richard II*. Most critics must form their judgments of these tricky, comic-and-pathetic-and-tense scenes wholly from their reading of the text, for they are seldom performed. They should be able to turn to theater research, but neither of the two stage-histories of *Richard II* is of any help. That in the Variorum edition of the play, published in 1955, does not mention the scenes; that in the New Cambridge Shakespeare, published in 1939, seems to infer that Benson's 1896 production at Stratford-upon-Avon presented them, but gives no further information. Finding that Professor Sprague has no comment in his *Shakespeare and the Actors,* the literary critic may pursue the question back to the Variorum and find three references to descriptions of the Benson production, and his hopes will rise; but one reference is back again to the New Cambridge Shakespeare, and the other two, when followed up, yield no information about the Aumerle scenes. The literary critic must instigate a search on his own behalf if he wants to learn about the theatrical effect of the fifth act of *Richard II* as Shakespeare wrote it. A mere reference to two or three reviews which the theater researcher will have read would not take much space in a footnote, and would be eagerly followed by the literary critic. The clown scenes in *Othello,* the spy scene in *Coriolanus,* the Lancelot-Jessica-Lorenzo scene in *The Merchant of Venice* are further examples of rarely performed parts of Shakespeare's plays in which the literary critic will be, or should be, especially interested.

These sugggestions are not meant to set a limit to a critic's interest in theater research; they are, rather, sprats to catch mackerel. Once an initial distrust is overcome, there is material for the critic in the wide range of theater research. Studies of the structure and management of all types of theater, descriptions of acting techniques and intentions, histories of scenic design, biographies of actors, analyses of audiences—all these can enrich the critic's knowledge of the theatrical life of plays, of their author's visual as well as verbal imagination, and his handling of time, emphasis, expectation, suspense; so they can lead the critic towards the fully theatrical criticism which the works of any author who chooses to write plays, and not poems or novels, necessarily demand.

Theater research has so many demands made upon it that a request for further information of a kind which may not be immediately interesting to anyone but the rare, theatrically-minded critic needs, perhaps, further recommendation. It must be remembered that the issue is a wide one. The study of Shakespeare as a "philosophic poet rather than a man of the stage" is symptomatic of an intellectual attitude which divorces literary criticism from the theater. The men who work in our theaters experiment along their own lines of interest, enquiry, and financial advantage, and critics and university scholars and students along theirs; despite honorable exceptions, rarely do they help each other, or know each other's language. Yet they could help each other and learn from each other, and so immeasurably enrich our theater. For this to happen literary critics must learn to consider the full theatrical life of the plays they study, so that they can analyse and judge a play as well as a poem, and speak of an image of life as well as of a theme, or pattern, or moral statement. If they could do this, theater directors, actors and audiences would recognize their own interests in the critics' deliberations, and would share in them. Here theater research can help, for, if it can respond to the first enquiries of literary critics, it can do much to establish and refine a consideration of plays in the element for which they were written.

* Based on a paper read to the Society for Theatre Research, March 15, 1960.

1 *Collected Plays* (1958), pp. 3–4.

2 *Some Shakespearean Themes* (1959), p. 14; the italics are mine.

3 *The Wheel of Fire* (4th ed., 1949), Preface, p. vi.

4 Crosse, p. 88.

5 *The Sunday Times*, March 9, 1947.

6 And more recently by Mr. E. L. Avery's *The London Stage, 1700-1729*, and Mr. Arthur H. Scouten's *The London Stage, 1729-1746*.

7 *The First Night of "Twelfth Night"* (1954), p. 119, etc.

8 Cf. A. C. Sprague, *Shakespeare and the Actors* (1944), pp. 90–91.

9 For details, cf. *The White Devil* (Revels Plays), ed. J. R. Brown (1960), pp. lx-lxi.

10 *Punch* (April 18, 1951) and *The Manchester Guardian* (October 5, 1951).

11 Cf. *Some Shakespearean Themes* (1959).

The Role of the
Shakespearean Producer

ALFRED HARBAGE

It is appropriate that Approaches to Shakespeare *should end with
this provocative warning by one of the most catholic and influential Shakespearean scholars against the dangers of criticism,
whether practiced by academic writers or translated into theatrical terms by a producer or director. Professor Harbage suggests
that the way in which a play becomes the expression of its producer's critical interpretation is a way of more than likely sub-
verting the wide range of possibilities Shakespeare gave it; and
it is only an extension of his argument to ask whether the reader
who decides that one critical view says all there is to be said
about a play does not similarly hamstring his own reading. Professor of English at Harvard University, critic, and historian,
Alfred Harbage has written a number of illuminating, important, and often controversial books on Shakespeare and on the
drama of the sixteenth and seventeenth centuries, among them*
Shakespeare's Audience *(1941),* Shakespeare and the Rival
Traditions *(1952), and* Theatre for Shakespeare *(1953), from
which this essay is taken.*

In Shakespeare's time there were neither dramatic critics nor
theatrical producers in the present sense of the terms. Criticism
consisted of approbation or disapprobation, usually moral and expressed in general terms, or of argument upon such technical principles as the unities. No one felt called upon to mediate between
the playwright and his auditors—to exhibit the beauties, analyse
the subtleties, or explain the *meaning* of a play. Similarly, pro-

duction consisted of converting the written word into the spoken word, the implied theatrical action into real theatrical action, by methods so simple and standardized as to be relatively neutral. A text might be revised between one series of performances and the next, but there is no evidence that by processes other than textual, plays were consciously reshaped upon successive revivals.

Today, of course, all this is changed. As we read Shakespeare, a hundred critical voices are whispering in our ears, voices of the present, voices from the past, many wise and harmonious, others simply insistent, but in either case introducing into the reading experience a factor other than the poet's page and our own susceptibilities. Our protection is that the voices are so many and various as to blend into an indistinguishable murmur almost as unobtrusive as silence. Against the producer, however, we have no like protection. We cannot attend a performance except in his personal custody. We cannot listen to Shakespeare except to the accompaniment of his single and penetrating voice. He is, alas, the one inescapable critic.

One need be inimical to neither critics nor producers in order to recognize that both, and especially the latter, are prone to rashness and are often too aggressive for our good. What follows is in essence a plea to the producer for self-restraint, based upon a reminder that from an historical point of view he is with us only upon sufferance.

That the modern "producer" (in America the "director" or "producer" *cum* "director") had no counterpart in Elizabethan England is perhaps best indicated by the fact that no word was created to designate his role. Even those most nearly in his authoritative position, such leaders of the juvenile troupes as Edwardes, Farrant, Mulcaster, Westcote, Evans, and Pierce retained only the designation "master," deriving from *school-master* or *chapel-master*. Since the repertories of the companies governed by these men consisted mainly of plays written by themselves or by poets closely associated with them in playhouse management, they can scarcely be equated with the non-writing, non-acting specialists of the present, and none of them gained a reputation from mere adroitness in guiding plays through rehearsal. Evidently such guidance was not considered "creative" or particularly difficult.

Even in the court masks, where the staging was sufficiently complex to evoke a technology of artificial lighting, and where a
diversity of specialized skills, poetic, musical, choreographic, cried
out for co-ordination, we hear nothing of a "producer" as distinct
from individual creative artists. The personnel of the Revels Office
was actively engaged, but as Jonson distributes "credits" through
the printed texts of his early masks, he commends only such men
as Masters Giles and Herne, for the choreography, Master Fer-
rabosco, for the musical score, Master Jones, for the scene and
costume designing, and himself for "the invention of the whole"
(*Hue and Cry after Cupid,* 1608). Presumably Jonson or Jones,
or both, came nearer to filling the role of "producer" than did
any staff sergeant of the Master of the Revels.

It is the adult professional troupes such as originally performed
Shakespeare that must chiefly engage our attention. As functions
in their theatres became sufficiently differentiated, words were
found to designate those who performed them: *player, poet,
house-keeper, sharer, hired-man, musician, gatherer, tireman,
book-keeper, stage-keeper.* The list, although nearly exhaustive,
is short; yet short as it is its items overlap. For instance, the *book-
keeper* (custodian of scripts, and prompter), who was a *hired-
man,* seems also to have functioned, at least in some companies,
as *stage-keeper* (stage-manager and -care-taker). It has even
been suggested that he was the counterpart of the modern producer or director. If so, his directing hand must have been tentative indeed, since the actors under his presumed direction were
his masters, employing him at six shillings a week and never, so
far as the records indicate, admitting him to a place as sharer in
a company.

No doubt the book-keeper's or stage-keeper's authority was only
minor, that tyranny in petty matters which all of us must suffer
from faithful aides. Someone else must have distributed the parts
of a new play and decided whether it was worthy of new costumes. These would have been the core considerations in any
Elizabethan "production," and the signs are unmistakable that
decisions were reached by the actor-sharers as a group or by one
of their number delegated by them. The latter, possibly Shakespeare as poet of the company, possibly Burbage as its principal

actor, possibly some lesser member distinguished only by a time-tried levelheadedness, may thus be envisioned as, in a sense, the "producer" in the Chamberlain's-King's Company. Since it is difficult for a group to make a series of minor decisions in concert, it is possible that this hypothetical producer may have arbitrated points of stage strategy. The simplicity of Elizabethan stage strategy has probably not yet been adequately recognized, but the present argument is independent of such an opinion. Whatever the emphasis and effects desired, and whatever the technical means of achieving them, and whatever the system of delegating immediate responsibility for the application of these means, the ultimate authority was vested solely in the actor-sharers as a group. In the circumstances the great arbiter would be the script. It would be the only agency for keeping a company of equals in step, and for ruling out repercussive distortions. The distortions of particular roles, with their disturbing effect upon other roles, are possible only in the type of production where some individual has an over-riding vote. The Elizabethan script might be altered in rehearsal, but between that script as finally endorsed and the acting company, no agency intervened; hence, between the playwright's original conception and the audience, no agency intervened except the acting company. It is for this reason that we may justifiably deny the existence of a "producer" in Elizabethan times.

The intervention of the actors themselves may seem, in the present context, too important to be lightly dismissed. The playwright's conception was not established and preserved as a thing holy and entire, and the lament of Dekker is by no means unique in its age: ". . . let the Poet set the note of his numbers even to Apollo's own lyre, the Player will have his own crochets, and sing false notes in despite of all the rules of music" ("Lectori," *The Whore of Babylon*, 1607). Nevertheless the tendency would have been to defer to the script, for the reason already given—the necessary conservatism of a democratic system of company organization—and for the additional reason that there was no occasion for doing otherwise. As free agents, the actors bought and staged only such plays as they wished to buy and stage. That the method of staging itself was not of a type calculated to alter the character of the text provided by the author cannot here be argued in detail, but it must strike anyone that, within a specified period, staging and stage-writing must be truly complementary. When plays were printed, their stage directions were rarely amplified. Laconic though they certainly are, they were nevertheless deemed a sufficient guide to visualization. It is safe to say that reading Shakespeare and seeing Shakespeare in the theatre were, in his own times, less disparate experiences than they have been at any time since. In the theatre the experience was not a different experience but the same experience intensified.

So long as the King's Men endured as an actor-sharer company, that is until 1642, the tendency, despite a few decorative interpolations like those in *Macbeth,* and the introduction at Blackfriars of *entr'acte* music and perhaps occasional experiments with scenery, was to perform the plays of Shakespeare in a manner established by tradition rather than to strive for new effects and altered emphasis. We may guess that between Shakespeare's death and the closing of the theatres the impulse to *produce* rather than simply *re-perform* the plays was, at any rate, only fitfully in evidence since there was not yet any authoritative individual to implement the impulse. The testimony of the Restoration prompter, John Downes, although unreliable in details, proves the existence of a conservative ideal. The part of Henry VIII, he avers, was "right and justly done by Mr. Betterton, he being instructed in it by Sir William, who had it from old Mr. Lowin, who had his instruction from Mr. Shakespeare himself." And again, concerning the performance of the role of Hamlet, "Sir William (having seen Mr. Taylor of the Blackfriars Company act it, who being instructed by the author, Mr. Shakespeare) taught Mr. Betterton in every particle of it. . . ." (*Roscius Anglicanus,* 1608, pp. 21, 24.)

The ideal, of course, did not survive the early Restoration period, and, curiously, the most conspicuous agent in its dissipation was that very Sir William mentioned by Prompter Downes. Sir William Davenant may with justice be called the first Shakespearean "producer." The present author has been inclined to deprecate the obloquy heaped upon Davenant in view of his real love of Shakespeare, but, like all things, "real love" must be judged by its consequences. As Professor Odell wittily put it, Davenant

"loved Shakespeare so much he could not leave him alone,"
whereas Killigrew, the rival playhouse manager, who was relatively indifferent to Shakespeare, was inclined to stage the plays
unaltered (*Shakespeare from Betterton to Irving*, 1920, 1, 24).
The paradox is not without significance. All of our contemporary
producers profess, and most of them no doubt have, a *tremendous
love of Shakespeare*.

Of course there were factors at work in the Restoration treatment of Shakespeare more potent than the mere personal inclina-
tions of Davenant or any other single individual. These factors
were two in number: first, the substitution of a managerial for
an actor-sharer system of company organization, with a consequent substitution of dictatorial radicalism for the democratic conservatism previously noted; and second, a spreading hiatus between the plays and the audience because of the passage of time
and the changing character of playgoers. Precisely these factors
have been operating ever since in giving us "productions" rather
than performances of Shakespeare.

We may without inappropriateness pass directly from the Restoration to the present day. The mid-twentieth century, at least
in the English and American theatrical worlds, is more *like* the
Restoration than like any other era. The adaptations, from
Davenant's to Cibber's, are no longer so frequently subjected to
condemnation (which would now sound somewhat hypocritical),
and the most notorious of them, the operatic *Tempest*, was of late
considered worth the trouble of a revival. Suffice it to say that
Davenant, from his day to ours, has been succeeded by a long
line of "producers," actor-managers and others, aided at first by
such authors as Tate, aided at last chiefly by stage technologists,
but early or late, relying mostly upon their own fertility. Some
of these producers, notably Garrick, achieved their most erratic
effects while purportedly restoring Shakespeare to his "true and
original form." Such claims might be traced as a subsidiary tradition in post-Restoration production, with a concluding survey of
the activity in twentieth-century "Globes."

No one would wish to deny the virtues of experiment or to dissipate the golden aura, not always spurious, hovering over three
centuries of Shakespeare in the restored English theatres. Fine

things have sometimes been done and great joy sometimes conveyed. It is not my present business to linger with these things, or with the fact that playhouses and players have an enticing glamour of their own quite apart from whatever they may do with or to a poet's dreams. Austerity of tone must inevitably accompany my attempt to make my point. My point is this: the best readers of Shakespeare, those who have gone to the theatre with the highest expectations, have long been the ones most cruelly disappointed there, and the responsibility lies at the door of the producers or the complex of production. Charles Lamb's indictment of Shakespeare-in-the-theatre is wrongly based, but his statement about the productions he saw (which only "brought down a fine vision") is the simple truth about *the productions he saw.* Coarser sensibilities than his were intervening between Shakespeare's text and himself. Mr. Eliot says essentially the same thing (*Elizabethan Essays,* p. 16):

> ... I know that I rebel against most performances of Shakespeare's plays because I want a direct relationship between the work of art and myself, and I want the performance to be such as will not interrupt or alter this relationship any more than it is an alteration or interruption for me to superpose a second inspection of a picture or building upon the first. I object, in other words, to the interpretation, and I would have a work of art such that it needs only to be completed and cannot be altered by each interpretation.

Unless one is committed to a faith in Mr. Eliot's infallibility, one must see that his error in laying his charge against the kind of plays these are equals Lamb's in laying his charge against performance rather than particular performances. At any rate both Lamb and Eliot, strange bedfellows, attest alike to the unfortunate accidents that so consistently befall Shakespeare's plays en route to us as spectators.

The features of a few recent productions and the attitudes of a few contemporary producers may be placed in evidence. In the 1953–54 production of *All's Well that Ends Well* at the Old Vic, the King of France was treated as a comic character. The phenomenon is indicative of the haphazard nature of theatrical "influences." In the undergraduate days of the present writer it was the custom among students to take turns in repeating the gnomic utterances of their academic elders to a chorus of artificial yawns. The exercise at the time seemed finely rebellious, sophisticated, and indescribably funny. In England, where for better and for worse, the literary and undergraduate worlds are more interpenetrable than elsewhere, a like custom must still prevail, judging from a scene in Christopher Fry's *The Lady's Not for Burning*, where several youths yawn away the wisdom of the world. From Fry to Shakespeare must seem a logical step—in the *All's Well* of the Old Vic the wisdom of the King of France was greeted by the exaggerated yawns of his young courtiers. By this (and less subtle means) he was converted into a figure of fun.

Now it is true that Shakespearean characters are susceptible to much diversity of evaluation. There is, however, a limit to its permissible range. No sane observer has ever mistaken Bottom for a dignitary or the King of France for a buffoon. That the actual words of Shakespeare were being repeated on the stage of the Old Vic is immaterial—the *producer* was composing this portion of the play. To proclaim that the language of Shakespeare is nowadays less frequently cut and no longer revised is to rejoice in a technicality.

The example will suffice for all those instances in which the producers consider the comedies insufficiently comic and the tragedies too tragic, and while honouring Hamlet's injunction to let the clowns speak no more than is set down for them, feel free to recruit their number—most commonly by transforming into a Polonius any available oldster in the dramatis personae. A different kind of directorial "touch" was illustrated in the 1953–54 production of *A Midsummer-Night's Dream* at the Shakespeare Memorial Theatre. The creatures of the fairy kingdom were made not comic but grotesquely sinister, especially Puck, who moved about either in somersaults or with a repulsively simian roll, like nothing so much as a stunted Caliban. True, Elizabethan fairies were commonly conceived of as malicious, but in this particular play by this particular author they are conceived of as reasonably genial. Puck, as a matter of fact, has struck generations of observers as not a little puckish, and when he ceases to be so, and when his co-spirits lose their charm, we are not compensated either by the evidence of research on Elizabethan fairies as a class or by the opportunities seized by the costume-designers.

It is invidious to point in this fashion to productions which err only in being typical. There is place for exploratory treatment surely, perhaps place for productions of precisely this kind; the calamity is that it is the only kind now available. The two have been cited because they were sponsored by the semi-official companies of Shakespeare's London and Shakespeare's Stratford, where if anywhere one might look for deference to the poet's conception. At both theatres a system of guest producers has been instituted. Since the same persons alternate as guests, forming literally an interlocking directorate, it is difficult to see the purpose of the system unless it be to allow time for the persons concerned to approach each new production with a new stock of notions.

To cite the views of particular producers, when these views are shared by all, is even more invidious than to cite the qualities of particular productions. I can only say that I have been guided in my choice by the desire to represent the three main types of apology by the three most distinguished spokesmen.

Mr. G. Wilson Knight, although relatively inactive in the professional theatre, is so influential as to be truly formidable. He may stand as spokesman for the *interpretive* producer. Mr. Knight believes that a Shakespearean production should be shaped to subserve the central philosophical idea of the play as conceived by the producer (*Principles of Shakespearian Production*, 1949 ed., pp. 35-36):

> Interpretation will always be a development in a new medium of some central idea of wholeness in the original; grasp of that central idea forcing a vital re-creation. It is the same with production. . . . The producer should be able to hold the play in jigsaw bits in his mind, to sort them all out, to build with them and recreate the whole from understanding of its nature. Such understanding gives him full powers to cut, adapt, even on rare occasions, transpose, according to circumstances; he has to consider his stage, his company, his audience.

Everything in fact, one is tempted to add, except his author. Mr. Knight does not tell us who is to vouch for this authoritative "understanding of its nature" or how we may distinguish between the play's idea and the producer's idea of the play. By rebuilding with "jig-saw bits" an interpreter may convert his idea of a Titian into his idea of a Picasso, and however masterful the original painting, the *contaminatio* may be merely vulgar. To those producers who would cut, adapt, and transpose in the happy assurance of their "grasp" we can only repeat Cromwell's cry to the prophets of the Kirk intoxicated with spiritual fulness: "I beseech you in the bowels of Christ think it possible that you may be mistaken."

Dr. Tyrone Guthrie, who has been kind enough to discuss these matters with me (with an admirable absence of cant), may speak for the *vitalizing* producers. Although he defended the Old Vic treatment of the role of the King of France, on the basis of the diversity in Shakespearean criticism, implying that since nothing is certain nothing is ruled out, his more serious view was expressed in a different connection. After professing admiration for the productions of Granville-Barker, he added that it would nevertheless be death just to go on in Granville-Barker's way. With this attitude one must have much sympathy, but whereas growth is evidence of vitality, change is not always evidence of growth. No one would advocate the servile imitation of anything, or a completely static tradition, but it remains true that all good productions of a particular play must have a great many features in common. On more philosophical grounds it may be argued that the work of art with which we are concerned is the play rather than the production, and the play is a *fait accompli*. It cannot be equated with a living organism. The organism can change; the play can only be changed. It cannot be *vitalized*; unless it retains its initial vitality it can only be animated. Fortunately those who have had in their custody the works of the master painters have felt no inclination to vitalize them. The analogy is not so pointless as it may seem. Although the Shakespearean plays are in a different category of art in that they invite manipulation, the manipulation was originally designed and might still be designed merely, in Mr. Eliot's phrase, to complete them; and although they are in the happy situation of having in their reproducible texts a more indestructible fabric than paintings, they can be at least *momentarily destroyed.*

Miss Margaret Webster's well-known views may be cited as those of the popularizing or *persuasive* producers. After passing adverse judgment, frequently acute, upon one of the works advocating production in "the original manner," she says (*Shakespeare Quarterly,* 1952, p. 64):

> It would be of great interest to scholars and students and some sections of the public who were already Shakespeare "convertites"; but in my view it would have the reverse effect on the large majority of audience who, at any rate in the United States, have to be persuaded that Shakespeare is anything but a dead "classic" without modern urgency or personal appeal.

To this we can only respond with anguished questions. Just what performances are now available to the "convertites"—those who need no persuasion and find it insufferable? Are *their* tears not wet, *their* sobs not audible in the night? Hath not a convertite senses, affections, passions? If you tickle them, do they not laugh? If you poison them, do they not die?

The views of the producers have not been fully and fairly represented, or adequately combated. It is enough to show that they exist. Presumably when there were no producers, there were no views, and the plays of Shakespeare were vital and persuasive in their own right, as well as self-interpretive. To the extent that they seem to us still so we must either shun the theatre or be encumbered with well-meant assistance. One may venture to say that the hiatus between plays and audience previously mentioned can be closed only by the effort of individual members of that audience. For those who cannot or will not make this effort there are modern plays to be seen. All producers shudder at the idea of productions merely archaeological, and properly, but it must be pointed out that selecting for performance a three-hundred-year-old script tends toward the archaeological and one should be willing to abide by the consequences. There is no use in pretending that the old play is a new play. It may be true that there is now no audience for the old play, but it is difficult to see how this may be determined unless it is occasionally performed.

The line that has been taken may seem unsympathetic. Nothing has been said of the producer's many troubles—with large and costly casts, theatre overseers and subventors, journalistic critics, the absence (or presence) of "stars," and the inexperienced younger actors, conning blank verse with one eye while watching with the other for emissaries from the West End, Broadway, or Hollywood. Let the quality of current productions be attributed to these troubles instead of to any cause suggested by me and the fact remains the same—that the quality is low. No one is compelled to produce Shakespeare, or to subscribe to the dubious principle that it is better to do a thing badly than not at all.

When all is said, however, even though they may with justice be considered the Davenants and Cibbers of our age, the producers are the ones with whom our hopes for immediate improvement must abide. We cannot summon Shakespeare to write modern plays or to modernize his own. We cannot reassemble the Elizabethan audience to exert upon twentieth-century performances those pressures that shaped both texts and performances in the first place. We cannot, unhappily, revive actor-sharer troupes with the traditions and competence of the King's Men. Since we must rely upon producers, we might profitably point out to them that their task is even more difficult than they think. A Shakespearean producer should be as reverent, knowledgeable, and technically expert as the conductor of a great symphony orchestra. He should either refuse to work with unqualified actors or else undertake to qualify them—in one way by concentrating upon their voices, articulation, and physical co-ordination the attention now directed towards their costumes, scenic background, and business, remembering that such elements in an undertaking as are least tractable may also be most important. He should know more about Shakespeare's language and frame of reference than the professors, and more about Shakespeare's theatre than the builders of models, not so much to imitate its methods as to understand their effects and to avoid a single-minded devotion to some rumoured aspect. At the same time he should regard the anxiety of the professors and model-builders to get the record straight with tolerance, and as relevant as his own conscience. Finally he should be a hopeful kind of person and assume that if he achieves the best, it will be appreciated, even in the United States, thus imitating Shakespeare's attitude in the unpromising purlieus of the Bankside.